AMERICAN LABOR

American Labor: A Documentary Collection

Edited by

Melvyn Dubofsky and Joseph A. McCartin

AMERICAN LABOR: A DOCUMENTARY COLLECTION
© Melvyn Dubofsky and Joseph A. McCartin 2004

First published 2004 by
PALGRAVE MACMILLAN™
175 Fifth Avenue, New York, N.Y. 10010 and
Houndmills, Basingstoke, Hampshire, England RG21 6XS
Companies and representatives throughout the world.

PALGRAVE MACMILLAN is the global academic imprint of the Palgrave Macmillan division of St. Martin's Press, LLC and of Palgrave Macmillan Ltd. Macmillan® is a registered trademark in the United States, United Kingdom and other countries. Palgrave is a registered trademark in the European Union and other countries.

ISBN 0–312–29565–0 hardback
ISBN 0–312–29564–2 paperback
ISBN 978-0–312–29564–6 paperback

Library of Congress Cataloging-in-Publication Data
American labor : a documentary collection / edited by Melvyn Dubofsky and Joseph A. McCartin.

   p. cm.
   Includes bibliographical references and index.
   ISBN 0–312–29565–0 (hc)—ISBN 0–312–29564–2 (pbk.)
      1. Labor—United States—History—Sources. 2. Work ethic—United States—History— Sources. 3. Labor movement—United States— History—Sources. 4. Labor unions—United States— History—Sources. I. Dubofsky, Melvyn, 1934– II. McCartin, Joseph Anthony.

HD8066.A728 2004
331'.0973—dc22   2003058099

A catalogue record for this book is available from the British Library.

Design by Newgen Imaging Systems (P) Ltd., Chennai, India.

First edition: October 2004
10 9 8 7 6 5 4 3 2 1

Printed in the United States of America.

Transferred to Digital Printing in 2010

Contents

ACKNOWLEDGMENTS

Many individuals helped make this volume possible and it is our pleasure to thank them here. First, we would like to acknowledge the help of several research assistants who aided us in gathering, reproducing, and formatting many of the documents used in this volume as well as carrying out other tasks essential to the book's completion. They are: Tina Braxton, Ed Donnelly, Nicole Manapol, Adam McKean, Kevin N. Powers, and Adam Smith. Without their help, the job of assembling this material would have been far more arduous than it turned out to be. We would also like to thank Eric Arnesen and the anonymous readers for Palgrave Macmillan for their comments on the plan for this volume. They helped us clarify our approach to this project in important ways. And we would especially like to thank our colleagues in the field of U.S. labor and social history, whose research helped direct us toward the most important evidence documenting the history of American workers. To those even marginally acquainted with the field, the influence of dozens of our fellow historians should be evident throughout this volume.

Without the early encouragement of Debbie Gershenowitz, our original editor at Palgrave Macmillan, we might not have undertaken this volume. We are indebted to Brendan O'Malley for stepping in to see the project to completion; his support was unflagging. We are indebted to Heather Van Dusen and Amanda Fernández for their invaluable help. Our thanks also to Emilye Crosby, Greg Guthrie, Roger Horowitz, and Maurice Jackson for furnishing important documents.

Finally, Joseph McCartin would like to thank his spouse, Diane Reis, and his daughters, Mara and Elisa, for their continuous love and support during the time this project preoccupied him.

INTRODUCTION

Nearly eighty years have passed since John R. Commons and his associates at the University of Wisconsin gathered and published the first multivolume collection of documents concerning the social history of American industrial society. As might be expected, their eleven-volume compilation, entitled *A Documentary History of American Industrial Society*, devoted several volumes to the subjects of workers, labor movements, and labor politics. For decades it provided a starting point for students of the history of American workers and their organizations. When we began this project, there was no documentary collection in print that aspired to provide even an introductory survey-level exposure to U.S. labor history.

The lack of such a collection is all the more glaring when one considers the dramatic scholarly resurgence that has redefined the field of labor history over the past three decades. Informed by the new social history, as well as by insights from the fields of anthropology, sociology, and political and legal history, that scholarly resurgence has generated not only a vast quantity of monographs reorienting labor history, but fine survey texts that offer overarching narratives of American working-class history. Two of those texts have been written by one of this volume's co-editors: Melvyn Dubofsky's *Industrialism and the American Worker, 1865–1920* (Harlan Davidson, 1996, 3rd ed.); and *Labor in America: A History* (Harlan Davidson, 2004, 7th ed.). Two other excellent surveys merit mention: James R. Green, *The World of the Worker: American Labor in the Twentieth Century* (Hill and Wang, 1980) and especially Robert Zieger and Gilbert Gall, *American Workers, American Unions: The Twentieth Century* (The Johns Hopkins University Press, 2002, 3rd ed.). The massive two-volume survey compiled by the American Social History Project, *Who Built America?* also offers much to students.

Yet, there is a dearth of supplemental documentaries that can introduce students to the history of American workers through more direct exposure to the voices and the records of the past. Indeed, no comprehensive collection of documents on the subject of American labor currently remains in print. Jerold Auerbach's excellent set of documents entitled *American Labor: The Twentieth Century* is now out of print. Leon Litwack's documentary history of American labor recently went out of print for a second time. Eileen Boris and Nelson Lichtenstein's book on labor for a series on "major problems" in United States history, includes a number of excellent documents yet it is not really a documentary collection; instead, it is a hybrid that devotes as much attention to historians' contradictory readings of the past as it does to the limited selection of documents it reprints. The American Social History Project has produced a CD-ROM to accompany *Who Built America?* that offers students an opportunity to read primary documents (as well as sample music, graphics, and visual evidence). But it does not easily lend itself to classroom use or provide documents of more than a page in length.

The lack of a viable one-volume documentary collection in American labor history is all the more glaring when one considers how much the study of labor history has changed since Commons's team did its work. Today the field of labor history encompasses culture as well as economics; household relations as well as industrial relations; women as domestic workers as well as factory workers; and black, Chicano, and Asian workers as well as white workers. In this comprehensive single-volume compilation of documents we seek to integrate institutional labor history with aspects of social history, to chart changes in both trade union and managerial practices, and to integrate the economics and politics of labor history.

In order to survey American labor history through the documentary evidence, we have divided the volume into six chronological periods, each of which has been chosen with an eye to its historical integrity as well as to facilitate classroom use.

The first period, which covers the years from the establishment of colonial North America to 1828, examines changes that occurred in the organization of work and the behavior of workers during this period of nation-building. It examines the varieties of labor—agricultural, artisanal, common, free, slave, and indentured—that coexisted in North America from its colonization by Europeans through the beginnings of the market revolution that would transform work life on the continent. And it reveals both the impact of the American Revolution and the outcome of workers' early struggles for the right to organize.

The second period, covering the years from 1828 to 1877, traces the rise of the factory system, the struggle between free and slave labor, the growth of national trade unions, and the emergence of a free labor economy. It was during this period that the United States emerged as a society within which industrial capitalism became the driving economic force. This section traces the process of proletarianization that led to the making of a U.S. working class; it examines the tensions between free and unfree labor that marked the beginning of this period, and the difficult and in some ways incomplete transition to free labor that was visible by its end. It also traces the emergence of the first national workers' organizations, from the National Union of Trades in the 1830s through the National Labor Union of the post–Civil War years. Finally, it introduces students to the dynamics of race, ethnicity, and gender that would shape workers' lives and efforts to organize during this formative period.

The third period, covering the years 1877 to 1914, encompasses the development of the United States as a mature industrial society in which workers struggled to come to terms with a new world of work and life. During that time both workers and their employers experimented with various institutional and organizational formulas to obtain greater control of the circumstances of their lives and futures, whether as wage-earners in the one case or capitalists in the other. By the end of this period, as the documents disclose, the most organizationally active workers had built national trade unions, the American Federation of Labor, and a political coalition with the Democratic party as their preferred institutions. For their part, employers had implemented forms of scientific management, welfare capitalism, and collective bargaining. In this period also, as the documents reveal, the state grew more directly concerned with and involved in industrial relations. Largely as a reaction to the turbulence, violence, and apparent anarchy of labor–capital relations, the state acted to promote social stability. The legislative and executive branches of government usually sought to mediate between labor and capital and to play the role of neutral party. A number of the documents that we have chosen for this section illustrate the persistent power of ethnicity, race, and gender in shaping the everyday substance of working-class life and also the character of workers' organizations.

During the years from 1914 through 1947, covered in the fourth section of the book, the United States built the world's first mass-production, mass-consumption society, ending the period as the globe's dominant economic power. Economic growth, however, did not occur painlessly, especially for workers. Even during the relatively prosperous 1920s, workers experienced persistent bouts of unemployment and earned real wages and a real standard of living that lagged far behind the growth in per capita productivity and corporate profits. And then during the 1930s, workers suffered from protracted and massive unemployment as the Great Depression ravished the national economy. Not until the outbreak of World War II did the economy recover fully from the ravages of depression, and it was the war that ushered the United States into a generation-long era of economic expansion and prosperity. The documents in this section explore the transition of the American nation from the economic expansion of the 1920s through the contraction of the Great Depression to the achievement of war-induced prosperity. These documents suggest how the structure of the labor force changed and how a mass-consumption economy brought both promise and frustration to workers. They show how insurgents within the house of labor built the new mass-production unionism through the Committee for Industrial Organization (renamed in 1938 the Congress of Industrial Organizations [CIO]), and how employers persisted in their strategies of antiunionism yet ultimately adjusted to the emergence of stable unions in the mass-production sector of the economy. Most important, the documents indicate how the state shifted away from hostility or bare toleration of independent unions to a policy of actively promoting the growth of trade unions and the practice of collective bargaining.

5ᵗʰ period:
1947-73

The years from 1947 through roughly 1973, covered in the fifth section of the book, reveal the United States at the height of its economic power and prosperity. These were years of ever-rising real wages and standards of living for most workers, a time when unions and management in most sectors of the economy bargained harmoniously. Unions signed long-term contracts that provided for job security; incorporated administrative law procedures to resolve workers' grievances; protected employees against rises in the cost of living through cost-of-living wage adjustments (COLAs); and offered workers paid holidays, health insurance, and retirement benefits. The documents in this section reveal how unions and management built their cooperative relationship with the encouragement and support of public policy, and also how the system many hailed as a new "people's capitalism" eliminated labor radicals and militants. Many observers saw this new era of affluence as marking an end both to ideology and labor–capital conflict. Yet, as some of the documents show, race and gender continued to affect working-class lives in all sorts of unexpected and complicated ways.

6ᵗʰ / final:
1973 -

The years since 1973, treated in the final section of the book, have been a time of crisis and transformation. On the one hand, during this period U.S. economic hegemony waned and prosperity become less of an everyday reality for many working people. For the first time since the decade of the 1920s, trade unions began to decline absolutely as well as relatively (i.e., they lost actual members and they represented an ever smaller proportion of the total labor force). In the altered economic environment brought about by the export of industrial jobs outside of U.S. borders, employers attacked trade unions in a manner not seen for almost fifty years. They did so at a moment when public policy for the first time since the year 1933 clearly shifted against the trade-union movement. The Republicans who controlled the White House throughout most of the period appointed people to the National Labor Relations Board and to the federal courts who increasingly ruled against individual workers and the organizations that represented them. On the other hand, these were years of tremendous transformations. The labor force changed in ways previously unimaginable, as the number and proportion of women wage-workers grew more rapidly than that of men. Nonwhite workers occupied an ever increasing proportion of the low-paid jobs at the bottom of the economy, partly as a consequence of a new wave of mass immigration that began after 1965 and drew workers primarily from the southern and eastern regions of the world. Simultaneously the number of so-called white-collar (also pink-collar) sales, service, and technical workers surpassed the total of blue-collar industrial, construction, transport, and mining employees while computers and the Internet began to reshape the economy. The documents in this section illustrate the transformation in the world of work and labor cited above and explore how the labor movement sought to cope with a situation that threatened its existence.

The documents selected for each of the six chronological periods are grouped into thematic sub-sections. Each documentary sub-section is introduced by brief headnotes that identify the documents selected and raise questions about them. It goes without saying that a one-volume collection of documents in labor history must be extremely selective. Surely we have slighted subjects of interest to many readers and omitted the favorite documents of others. Nevertheless, we trust that the documents we chose to reprint in this volume distill primary characteristics, beliefs, and behavioral patterns that have marked the history of work and workers in the broad sweep of U.S. history. They are intended, moreover, not to tell the complete history of the subject but rather to serve as a documentary supplement to narrative and analytical histories of American labor and to enable readers to glimpse the past directly without the intercession of intermediaries, whether scholars, teachers, or journalists. Thus, in each section we have sought to enable ordinary working men and women to speak for themselves and to give space to diverse peoples and voices.

Unless otherwise noted, all italics, boldfaces, and underlining in the documents are as they appeared in the original.

1

LABOR IN THE COLONIAL AND EARLY
NATIONAL PERIODS, TO 1828

The colonies established on the North American mainland and the Caribbean islands by rival European empires in the sixteenth and seventeenth centuries, an age of mercantilism, aimed at enriching the colonial powers. The Spanish, who led the way, wrested silver, gold, and other precious materials from their Western Hemisphere possessions. The Portuguese, Dutch, French, and British who followed sought similar riches but failed to find the precious metals dug from the earth by indigenous and imported slave labor under Spanish domination. Instead, the Dutch, French, and British relied on other avenues of trade and exploitation to amass wealth. All three imperial nations, the Dutch and the British most especially and the French less so, turned to private entrepreneurs in the form of joint-stock companies to nourish the streams of trans-Atlantic commerce that would fill the coffers of the home country with bullion, the residue of a positive balance of trade.

These three nations found one source of the wealth that they sought in the furs trapped and traded to them by various Indian nations and tribes. Such commerce required no large body of labor employed by the Europeans, other than their traders in the field, nor a large capital stock, other than the relatively inexpensive European goods that they bartered for pelts. The indigenous peoples could organize trapping on their own terms, maintain their customary cultures and material lives, and barter with the foreigners on mutually acceptable and advantageous terms. The French, British, and Dutch to a lesser extent found another source of riches in the cultivation of staple crops, especially sugar in the Caribbean and tobacco on the mainland. Forest products and fisheries provided other means of income. Whether staple-crop agricultural production, timber and its by-products, or fish for colonial and European markets, each of those economic ventures required an abundant supply of labor.

Labor, however, proved scarce. In the British, Dutch, and French mainland and island colonies the indigenous peoples were relatively few (even before disease ravaged Indian peoples) in relation to land mass and demand for labor. Most indigenous people, moreover, were content within their traditional societies and loath to make their labor available to Europeans.

Some colonists tried to exploit Indian labor through forms of slavery and harsh indenture but such exploitation failed to solve the demand for a disciplined and productive labor force. Without adequate labor, joint-stock enterprises or individual entrepreneurs and planters could not turn a profit.

Two different streams of labor provided the hands to harvest crops, fell trees, manufacture goods, transport the commodities of commerce, and attend to domestic responsibilities in the homes of the wealthy. In the sixteenth and seventeenth centuries, the British Isles and several of the German principalities in the Rhineland experienced a glut in their labor markets. Too many casual laborers, artisans, and domestics chased too few jobs; too many rural folk found their labor no longer desired or the lands that they worked inadequate to support them and their dependents. For them, the colonies offered hope, the prospect for employment, and some economic advance. Few of them, however, could afford to finance their voyage across the ocean. In order for them to pay their way, most of Europe's surplus laborers signed contracts of indenture with future employers (masters) in the colonies or with ships' captains who auctioned them to buyers in the port of arrival (redemptioners). According to the historian Bernard Bailyn, the indentured laborers from Britain represented the entire spectrum of the British urban and rural workforce, although the Celtic fringe—Wales, Scotland, and Northern Ireland (Ulster)—was probably overrepresented. The British also transported thousands of convicts and many orphaned or destitute youngsters and adolescents to the colonies. The poorest and sorriest in the stream of indentured laborers ended up at work on the sugar plantations of the Caribbean and in the tobacco fields of the Chesapeake. There work was harsh, conditions primitive, and life often nasty, brutish, and short. The more fortunate worked for artisan masters in the handicraft trades, as laborers on mixed crop farms, or as domestics in urban and rural households. Well into the eighteenth century indentured servants remained the primary source of labor in the Middle and New England colonies.

Unlike the British who were scattered from one end to the other of Britain's American colonies, the Germans tended to concentrate in the Middle Colonies, especially Pennsylvania. They proved themselves diligent and productive laborers, who did well when they completed their terms of indenture and gained their freedom from service. Germans played perhaps the major role in transforming the fields, towns, and villages of southeastern Pennsylvania into what one historian has called "the best poor man's country."

Indentured servitude alone failed to solve the colonial labor shortage. Indentures served for specified periods, almost never more than seven years and in many cases even fewer. Nearly all contracts required masters to provide their servants with "freedom dues" at the satisfactory termination of service. The survival of the indenture system required an endless stream of new recruits from overseas, the continuation of which was never a certainty. Furthermore, indentured servitude on the sugar plantations and in the tobacco fields proved increasingly unattractive to even the most desperate of European emigrants.

Another source of labor proved especially attractive to colonial employers: that of unfree, involuntary emigrants from the African continent. Soon after Portuguese explorers first charted the coast of West Africa, Europeans began to exploit the institution of African slavery, one of the customary effects of wars and conflicts on that continent. First the Portuguese, and then the Dutch, and finally the British came to dominate the trade in captive Africans. African slaves proved a far more efficient and economical source of labor on Caribbean sugar plantations than European indentured servants, where mortality and morbidity among field hands was exceptionally high. On the North American mainland by the eighteenth century Africans had come to replace Europeans in the tobacco fields of the Chesapeake. And in the Carolina and Georgia low country, African laborers, familiar with rice culture in their places of origin, proved adept at working the region's rice plantations.

At first, the distinction between indentured servitude and slavery was far from evident. Both white European and black African laborers worked together on sugar and tobacco plantations and in various occupations in seaport cities. Over time, however, the various colonies, both in the Caribbean and on the mainland from Massachusetts to Georgia, enacted laws that established a separate legal category for African laborers, one that bound them to their masters for life and condemned their children to a similar status. By the middle of the eighteenth century, most African laborers (all the colonies included a small minority of Africans who enjoyed a free status) were not only legally enslaved but were defined by the law as chattel property, their bodies, and sometimes their lives, at the absolute disposal of their masters. While the law fastened slavery on nearly all Africans and their descendants, indentured servitude among white immigrants and their offspring steadily declined. As the historian Edmund Morgan observed about the colony of Virginia, citizenship for whites (democracy) flourished as slavery for blacks solidified.

Throughout the colonial era the European settlements remained overwhelmingly agrarian and rural. In the staple-crop colonies, slaves came to dominate the labor force, responsible for nearly all the field labor required to produce cash crops, a monopoly of domestic labor in plantation households, and much of the skilled labor on plantations and also in towns. African and African American slaves also worked on the farms of the Middle Colonies, especially New York where Dutch landholders employed many slaves, and as domestics, artisans, and day laborers in the seaport cities of all the northern colonies. In the countryside of the Middle and New England colonies, farm families had to satisfy nearly all their own consumption needs, not just food and shelter but also clothes, household furnishings, even soap and candles; thus in what has been characterized as "an age of homespun," farm women toiled as hard, if not harder, than their men. Idle hands, even among children, proved a luxury in the countryside. As markets for farm products developed, however, and those farmers closest to towns and cities sold their surplus, they obtained the funds to purchase goods produced by artisans abroad or in colonial cities and to hire the services of traveling artisans.

In the colonial cities the production of goods and the provision of services replicated European patterns. Most goods were produced in small workshops on a custom-order basis for specific customers. In this handicraft or artisan system of production, masters owned the workshops and employed one or two journeymen and an apprentice (usually an early adolescent indentured by his parents in order to learn a useful trade). Theoretically, the journeymen refined their skills as craftsmen prior to rising to the status of master while the apprentices acquired the skill to serve as journeymen. This traditional guild system of production, already in decline in Europe, failed to solidify itself in the colonies. The acquisition of a craft or skill remained looser in the colonies and self-identified skilled artisans appeared everywhere within the interstices of the traditional guild system. Cities also required a mass of unskilled laborers to unload and load ships; cart goods to and from the waterfront and also to and from workshops; and to remove the nightsoil of urban residents. Most of the carting or transport trades, though less than skilled and certainly not artisanal, were licensed by local authorities and hence not open to all. A carting license was in many ways as precious to its possessor as was a dearly learned skill to an artisan.

In an economy of perpetual labor scarcity, idle hands could not be tolerated. Even worse were idle hands who failed to support themselves. As the colonial population grew and the economy expanded and contracted to the rhythms of an increasingly capitalistic world economy and conflictual imperial order, poverty emerged as a considerable social problem. Colonials perceived such poverty as particularly the plight of dependent women and children; women whose husbands had died or abandoned them; spinsters and girls without men to support them; orphaned children and offspring of penurious parents. Such people were not only a drain on the material resources of the communities in which they dwelled; their social betters saw idleness as the work of the devil and searched for the best means to insure that the poverty-inflicted could support themselves by forms of labor that would teach them discipline and productivity.

The American Revolution and its aftermath not only created a new nation, it also altered basic aspects of working-class lives. The ideology of the revolutionaries as expressed in the Declaration of Independence and other documents as well as wartime British policies imperiled slavery as a system. Britain offered freedom to slaves who chose to fight on their side, and thousands of slaves took that option. Other slaves insisted that they, too, were part of the human mass that the Declaration said was equal. Moreover, during and after the Revolutionary War, many of the new northern states wrote constitutions or enacted laws that ended slavery, in most cases gradually. The conflict with Britain affected urban workers as well. In the struggles that preceded the Declaration and during the actual war, residents of the former colonies no longer enjoyed access to British consumer goods, whether as a result of voluntary boycotts or military necessity. As a result, both domestic homespun and artisan workshop production surged. With the war's end, however, British goods again flooded mainland markets, imperiling the security and employment of masters and journeymen. During the war waterfront laborers saw diminished work opportunities and seamen endured seizure and impressment by the British Royal Navy. Even after the treaty of peace that ended the war, the British continued to impress sailors on U.S. merchant ships, one of the persistent grievances that would later precipitate the War of 1812. The dual threats posed to American workers by British competition for domestic markets and the impressment of sailors caused workers, journeymen, and the unskilled as well as masters to be among the more enthusiastic advocates of the new national (or federal) government as proposed by the Constitution of 1787.

As the new nation took shape between 1789 and the 1820s, indentured labor faded almost everywhere, slavery solidified itself in the plantation, staple-crop states and disappeared elsewhere, and the traditional artisanal trades slowly changed. Among these changes, the latter proved most important. As the population grew, partly as a result of natural increase and partly owing to increased immigration, the market for domestically produced goods deepened and broadened. Some master artisans responded to market changes by shifting from custom-order production to manufacture for future demand. They became merchant-manufacturers, creating new markets for their goods, and they often no longer worked alongside their journeymen and apprentices in the traditional workshop style. Such new-style capitalists, and that is what they should be called, sought to increase productivity among their employees, hence lowering the cost of production and widening profit margins. Where the merchant-manufacturers succeeded in their aims, the gap between master and journeyman, employer and employee, widened; increasing numbers of journeymen saw their access to the status of master and personal independence foreclosed. In response, they created the first trade unions and resorted to turnouts or strikes in order to defend their earnings, their autonomy, and their prospects for the future. In return, their employers, or masters, used the law as well as economic power to thwart the journeymen. By the end of this protracted era of colonialism and early nationhood, one could glimpse the lineaments of the industrial nation to be, its diverse labor force, and the different means by which workers would seek to defend and better themselves.

NEW WORLD ENCOUNTERS

The following documents (1.1–1.3) describe European perceptions of the societies, economies, and cultures of the native peoples (the Indians) whom they observed. Both the French and English observers commented on similar aspects of Indian society, noting especially what from their perspective was an unusual gendered division of labor. Are there any observations in these three documents that enable you to explain why, as a rule, ~~Indians provided~~ an ~~inadequate solution to colonial labor scarcity?~~ How would you characterize the European attitude toward the native peoples?

1.1   Observing a Different System of Gender and Labor, 1633. From the relation of Father Paul Le Juene, S.J., 1633, in Rueben Gold Thwaites, ed., *The Jesuit Relations and Allied Documents: Travels and Explorations of the Jesuit Missionaries in New France*, Vol. 5 (Cleveland: The Burrows Brothers, 1897), p. 133.

It is true that the Savages are very patient, but the order which they maintain in their occupations aids them in preserving peace in their households. The ~~women know what they are to do,~~ and the men also; and one never meddles with the work of the other. The men make the frames of their canoes, and the women sew the bark with willow withes or similar small wood. The men shape the wood of the raquettes, and the women do the sewing on them. Men go hunting, and kill the animals; and the women go after them, skin them, and clean the hides. It is they who go in search of the wood that is burned. In fact, they would make fun of a man who, except in some great necessity, would do anything that should be done by a woman. Our Savage, seeing Father de Nouë carrying wood, began to laugh, saying "He's really a woman;" meaning that he was doing a woman's work. But a short time afterward, his wife falling sick, and having no one in his cabin who could assist him, he was compelled to go out himself in search of supplies; but in truth he went only at night when no one could see him.

1.2   Impressions of Indian Agricultural Labor. An account of Indian labors by Father Joseph Lafitau, S.J., the Jesuit missionary to the converted Iroquois near Montreal, in James Axtell, ed., *The Indian Peoples of Eastern America: A Documentary History of the Sexes* (New York: Oxford University Press, 1981), pp. 124–25. Reprinted with permission from the Campion Society.

The Indian women as well as the Amazons, the Thracian, Scythian and Spanish women and those of the other ~~barbarian races of antiquity,~~ ~~work the fields~~ as women do today in Gascony, Bearn and Bresse [in France] where we often see them running the plough while their husbands ply the distaff. The grain which they sow is maize, otherwise known as Indian or Turkish or Spanish wheat. It is the basis of the food of almost all the sedentary nations from one end of America to the other . . . In Canada, the moment that the snows are melted the Indian women begin their work. The first work done in the fields is gathering and burning the stubble. Then the ground is ploughed to make it ready to receive the grain which they are [going] to throw there. They do not use the plough [for this], any more than they do a number of other farming implements whose use is unknown to them and unnecessary for them. All that they need is a piece of bent wood three fingers wide, attached to a long handle which serves them to hoe the earth and stir it lightly. The fields which they are to sow are not arranged in headlands and furrows as they are in Europe, but in little round hillocks three feet in diameter. They make nine holes in each of these mounds. They cast into each hole a grain of Indian corn which they cover over carefully.

All the women of the village join together for the heavy work. They make numerous different bands according to the different quarters where they have their fields and pass from one field to the other helping each other. This can be done with less difficulty and the more quickly in that the fields are not separated by hedges and ditches. All together these [fields] give the appearance of only a single farm where there are no disputes over boundaries because every one knows how to recognize them clearly.

The mistress of the field where they are working distributes to each one of the workers the grain or seed for sowing which they receive in little *mannes* or baskets four or five fingers high and as wide, so that they can calculate the number of grains given out. Beside maize, they sow horse beans or little lima beans, pumpkins of a species different from those of France, watermelons and great sunflowers. They sow the lima beans next to the grains of their Indian corn, the cane or stalk of which serves them [the lima bean plants] as support as the elm does to the vine. They prepare special fields for their pumpkins and melons, but before sowing them in these fields, they plant the seeds in a preparation of black, light soil between two sheets of bark and place them above their hearths where they germinate. They keep their fields very clean. They are careful to pull up the grass in them until harvest time. There is also a set time for this [task] when they work all in common. Then each one carried with her a bundle of little sticks a foot or a foot and a half long, with her individual mark and gaily decorated with vermilion. They use these to mark their accomplishments and to make their work show up. When harvest time has come, they gather Indian corn which they pull off with the leaves around the ears so that they form the husk. These husks, strongly attached as they are serve for braiding them in bunches or in strings as is done with onions. The festival of binding together corn shocks is doubtless one of those which the ancients called <u>Cereales</u> which they celebrated in honour of Ceres. It takes place at night in the fields and is the only occasion when the men, who do no work either in the fields or with the harvest, are called upon by the women to help.

1.3 Trying to Understand Indian Notions of Property and Work. "The Description of Virginia by Captain John Smith, in Edward Arber, ed., *Captain*

John Smith, Works, 1608–1631 (Birmingham England, 1884), 65–70; quoted in Sylvia Frey and Marian J. Morton, eds., *New World, New Roles: A Documentary History of Women in Pre-Industrial America* (Westport: Greenwood Press, 1986), p. 49.

[handwritten annotation: That Why they weren't to labour good Solution prob?]

The ~~land is not populous, for the men be few~~; their far greater number is of women and children. Within sixty miles of Jamestown there are about some 5000 people, but of able men fit for their wars scarce 1500. To nourish so many together they have yet no means, because they make so small a benefit of their land, be it never so fertile.

Some being very great, as the Susquehannocks, others very little, as the Wighcocomocos; but generally tall and straight, of a comely proportion, and of a color brown when they are of any age, but they are born white. Their hair is generally black, but few have any beards. The men wear half their beard [heads] shaven, the other half long; for barbers they use their women, who with two shells will grate away the hair, of any fashion they please. The women's [heads] are cut in many fashions, agreeable to their years, but ever some part remains long.

They are very strong, of an able body and full of agility, able to endure to lie in the woods under a tree by the fire in the worst of winter, or in the weeds and grass. They are inconstant in everything but what constrains them to keep. Crafty, timorous, quick of apprehension, and very ingenious. Some are of disposition fearful, some bold, all savage. They are covetous of copper, beads, and such like trash. They are soon moved to anger, and so malicious that they seldom forget an injury. They seldom steal from one another, lest their conjurers should reveal it and so they be pursued and punished. That they are thus feared is certain, but that any can reveal their offenses by conjuration, I am doubtful. Their women are careful not to be suspected of dishonesty without the leave of their husbands.

Each household knows their own lands and gardens, and most live off their own labors. Their houses are in the midst of their fields or gardens, which are small plots of ground—some twenty acres, some forty, some one hundred, some two hundred, some more, some less. In some places from two to fifty of those houses [are] together or but a little separated by groves of trees. Near their habitations is little small wood or old trees on the ground by reason of their burning of them for fire. So that a man may gallop a horse among those woods any way but where the creeks or rivers shall hinder.

The men bestow their time in fishing, hunting, wars, and such man-like exercises, scorning to be seen in any women-like exercise, which is the cause that the women be very painful [toiling] and the men often idle. The women and children do the rest of the work. They make mats, baskets, pots, mortars, pound their corn, make their bread, prepare their victuals, plant their corn, gather their corn, bear all kind of burdens, and such like.

Their fire they kindle presently by chafing a dry pointed stick in a hole of a little square piece of wood, that firing itself will so fire moss, leaves, or any such like dry thing that will quickly burn.

In March and April they live much upon their fishing weirs, and feed on fish, turkeys, and squirrels. In May and June they plant their fields and live most off acorns, walnuts, and fish. But to amend their diet, some disperse themselves in small companies and live upon fish, beasts, crabs, oysters, land tortoises, strawberries, mulberries, and such like. In June, July, and August, they feed upon the roots of tuckahoe, berries, fish, and green wheat.

Betwixt their hands and thighs, their women use to spin the barks of trees, deer sinews, or a kind of grass they call pemmenaw; of these they make a thread very even and readily. This thread serves for many uses, as about their housing, apparel, also they make nets for fishing, for the quantity as formally braided as ours. They make also with it lines for angles.

Their hunting houses are like unto arbors covered with mats. These their women bear after them, with corn, acorns, mortars, and all bag and baggage they use. When they come to the place of exercise, every man does his best to show his dexterity, for by their excelling in those qualities they get their wives.

INDENTURE

What, if anything, do the following three documents (1.4–1.6) tell you about the people who signed indentures, the sorts of work and services that they provided their masters, and the treatment that they received? As you can see from these documents, labor was scarce in all regions of the colonies, indentures were much in demand, and indentured servants provided such skilled services as tutoring the children of masters and mistresses. Document 1.5, the diary of an indentured tutor, illustrates that even educated and married adult men sometimes had no choice but to sign articles of indenture. Document 1.6, by way of contrast, shows how colonial courts assigned dependent females and children to terms of indenture.

1.4   Evidence of Labor Shortages, 1743. An excerpt from the diary of William Stephens of Georgia, reproduced in E. Merton Coulter, ed., *The Journal of William Stephens, 1743–1745* (Athens: University of Georgia Press, 1958–59), pp. 24, 28.

October 4 [1743]. Tuesday. Upon making particular Enquiry what our New Settlers at Vernonburgh and Acton were doing, this being the best Season for clearing the land, I found there were employd to good purpose, and had already made good progress. . . . But I was sorry to see so little done on other such Tracts, where the Occupiers who had (divers of them) a good will to be doing, seemed utterly at a Stand for want of hands, and their hopes were in being suppled with some Assistance of Servants pursuant to the Trustees Intention before the Season was too far gone. All the Strength I could employ at Bewlie, was only two Boys with an Overseer to help; and that was precarious too, Wages being so exorbitant, that Day Labourers were in a manner to become our masters. In a melancholly mood under these thoughts, I pursued what was my present Business to get forward what I had to send in my packett.

October 15 [1743]. Saturday. A New York Sloop that had been trading at Barbadoes, and the Leeward Islands, Dubois Master, Springing a Leak, put in at Tybee on her way home, and the Master came up in his Boat to get help, and provision, which also he was in want of, having met with bad weather and Contrary Winds. The indented time of those three or four families of the Trusts Servants now expiring which hitherto they were bound by, now were preparing to go and Settle at Vernonburgh, where some fifty Acre Tracts were provided for them, among their Countrymen. And now we were reduced to a very helpless Condition, in Town as well as in Country, not knowing where to find working hands, Male or Female, either for the Field or the most necessary Domestick Uses, which to enlarge upon would be grievous; but tis yet to be hoped some Relief will be found in good time.

1.5   Diary of Indentured Servant John Harrower, 1774. An excerpt reproduced in John R. Commons et al., *Documentary History of American Industrial Society*, Vol. 1 (Cleveland: The A. H. Clark Company, 1910), pp. 366–69.

Wednesday, 26th. [January 1774] This day I being reduced to the last shilling I hade was obliged to engage to go to Virginia for four years as a schoolmaster for Bedd, Board, washing and five pound during the whole time. I have also wrote my wife this day a particular Acco't of everything that has happened to me since I left her until this date; at 3 pm this day I went on board the Snow Planter Cap't Bowers Com'r for Virginia now lying at Raliff Cross, and immediately I cam Onb'd I rec'd my Hammock and Bedding.

Munday, 31st. . . . It is surprising to see the No of good trades men th't come on b'd every day.

Sunday, [February] 6th. At 7 AM got under way with a fair wind and clear w'r. . . . with seventy Servants on board and all indented to serve four years there at their differint Occoupations myself being one of the Number and I Indented for a Clerk and Bookkeeper. . . .

Tuesday [May] 3rd. . . . we made Entry of the Rappahannock River, which we did at 10 AM, proceeding up the same for Fredericksburgh. . . .

Wednesday [May] 11th. At 10 AM Both Coopers and the Barker from our Mace went ashore upon tryall. At night one Daniel Turner a serv't returned onb'd from Liberty so drunk that he abused the Cap't And Chief

Mate and Boatswan to a verry high degree, which made to be horse whip'd, put in Irons and thumb screwed. On houre afterward he was unthumscrewed, taken out of Irons, but then he was handcuffed, and gagged all night. . . .

Munday, [May] 16th. This day severalls came onb'd to purchase serv'nts Indentures and among them there was two Soul drivers. They are men who make it their business to go onb'd all ships who have in their Servants or Convicts and buy sometime the whole and sometimes a parcell of them as they can agree, and then they drive them through the Country like a parcell of Sheep untill they can sell them to advantage, but all went away without buying any. . . .

Thursday, [May] 26th. This day at noon . . . Colonel [Daingerfield] send a Black with a cuple of horses for me and soon after I set our on Horseback and aravied at his seat of Belvidera. . . .

Freiday, [May] 27th. This morning about 8 AM the Colonel delivered his three Sons to my Charge to teach them to read, write and figure. . . . My school hours is from 6 to 8 in the morning; in the forenoon from 9 to 12, and from 3 to 6 in the afternoon.

1.6   Servants in Court, Chester County, Pennsylvania, 1697–98. From Sylvia R. Frey and Marian J. Morton, *New World, New Roles* (Westport: Greenwood Press, 1986), pp. 54–55.

John Wood had a servant maid whose name is Elizabeth Allen, who was adjudged to serve five years from the Court to the said John Wood or his assigns. Francis Chadsey brought a boy whose name is Alexander Steward, who was adjudged to serve eight years from the 14th day of September last past, if he be taught to read or write or else to serve but seven years. Also he had a servant maid whose name is Ann Bean, who was adjudged to serve five years from this Court to said Francis or his assigns.

William Cope brought a boy whose name is Thomas Harper, who was adjudged to serve five years and three quarters from the 14th day of September last past. If he be taught to read and to write or else to serve but five years from the said time to him or his assigns. William Coeburn's servant lad whose name is James Canadee was brought to this Court to answer for the getting of his servant woman with child, whose name is Margaret Adamson, and being examined about it, he denied it, and she being called and strictly examined, declared that he was the father of the child and no other and that it was one day that her master and dame was here at meeting and left them both at home together, and after some debate, it was reserved till the next Court that the same James Canadee shall appear at the next County Court. William Coeburn preferred a petition to the Court for to have satisfaction made him by the servant woman Margaret Adamson for what charges he had been had and expenses and for the loss of her time while she lay in and for her running away diverse times, and the said William Coeburn and Martha Reston were both attested and declared that they heard the said Margaret.

SLAVERY

Because slavery quickly became the preferred colonial solution to labor scarcity and existed in all of the colonies, we have chosen to include a larger number of documents on this subject. Scholars recently have raised a number of questions about the authenticity of Document 1.7, but we have included it because, despite what may be its semi-fictional character, it does contain revealing reflections on the "middle passage"—the ocean journey from Africa to the colonies—the ethnic and linguistic diversity among the African captives, and the strangeness of the "new world" and the white masters who dominated it. Document 1.8 provides support to a part of the reflections in the preceding document, suggesting how difficult it actually was to accustom African captives to the demands of slave labor. Documents 1.9– 1.11 illustrate the means by which some slaves resisted their bondage and how they were punished for their resistance—punishment that could include execution. Document 1.12 simultaneously indicates the power held by masters to sell their slaves and the residual ability of slaves to influence the terms of their sale. Document 1.13 offers evidence about one of the most common types of slave resistance, flight. Based on these ads for runaways, which slaves were most likely to flee? Finally, Document 1.14 illustrates how the ideology of the American Revolution prompted some slaves to draft petitions demanding their freedom.

1.7   An Account of the Middle Passage by a Slave. From Olaudah Equiano, *The Interesting Narrative of the Life of Olaudah Equiano* (London: X Press, 1998 [orig. 1791]), pp. 32–33.

One day, when we had a smooth sea and moderate wind, two of my wearied countrymen, who were chained together, (I was near them at the time) preferring death to such a life of misery, somehow made through the nettings and jumped into the sea. Immediately another quite dejected fellow, who on account of his illness was suffered to be out of irons also followed their example, and I believe many more would very soon have done the same, if they had not been prevented by the ship's crew, who were instantly alarmed. Those of us who were the most active were in a moment put down under the deck and there was such a noise and confusion amongst the people of the ship as I never heard before, to stop her and get the boat out to go after the slaves. However two of the wretches were drowned; but they got the other and afterward flogged him unmercifully, for thus attempting to prefer death to slavery. In this manner we continued to undergo more hardships than I can now relate, hardships which are inseparable from this accursed trade. Many a time we were near suffocation from the want of fresh air, being deprived thereof for days together. This and the stench of the necessary tubs, carried off many. . . .

We eventually came in sight of the island of Barbados, at which the whites on board gave a great shout and made many signs of joy to us. We did not know what to think of this, but as the vessel drew nearer we plainly saw the harbour and other ships of different kinds and sizes, and we soon anchored amongst them off Bridge Town. Many merchants and planters now came on board, though it was in the evening. They put us in separate parcels and examined us attentively. They also made us jump and pointed to the land, signifying we were to go there. We thought by this we should be eaten by these ugly men, as they appeared to us and, when soon after we were all put down under the deck again, there was much dread and trembling among us and nothing but bitter cries to be heard all the night from these apprehensions, insomuch that at last the white people got some old slaves from the land to pacify us. They told us we were not to be eaten, but to work and were soon to go on land, where we should see many of our country people. This report eased us much and, sure enough, soon after we landed, there came to us Africans of all languages.

We were conducted immediately to the merchant's yard, where we were all pent up together like so many sheep in a fold, without regard to sex or age.

As every object was new to me, everything I saw filled me with surprise. What struck me first was that the houses were built with bricks in stories and were in every other respect different from those I had seen in Africa; but I was still more astonished at seeing people on horseback. I did not know what this could mean, and indeed I thought these people full of nothing but magical arts. While I was in this astonishment one of my fellow prisoners spoke to a countryman of his about the horses, who said they were the same kind they had in their country. I understood them, though they were from a distant part of Africa and I thought it odd I had not seen any horses there, but afterwards, when I came to converse with different Africans, I found they had many horses amongst them and much larger than those I then saw.

We were not many days in the merchants' custody before we were sold after the usual manner, which is this: On a signal given, such as the beat of a drum, the buyers rush at once into the yard where the slaves are confined and make choice of that parcel they like best. The noise and clamour with which this is attended and the eagerness visible in the countenances of the buyers, serve not a little to increase the apprehensions of the terrified Africans, who may well be supposed to consider them the ministers of that destruction to which they think themselves devoted. In this manner, without scruple, are relations and friends separated, most of them never to see each other again. I remember in the vessel in which I was brought over, in the man's apartment, there were several brothers who, in the sale, were sold in different lots, and it was very moving on this occasion to see their distress and hear their cries at parting.

1.8 "Breaking In" New Slaves, ca. 1800. Extract from C. C. Robin's *Voyages . . . de Louisiane* (Paris, 1807), reproduced in John R. Commons et al., *Documentary History*, Vol. 2 (Cleveland: The A. H. Clark Company, 1910), pp. 31–41.

Negroes bought from the importers and carried home by the purchasers are ordinarily treated differently from the old ones. They are only gradually accustomed to work. They are made to bathe often, to take walks from time to time, and especially to dance; they are distributed in small numbers among old slaves in order to dispose them better to acquire their habits. These attentions are not usually due to sentiments of humanity. Interest requires them. It happens too often that poor masters, who have no other slaves, or are too greedy, require hard labor of these fresh negroes, exhaust them quickly, lose them by sickness and more often by grief. Often they hasten their own death; some wound themselves, others stifle themselves by drawing in the tongue so as to close the breathing passage, others take poison, or flee and perish of misery and hunger. The Africans imported into Louisiana are still more exposed to diseases than those of the other colonies [the French West Indies]. The winter bringing sharp and sudden frosts, is extremely hurtful to the negroes, especially when they are not young. They must always be covered and kept warm. The parsimony of some planters whom I could mention has cost them dear.

1.9 Execution of Rebellious Slave, 1681. The case of Maria Negro in *Publications of the Colonial Society of Massachusetts*, Vol. vi (Boston, 1904), 321; reproduced in Frey and Morton, eds., *New World, New Roles*, pp. 58–59.

AT A COURT OF ASSISTANTS HELD AT BOSTON,

6 September, 1681
Maria Negro, servant to Joshua Lamb of Roxbury in the County of Suffolk in New England, being presented by the Grand Jury, was indicted by the name of Maria Negro for not having the fear of God before her eyes and being instigated by the Devil at or upon the eleventh day of July last in the night did wittingly, willingly and feloniously set on fire the dwelling house of Thomas Swann of said Roxbury by taking a coal from under a sill and carried it into another room and laid it on the floor near the door and presently went and crept into hole at a back door of thy master Lamb's house and set it on fire. Also taking a live coal between two chips and

carried it into the chamber by which also it was consumed as by your confession will appear contrary to the peace of our Sovereign Lord the king, his Crown and dignity, the laws of this jurisdiction. The prisoner at the bar pleaded and acknowledged herself to be guilty of this fact. And accordingly, the next day being again brought to the bar, had sentence of death pronounced against her by the Honorable Governor, yet she should go from the bar to the prison whence she came and thence to the place of execution and there be burned.

1.10   Slaves' Resistance, 1833. Extract from a letter of Elisha Cain, overseer on Retreat Plantation, Jefferson County, Ga., to his employer, Alexander Telfair, Savannah, Ga., Nov. 4, 1833; in John R. Commons et al., *Documentary History*, Vol. 2 (Cleveland: The A. H. Clark Company, 1910), pp. 31–41.

I get on Pretty well with all the negroes Except Darkey she is the most troublesome one on the place Making disturbances amongst the Rest of the negroes and there is hardly any of them will Even go near the yard, she is of such a cruel disposition, not Even her sister's family. She could not stay in the yard with the girls you sent up without making an interruption with them, at length she got so high I went there and give her a moderate correction and that had a Bad affect she then threatened their lives and said that she would poison them they become alarmed and ask me permission to move to the Quarter I give them leave they have Been in the Quarter about one weeke. as I have commenced the subject I will give you a full history of my Belief of Darkey. to wit I believe her disposition as to temper is as Bad as any in the whole world I believe she is as unfaithful as any I have Ever Been acquainted with in every respect I believe she has Been more injury to you in the place where she is than two such negroes would sell for. I do not believe there is any negro on the place But would do Better than she has Ever done since I have been acquainted with her. I have tryed and done all I could to get on with her hopeing that she would mend. but I have Been disappointed in Every instant. I can not hope for the better any longer.

1.11   Slaves Influencing the Terms of Their Bondage, 1817. From M. G. Lewis, *Journal of a West India Proprietor* (London, 1834), the diary of the author while on a visit to his Jamaica plantation in 1817. Reproduced in John R. Commons et al. *Documentary History*, Vol. 2 (Cleveland: The A. H. Clark Company, 1910), pp. 31–41.

May 1, This morning I signed the manumission of Nicholas Cameron, the best of my mulatto carpenters. He has been so often on the very point of getting his liberty, and still the cup was dashed from his lips, that I had promised to set him free, whenever he could procure an able negro as his substitute; although being a good workman, a single negro was by no means an adequate price in exchange. On my arrival this year I found that he had agreed to pay £150 for a female negro, and the woman was approved of by my trustee. But on enquiry it appeared that she had a child, from which she was unwilling to separate, and that her owner refused to sell the child, except at a most unreasonable price. Here then was an unsurmountable objection to my accepting her, and Nicholas was told to his great mortification, that he must look out for another substitute. The woman on her part, was determined to belong to Cornwall estate and no other: so she told her owner that if he attempted to sell her elsewhere she would make away with herself, and on his ordering her to prepare for a removal to a neighboring proprietor's she disappeared, and concealed herself so well, that for some time she was believed to have put her threats of suicide into execution. The idea of losing his £150 frightened her master so completely, that he declared himself ready to let me have the child at a fair price, as well as the mother, if ever she should be found and her friends having conveyed this assurance to her, she thought proper to emerge from her hiding-place, and the bargain was arranged finally.

1.12   Slave for Sale. Letter of Billy Proctor, a slave, to John B. Lamar, Macon, Ga.; Americus, Ga., Dec. 1, 1854; in John R. Commons et al., *Documentary History*, Vol. 2 (Cleveland: The A. H. Clark Company, 1910), pp. 31–41.

MR. JOHN B. LAMAR, Macon, Ga.

Sir, As my owner, Mr. Chapman has determined to dispose of all his Painters, I would prefer to have you buy me to any other man. And I am anxious to get you to do so if you will. You know me very well yourself, but as I wish you to be fully satisfied, I beg leave to refer you to Mr. Nathan C. Monroe Dr. Strohecker and Mr. Bogg. I am in distress at this time, and will be until I hear from you what you will do. I can be bought for $1000—and I think that you might get me for 50 Dolls less if you try, though that is Mr. Chapman's price. Now Mas John, I want to be plain and honest with you. If you will buy me I will pay you $600—per year untill this money is paid, or at any rate will pay for myself in two years. I knew nothing of this matter last night when at your house, or I would have mentioned it while there. I am fearfull that if you do not buy me, there is no telling where I may have to go, and Mr. C. wants me to go where I would be satisfied—I promise you to serve you faithfully and I know that I am as sound and healthy as any one you can find. You will confer a great favour sir, by Granting my request, and I would be very glad to hear from you in regard to the matter at your earliest convenience—I would rather you would not say anything to Mr. C—about this matter untill I can hear from you, for I assure you I am in great distress and trouble at this time, but if you will grant my request—you will please write me a few lines, and I will come immediately to Macon to see you.

Your obedient & Humble Svt

BILLY PROCTOR

Americus, Ga. December 1, 1854.

1.13   Sample Runaway Slave Advertisements, Annapolis, Maryland, 1764. From *Runaway Slave Advertisements: A Documentary History from the 1730s to 1790*, Vol. 2, *Maryland*, compiled by Lathan A. Windley (Westport, CT: Greenwood Press, 1982), p. 55.

Annapolis *Maryland Gazette*, June 7, 1764.

RAN away from the Subscriber, living in Annapolis, a strong, well set Negro Man, named Charles*, about 5 Feet 9 Inches high, he was born in Dorchester County, and brought up in Mr. Nevit's Family, a waiting Man: He had on and with him when he went away, a grey Fearnought Jacket, one coarse white Cotton, and one blue Ditto, without Sleeves, Cotton Breeches, Yarn Stockings, and Country made Shoes, with Straps: He took with him his Blankets, is a sensible Fellow, tells his Story plausibly, was lurking about Annapolis some Time after he ran away, and may possibly now be in it's Neighbourhood.

Whoever will bring him to us, if taken within Ten Miles of Annapolis, shall have Twenty Shillings; and if taken in this County beyond that Distance, Twenty Shillings and what the Law allows; and if taken out of the County, and secured in the County Goal where taken, Twenty Shillings besides what the Law allows.

LANCELOT JACQUES,

THOMAS JOHNSON, junr.

Annapolis *Maryland Gazette*, August 23, 1764.

RAN away from the Subscriber, living near the Head of South-River, some Time last June, a Country born Negro man named Toney, about 6 Feet high, has a small Scar in his Forehead, a down Look, and is slow of Speech: Had on when he went away, an Oznabrigs Shirt, and a Cotton Jacket and Breeches. It is likely he has other Cloathings, as some are missing. He has been used to work on board of Ships, and it is thought he is lurking about in order to get on board a Vessel. All Masters of Vessels are forbid carrying him off at their Peril.

Whoever will deliver the said Negro to me, shall receive Four Dollars Reward.

JOHN WILMOT.

Annapolis *Maryland Gazette,* September 6, 1764.
RAN away from the Subscriber, on the 23d of August last, a Country born Mulatto Slave, named James, who formerly belonged to Capt. Richard Boone; he is about 30 Years of Age, near 6 Feet high, an able brisk Fellow, understands Plantation Work, Sawing, and has been used to go by Water, is a cunning artful Fellow, and will deceive any Person that give Credit to what he says. His Apparel is an Oznabrigs Shirt, and black and white Country Cloth Breeches; but them he will change, if he has an Opportunity of Stealing. Masters of Vessels and Others are forewarned not to employ him, as they will answer it at their Peril. Whoever takes him up, and delivers him to the Subscriber in Broad-Neck, on the North Side of Severn River, shall have Twenty Shillings Reward, paid by
PHILIP PETTIBONE.

Annapolis *Maryland Gazette,* September 13, 1764.
RAN away from the Subscriber at Bladensburg; on the first of this Instant September, a Negro Man named Joe, about 35 Years old, of a low Stature, and has a very wide Walk. His Breeches are red; but the other Parts of his Dress is not certainly known. He is by Trade a Ship Carpenter or Caulker, and when he lived with some Masters, he was allowed to look for Work in different Rivers. Whoever will bring him to his Master, shall have Twenty Shillings more than the law allows. All Masters of Vessels and Others are desired not to employ or entertain him. He is very artful, and probably may endeavour to pass as a Freeman. Should he be brought any considerable Distance, Satisfaction will be made in Proportion. It will be necessary to tie him securely.
CHRISTOPHER LOWNDES.

1.14   Slaves' Petition for Freedom, 1773. From Herbert Aptheker, ed., *A Documentary History of the Negro People in the United States,* Vol. 1 (New York, Citadel Press, 1951), pp. 7–8.

[For the Representative of the town of Thompson]
Boston, April 20th, 1773
Sir, The efforts made by the legislative of this province in their last session to free themselves from slavery, gave us, who are in that deplorable state, a high degree of satisfaction. We expect great things from men who have made such a noble stand against the designs of their *fellow-men* to enslave them. We cannot but wish and hope Sir, that you will have the same grand object, we mean civil and religious liberty, in view in your next session. The divine spirit of *freedom,* seems to fire every human breast on this continent, except such as are bribed to assist in executing the execrable plan.

We are very sensible that it would be highly detrimental to our present masters, if we were allowed to demand all that of *right* belongs to us for past service; this we disclaim. Even the *Spaniards,* who have not those sublime ideas of freedom that English men have, are conscious that they have no right to all the services of their fellow-men, we mean the *Africans,* whom they have purchased with their money; therefore they allow them one day in a week to work for themselves, to enable them to earn money to purchase the residue of their time, which they have a right to demand in such portions as they are able to pay for (a due appraizement of their services being first made, which always stands at the purchase money.) We do not pretend to dictate to you Sir, or to the Honorable Assembly, of which you are a member. We acknowledge our obligations to you for what you have already done, but as the people of this province seem to be actuated by the principles of equity and justice, we cannot but expect your house will again take our deplorable case into serious consideration, and give us that ample relief which *as men,* we have a natural right to.

But since the wise and righteous governor of the universe, has permitted our fellow men to make us slaves, we bow in submission to him, and determine to behave in such a manner as that we may be reason to expect the divine approbation of, and assistance in, our peaceable and lawful attempts to gain our freedom.

We are willing to submit to such regulations and laws, as may be made relative to us, until we leave the province, which we determine to do as soon as we can, from our joynt labours procure money to transport ourselves to some part of the Coast of *Africa,* where we propose a settlement. We are very desirous that you should have instructions relative to us, from your town therefore we pray you to communicate this letter to them, and ask this favor for us.

In behalf of our fellow slaves in this province, and by order of their Committee.
Peter Bestes
Sambo Freeman
Felix Holbrook
Chester Joie

WOMEN AND WORK

As we noted in the introduction to this section, the labor of women was as vital to the colonial economy and society as that of men. Women provided a remarkable array of services and provisions for society as Document 1.15 illustrates. Document 1.16 offers evidence of a persistent peril of dependent female domestic labor, the tendency or ability of exploitative masters to harass sexually their female employees. The excerpts from the diary of the Maine midwife, Martha Ballard (Document 1.17) show even more fully how hard colonial and early national women labored; how difficult it would have been to reproduce the colonial population without the medical services offered by such women as Martha; and how common and everyday were occurrences such as severe illness and death.

1.15   Colonial Women Advertise for Work, ca. 1760. Advertisements gathered and reproduced in Julia Cherry Spruill, *Women's Life and Work in The Southern Colonies* (Chapel Hill: The University of North Carolina Press, 1938), 286–87.

"Quilting, Plain or Figur'd, coarse or fine performed in the best and cheapest manner."

"Dyeing in all Colours, and Scowering of all Sorts, is performed as usual by Mrs. Bartram. N. B. Chints's and Callicoes are cleaned and glazed after the best Manner."

"Rich plumb cake at 10s. per pound, biscuit and seed ditto, syllybubs and jelleys, 20s. per dozen, white custards in glasses at *15s.* per dozen, lemon and orange cream blomage, 20s. per plate, rice cups, at 12s. 6d. per plate, lemon, orange, citron, and almond pudding, 20s. a piece, orange pye, 30s., snow cheese, 30s., apple tarts, curd, and apple cheese cakes, 24S. per dozen, almond and lemon ditto, 30s. per dozen, minced pies, 3s. 9d. a piece, a piece, apples 15s. per."

1.16   Sexual Harrassment of a Servant. From Frey and Morton, eds., *New World, New Roles*, p. 53.

TESTIMONY OF ELIZABETH STURGIS

First, I, Elizabeth Sturgis, do affirm that when I lived with my master Cummings, I was sent to Captain Patrick's to help his wife, and having business in the cellar, he came down presently after me and took me about the middle and would kiss me and put his hand into my bosom, at which I was much amazed at his carriage to me, being but young, yet striving with him, he let me go then presently. After I went home to my master's and being troubled at it when we were in bed, I acquainted my dame's sister with his carriage to me. Afterwards my dame sending me thither again, I refused to go. My dame desirous to know the reason, her sister standing by told her, and she made her husband acquainted with his carriage to me, and her husband told a neighbor of it and that man told master Carter and Mr. Carter deals with him about it, whereupon he comes to my master and calls him to speak with him. Then my master calls me out and said to me, I wonder you should deal so with me, and I replied to him and said you cannot be ignorant of these things. And after many passages, he said if these things be true, I was in great temptation, and then he said to me, he could trouble me, but he would not and so he left.

Secondly, some time after I living at home with my father, I went into the lot to gather sucking stalks and he [Patrick] came suddenly upon me and asked me whether I spake those things that I had spake for any hurt to him or not. I said no, I aimed not to hurt him nor any other and the things being past, I intended to speak no more of them. Then he offered to kiss me. I refusing, he said unless I would kiss him, he would not believe but that I would speak of it again.

Thirdly, some time after, I being married, upon some occasion coming into the bay to my father's, I going to Watertown to the lecture, he [Patrick] overtook me on the way and spake to me to call in as I went back to see his wife, which I did. And suddenly he came in and desired me to go into the next room to speak with me about our plantation, and I was there, he came to kiss me. I desired him to forbear and told him such things were not fit, but he would and did and would have had me to set on his lap, but I did not. Then he replied to me that it was lawful so to do to express love one to another. Then I rose up to go away, but he said I should tarry, for he had sent for sack [wine] and I should drink with him. I told him I must be going. He told me if he had time and opportunities, he would make it appear to me the lawfulness of it. I still desiring to be gone, he wished me not to be offended, for if I did love him but as well as he did love me, I would not take it so ill but would rather pity him than be offended. Then he was at me to meet him in the evening and he would further labor to convince me of his love to me, but with much ado I got away and presently made my father and all the house acquainted with it and durst not go out that night for fear.

1.17 Two Weeks in the Life of Midwife Martha Ballard, 1787. From Laurel Thatcher Ulrich, *A Midwife's Tale: The Life of Martha Ballard, Based on Her Diary, 1785–1812* (New York: Vingtage Books, 1990), pp. 36–39.

[Friday, Aug. 3, 1787] Clear & very hot. I have been pulling flax. Mr Ballard Been to Savages about some hay.

[Sat. Aug. 4] Clear morn. I pulld flax till noon. A very severe shower of hail with thunder and Litning began at half afer one continud near 1 hour. I hear it broke 130 panes of glass in fort western. Colonel Howard made me a present of 1 gallon white Rhum & 2 lb sugar on acount of my atendance of his family in sickness. Peter Kenny has wounded his Legg & Bled Excesivily.

[Sunday, Aug. 5] Clear morn. Mr Hamlin Breakfastd here. Had some pills. I was calld at 7 O Clok to Mrs Howards to see James he being very sick with the canker Rash. Tarried all night.

[Monday, Aug. 6] I am at Mrs. Howards watching her son. Went out about day, discovered our saw mill in flames. The men at the fort went over. Found it consumed with some plank & Bords. I tarried till Evinng. Left James Exceedingly Dangerously ill. My daughter Hannah is 18 years

old this day. Mrs. Williams here when I came home. Hannah Cool gott
Mrs Norths web out at the Loome. Mr Ballard complains of a soar throat
this night. He has been to take Mr gardners hors home.

[Tuesday, Aug. 7] Clear. I was Calld to Mrs. Howards this morning for
to see her son. Find him very low. Went from Mrs Howard to see
Mrs Williams. Find her very unwell. Hannah Cool is there. From thence
to Joseph Fosters to see her sick Children. Find Saray & Daniel very ill.
Came home went to the field and got some Cold water root. Then calld
to Mr. Kenydays to see Polly. Very ill with the Canker. Gave her some of
the root. I gargled her through which gave her great Ease. Returned home
after dark. Mr Ballard been to Cabesy. His throat is very soar. He gargled
it with my tincture. Find relief & went to bed comfortably.

[Wednesday, Aug. 8] Clear. I have been to see Mary Kenida. Find her
much as she was yesterday. Was at Mr. McMasters. Their children two of
them very ill. The other 2 recovering. At Mr Williams also. She is some
better. Hear James Howard is mending. Hannah Cool came home.

[Thursday, Aug. 9] Clear. I workd about house forenoon. Was Calld to
Mrs Howards to see James. Found him seemingly Expireing. Mrs Pollard
there. He revived.

[Friday, Aug. 10] At Mrs Howards. Her son very sick. Capt Sewall &
Lady set up till have after 4. Then I rose. The Child seems revivd.

[Saturday, Aug. 11] Calld from Mrs Howard to Mr. McMasters to see
their son William who is very low. Tarried there this night.

[Sunday, Aug. 12] Loury. At Mr. McMasters. Their son very sick. I set
up all night. Mrs Patin with me. The Child very ill indeed.

[Monday, Aug. 13] William McMaster Expird at 3 O Clock this morn.
Mrs Patin & I laid out the Child. Poor mother, how Distressing her Case,
near the hour of Labour and three Children more very sick. I set out for
home. Calld at Mrs. Howards. I find her son very low. At Mr Williams.
Shee very ill indeed. Now at home. It is nine O Clok morn. I feel as if I
must take some rest. I find Mr Ballard is going to Pittston on Business.
Dolly is beginning to weave three handkerchiefs. Ephraim & I went to see
Mrs Williams at Evining. I find her some Better. . . .

[Tuesday, Aug. 14] Clear & hott. I pikt the safron. Mrs Patten here.
Mr Ballard & I all the girls attended the funeral of William McMaster.
Their other Children are mending. James Howard very low. I drank Tea at
Mr Pollards. Calld at Mr Porters.

[Wednesday, Aug. 15] Clear mon. I pulld flax the fornon. Rain afternoon. I am very muich fatagud. Lay on the bed and rested. The two
Hannahs washing. Dolly weaving. I wast called to Mrs Claton in trail at
11 O Clok Evening.

[Thursday, Aug. 16] At Mr Cowans. Put Mrs Claton to Bed with a
son at 3 pm. Came to Mr Kenadays to see his wife who has a sweling
under her arm. Polly is mending. I returned as far as Mr Pollards by water.
Calld from there to Winthrop to Jermy Richards wife in Travil. Arivd about
9 O Clok Evin.

[Friday, Aug. 17] At Mr. Richards. His wife Delivered of a Daugher 10 O Clok morn. Returned as far as Mr Pollards at 12. Walked from there. . . .

[Saturday, Aug. 18] I spun some shoe thread & went to see Mrs. Williams. She has news her Mother is very sick. Geny Huston had a Child Born the night before last. I was Calld to James Hinkly to see his wife at 11 & 30 Evening. Went as far as Mr Weston by land, from thence by water. Find Mrs Hinkly very unwell.

WORK, WELFARE, AND COMMUNITY VALUES

The alleviation of poverty without draining the material resources of local communities intensified in the colonies as the population expanded rapidly and the dependent portion of it, especially women and children, grew substantially. The following three documents (1.18–1.20) indicate how in colonial New England the region's dominant citizens, often men of the cloth, amalgamated charity and Christianity to solve the dual problems of poverty and unemployment. What methods were proposed in these documents to fight poverty among dependent women and children and to train them to become disciplined and productive members of society?

1.18 Linking Christian Charity to Enterprise, 1754. From the *Articles of the Society for Encouraging Industry and Employing the Poor* (Boston: Society for Encouraging Industry and Employing the Poor, 1754), pp. 2–3.

Rules of the Society for Encouraging Industry and Employing the Poor

This Town has remarkably signalized itself, for its Charity and Compassion to the Poor, who for some Years past have been an encreasing Burthen, and yet the Supplies that are annually furnish'd, are very far from being an adequate Relief to their Necessities; and what is worse, there is no Prospect of diminishing this Burthen in the present Way of distributing our Charity; on the contrary, it must be expected to increase by the continual Addition of new Objects, from which nothing but their Death will be likely to release us, which a new Succession of them will daily present themselves in the Room of those who are at rest from their Miseries; Every Man of Sense must see and every Lover of his Country will deplore the Calamities that must arise from increasing Poverty, Idleness, and Vice; but every Christian will feel the Miseries of such a State, almost as if they were his own, and be uneasy till some Method be entered upon, for providing an effectual Remedy against them—Temporary Methods of Relief are very commendable, till something better can be established; but these are of the Nature of Palliatives only, it must be a lasting and permanent Scheme, that may be expected to reach the Root of this Malady; The Linen Manufacture, when thoroughly understood, will appear to be such a Scheme, and under proper Cultivation will, it is apprehended, enlarge itself into a noble Design, so as not only to yield present Relief to great Numbers of poor People, but by gradually extending itself to all parts of the Province, seems to promise a perpetual Establishment; and it is to be enter'd upon with a proper Spirit, and vigorously supported in the Beginning, it will soon add a new branch of Riches to the Province, will cloathe the Naked, find Bread for the Hungry, and Employment for the Idle.

1.19   The Deserving and Undeserving Poor, 1752. From Charles Chauncy, *The Idle Poor Secluded from the Bread of Charity by Christian Law: A Sermon Preached* in *Boston, Before the Society for Encouraging Industry and Employing the Poor, August 12, 1752* (Boston: T. Fleet, 1752), pp. 16–18.

You are hereby, my Brethren, restrained as to the Distributions of your Charity; not being allowed to dispense it promiscuously, but obliged to take due Care to find out suitable Objects; distinguishing properly between those needy People who are *able*, and those who are *unable*, to employ themselves in Labour.

You can scarce be too liberal in your Charities to those, who, in the Providence of God, are reduced to Straits, not thro' Slothfulness, but real Incapacity for Work. The Christian Law, requiring Charity, was made with a special View to this Kind of needy People: and you may under no Pretence, shut up the Bowels of your Compassion against the Cry of their Wants. . . .

But tho' you can't be too generous in your Charities to the poor, yet, as I said, you must take Care to distinguish between them. For as to them who *can*, but *won't*, work; who have the Ability for Labour but no Disposition, you are restrained from supporting them in *Idleness.*

And in what more proper Way can we shew Kindness to the poor . . . than by contributing to such a generous Design of setting them to Work, that with quietness they may Labour, and, as the Fruit thereof, eat their own Bread. We shall herein concur with the infinitely good God himself, who does not give Men Food and Raiment, and other Necessaries immediately from Heaven, but by adding his Blessing to their laborious Industry. . . .

According to Information I have received, some thousands of Yards of good *Linen Cloth,* have been already fitted for Market; a Specimen whereof, you have there before your Eyes. And it is easy to determine, that, in order to this, Employ must have been given to a very considerable Number of Labourers, in raising Flax, in preparing it for the Wheel, in spinning it into Thread, and then in weaving into Cloth. Some hundreds of Women and Children have, by this Means, been kept at Work, whereby they have done a great deal towards supplying themselves with Bread, to the easing the Town of its Burthen in providing for the poor. And, as one good Effect of the setting up of this *Linen Manufacture,* it may with Truth be said, there is now to be found, in the Town, many a virtuous married Woman, and young Maiden (some Instances whereof are there presented to your View) who may be characterized in the Words of Solomon, *She seeketh Flax, and working willingly with her hands She Layeth her hands to the Spindle, and her Hands hold the Distaff. She maketh fine Linen, and selleth it to the Merchant.*

Perhaps, scarce any Design of this Nature has afforded a more hopeful Prospect in its beginning . . . finding Employ for great Numbers of Women and Children, and by this Means enabling them to assist in the support of the Families to which they belong, to the great Advantage of the Community.

1.20   Rooting Out "Evil Habits," 1758. Thomas Barnard, *A Sermon Preached in Boston, New-England, before the Society for Encouraging Industry and Employing the Poor, September 20, 1758* (Boston: S. Kneeland, 1758), pp. 10–24.

An Industrious Prosecution of the Arts of civil Life is very friendly to social Virtue, and begets and maintains relative Happiness. . . . Religion will most flourish where the Arts of Peace are cultivated, especially Industry, among those born for Labour. For by Means of this quiet, this social State, this steady Kind of Life, Men's Attention is less dissipated, their Minds more open to Instruction, a Regard to whatever is virtuous & pious kept alive. . . .

The Design therefore of the Society for Encouraging Industry and employing the Poor is wise & generous. To rescue Youth of the lower Sort from the Temptations Idleness exposes to—To add as it were, so many useful Members to the Common-wealth—To relieve the Dispirited, and at the same Time serve the Public, is a noble Purpose; in the Execution of which, *Gentlemen,* we heartily *bid you God speed.*

Though your particular Institutions have a special Regard to the female Sex, they have never the less Utility. We know what an Influence that Sex has had on us, from the Days of the first Woman. When they have contracted evil Habits, they will be bad Wives, bad Mothers, and nurse up a useless Race in their own Likeness. Your Measures rescue tender Modesty from Snare, promote Virtue, the Happiness of particular Relations, as well as the general Good. But they are not confined to these Females. The Manufactures they are employed in, give Rise to the Labour & Earnings of Multitudes, from the plowing the Ground for Flax, to the exporting the Seed. We hope that Love to your Country and your Species, will carry you thro' every Difficulty attending your Scheme in its early Days.

ARTISAN LABOR

Artisan laborers in the colonial and early national periods shared a particular culture, a style of work, and aspirations for the future. Perhaps the most famous of colonial artisans and the one whose many writings best exemplify the culture of such workers was Benjamin Franklin. The following excerpt (Document 1.21) from one of his most famous pieces defines the essence of the artisan work ethic as well as the artisan's independent nature. Document 1.22 illustrates how artisans sought to distinguish themselves from aristocrats or gentlemen who strutted about with fancy manners and did no productive labor. Finally, Document 1.23 explores one of the darker sides of artisan culture, the penchant of such workers for the prolific consumption of strong alcohol, a habit that coexisted alongside strong strictures within the culture against the dependency that overindulgence in drink could foster.

1.21   Ben Franklin Espouses the Work Ethic, 1757. An excerpt from *Poor Richard's Almanac* in Jared Sparks, ed., *The Works of Benjamin Franklin*, Vol. 2 (Boston: Hilliard, Gray, and Company, 1840), pp. 95–96.

unlike aristocrats!

Let us then be up and doing, and doing to the purpose; so by diligence shall we do more with less perplexity. *Sloth makes all things difficult, but industry all easy;* and *He that riseth late must trot all day, and shall scarce overtake his business at night;* while *Laziness travels slowly so poverty overtakes him....* He that hath a trade hath an estate; and he that hath a calling, hath an office for profit and honor, as Poor Richard says; but then the trade must be worked at, and the calling followed, or neither the estate nor the office will enable us to pay our taxes. If we are industrious, we shall never starve; for *At the working man's house hunger looks in, but dares not enter....* If you were a servant, would you not be ashamed that a good master should catch you idle? Are you then your own master? Be ashamed to catch yourself idle, when there is so much to be done for yourself, your family, your country, your king. Handle your tools without mittens; remember, that *The cat in gloves catches no mice,* as Poor Richard says. It is true there is much to be done, and perhaps you are weak-handed; but stick to it steadily, and you will see great effects for *Constant dropping wears away stones;* and *By diligence and patience the mouse ate in two the cable;* and *Little strokes fell great oaks.*

don't be idle

1.22   The Artisan's Pride in Manual Labor, 1811. A letter to the Independent Mechanic, May 25, 1811, reprinted in Howard B. Rock, ed., *The New York City Artisan, 1789–1825: Documentary History* (Albany: State University of New York Press, 1989), pp. 50–51.

Mr. Editor, there is an evil which I should extremely well like to see some notice taken of. I allude to a certain class of men whom I often observe in my route to my daily labour (being a mechanic) walking with slow and solemn pace, perusing their letters on their way from the post office. I do not mean to complain, Mr. Editor, at their anxiety to see the contents of their letters, for that I know is natural to us all; but it is the affectation and self consequence displayed in the manner. I know, indeed, that men of business have not time to go home to read their letters, and therefore, their looking at them in the street, is often necessary. But as soon as they read them over, they put them into their pockets; this is as it should be. But, Mr. Editor, is it not ridiculous to see a young fellow, who wishes to attach a degree of consequence to himself, stand for an hour posing over half a dozen lines from a country friend, and not even content with that he takes up his line of march, with his letter up to his eyes, and his head bent in the attitude of deep study and meditation, and thus continues, probably, until he reads within a few doors of his master's shop. But perhaps, Mr. Editor, you will say that it may be a long letter, and wrote in a poor hand, and therefore that it would require some time to feret it out. This, indeed, might be the case, I readily grant; though that is not always so. I know from experience: for having accidentally got a peep at one of those consequential blade's letters, I discovered to my satisfaction, that his letter amounted to but five lines, written in quite large and legible hand; so coaxing my patience to watch his manoevres at the post office door for half an hour, and being not yet satisfied, I actually waited till he moved, and then took up my march after him. After having followed him for a mile and a half (during the whole of which time he was deeply concerned in perusing his five lines) I abandoned him, concluding, that instead of a quarter, I should lose half a day, if I kept on any longer.

It is to be hoped, Sir, that by thus noticing these pompous, vain and ridiculous practices of a certain class of young men . . . [we can] put a stop to a foolish pride in which they too far indulge themselves, and teach them a lesson, that the honest, blunt, and unaffected manners of a young mechanic, is far more praise-worthy, than the pedantic foppish airs of a would-be gentleman.

Ariel Mechanic

1.23   Artisans and Alcohol, 1811. From the Independent Mechanic, August 10, 1811, reprinted in Rock, ed., *The New York City Artisan, 1789–1825*, p. 49.

FOR THE INDEPENDENT MECHANIC ON DRUNKENNESS

being called a drunk is really offensive?

Of all the vices to which the fallibility of our nature has subjected us, this is the most disgustful. It brings with it numberless disorders, accumulating both on the body and conscience, and renders us not only detested by society, but hateful even to ourselves. From the brightest prospects of earthly fame and happiness, it plunges us into the darkest depth of misery and despair, closing the bright scenes of happiness hereafter from view forever. How miserable must be the man addicted to this vice! How wounding to the feelings of an innocent man to be accused of it!—I have written this for the purpose of introducing a letter written from a man who was accused of habitual drunkenness, to his accuser. The former had indeed given some ground for suspicion, but was far from being guilty of the charge.
Mr. W.

Reports have circulated abroad which owe their origin to you, stamping upon the unblotted page of my charachter, in letters of the blackest dye, the name of drunkard! Christian forebearance teaches the expostulation, although the silver voice of friendship has by this report become discordant, and the hand of confidence is dubiously extended towards men. Sir, I am young, and an adventurer, my prospects all depending on my character. I have mother, brothers, sisters, and friends. The man who becomes a drunkard, sacrifices his youth and health, his prospects and his fame; he brings the grey hairs of his parents "with sorrow to the grave;" he brings disgrace upon his brothers and dishonour upon his sisters; and freezes the warm current of friendship, the nourisher of life and hope, the soother of sorrow, and the comforter in misfortune.

A drunkard is a being who bears no connexion to this world; with whom the world has no connexion. Living in himself, he loaths mankind, and still is sickened with the food he lives on. A wretch, who stands a mark for scorn to point her slowly moving finger at. Compassion exercises her functions with indifference, and charity, even charity, weeps, that the object is unworthy the exercise of her grace. Do I deserve this?

WORKERS' GRIEVANCES AND EARLY UNION ORGANIZATION DEBATES

As the gap between poor and rich widened in the late colonial period and more especially the gap between masters and journeymen in the early national period, the poorer and less successful economically expressed their discontent and also acted to remedy it. The excerpt from Benjamin

Franklin's writings (Document 1.24) partly defends the existing distribution of income and wealth and indicts the poor for being both envious and their own worst enemies, for example by celebrating "St. Monday," an extra day of rest following a weekend of debauchery. The final four documents (1.25–1.28) show how journeymen shoemakers (cordwainers in early national Philadelphia) sought to defend their status, income, and independence through collective action, and also how their employers attacked them. Document 1.25 indicates how masters sought to use the law to combat collective action by their journeymen while Document 1.26 provides the legal defense offered by the journeymen. Document 1.27 gives the legal testimony of one loyal member of the shoemakers' union who participated in the turnout (strike) against the masters, while Document 1.28 offers the testimony of a journeyman shoemaker who chose to breach society (union) rules, stay at work, and "scab" on his fellow journeymen.

1.24 Benjamin Franklin on the "Laboring Poor," 1768. In Sparks, ed., *The Works of Benjamin Franklin*, Vol. 2, pp. 367–71.

I have met with much invective in the papers, for these past two years, against the hard-heartedness of the rich, and much complaint of the great oppressions suffered in this country by the laboring poor. . . . But when I see that the poor are . . . exasperated against the rich, and excited to insurrections, by which much mischief is done, and some forfeit their lives, I could wish the true state of things were better understood. . . .

If it be said that their wages are too low, and that they ought to be better paid for their labor, I heartily wish that any means could be fallen upon to do it, consistent with their interest and happiness; but, as the cheapness of other things is owing to the plenty of those things, so the cheapness of labor is in most cases owing to the multitude of laborers, and to their underworking one another in order to obtain employment. How is this to be remedied? A law might be made to raise their wages; but, if our manufactures are too dear, they will not vend abroad, and all that part of employment will fail. . . .

Among ourselves, unless we give our working people less employment, how can we . . . pay them higher for what they do? . . . Should they get higher wages, would that make them less poor, if, in consequence, they worked fewer days of the week proportionably? I have said, a law might be made to raise their wages; but I doubt much whether it could be executed . . . unless another law, now indeed almost obsolete, could at the same time be revived and enforced; a law, I mean, that many have often heard and repeated, but few have duly considered. *SIX days shalt thou labor.* This is as positive a part of the commandment, as that which says, *The SEVENTH thou shalt rest.* But we remember well to observe the indulgent part, and never think of the other. *Saint Monday* is generally as duly kept by our working people as *Sunday;* the only difference is, that, instead of employing their time cheaply at church, they are wasting it expensively at the alehouse.

1.25   Indictment Against the Philadelphia Cordwainers, 1806. From the case of *Commonwealth v. Pullis*, 1806. Reproduced in John R. Commons et al., *Documentary History*, Vol. 3 (Cleveland: The A. H. Clark Company, 1910), pp. 62–67.

The grand inquest of the commonwealth of Pennsylvania, inquiring for the city of Philadelphia upon their oaths and affirmations, respectively, do present that George Pullis, Peter Pollen, John Harket, John Hepburn, Underi Barnes, John Dubois, George Keimer, and George Snyder, late of the city of Philadelphia, aforesaid, being artificers, workmen and journeymen in the art and occupation of a cordwainer, and not being content to work, and labour in that art and occupation, at the usual prices and rates for which they and other artificers, workmen and journeymen, in the same art and occupation were used and accustomed to work and labour; but contriving, and intending unjustly and oppressively, to increase and augment the prices and rates usually paid and allowed to them and other artificers, workmen, and journeymen, in the said art, and occupation, and unjustly to exact and procure great sums of money, for their work and labour, in the said art and occupation, on the first day of November in the year of our Lord one thousand eight hundred and five, with force and arms did combine, conspire, confederate, and unlawfully agree together, at the city of Philadelphia, aforesaid, that they, the said . . . [defendants], or any of them would not, nor should work and labour, in the said art and occupation, but at certain large prices and rates, which they the said George Pullis [et al.] then and there insisted on being paid, for their future work and labour in the said art and occupation, for and upon, and in respect of certain particular sorts of work and labour in the said art and occupation, that is to say: for making fancy boots, the sum of five dollars for making back strap boots the sum of four dollars, for making long boots the sum of three dollars, for making cossacks the sum of three dollars, and for making bootees the sum of three dollars, which, said several rates and prices which were so as aforesaid, fixed and insisted on by the said George Pullis [et al.] were at the time of their being so fixed and insisted on by them the said George Pullis [et al.], more than the several and respective prices and rates, which had been, and which were then used and accustomed to be paid and allowed to them, the said George Pullis [et al.], and other artificers, workmen, and journeymen employed in the said art and occupation of a cordwainer, for and upon and in respect of the said particulars and respective sorts of work and labour, for and upon and in respect of which the same were so respectively fixed and insisted on by the said George Pullis [et al.], as aforesaid, to the damage, injury, and prejudice, of the masters employing them in the said art and occupation, of a cordwainer and of the citizens of the commonwealth generally, and to the great damage and prejudice of other artificers, and journeymen, in the said art and occupation of a cordwainer, to the evil example of others, and against the peace and dignity of the commonwealth of Pennsylvania.

And the inquest aforesaid upon their oaths, and affirmations aforesaid, do further present that the said George Pullis [et al.] being artificers, work-men, and journeymen, in the said art and occupation of a cordwainer, and not being contented to work and labour, in that art, and occupation, at the usual prices and rates, for which they and other artificers, work-men, and journeymen, in the same art and occupation, were used and accustomed to work and labour, but contriving and intending, unjustly and oppressively to increase and augment the prices, and rates usually paid, and allowed to them and other artificers, workmen, and journeymen, in the said art and occupation, and unjustly to exact and procure great sums of money for their work and labour, on the said first day of November one thousand eight hundred and five, with force, and arms, at the city of Philadelphia, aforesaid, unlawfully did combine, conspire, confederate, and agree together, that they the said George Pullis [et al.], or any of them would not, nor should, and also that they the said George Pullis [et al.], and each, and every of them should and would endeavour to prevent by threats, menaces, and other unlawful means, other artificers, workmen, and jour-neymen, in the said art and occupation, from working and labouring in the said art and occupation, but at certain large prices, and rates which they the said George Pullis [et al.], then and there fixed and insisted on being paid for their future work and labour. . . .

And the inquest aforesaid, upon their oaths and affirmations aforesaid, do further present, that, the said George Pullis [et al.] . . . in pursuance of the said unlawful conspiracy, combination, and agreement, refused to work at the usual rates and prices given to artificers, workmen and journeymen in the said art and occupation of a cordwainer, and still do, and each of them doth refuse to work and labour at the usual rates and prices accustomed to be given to them, the said George pullis [et al.], and other artificers, workmen and jour-neymen in the said art and occupation of a cordwainer, to the great damage and prejudice of the masters employing them in the said art and occupation of a cordwainer, and of the citizens of the commonwealth generally, and to the great damage and prejudice of other artificers and journeymen in the said art and occupation of cordwainer, to the evil example of others, and against the peace and dignity of the commonwealth of Pennsylvania.
For the attorney general.—Jos. REED.

1.26   Philadelphia Cordwainers Defended, 1806. Opening statement of the defense in *Commonwealth v. Pullis*, from Commons et al., *Documentary History*, Vol. 3, pp. 107–12.

If the court pleases, and you gentlemen of the jury, it is my duty to open the case on the part of the defendants and to state the grounds on which we mean to rely for their acquittal. . . .

The defendants, with a number of other persons, who go under the denomination of journeymen shoemakers, are members of an association, called the "federal society of journeymen cordwainers," which was been established in this city for a considerable time past. For fifteen years and more, the members of that society have been accustomed to the enjoyment of the privilege secured to them and all other citizens, by the constitution of the commonwealth of Pennsylvania, to assemble together in a peaceable manner for their common good. The object of their thus uniting, and meeting together, were the advancement of their mutual interests; the relief of the distressed, and indigent members; and generally, to promote the happiness of the individuals, of which their society was composed. These purposes were, certainly, innocent and legal: even in the eyes of the master workmen, they must appear to be laudable and meritorious. But, unfortunately for these poor and ignorant men! they thought they had a right, to determine for themselves the value of their own labour! and among other acts of their association, committed the unpardonable sin of settling and ascertaining the price of their own work!!!

If this offence, against the master workmen were really an offence against the laws of their country, how were these journeymen to know it? They know, that their would-be-masters had united against them; they had set the example of combining, and confederating together. They [the masters] had their meeting, and passed their resolutions; they had joined all their forces: not for the purpose of establishing the prices of their own goods; but also, for the purpose of determining the rate at which the journeymen should work. They assumed the right of limiting those whom they employed, at all times . . . without consulting the interests, or wishes of the journeymen, or permitting them to have a voice upon the question. . . .

The society of journeymen here appointed delegates to reason the matter with the masters; but a conference was refused; and, shortly afterwards, was sent to the journeymen, the result of a meeting held by the masters among themselves . . . a paper . . . announcing their unanimous determination not to pay any higher wages than they had before given . . . much lower than is paid in some other places.

These . . . journeymen, in self defence, were compelled to resort to the measures which they adopted . . . not inconsistent with any law, or known institution of the land. These were measures, however, for which the defendants were arrested and committed to jail!

1.27   A Shoemaker on Strikers and Scabs, 1806. Excerpt from *Commonwealth v. Pullis.* Reproduced in Commons et al., eds., *A Documentary History*, Vol. 3, pp. 113–16.

James Geoghan, *sworn.*
Q.   Do you know anything of the turn-out about 1799?
A.   Yes; the turn-out you allude to . . . was not a turn-out on the part of the journeymen, but of the masters who were about to reduce the wages the journeymen then received.

Q.   Were the measures pursued at that time, taken in order to induce the employers to give the old prices?
A.   Yes. We assembled then at the corner of Race and Fifth Streets, and agreed that we would not set down to work, under the wages we have been accustomed to receive. In consequence of the resolutions, there was a most obstinate turn-out on both sides; this went on a considerable time, and the employers had a number of handbills printed; purporting, that they would give the wages they offered, to any journeyman of the body, who would set down and work for one year round. Some of the bills found the way into the society of journeymen, but they did not answer the desired effect. . . . Some time after this the employers began to waver, and various reports came to the society that some of them were about to fall off. One morning early, before I was up, Mr. Ryan, accompanied with Mr. Case, came to the place I lodged at; he had a paper importing, that they would give the wages we asked, with one proviso; that we would take no measures against scabs . . . I never recollect that the society went into any resolution about the scabs. . . .
Q.   Was there any personal violence threatened to them?
A.   What am I to understand by personal violence?
Q.   Why, to hurt or beat them?
A.   Never to my knowledge; there is no punishment inflicted on a scab, it is his own act which excludes him from the society. He has only to pay a fine if he becomes a member again; but unless he becomes a member, the constitution declares that no one of the society shall work with him.
Q.   Any person has a right to exclude himself from the society?
A.   Yes; he excludes himself if he deviates from their rules.

1.28   A Shoemakers Decides to Scab, 1806. Excerpts from the testimony of Job Harrison in *Commonwealth v. Pullis* in Commons et al., *A Documentary History*, Vol. 2, 71–83.

Job Harrison, *sworn.*
Question, by Mr. Hopkinson. Are you a journeyman shoemaker?
A.   Yes.
Q.   Do you know whether the journeymen cordwainers in this city, are associated together for particular purposes, and do you belong to them?
A.   Yes they are formed into a society, and I belong to them . . .
Q.   Did you join the association of you own free will, or were you compelled to join it?
A.   I was notified that there was such a society, when in 1794 I came into this country, from England: I had tarried some considerable time in the city before I removed up to this side of Germantown at the place of the Calico printer. The wages were then at that time 6s. a pair to the journeymen: I tarried at Germantown six or seven weeks; during which time I worked for Mr. Bedford, one time when I came in, (for I used to fetch in

my work once a week), it was on Saturday, (for I always came in on Saturday), Mr. Bedford, told me that the wages had been raised, to I forget whether a dollar a pair or something under, but, he gave me what they were raised to, for my work. At this time I knew none of the journeymen, in the city, nor that there was any body of them associated. In the course of a little time I came into the city again, and I was told the wages were raised again; if they were not at the first time raised to a dollar, they were raised immediately after, and he told me of this rise again, and gave me the wages that had been asked. In a few weeks, some of the journeymen, who knew me, called upon me and requested me to join the body. It might be five or six weeks after the rise of wages.

Q. Do you know who they were that called on you?

A. I do not, I believe they knew me, when I did not know them, for I had been at the shop, several times they notified me that it was my duty to come to the body. I told them I knew nothing about the body, I did not know there was such a thing. They told me if I did not come to the body, I was liable to be scabb'd; I did not know at that time what it was to be scabb'd; but some of the men explained it, and I told them that I was willing to be as good a member of their body as any other man.

MR. RECORDER. Q. How did they explain themselves?

A. Their meaning was, that if I did not join the body, no man would set upon the seat where I worked; that they would neither board or work where I was unless I joined. By a seat I mean they would not work in the same shop, nor board or lodge in the same house, nor would they work at all for the same employer. I was a man with a large family, and wished to conform to the laws and be a good member. A notification came shortly after from the Secretary, that I must attend the body-meeting at a certain time, and I accordingly did so. And then I learned the nature of the institution. I had another notification after, which was signed by, both the chairman and secretary but I have not kept it.

MR. HOPKINSON. Q. Did you ever fall under the displeasure of the body, and what was their conduct towards you?

A. After I had become a member I was as willing as any one to support the body. I had been with them a considerable time when in the year 1799 or 98 I do not recollect exactly . . . but I should first observe, that, I always worked upon shoes, for Mr. Bedford, I had not long worked for him before I got on to light dress-shoes. He told me if he could make some light dress-shoes after the London fashion, he would pay extra wages for them. I tried to imitate the London fine shoes, but I could not imitate them exactly, yet I did the best I could, and he told me that they deserved six pence more than the common wages; as I continued on this light work my hand got better in, and he told me if I would side line them with silk, he would give me six pence a pair more; this was a shilling advance. He told me if I would endeavour to make them lighter still, so as to come nearer to the London dress-shoes, accordingly I tried and found that I could now imitate them tolerably well, and he was satisfied to give me 9s. a pair, if I did them no worse. In a little time there came a turn-out to raise the wages upon boots; knowing I had my full terms for my own work and that I had no interest in the turn-out upon boots, that I have everything to lose but nothing to gain; I remonstrated with the society at large, of which I was still a member. I stated that they ought not to include me with them, in the turn-out, as I worked altogether upon shoes, and their ~~human~~ measure, was, to raise the wages on boots. I mentioned that I had a ~~sick wife~~ ~~reason for why didn't strike~~ and a ~~large young family~~, and that, I knew I was not able to stand it: they ~~strike~~ would grant me no quarters at all, but I must turn-out. All the remonstrances I could make were of no use. I must turn-out; unless my employer would pay their price for making boots I must refuse to make shoes. At that time I was from hand to mouth, and in debt, owing to the sickness of my family, and market work was only from 3S. to 3s. 6d. per pair. I concluded at that time I would turn a scab, unknown to them, and I would continue my work and not let them know of it. I did not desire more wages than I then got, more could not be looked for, nor more could not be given. I had a neighbor, who I was acquainted with, and thought a good deal of, I knew I could not deceive him, for he knew Bedford's work, as well as I did myself, and he was frequently to see me, and must have observed the work I was upon. He was a shoemaker and upon the turn-out. I said to him Swain, you know my circumstances, my family must perish, or go to the bettering house, unless I continue my work. He said he knew my case was desperate, but a man had better make any sacrifice than turn a scab at that time. I reasoned with him as I had done to the body, that my turning out would be of no advantage to them, but certain ruin to myself, but he was as unreasonable as they had been, and would take no apology for my conduct.

MR. RECORDER. Q. How many persons were at the meeting when you remonstrated against being compelled to join the turnout in 1799?

A. Perhaps one hundred. The body was composed of upwards of one hundred. The names were called over but the number present are not mentioned. John M'Curdy, John Waltar, and one Cooke, were a tramping committee, that I know . . . their business was to watch the Jers* that they did not scab it. They go round every day, to see that the Jers are honest to the cause; I was a scab myself, yet I was upon the committee to go round and watch other scabs, but then the members did not know I was a scab at the time. And we were obliged to serve on this Committee or pay a fine, we had no compensation that I recollect, we served for the good of the cause and I think the tramping committee were changed every day by the body. I had the extent of my wages during the whole time. I am speaking of the turn-out in 1799. When the tramping committee came round they went to Swain, and he informed them that I was scabbing it: to deceive them I had got a side of leather and a skin or two to make shoes of, as a pretence of working for myself, as they must know I should be in want of money; but M'Curdy was too deep for me, for he knew Bedford's work, they pinned me so close that I could not get over it, and was forced to confess, at last I got angry and ordered them out of the house and told them I would scab it whatever consequences might follow. The body after this

---

* Journeymen.

thought it requisite to take one man instead of three for the tramping committee and they paid him: they took one Nelson for the business. He had nobody but himself when he called upon me the day after. I told him I was scabbing of it, he replied I don't believe you. Depend upon it I am, he still seemed as if he did not believe me, he went away and called again the next day. I said so you will come again for all I tell you I am scabbing of it, and depend upon it I am . . .

(Some noise being heard in court at this moment, Mr. Recorder asked who it was made that noise. Mr. Ryan, pointing to a person just behind him, said it was him, and on being asked by Mr. Recorder, what the person said, Mr. Ryan replied . . . "A scab is a shelter for lice."

Mr. Recorder directed Mr. Ryan to be sworn, which being done, he declared that he heard George Alcorn say, a scab is a shelter for lice, in a distinct tone of voice, there was some little addition muttered in such a manner that he could not understand it.

After a short consultation on the bench, Mr. Recorder said, "George Alcorn, for this contempt of court in interrupting a witness, the court fine you ten dollars, and order you to pay the money immediately or be committed." The money was paid immediately.)

2

The Rise of Free Labor, the Factory System, and Trades Organization, 1828–1877

The middle decades of the nineteenth century witnessed profound changes in the size and structure of the U.S. economy, the arrangement of work-places, the methods by which workers labored, and the organizations through which workers responded to all of these changes. These years provided the seedbed for an industrializing nation. During this time one finds the origins of an industrial working class in the United States, the end of pre-industrial work patterns of slavery and artisan labor, and the emergence of the first national workers' organizations that sought to challenge the inequities of the emerging industrial system.

The years during which the American industrial working class emerged were characterized by contradiction and disjuncture. In 1828 much of the U.S. economy still rested on two deeply contradictory forms of production. On the one hand, artisan labor, which valued the manly independence of skilled producer-citizens, continued to thrive in many fields of production. On the other hand, slavery, which was based on a negation of independence and citizenship for the millions who toiled in bondage, was in the process of consolidation and westward expansion. By 1877, however, these two pillars upon which so much of the social structure of the antebellum United States rested were gone. Slave labor had been eliminated by the Civil War and Reconstruction, and artisan labor was well along the road toward extinction as a new factory-based economy increasingly altered traditional work patterns with machinery. The rise of industrial capitalism symbolized by the textile and shoe factories of pre–Civil War New England in many ways foreshadowed the end of the "artisan republic" or "agrarian republic," and its visions of political order in which power and virtue rested in the hands of economically independent white citizen-producers. In place of these waning visions emerged the reality of a class-divided industrial society, whose white working class, increasingly immigrant in its make-up, lacked the hope of ever attaining the economic independence of erstwhile artisans or yeomen farmers. As the members of that emerging working class grappled with the realities of wage labor, they cast about for alternatives to the emerging system and for ways of organizing for their self-protection. Out of such efforts emerged a variety of utopian schemes as well as workers' first sustained efforts to build national trade unions and union federations.

At the outset of this period, few could have anticipated the extent of the social upheaval that lay ahead. In the 1820s artisan crafts continued to thrive in many fields, such as shoemaking, hand-loom weaving, tailoring, and cabinet making. Artisans who worked in such fields continued to follow pre-industrial work patterns in which intense bouts of labor alternated with periods of comparative idleness. Like the shoemakers whose "ten footer" shops were usually set up in their own backyards, most artisans owned their workshops and tools. They tended to do special order "bespoke work" rather than mass producing for a market. They effectively controlled entry to their trade through the process of apprenticeship. They prized their manly independence, their sobriety and good citizenship, and their role in maintaining the standards of work in their trades.

But the market revolution triggered by the building of canals and railroads between 1820 and 1860 undermined the artisan's world. Between the completion of the Erie Canal in 1825 and the outbreak of the Civil War in 1861, the nation's economy was transformed in ways that weakened marginally profitable family farms in the East and sent farmers' sons and daughters in search of new work, while simultaneously providing a vast market for New England manufacturers who could mass produce shoes or cloth for clamoring customers to the west and south. During this period the factory model of production evolved from its roots in the textile mill opened by Samuel Slater in Pawtucket, Rhode Island, in 1790. The "Waltham System," inaugurated by the Boston Manufacturing Company in Waltham, Massachusetts, in 1813, relied on large numbers of young women recruited from the economically strapped farms of New England for its workforce. By 1822 the company had established large mills on the Merrimac River in Lowell, which became the cockpit of the American industrial revolution. By 1847 steam power was being successfully employed in textile production. As the factory rose, home-based production declined. Indeed, household manufactures dropped from a value of $1.70 per capita in 1840 to $0.78 in 1860.

The role of women's waged labor was crucial to American industrialization in these years. Women increasingly worked in the market economy as millhands, or as outworkers who accepted piecework in such industries as shoemaking or hatmaking. (Even more common was the decision of a young woman to work as a paid domestic laborer in the homes of the emerging urban middle class. Domestic labor was the largest sector of women's paid employment by 1877.)

Whether factory machinery was tended by women or men, the rise of the factory production was not uncontested. Many Americans viewed the emergence of large-scale, machine-driven plants owned by absentee investors, governed by paternalistic managers, and staffed by a permanent class of hirelings as inimical to the idea of a democratic republic. Average workdays in these early factories ranged between 11.5 and 13.5 hours, depending upon the season (for the factories generally relied upon natural lighting). Six-day workweeks were also common, leaving factory laborers little waking time for anything but their labor. Although instances of machine-breaking (known as Luddism) were rare, peaceful protests against the injustices of the factory system became increasingly common in the 1830s. And episodic strikes, or "turn-outs" as they were called, afflicted textile factories by the 1840s.

Between 1830 and 1850, the arrival of waves of immigrants, especially from Ireland and Germany, only deepened the concerns that many Americans had about the factory system, which drew upon an increasingly foreign-born labor force. Pressured by the competition of low-waged immigrant workers, the introduction of machinery, and the extension of the market, skilled artisan producers saw their way of life imperiled. Once proud journeymen hatters were among the hardest hit. They saw their average weekly pay fall from $12 in 1835 to $8 in 1845. What hatters experienced was typical of the transition faced by a wide range of artisan workers in the decades prior to the Civil War.

As they railed against the deterioration of the artisanal way of life, many of the workers adversely affected by industrialism grasped for a political language to express their grievances. They contended that a form of "slavery" was being visited upon them and they called for an end to their "wage slavery." Their fears of enslavement were only reinforced by the real consolidation and expansion of the actual institution of African American slavery in the southern states between 1830 and 1860.

Slavery's fortunes had experienced a revival beginning in the early years of the nineteenth century as the invention of the cotton gin suddenly made cotton culture handsomely profitable, and as textile mills from Lowell to Manchester, England, fed the seemingly insatiable demand for baled cotton. The Louisiana Purchase, the opening of Mississippi, and the settlement of Texas introduced new areas for slavery's spread. Although the legal importation of slaves was forbidden in 1808, as provided in the U.S. Constitution, a large internal market in enslaved people developed. The enslaved daily contested the control of their lives by masters in a variety of subtle ways during this period. Periodic slave rebellions also shook the slave South. The most important of these was led by Nat Turner, a black preacher, in Southampton County, Virginia, in August 1831. It led to the deaths of 57 whites, and at least 100 blacks, and resulted in the subsequent execution of 20 more blacks (including Turner). The rebellion marked a turning point for slavery. In the South, slaveholders' determination to defend and extend the system grew markedly after 1831. In response, slave codes restricting the mobility of the enslaved were tightened, and over time slaveholders developed a positive defense of their system as morally superior to that of free labor. Meanwhile, the 1830s saw the emergence of the first significant abolitionist agitation among Northerners, as petitions, newspapers, pamphlets, and sermons increasingly denounced slavery's depredations. By the 1840s an "Underground Railroad" had come into existence through which abolitionists helped those who ran away from their enslavement escape to freedom in Canada.

By the 1850s the debate between pro- and anti-slavery forces intensified, with each side imputing conspiratorial motives to their opponents. Northern white working people were increasingly drawn into the debate, yet it is hard to generalize about their responses to it. Many white workers attacked the "slave power" as a direct threat to their economic and political status. Others, most likely including a majority of Irish immigrants, feared that abolition would place them in competition with free black workers whom they had already come to view as beneath them.

The outbreak of war and the launching of Reconstruction settled such debates. But the destruction of slavery simultaneously opened as many questions as it settled. The disappearance of slavery created the possibility for the development of a biracial working class of free laborers. But it scarcely determined the ways in which white and black working people would come to terms with each others' aspirations following the war. Whether or not white and black workers could cooperate effectively for their joint emancipation from industrial exploitation remained to be seen.

As the contradictory worlds of free artisans and enslaved African Americans came under strain after 1828, white workers were beginning to adapt organizationally to the changes wrought by the emerging industrial economy. Trade unions had been long established in the United States by this point. But in the decade after 1828 three new tendencies emerged among the unions. The first was toward workers' organization on the city-wide level. In 1827, the first "city central" federation came into being with the founding of the Philadelphia Mechanics' Union of Trade Associations. By 1836, 13 cities had established such local union federations. The second trend was toward the establishment of workers' political parties. In 1828, workers in New York, Philadelphia, and Boston launched labor parties. These parties championed legislation to limit work to ten-hour days, abolish debtors' prisons, enact mechanics' lien laws, curb monopolies, and create a universal free education system. The third tendency was toward national trades organization. In 1834, the New York General Trades Union launched a movement to create a national federation of unions, the National Trade Union. This effort in turn encouraged the emergence of national organizations within individual trades, many of which held conventions between 1834 and 1837. Between 44,000 and 131,000 workers unionized in the mid-1830s. Women occasionally established their own organizations during this period, such as Baltimore's Ladies Shoebinders and Female Bookbinders and Philadelphia's Female Improvement Society.

The financial panic of 1837 and the resulting depression undercut all of these initiatives, however, and in the decade that followed workers experimented with other reform ideas. One of those was the vision of agrarianism promoted in the 1840s by George Henry Evans, a veteran of the New York Workingman's Party, who had retired to a farm in New Jersey after the defeat of worker political action. In 1845 Evans helped found the National Reform Association, which was dedicated to bringing about land reform that would ensure the survival of the form of agrarian republic Thomas Jefferson had extolled. Although Evans's vision never came to fruition, it proved stubbornly attractive to Americans and it ultimately helped influence debate that led to passage of the Homestead Act in 1862. The 1840s also saw workers look for relief from onerous working conditions through demands for the passage of ten-hour workday legislation. By the early 1850s, energetic worker-led campaigns had led to the passage of ten-hour laws in a half-dozen states. Each law contained glaring loopholes, however, and none of them were successfully enforced.

As a result, when economic conditions improved in the 1850s and 1860s, those workers who were able to do so, increasingly turned to union organization as the best solution to their problems. A host of national unions were launched in these years, including the National Typographical Union (1854), United Cigar Makers (1856), and Iron Molders (1859). During the Civil War, labor shortages strengthened the hands of workers in the north and led to the proliferation of these trade unions.

At the end of the war, a more successful attempt to build a national union federation was launched with the creation of the National Labor Union (NLU) in 1866. The NLU championed labor's new demand for the eight-hour workday and promoted the creation of worker-owned cooperatives as an alternative to the rapidly proliferating model of factory-based capitalism. The NLU also attempted to enlist working women and African American workers in its ranks. Yet the NLU did not survive an ill-fated venture into national presidential politics in 1872 and the financial panic of 1873 that precipitated a shattering depression in the mid-1870s.

As Reconstruction came to an end and the nation moved into the second century of its history in 1877, workers inhabited a world far different than their parents and grandparents had inhabited only 50 years earlier. It was increasingly clear that industrialism had refashioned the nation's social fabric in fundamental and probably irreversible ways. In response to these changes, recognizably modern patterns of workers' organization and struggle were already emerging.

THE ARTISANS' WORLD

Many skilled artisans of the 1820s maintained traditions that dated back to the eighteenth century and earlier. As Horace Greeley's remembrance in

Document 2.1 makes clear, the tradition of apprenticeship usually meant hard labor for the boys who signed up to learn their trades under skilled craftsmen. Yet in most artisan shops, bouts of hard labor often alternated with periods of leisure and even drinking in a workday that corresponded to traditional rhythms rather than a time clock. In Document 2.2, nineteenth-century chronicler David Johnson notes that drinking during the workday was a common feature of life in a shoemaker's shop; and Document 2.3 notes that frequent breaks, eating, and drinking characterized the shipwright's workday. If drinking and bouts of idleness and play were often features of an artisan's workday, artisans also generally prided themselves on their craftsmanship, manliness, and sobriety. Indeed, artisans frequently led campaigns for temperance of the sort celebrated by the poem in Document 2.4. How might the attitudes toward work and leisure suggested in these documents have reinforced the artisans' pride and sense of independence?

2.1 A Printer's Apprenticeship, 1826. Horace Greeley, *Recollections of a Busy Life* (New York: J. B. Ford and Company, 1868), pp. 61–63.

When I was but eleven years old, hearing that an apprentice was wanted in the newspaper office at Whitehall [N.Y.], I accompanied my father to that office, and tried to find favor in the printer's eyes; but he promptly and properly rejected me as too young, and would not relent; so I went home downcast and sorrowful. No new opportunity was presented till the Spring of 1826, when an apprentice was advertized for by the publisher of *The Northern Spectator*, at East Poultney, Vt. . . . I walked over to Poultney, saw the publishers, came to an understanding with them, and returned; a few days afterward . . . my father took me down, and verbally agreed with them for my services. I was to remain till twenty years of age, be allowed my board only for six months, and thereafter $40 per annum in addition to my clothing. So I stopped, and went to work . . .

The organization and management of our establishment were vicious; for an apprentice should have one master; while I had a series of them, and often two or three at once . . . we had a succession of editors and of printers. I had not been there a year before my hands were blistered and my back lamed by working off the very considerable edition of the paper on an old-fashioned, two pull Ramage (wooden) press,—a task beyond my boyish strength,—and I can scarcely recall a day wherein we were not hurried by our work. . . . While I lived at home, I had always been allowed a day's fishing, at least once a month in Spring and Summer, and I once went hunting; but never fished, nor hunted, nor attended a dance, nor any sort of party or fandango in Poultney. I doubt that I even played a game of ball.

2.2   Work and Play in a Shoemaker's Shop, ca. 1830. From David N. Johnson, *Sketches of Lynn. The Changes of Fifty Years* (Lynn: Thomas P. Nichols, 1880), pp. 47–48.

The shoemaker's vocabulary of terms applied to drinking and drunkenness was quite extensive, and some were peculiar to the locality and the craft. If a man was very drunk, he was "blind as a bat," or "well corned," or "well stove in," or "slewed," or "cocked," or "well smashed." In later times such were said to "carry a heavy turkey," or a "brick in their hat." . . .

Various expedients were resorted to, to keep up the supply of black-strap [a rum drink]. The one who made the most or the fewest shoes, the best or the poorest, paid the "scot." Bets were made on all occasions. . . . Small games of chance, the stakes of which were black-strap were frequently made. A common game was played with a "shoulder-stick." This was called "trolling the tog." These sticks were marked on several sides, beginning with one, and going up to four, making ten in all. Each player was allowed three twirls, or "trolls," of the "stick" as his turn came, an arrangement that made twelve the highest number attainable at a single trial, and whoever showed the lowest figures, paid the bet. When a young man attained his majority, on birthdays . . . and many other days, the supply was expected to be ample.

2.3   Pre-industrial Work Habits, ca. 1820s. From "A Workingman's Recollections of America," *Knight's Penny Magazine*, 1 (1846), 97–112, quoted in Herbert G. Gutman, *Work, Culture, and Society in Industrializing America: Essays in American Working-class and Social History* (New York: Vintage Books, 1976).

In our yard, at half-past eight A.M., Aunt Arlie McVane, a clever kind-hearted but awfully uncouth, rough sample of the "Ould Sod," would make her welcome appearances in the yard with her two great baskets, stowed and checked off with crullers, doughnuts, gingerbread, turnovers, pieces, and a variety of sweet cookies and cakes; and from the time Aunt Arlie's baskets came in sight until every man and boy, bosses and all, in the yard, had been supplied . . . trade was a brisk one. Aunt Arlie would usually make the rounds of the yard and supply all hands in about an hour, bringing the forenoon up to half-past nine, and giving us from ten to fifteen minutes "breathing spell" during lunch; no one ever hurried during cake time. . . .

After this was over we would fall to again, until interrupted by Johnnie Gogean, the English candyman, who came in always at half-past-ten, with his great board, the size of a medium extension table, slung before him, covered with all sorts of "stick," and several of sticky candy, in one-cent lots. Bosses, boys, and men—all hands, everybody—invested one to three cents in Johnnie's sweet wares, and another ten minutes in consuming it. Johnnie usually sailed out with a bare board until 11 o'clock at which time there was a general sailing out of the yard and into convenient grog-shops after whiskey; only we had four or five men among us . . . who use to sail out pretty regularly ten times a day on the average, two that went for whisky only when someone invited them to drink, being too mean to treat themselves; and two more who never went at all.

In the afternoon, about half-past three, we had a cake-lunch, supplied by Uncle Jack Gridder, an old, crippled superannuated ship's carpenter . . .

At about five o'clock P.M., always, Johnnie used to put in his second appearance; and then, having expended money in another stick or two of candy, and ten minutes in its consumption, we were ready to drive away again until sundown; then home to supper.

2.4 Workers' Temperance Poem, 1835. Albert Barnes, *The Connexion of Temperance with Republican Freedom: An Oration Delivered on the 4th of Jul, 1835, before the Mechanics and Workingmens Temperance Society of the City and County of Philadelphia* (Philadelphia: Boyles and Benedict, 1835), quoted in Bruce Laurie, *Working People of Philadelphia*, 1800–1850 (Philadelphia: Temple University Press, 1981), p. 90.

"The Temperance Strike"

His chains the tyrant rum, too long
Has tried to cast around us,
Shall not Mechanics prove too strong,
When any would confound us?
We shall! we shall! we feel our strength
And who no sword will draw,
When we for freedom strike a length?
Hurrah! hurrah! hurrah!

Our fathers—who may see their like!
When trodden down as cattle,
For liberty knew how to strike,
And win the righteous battle!

And shall their sons be slaves to drink?
O never! never! Nor
Will Working Men like cowards shrink,
No boys!—hurrah! hurrah!

. . .

Some strike for wages, some for hours,
Shall we refuse?—O never!

For time and cash we pledge our powers,
And strike for both for ever!
Then strike who will for "6 to 6,"
We flinch not in the war;
For Temperance and for Seventy-six
We strike—hurrah! hurrah!

THE WORLD OF SLAVE LABOR

The heartrending letter from an enslaved woman reproduced in Document 2.5 exposes a reality that enslaved people feared as the internal market for slaves sent increasing numbers of slaves westward after 1820, thus shattering families that they painstakingly tried to hold together under slavery. One thing slavery did not take from its victims was the sense of injustice they felt at their treatment, a sense memorably invoked by the slave song remembered by Frederick Douglass in Document 2.6. While slave rebellions were relatively uncommon, the enslaved often did resist their bondage either by running away or engaging in subtle forms of resistance hinted at in Documents 2.7 and 2.8. What did it mean to be an "eye servant"? And what do these documents suggest about the nature of the master-slave relation?

2.5   An Enslaved Woman Seeks Help, 1852. Reproduced in Ulrich B. Phillips, *Life and Labor in the Old South* (Boston: Little, Brown and Company, 1929), p. 212.

Charlottesville, Oct. 8th, 1852
Dear Husband I write you a letter to let you know my distress my master has sold albert to a trader on Monday court day and myself and other child is for sale also and I want you to let [me] hear from you very soon before next cort if you can I don't know when I don't want you to wait until Christmas I want you to tell dr. Hamelton and your master if either will buy me they can attend to it know and then I can go afterwards. I don't want a trader to get me they asked me if I had got any person to buy me and I told them no they took me to the court houste too they never put me up a man buy the name of brady bought albert and is gone and I don't know where they say he lives in Scottesville my things is in several places some is in staunton and if I should be sold I don't know what will become of them I don't expect to meet with the luck to get that way till I am quite heartsick nothing more I am and ever will be your kind wife Maria Perkins
To Richard Perkins.

2.6   They Give Us the Husk, ca. 1830. From Frederick Douglass, *The Life and Times of Frederick Douglass* (New York: Pathway Press, 1941), 164–65.

We raise de wheat,
Dey gib us de corn;
We bake de bread,
Dey gib us de crust;
We sif the meal,
Dey gib us the huss;
We peel de meat,
Dey gib us de skin;

And dat's de way
Dey take us in;
We skim de pot,
Dey giv us de liquor

And say dat's good enough for nigger
Walk over! Walk over!
Your butter and de fat;
Poor nigger, you can't get over dat!
Walk over—

2.7   Slave Supervision on a Virginia Plantation, ca. 1853. Frederick Law Olmsted's *A Journey in the Seaboard Slave States in the Years 1853—1854,* reproduced in John R. Commons et al., eds., *A Documentary History,* Vol. 2 (Cleveland: The A. H. Clark Company, 1910), p. 34.

The labor of this farm was entirely performed by slaves. I did not inquire their number, but I judged there were from twenty to forty. . . . During the three hours, or more, in which I was in company with the proprietor, I do not think there were ten consecutive minutes uninterrupted by some of the slaves required his personal direction and assistance. He was even obliged, three times, to leave the dinner-table.

2.8   The Difficulty with "My Man Ned," 1846. Letter of John B. Lamar, Macon, Ga., to his sister, Mrs. Howell Cobb; April 27, 1846, reproduced in Commons, et al., *Documentary History,* Vol. 2, pp. 31–41.

Yours of the 22nd Came duly to hand. With reference to the building of your negro house, I expect it would be best under all the circumstances to have it done as John proposed, let some one find all the materials & do the work at a specific price. But $250 is a high price for a negro house & unless it is to be a mighty fine negro house.

Whoever does the work ought to furnish certain specifications, such as the dimensions of the house, the number of lights &c so that you can have some means of judging if you are not paying double price.

My man Ned the carpenter is idle or nearly so at the plantation. He is fixing gates & like the idle groom in Pickwick trying to fool himself into the belief that he is doing something. But on considering his general character for intemperance & disobedience, & quarrelsomeness I have concluded it would be best to pay a little too much for the house, rather than inflict him on you at this time. While I was gone I had him in town & on returning found that he had been drunk & fighting, and misbehaving in every way, so that I have banished him to rural life. He is an eye servant. If I was with him I could have the work done soon & cheap, but I am afraid to trust him off where there is no one he fears. He is doing literally nothing at home, and sparing him would not be a cents expense as to that, but I conclude that you do not feel like being annoyed, just now, as I fear & almost know he would annoy you, by getting drunk & raising a row on the lot. I shall sell the rascal the first chance I get.

[handwritten margin note: Someone who only does work when watched]

EARLY FACTORY LABOR

The emergence of factories in the antebellum Northeast raised a variety of concerns among working people. The boarding house and factory rules noted in Documents 2.9 and 2.10 illustrate mill managers' efforts to establish a form of paternalistic control that increasingly elicited protest from workers. By the 1830s, workers' organizations were undertaking their own investigations of factory conditions. As Documents 2.11 and 2.12 point out, one of the features that elicited the most concern was the mills' employment of children. In general, as Documents 2.13 and 2.14 indicate, workers were suspicious that factory labor would evolve into a form of slavery. What features of factory labor prompted these suspicions?

2.9   Boarding-house Rules, 1848. Excerpts from the *Handbook to Lowell* (1848) quoted in John R. Commons et al., eds., *Documentary History,* Vol. 7 (Cleveland: The A. H. Clark Company, 1911), pp. 137–38.

REGULATIONS FOR THE BOARDING-HOUSES of the Hamilton Manufacturing Company.

The tenants of the boarding—houses are not to board, or permit any part of their houses to be occupied by any person, except those in the employ of the company, without special permission.

They will be considered answerable for any improper conduct in their houses, and are not to permit their boarders to have company at unseasonable hours.

The doors must be closed at ten o'clock in the evening, and no person admitted after that time, without some reasonable excuse.

The keepers of the boarding-houses must give an account of the number, names and employment of their boarders, when required, and report the names of such as are guilty of any improper conduct, or are not in the regular habit of attending public worship.

The buildings, and yards about them, must be kept clean and in good order; and if they are injured, otherwise than from ordinary use, all necessary repairs will be made, and charged to the occupant.

The sidewalks, also, in front of the houses, must be kept clean, and free from snow, which must be removed from them immediately after it has ceased falling; if neglected, it will be removed by the company at the expense of the tenant.

It is desirable that the families of those who live in the houses, as well as the boarders, who have not had the kine pox, should be vaccinated, which will be done at the expense of the company, for such as wish it.

Some suitable chamber in the house must be reserved, and appropriated for the use of the sick, so that others may not be under the necessity of sleeping in the same room.

John Avery, Agent.

2.10   Factory Rules, 1848. Excerpts from *Handbook to Lowell* (1848), reproduced in Commons et al., *Documentary History*, Vol. 7, 135–36.

REGULATIONS TO BE OBSERVED by all persons employed in the factories of the Hamilton Manufacturing Company. The overseers are to be always in their rooms at the starting of the mill, and not absent unnecessarily during working hours. They are to see that all those employed in their rooms, are in their places in due season, and keep a correct account of their time and work. They may grant leave of absence to those employed under them, when they have spare hands to supply their places, and not otherwise, except in cases of absolute necessity.

All persons in the employ of the Hamilton Manufacturing Company, are to observe the regulations of the room where they are employed. They are not to be absent from their work without the consent of the over-seer, except in cases of sickness, and then they are to send him word of the cause of their absence. They are to board in one of the houses of the company and give information at the counting room, where they board, when they begin, or, whenever they change their boarding place; and are to observe the regulations of their boarding-house.

Those intending to leave the employment of the company, are to give at least two weeks' notice thereof to their overseer.

All persons entering into the employment of the company, are considered as engaged for twelve months, and those who leave sooner, or do not comply with all these regulations, will not be entitled to a regular discharge.

The company will not employ any one who is habitually absent from public worship on the Sabbath, or known to be guilty of immorality.

A physician will attend once in every month at the counting room, to vaccinate all who may need it, free of expense.

Any one who shall take from the mills or the yard, any yarn, cloth or other article belonging to the company, will be considered guilty of stealing and be liable to prosecution.

Payment will be made monthly, including board and wages. The accounts will be made up to the last Saturday but one in every month, and paid in the course of the following week.

These regulations are considered part of the contract, with which all persons entering into the employment of the Hamilton Manufacturing Company, engage to comply.

John Avery, Agent.

2.11   Child Labor, Philadelphia, 1830. From a report by "Many Operatives" printed in the *Mechanics' Free Press*, Aug. 21, 1830, and reproduced in John R. Commons et al., eds., *Documentary History*, Vol. 5 (Cleveland: The A. H. Clark Company, 1910), pp. 61–63.

In looking over one of your late numbers, I was rejoiced to find that some friend has noticed the sufferings of people employed in our manufactories; particularly in that of cotton. It is a well known fact, that the principal part of the helps in cotton factories consist of boys and girls, we may safely say from six to seventeen years of age, and are confined to steady employment during the longest days in the year, from daylight until dark, allowing at the outside, one hour and a half per day. In consequence of this close confinement, it renders it entirely impossible for the parents of such children to obtain for them any education or knowledge, save that of working that machine, which they are compelled to work, and that too with a small sum, that is hardly sufficient to support nature, while they on the other hand are rolling in wealth, of[f] the vitals of these poor children every day. We noticed the observation of our Pawtucket friend in your number of June 19th, 1830, lamenting the grievances of the children employed in those factories. We think his observations very correct, with regard to their being brought up as ignorant as Arabs of the Desert; for we are confident that not more than one-sixth of the boys and girls employed in such factories are capable of reading or writing their own name. We have known many instances where parents who are capable of giving their children a trifling education one at a time, deprived of that opportunity by their employer's threats, that if they did take one child from their employ, (a short time for school,) such family must leave the employment—and we have even known these threats put in execution. Now as our friend observes, we may establish schools and academies, and devise every means for the instruction of youth in vain, unless we also give time for application; we have heard it remarked to some employers, that it would be commendable to congress to shorten the hours of labour in factories; the reply was: it would be an infringement on the rights of the people. We know the average number of hands employed by one manufacturer to be, at the lowest estimate, fifty men, women and children. Now the query is: whether this individual, or this number employed by him, is the people.

It is not our intention at present, to undertake a thorough discussion of this interesting subject, but rather to give some hints on the subject, which, we hope, may attract the notice of your readers, and be the means of arrousing some abler pen to write on the matter; for we think it is high time the public should begin to notice the evil that it begets. We see the evil that follows the system of long labor much better than we can express it; but we hope our weak endeavors may not prove ineffecutal. We must acknowledge our inability prevents us from expressing our sentiment fluently, at present but we hope to appear again in a more correct manner.

2.12 Child Labor, Paterson, N.J., 1835. A report from the *Paterson Courier* published in the *National Trades' Union* (New York), Aug. 15, 1835, and reproduced by Commons et al. eds., *Documentary History*, Vol. 5, pp. 63–66.

Paterson, Aug. 11th, 1835.
Messrs. Schenck & Hewson, Newark Delegates.
Gentlemen, The accompanying document is in reply to the queries proposed by yourselves and Mr. Scott of New York, in relation to the present state of the population of this town. . . . We have based part of our Report besides other information, on the attested evidence of two individuals, each having five children of his family employed in the factories. With great respect we subscribe ourselves, yours sincerely,
John Tilby, John K. Flood.

Question 1st. What number of mills are idle in consequence of the strike? Answer. The number is 19 cotton mills, and 1 woolen factory.

Question 2d. What number of children are idle in consequence of the strike? Answer. It would be take some weeks to ascertain the number of minors; the whole number employed in these factories, is from 19 to 20 hundred; the number of hand-loom weavers and others dependent on the factories would swell the amount of persons thrown out of work, much more.

Questions 3 and 4. What number of children are under 12 years? What number are over 12 years? Answer. We have placed these two queries together, because, like the question above, we could not ascertain without an actual personal survey of the town. Doctor Fisher, who formerly took the census, and which he has said employed him nearly six weeks, reported in 1832, the whole number of population under 16 years of age, at 3949; we consider it would be within compass to take the sixth part as engaged in manufacturing—say 600 under 16 years.

Question 5. What average compensation for those under 12? Answer. From 50 cents to $1.75 per week—average $1.12 1/2.

Question 6. What average compensation for those over 12? Answer. Many of those work by the piece, as rulers, weavers, warpers, &c. As near as we can learn, the average is $2.12 1/2 per week. In reference to this question, we send you two statements on oath of the wages obtained by the individuals in those two families (five in each) in one of which you will see they are all over 12 years and average $2.10. In this statement we do not include spinners and sub bosses, but only such as may be considered minors among the male sex; but also includes among the females, many grown women.

Question 7. What time do they commence work in summer? Question 10. What time do they quit in the evening? Answer. From sun-rise to sun-set from March first to October 1st.

Question 8. What time is allowed for breakfast? Answer. In summer, half an hour. From October 1st to the 15th March, no time allowed. The hands breakfast by candle-light before going to work.

Question 9. What time is allowed for dinner? Answer. Three quarters of an hour, the year round.

Question 11. The same queries in reference to the winter season. Answer. From October 1st to March 1st, commence at daylight to quit at 8 o'clock; in which some mills are very precise; others overrun that time, probably on account of the difference of clocks.

Question 12. What number are in destitute circumstances? Answer. In consequence of the strike, many have left town. The whole who remain may be said to be destitute. Doctor Fisher in his last census, 1831, stated the number of widows to be 163, and the amount of their families to be 834. Now these are precisely the class of persons who cannot remove in case of a strike, or of being thrown out of work from any other cause; and as the town was more populous as well as more prosperous at the commencement of the strike, than it was in 1832, being the time of cholera, we believe we are within compass to say there are 1000 persons in need of assistance.

State of New Jersey, Essex County, ss.

2.13 A Report on Women's Factory Labor, 1835. Discussion on Conditions of Females in Manufacturing Establishments, National Trades' Union Convention, 1835, reproduced in John R. Commons et al., eds., *Documentary History,* Vol. 6 (Cleveland: The A. H. Clark Company, 1910), pp. 218–19.

We talk, said Mr. D., of the rising generation! What must that generation be, coming from such a stock of disease and deformity? What a race, in comparison to our hardy forefathers, whose iron nerves could second their resolute souls to meet any emergency! It is of little use for us to legislate here, said Mr. D., while this factory system is undoing more than our united exertions can possibly build up. It was his confirmed opinion, that this system was laying the foundation of an aristocracy; and is so intended by its projectors. He believed it to be a deliberate plot of the enemies of freedom and equality, to ruin the farmers, to break down that sturdy, independent spirit, so characteristic of the former race, so unpropitious to the future schemes of aristocrats. They can command more money than the farmer, and are applying their "facilities" to draw his sons and daughters from the farm to the factories. For a few years past, the sons of our farmers, as soon as they are of sufficient age, have been induced to hasten off to the factory, where for a few pence more than they could get at home, they are taught to become the willing servants, the servile instruments of their employer's oppression and extortion! The daughters, too, must quit the farm house, the seat of ruddy health and former content, for a confined and baneful workshop, where, to be sure, she earns a little more money, for a short time; but as surely loses health, if not her good character, her happiness!

What is the course the managers of these establishments pursue? Knowing these adventurers have come for gain, they commence a direct appeal to their feelings of avarice—persuade them to work overhours. After a few months spent in excessive labor, these unfortunate young people most frequently find, too late, their constitutions destroyed—their health gone, and ere long, they go down to the grave, to swell the list of yearly victims of this pernicious system.

Mr. D. mentioned an instance he had lately heard of; it was of a hale New Hampshire girl, who came to Lowell for work. She, like others, was induced to commence overwork, which she pursued for four months. At the end of this term, she was compelled to quit: the blight of disease had fastened upon her—the rose of health had departed. She returned to her once happy home; and, in two months more, was carried to her grave. This was an example of many regularly occurring.

It is our duty, sir, to look to these establishments; to calculate the consequences of their further spread. We must look after these men of high percentage, bred to that, and who care for nothing else. Who shall reform this system but the working men? This is, indeed, the most important work we have to do. How shall we avert the evil? They resort to piece work, that we may not be able to reach them. But we must devise a remedy; we must appeal to the people to join, to set their faces against this system, as one pregnant with our certain destruction. We must go before our legislatures—must expose these "beings"—not to use a harsher term— who destroy life for gain—who make their enormous percentage at a yearly expense of hundreds of lives! They must be forced to shut their mills at a regular hour; there must be a certain time over which they shall not work; that all the inmates may have an opportunity to rest their weary limbs, and to enjoy free and wholesome air.

2.14 The Factory System Described, 1846. A working-class investigator reports in *The Harbinger,* Nov. 14, 1846, from Commons et al., eds., *Documentary History,* Vol. 7, pp. 132–38.

We have lately visited the cities of Lowell and Manchester, and have had an opportunity of examining the factory system more closely than before . . .

We went through many of the mills, talked particularly to a large number of the operatives, and ate at their boarding-houses, on purpose to ascertain by personal inspection the facts of the case. We assure our readers that very little information is possessed, and no correct judgments formed, by the public at large, of our factory system, which is the first germ of the Industrial or Commercial Feudalism, that is to spread over our land.

In Lowell live between seven and eight thousand young women, who are generally daughters of farmers of the different States of New England; some of them are members of families that were rich the generation before . . .

The operatives work thirteen hours a day in the summer time, and from daylight to dark in the winter. At half past four in the morning the factory bell rings, and at five the girls must be in the mills. A clerk, placed as a watch, observes those who are a few minutes behind the time, and effectual means are taken to stimulate to punctuality. This is the morning commencement of the industrial discipline—(should we not rather say industrial tyranny?) which is established in these Associations of this moral and Christian community. At seven the girls are allowed thirty minutes for breakfast, and at noon thirty minutes more for dinner, except during the first quarter of the year, when the time is extended to forty-five minutes. But within this time they must hurry to their boarding-houses and return to the factory, and that through the hot sun, or the rain and cold. A meal eaten under such circumstances must be quite un-favorable to digestion and health, as any medical man will inform us. At seven o'clock in the evening the factory bell sounds the close of the day's work.

Thus thirteen hours per day of close attention and monotonous labor are exacted from the young women in these manufactories. . . . So fatigued—we should say, exhausted and worn out, but we wish to speak of the system in the simplest language—are numbers of the girls, that they go to bed soon after their evening meal, and endeavor by a comparatively long sleep to resuscitate their weakened frames for the toils of the coming day. . . .

Now let us examine the nature of the labor itself, and the conditions under which it is performed. Enter with us into the large rooms, when the looms are at work the largest that we saw is in the Amoskeag Mills at Manchester. It is four hundred feet long, and about seventy broad; there are five hundred looms, and twenty-one thousand spindles in it. The din and clatter of these five hundred looms under full operation, struck us on first entering as something frightful and infernal, for it seemed such an atrocious violation of one of the faculties of the human soul, the sense of hearing. After a while we became somewhat inured to it, and by speaking quite close to the ear of an operative and quite loud, we could hold a conversation, and make the inquiries we wished.

The girls attend upon an average three looms; many attend four, but this requires a very active person, and the most unremitting care. However, a great many do it. Attention to two is as much as should be demanded of an operative. This gives us some idea of the application required during the thirteen hours of daily labor. The atmosphere of such a room cannot of course be pure; on the contrary it is charged with cotton filaments and dust, which, we were told, are very injurious to the lungs. On entering the room, although the day was warm, we remarked that the windows were down; we asked the reason, and a young woman answered very naively, and without seeming to be in the least aware that this privation of fresh air was anything else than perfectly natural, that "when the wind blew, the threads did not work so well." After we had been in the room for fifteen or twenty minutes, we found ourselves, as did the persons who accompanied us, in quite a perspiration, produced by a certain moisture which we observed in the air, as well as by the heat. . . .

The young women sleep upon an average six in a room; three beds to a room. There is no privacy, no retirement here; it is almost impossible to read or write alone, as the parlor is full and so many sleep in the same chamber. A young woman remarked to us, that if she had a letter to write, she did it on the head of a band-box, sitting on a trunk, as there was not space for a table. So live and toil the young women of our country in the boarding-houses and manufactories, which the rich and influential of our land have built for them.

WOMEN'S WORK: SERVANTS AND MILLGIRLS

Women provided an indispensable source of labor for American industrialization. New England farm women found that mill work offered opportunities for money and adventure that were unavailable to them elsewhere. Priscilla Howe's letter to her sister, excerpted in Document 2.15, gives one woman's reasons for seeking employment in the Lowell textile mills. If mill work did provide a modicum of adventure and income, it also required adapting to a loud and sometimes dehumanizing, mechanized workplace. But as millworker Lucy Larcom eloquently recalls in Document 2.16, mill women found ways to humanize their new environments. More women worked as domestic servants than as millgirls in the nineteenth century. Yet, as European visitor Frances Trolloppe found to her amazement, American servants did not submit easily to the social hierarchy implied by domestic service (Document 2.17). What do these documents suggest about women's ambivalence toward waged labor in this period?

2.15   Deciding to Work in a Lowell Mill, 1851. From David A. Zonderman, "From Mill Village to Industrial City: Letters from Vermont Factory Operatives," *Labor History,* Vol. 27 (Spring 1986), pp. 283–84.

[To Laura Howe Ford, Granville, Vt.]

Lowell, Mass.
Oct 5th 1851.

Dear Sister,

Good morning to you, how do you get along, I suppose you are very much surprised to see my letter mailed in Lowell and suppose Mother will feel very bad, as she was thinking of seeing me there this fall, and I thought myself I should go there, I have had everything to do and more to, this summer . . . [working for] a family of nine or ten most of the time, and the milk of six cows to take care of . . . I suppose I should have stayed there if they had payed me regular wages, I did not ask them to I presume they would if I had, I had what clothes I needed but I had got tired of house work, and thought I would try the mill a while. Business is very dull this fall they do not make as much as they used to. I have not the least idea of staying longer than Spring perhaps not more than three months it don't seem as pleasant here as it used to. I am sorry to disappoint you so much but it seemed rather necessary that I should come here first, I came here last week but have not gone to work yet but expect to tomorrow or next day. . . . My health was never better than at the present and I am in hope it will remain so if I think the work is too hard or wont agree with me I shall leave and go into the country, to do something else, for good health is better than any thing else with out it, do write to me as soon as possible. Please accept this from your sister Priss [Priscilla Howe]

2.16   Coping with the Factory Regime, ca. 1840s. From Lucy Larcom, *A New England Girlhood: Outlined From Memory* New Edition (Boston: Houghton Mifflin Company, 1924 [orig. 1889]), pp. 175–83.

At this time I had learned to do a spinner's work, and I obtained permission to tend some frames that stood directly in front of the river windows, with only them and the wall behind me, extending half the length of the mill,—and one young woman beside me, at the farther end of the row. She was a sober, mature person, who scarcely thought it worth her while to speak often to a child like me; and I was, when with strangers, rather a reserved girl; so I kept myself occupied with the river, my work, and my thoughts. And the river and my thoughts flowed on together, the happiest of companions. . . . When the work "went well," I sat in the window-seat, and let my fancies fly whither they would,—downward to the sea, or upward to the hills that hid the mountain-cradle of the Merrimack.

The printed regulations forbade us to bring books into the mill, so I made my window-seat into a small library of poetry, pasting its side all over with newspaper clippings. In those days we had only weekly papers, and they had always a "poet's corner," where standard writers were well represented, with anonymous ones, also. I was not, of course, much of a critic. I chose my verses for their sentiment, and because I wanted to commit them to memory. . . .

Some of the girls could not believe that the Bible was meant to be counted among forbidden books. We all thought that the Scriptures had a right to go wherever we went, and that if we needed them anywhere, it was at our work. I evaded the law by carrying some leaves from a torn Testament in my pocket.

The overseer, caring more for law than gospel, confiscated all he found. He had his desk full of Bibles. It sounded oddly to hear him say to the most religious girl in the room, when he took hers away, "I did think you had more conscience than to bring that book in here." . . . It was a rigid code of morality under which we lived. . . .

The last window in the row behind me was filled with flourishing houseplants—fragrant leaved geraniums, the overseer's pets. They gave that corner a bowery look; the perfume and freshness tempted me there often. Standing before that window, I could look across the room and see girls moving backwards and forwards among the spinning-frames, sometimes stooping, sometimes reaching up their arms, as their work required, with easy and not ungraceful movements. . . .

I loved quietness. The noise of the machinery was particularly distasteful to me. But I found that the crowd was made up of single human lives, not one of them wholly uninteresting, when separately known. I learned also that there are many things which belong to the whole world of us together, that no one of us, nor any few of us, can claim or enjoy for ourselves alone. I discovered too that I could so accustom myself to the noise that it became like a silence to me. And I defied the machinery to make me its slave. Its incessant discords would not drown the music of my thoughts if I would let them fly high enough.

2.17 The American Servant Problem, 1832. Frances Trolloppe, *Domestic Manners of the Americans* (New York: Dodd, Mead [1927]), pp. 43–45.

The greatest difficulty in organising a family establishment in Ohio, is getting servants, or, as it is there called, "getting help," for it is more than petty treason to the republic to call a free citizen a *servant*. The whole class of young women, whose bread depends upon their labour, are taught to believe that the most abject poverty is preferable to domestic service. Hundreds of half-naked girls work in the paper-mills, or in any other manufactory, for less than half the wages they would receive in service; but they think their equality is compromised by the latter, and nothing but the wish to obtain some particular article of finery will ever induce them to submit to it. A kind friend, however, exerted herself so effectually for me, that a tall stately lass soon presented herself, saying "I be come to help you." The intelligence was very agreeable, and I welcomed her in the most gracious manner possible, and asked what I should give her by the year.

"O Gimini!" exclaimed the damsel, with a loud laugh, "you be a down-right Englisher, sure enough. I should like to see a young lady engage by the year in America! I hope I shall get a husband before many months, or I expect I shall be an outright old maid, for I be most seventeen already: besides, mayhap I may want to go to school. You must just give me a dollar and a half a week, and mother's slave Phillis must come over once a week, I expect, from t'other side the water, to help me clean."

I agreed to the bargain, of course with all dutiful submission; and seeing she was preparing to set to work in a yellow dress, *parsemé* with red roses, I gently hinted, that I thought it was a pity to spoil so fine a gown, and that she had better change it.

" 'Tis just my best and my worst" she answered; "for I've got no other."

And in truth I found that this young lady had left the paternal mansion with no more clothes of any kind than what she had on. I immediately gave her money to purchase what was necessary for cleanliness and decency, and set to work with my daughters to make her a gown. She grinned applause when our labour was completed; but never uttered the slightest expression of gratitude for that, or for any thing else we could do for her. She was constantly asking us to lend her different articles of dress, and when we declined it, she said: "Well, I never seed such grumpy folks as you be; there is several young ladies of my acquaintance what goes to live out now and then with the old women about the town, and they and their guns always lends them what they asks for; I guess you English thinks we should poison your things, just as bad as if we was negurs." Here I beg to assure the reader, that whenever I give conversations, they were not made *à loisir,* but were written down immediately after they occurred, with all the verbal fidelity my memory permitted.

This young lady left me at the end of two months; because I refused to lend her money enough to buy a silk dress to go to a ball, saying: "Then 'tis not worth my while to stay any longer."

I cannot imagine it possible that such a state of things can be desirable, or beneficial to any of the parties concerned. I might occupy a hundred pages on the subject, and yet fail to give an adequate idea of the sore, angry, ever-wakeful pride that seemed to torment these poor wretches. In many of them it was so excessive, that all feeling of displeasure, or even of ridicule, was lost in pity. One of these was a pretty girl, whose natural disposition must have been gentle and kind; but her good feelings were soured, and her gentleness turned to morbid sensitiveness, by having heard a thousand and a thousand times that she was as good as any other lady; that all men were equal, and women too; and that it was a sin and a shame for a free-born American to be treated like a servant.

When she found she was to dine in the kitchen, she turned up her pretty lip, and said: "I guess that's cause you don't think I'm good enough to eat with you. You'll find that won't do here." I found afterwards that she rarely ate any dinner at all, and generally passed the time in tears. I did everything in my power to conciliate and make her happy, but I am sure she hated me. I gave her very high wages, and she stayed till she had obtained several expensive articles of dress, and then, *un beau matin,* she came to me full dressed, and said: "I must go." "When shall you return, Charlotte ?"—"I expect you'll see no more of me." And so we parted. Her sister was also living with me; but her wardrobe was not yet completed, and she remained some weeks longer, till it was.

IMMIGRANTS

The United States was inundated with immigrant laborers from Ireland and Germany in the decades before the Civil War. The Irish, fleeing intense poverty and even famine, arrived in America with few resources. European traveller Captain Frederick Marryat was stunned by the conditions he found among some Irish laborers living in shanties on the outskirts of Troy, New York, around 1838 (Document 2.18). Nonetheless the Irish provided a key source of labor for the building of America's canals, dangerous and disease-ridden work, which the Irish viewed with the mixture of pride and indignation captured in the canal diggers' ballad reproduced in Document 2.19. German immigrants, especially those who arrived following the revolutionary upheavals that shook Europe in 1848, tended to be better acquainted with industrialism. As Document 2.20 suggests, they brought with them a strong organizational impulse, building a variety of self-help agencies that cushioned their transition to labor in industrializing America with provisions such as sickness and death benefits. What do these documents indicate about the variability of immigrants' preparation for entry into an industrializing society, their encounters with waged labor, and their responses to it?

2.18   Recent Irish Arrivals, ca. 1838. Captain Frederick Marryat, *Diary in America*, ed. Jules Zanger (Bloomington: Indiana University Press, 1960 [orig. 1839]), pp. 92–93.

Close to the Falls, I perceived a few small wooden shealings, appearing, under the majestic trees which overshadowed them, more like dog-kennels than the habitations of men: they were tenanted by Irish emigrants, who had taken work at the new locks forming on the Erie canal. I went up to them. In a tenement about fourteen feet by ten, lived an Irishman, his wife, and family, and seven boys as he called them, young men from twenty to thirty years of age, who boarded with him. There was but one bed, on which slept the man, his wife, and family. Above the bed were some planks, extending half way the length of the shealing, and there slept the seven boys, without any mattress, or even straw, to lie upon. I entered into conversation with them: they complained bitterly of the times, saying that their pay was not 2s. 6d. of our money per day, and that they could not live upon it. This was true, but the distress has been communicated to all parts, and they were fortunate in finding work at all, as most of the public works had been discontinued. I mentioned to them that the price of labour in Ohio, Illinois, and the West, was said to be two dollars a-day, and asked them, why they did not go there? They replied, that such were the price quoted, to induce people to go, but that they could never find it when they arrived; that the clearing of new lands was attended with ague and fever; and that if once down with these diseases there was no one to help them to rise again. I looked for the pig, and there he was, sure enough, under the bed.

2.19 "Paddy on the Canal," a folk ballad, ca. 1830s. From Glasgow Broadside Ballads, Special Collections, University of Glasgow Library.

When I came to sweet Philadelphia,
  It happened to be in the fall,
Never gave way to my rigging,
  Until I landed on the Canal.
To look at such a terrible rumour,
  It filled my heart with surprise,
To see such great undertakings—
The like I ne'er saw with my eyes,
  So farewell father and mother,
    And fare-you-well Ireland too.
  For fare-you-well sister and brother,
    So kindly I bid you adieu.
I being a poor Irish stranger,
  And knowing not what for to say,
When the ganger came up in the hurry,
  Saying "boys it is gay time today."
They all stood up in good order.
  You'd thought he was father of all,
I was wishing that very same moment,
  I was digging upon the Canal.
I fell in love with a rich farmer's daughter.
  And she was right proud do you see,
I caught her close round by the middle,
  And set her right down on my knee.

The old woman got up in a hurry,
    And loudly began for to bawl.
Saying, "get out you saucy bould jade.
    For Paddy will prove your downfall."
The girls they do all love me here,
    or wherever that I do go,
There's Sarah, Betsy, and Polly,
    They all call me their beau,
The ould woman got up in a fury,
    And loudly began for to bawl,
Saying, "We've got no good of our daughter,
    Since Paddy came on the Canal."
I learned the art of Navigation,
    I thought it was a very fine trade,
I could handle the pick and shovel,
    Likewise the wheelbarrow and spade.
I learnt to be very handy,
    Although I am not very tall
I could handle the sprig of shillalah
    With ever a boy on the Canal.
So now to conclude and finish
    And publish in every degree
I am just as true-hearted an Irishman,
    As ever your country did see.
So fill up a glass and be hearty
    And drink a good health to us all
And to every true-hearted Irishman,
    That's digging upon the Canal.

2.20   Bylaws of a German Workers Fraternal Society, 1849. Excerpts from the Constitution of Robert Blum Lodge, No. 58, of the Order of the Odd Fellows, Reprinted in Hartmut Keil and John B. Jentz, eds., *German Workers in Chicago: A Documentary of Working-Class Culture from 1850 to World War I* (Urbana: University of Illinois Press, 1988), pp. 176–79.

Preamble
The Odd Fellows are . . . a society united in a holy and indivisible bond, comprised of true friends and brothers who are bound—to the extent that honor and duty allow—to stand by one another in good time as in bad times, to support those in need to rush to the aid of the sick, to care for the widows and orphans of their deceased brothers, and to do everything in their power to give the latter their advice and protection.

    To do good deeds must be considered to be and should be recognized as the sole intention of the Odd Fellows, and Friendship, Love and Fidelity their motto . . .

Constitution

Article 2. Concerning the Members

1. The candidate is to believe in an Absolute Being, in a Creator, Preserver, and Governor of the Universe; he is to have reached his twenty-first year; he is to be a white male of sturdy moral character; he is to be industrious, able to prove an honorable means to earn his livelihood, and free of all shortcomings which could hinder him from earning his living.

. . .

Article 7: Benefit Recipients

1. Any Brother who has been a member of this Lodge for three months and who, due to sickness or accident, becomes unable to earn his living, is to receive a weekly allowance amounting to $4, and should he have reached the scarlet degree, is entitled to $5 for the duration of his sickness or inability, provided that this sickness or inability has not been brought about by his own immoral actions, and that the Brother has not forfeited his clam by having violated any of these bylaws.

3. In the case of the death of any Brother who is no more than four months behind in payments, a sum of thirty dollars is to be allotted for burial costs and paid to his widow or next of kin living anywhere in the United States.

4. Should a Brother die in the city of Chicago, the president and vice-president are responsible for extending the last worldly tributes in a proper and solemn manner, and the secretary is responsible for inviting all the members to the funeral ceremony.

5. Should the deceased not be survived by family or relatives in the city, a committee comprised of three members is to ensure that his effects or an equivalent sum be sent to the proper heirs, and to give an exact account to the Lodge.

8. Widows and orphans surviving Brothers of the Lodge who find themselves in need and who qualify according to the laws, are entitled to assistance appropriate to the circumstances as determined by the Lodge.

ORGANIZING TRADE UNIONS

Between 1828 and 1837, the United States witnessed an upsurge in union organization. Employers often attacked union workers for attempting to monopolize labor, using arguments like those deployed by Philadelphia's master carpenters in 1836 (Document 2.21). Workers often answered those arguments with vigorous rebuttals of the sort that Philadelphia's journeymen carpenters use in Document 2.22, and with the same degree of passion that the famed 1830s labor agitator Seth Luther displays in Document 2.23.

Courts tended to side with the employers in labor disputes of this period, using the kind of reasoning advanced in the sentencing of some New York journeymen tailors in 1836 on conspiracy charges for their role in a strike (Document 2.24). Once the 1837 depression weakened labor organizations, employers turned to more militant tactics to battle unions, including the blacklisting of strikers, which is protested by the New England mill workers in Document 2.25. In what ways did trade unionism's advocates and critics make their respective cases?

2.21   Employers Attack Trades Unions, 1836. The resolutions adopted by master carpenters in response to the organization of their journeymen in November 1835 to demand a $1.25 a day wage, reprinted in the *Pennsylvanian*, March 17, 1836, and reproduced in Commons et al., eds., *Documentary History*, Vol. 6., pp. 50–54.

Whereas it is the mutual interest of the employer and the employed, that good feeling, friendship and confidence should exist between them, and whereas a combination of Journeymen Mechanics has been formed, under the name of the Trades' Union, arbitrary in its measures, mischievous in its effects, subversive of the confidence and good feeling that formerly existed, and equally calculated to destroy the independence of both the master workmen and journeymen in their contracts and private relations, we, the Master Carpenters, of the City and County of Philadelphia, in self defence, deem it expedient to make known the grievances we labor under, and to take such measures as may, in some degree, remedy the evil. Under the existing state of things, no master workman can make a contract with any safety or security, that he will be able to fulfill his engagements, while his operations are under the control of a combination of men, who at a moment's notice may alter the established wages, the hours for working, and even prescribe to him what hands he shall employ, and he must accede to the most arbitrary measures, at the risk of his work standing still.

The Trades' Union is composed of Journeymen in every branch of Mechanics. Each member contributes weekly or monthly a portion of his earnings, to carry into effect the objects of the Institution. Some branches of Mechanics have some supposed grievances to complain of, and in secret conclave it is settled how and when it shall be remedied. The time selected is when their employers have large contracts on hand; a demand is made and if not promptly acceded to, no matter how unreasonable, the malcontents strike, throw down their tools, and quit their work, thus subjecting their employers to a breach of their contract and loss of time. Should the master workmen resist being coerced into the measure, and the Journeymen in that branch are thrown out of employ, they are supported from the Funds of the Society until the difficulty be reconciled. . . . Combinations of this description are indebted for their origin to the discontented and disorganizers in a monarchical government; they are not of American birth; they are arbitrary and oppressive in their operations, subversive of all regularity in business, and destructive of confidence in the parties concerned; it is the mother of countless evils, and the source of no good. They have been discountenanced in Europe, their birth place; but how they have ventured to raise their heads to breathe and exist in a republican atmosphere, is indeed wonderful.

Such being the evils imposed upon us, we, the Master Carpenters of the city and county of Philadelphia, find ourselves compelled in self-defence to form an Association for the purpose of putting down the combination called the Trades Union, and cordially invite the other branches to assist in the undertaking. Therefore,

RESOLVED, that the Trades' Union is arbitrary, unjust and mischievous in its operation, inasmuch as it forcibly compels the well disposed journeymen to become members, as there is a By Law of this Association prohibiting all members from working at the same building or in the same shop with any journeyman who is not a member, thus compelling him to join the Association and contribute weekly his earnings for the support of the idle and discontented, or he will be thrown out of work himself as his employer will be compelled to discharge him, fearing that all his other hands will strike.

RESOLVED, that we view the Trades' Union as a powerful engine of the levelling system; its operation is calculated to reduce the employer to the condition of a journeyman, and to keep the well disposed and industrious journeyman a journeyman all the days of his life, as he is restricted from doing over work, even though he is so disposed.

RESOLVED, that the Trades Union is calculated to weaken and destroy the harmony and ties of mutual interest that formerly existed between the master and apprentices; the boys have their minds poisoned by the members of the association, until they no longer consult their masters' interest, and finally look upon him as a hard task master and oppressor, instead of a friend and protector.

RESOLVED, that the Trades' Union is the growth of Monarchial Government, and ill adapted to our Republican Institutions.

RESOLVED, that we claim the right as Free Citizens, to make our contracts with the journeymen mechanics themselves, without the intervention of the Trades' Union; and that we do not recognize the right of any association or combination of men, to interfere in the ordinary transaction of our business.

RESOLVED, that we are willing, owing to the advanced price of living, to increase the wages to good workmen, provided they furnish themselves with tools, as is the custom of other cities, and that we deem it inexpedient to name any sum, preferring that every man be at liberty to make his own bargains, and be master of his own shop or building.

RESOLVED, that the Master Mechanics of the city and county of Philadelphia, be invited to attend a meeting, for the purpose of forming an association to be called the Anti-trades' Union Association, the object will be to protect us from the mischievous effects arising from that combination.

RESOLVED, that a committee of seven persons be appointed to carry into effect the last resolution.

James Leslie, President. John Northrop, Jr., John Longstreth, Vice Pres'ts. John Lindsay, Wm. C. Hancock, Secretaries.

2.22 Journeymen Carpenters Defend Trade Unionism, 1836. Preamble and resolutions adopted at a meeting of journeymen house carpenters, March 18, 1836, published in the *Pennsylvanian*, March 21, 1836, and reproduced in Commons et al., eds., *Documentary History*, Vol. 6, pp. 54–57.

Whereas, at a meeting of the employing carpenters of the city and county of Philadelphia, held pursuant to public notice, at the Carpenters' old Hall, on Monday, March 14th, 1836, have in their published proceedings made charges against the Trades' Union and this Association, accompanied with threats to put down all combinations that may be formed by mechanics, for the promotion and protection of their own interests, which charges, unsupported as they are by any evidence of their truth, are as malicious as their threats against the Trades' Union *are* vain and ridiculous. The constitution of our country secures to all its citizens the right to associate for the promotion of their own interests. All the various professions and callings, that compose society, have always exercised and enjoyed this right unmolested. Such a course of proceedings on the part of the employing carpenters is ill calculated to produce that mutual good feeling, which they say is so essential to our mutual interests. The employers say some branches of mechanics have some supposed grievances to complain of. A plain statement of facts will, we think, convince the public that our grievances are real. The average wages of our trade have been, before the strike of the ten hour system, one dollar and twenty five cents per day, from the first of April to the first of November, and one dollar and twelve and a half cents for the remaining part of the year. Not more than one half of the journeymen have employment more than nine months in the year, we are very much exposed to the heat of the summer sun while roofing or framing, and in the winter time to work in cold bleak shops or in open buildings without fire, or are compelled to lose time. The cost of journeymen's tools is from ten to a hundred dollars, which they are obliged to carry very often on their backs like pack horses, from shop to shop, and from building to building, and which they are liable to have stolen from them or destroyed by fire. Many employers have been in the habit of employing hands only during the long days of summer, discharging them as soon as the days become short; an unjust, but almost general custom has long since been established in the city of withholding one third of our wages, paying us only five dollars per week for months and sometimes years, without allowing us any interest for what is withheld, by which means we are often compelled to take orders in payment. A member of the committee that drafted resolutions for the meeting of the employers, has been known to purchase fifty dollars worth of hats at a discount of thirty per cent, and palm them on his journeymen in payment for their labor. Many of us would prefer working piece-work if we could know the price that would be put on our work; but we cannot know it in consequence of the employers' book of prices being secret; that it is unjust, numbers of us have learned to our cost: nor are we the only ones that have paid dearly for learning the fact. We have the evidence of citizens that have had work done for them, valued by the book in question, that it is unjust. A book of prices that is secret cannot be impartial or just. These are some of the grievances of which we have to complain. Our country and city are in a very flourishing condition; the increase in the price of living every body knows is great; we have in consequence asked an increase of 25 cents on last years' wages, to take place on the 20th of March, and have given our employers three months' notice of our intention, for this just and reasonable request, we are indebted for the base and malicious charges and threats, against the Trades' Union and this Association. Therefore

RESOLVED, that the resolutions of the employers have more than ever convinced us of the danger we would be exposed to without our union.

RESOLVED, that we earnestly recommend to the journeymen in every branch of business, that have not yet become members of the Trades' Union, to organize speedily for that purpose, and thus participate in a right, guaranteed by the constitution of the United States to all citizens of this Republic.

2.23 Seth Luther on "Combinations" and Equal Rights, 1832. Seth Luther, *An Address to the Working-Men of New-England on the State of Education and on the Condition of the Producing Classes in Europe and America* (Boston: Published by the Author, 1832), pp. 26–27.

Men of property find no fault with combinations to extinguish *fires* and protect their *precious persons* from danger. But if *poor men* ask JUSTICE, it is a most HORRIBLE COMBINATION. The Declaration of Independence was the work of a combination, and was hateful to the TRAITORS and TORIES of those days, as combinations among working men are now to the *avaricious* MONOPOLIST and *purse-proud* ARISTOCRAT.

Think you . . . there was no combination, when some of the inhabitants of Providence *commenced* the revolution, in 1772, by burning the British tender Gaspee in Providence River? Was there no combination, when the leather apron of the farmer and mechanic were seen mingling with the shining uniform of the "British Regulars," and when that class, who are *now* so much *despised* by the HIGHER ORDERS, achieved our "independence?" Was there no combinations, when the Bostonians, in the disguise of Mohawk Indians, made a dish of TEA at the expense of *King George the Third,* using Boston harbour for a tea-pot?

When monopolists, and others, belonging to the HIGHER ORDERS, wish to carry any of their measure into effect, they *can* and *do* form *"combinations"*; they *can* and *do* talk of supporting *their* views at the point of the *bayonet,* and of exterminating such citizens of this free country as oppose *their* views. . . . So much for combinations. . . .

It has been said, that the speaker [Luther himself] is opposed to *the* American System. It turns on one single point,—If these abuses are *the* American System, he is opposed. But let him see *an* American System, where education and intelligence is generally diffused, and the enjoyment of *life,* and *liberty* secured to all; he then is ready to support *such* a system. But so long as our government secures exclusive privileges to a *very small part of the community* and leaves the majority *"lawful prey"* to avarice—so long does he contend against *any* "System" so exceedingly unjust and unequal in its operation. . . . Must we fold our arms and say, It always was so, and always will be. If we did so, would it not almost rouse from their graves the heroes of our revolution? Would not the cold marble, representing our beloved Washington, start into *life,* and reproach us for our *cowardice?* Let the word be—Onward! onward! We know the difficulties are great, and the obstacles many; but, as yet; "we know our rights, and knowing, dare maintain." We wish to injure no man, and we are determined not to be injured as we have been; we wish nothing, but those equal rights, which were desired for us all. And although wealth, and prejudice, and slander, and abuse, are all brought to bear on us, we have one consolation—*"We are the Majority."*

2.24   Journeymen Tailors Sentenced, 1836. From the New York *Evening Post,* June 13, 1836, copied from *The Times.* In John R. Commons et al., eds., *Documentary History,* Vol. 4 (Cleveland: The A. H. Clark Company, 1910), pp. 325–33.

COURT OF OYER AND TERMINER. *Present—Judge* Edwards, Aldermen Banks, Ingraham, Benson and Randall.

SENTENCE OF THE TAILORS. The Court room was thrown open a few minutes past eleven o'clock. A large number of persons, who had previously assembled in the passages of the hall, immediately entered, and completely filled the large room. . . .

The names of the defendants were then called. . . .

The Judge then proceeded to pass sentence, which was done in the following words:

You have been convicted of a conspiracy. The bill of indictment charges substantially that you and others, being journeymen tailors, did perniciously form and unite yourselves into an unlawful club or combination to injure trade, and did make certain arbitrary bylaws, rules and orders, intending to govern not only yourselves but other journeymen tailors, and persons engaged in the business of tailors, and to oppress and injure them, and to injure trade and commerce. And also to prevent any journeymen tailors from working for any tailor who would not assent to said by-laws, that the said by-laws were to the effect following, viz. That you would not work for any tailor who would employ a journeyman tailor who was not a member of the said combination, or who would refuse to keep a slate hanging up in a public part of his store or shop, on which should be entered the name of every journeyman taking a job from his store, and that no journeyman should take one out of his turn. And also that no member of the said confederacy should go to any such shop for the purpose of getting a job, unless in his turn, under the penalty of forfeiting the price of the job. And also that no member should work for less than the bill of prices established by the club; nor for any tailor who employed a person who worked at a less price than the said bill of prices.

Also that during the period when there should be a strike, or turn out among such club, that a certain number of it should daily watch the shops of the persons against whom such strike or turn out was made, and that the person so appointed should serve, under the penalty of five dollars.

The indictment also charges, that you did, in presence of such combination, refuse to work, and did in a violent and tumultuous manner assemble together, and did go about from place to place, and to the workshops of certain tailors, with the intent to alarm and terrify them and with the intent to persuade and deter other journeymen to leave and desist from their work, and did compel divers journeymen tailors to quit their employment.

Combining to do an act injurious to trade, is declared by a statute of this State, to be a misdemeanor.

That such combinations are injurious to trade, has been fully verified in this city. Various trades have from time to time been brought to a stand, and the community extensively inconvenienced and embarrassed by them. . . .

The law leaves every individual master of his own individual acts. But it will not suffer him to encroach upon the rights of others. He may work or not, as suits his pleasure, but he shall not enter into a confederacy with a view of controlling others, and take measures to carry it into effect. The reason for the distinction is manifest. So long as individual members of the community do not resort to any acts of violence, their hostility can be guarded against. But who can withstand an extensive combination to injure him in his calling? When such cases, therefore, occur, the law extends its protecting shield.

Your case affords a striking manifestation of the necessity of the law extending its protection to the individual aimed at. The object of your combination was not only to control the merchant tailors, but even the journeymen. Your rules were craftily devised to accomplish this object, by throwing out of employment any master or journeyman who would not submit to your dictation.

But you were not content to stop here. You appointed committees to act as spies upon those whom you wished to subject to your will. Their premises were placed, day and night, under their vigilant inspection. You thronged around their shops, and were guilty of gross acts of indecorum. The journeymen who took jobs, were followed to their dwellings, and otherwise annoyed by you. In short, every ingenious device was resorted to by this extensive combination to which you were attached, to effect your object. Your conduct became insupportable, and the individuals aggrieved have found it necessary to appeal to the laws for protection; and a jury of your country has pronounced you guilty.

Associations of this description are of recent origin in this country. Here, where the government is purely paternal, where the people are governed by laws of their own creating; where the legislature proceeds with a watchful regard to the welfare not only of the whole, but of every class of society; where the representatives even lend a listening ear to the complaints of their constituents, it has not been found necessary or proper to subject any portion of the people to the control of self-created societies. . . .

Self-created societies are unknown to the constitution and laws, and will not be permitted to rear their crest and extend their baneful influence over any portion of the community. . . .

We have had in this country so little experience of these combinations, that we are at a loss to know what degree of severity may be necessary to rid society of them. From the considerations which I have before stated, and from a hope that the explicit declarations will have the effect to prevent such practices, we are disposed to impose a very mild punishment, compared to the offence. But if this is not found to answer the purpose, we shall proceed from one degree of severity until the will of the people is obeyed; until the laws are submitted to.

Henry Faulkner, who was President of the society, shall be fined $150; Howell Vail, who made himself particularly conspicuous, $100—all others $50 each; and stand committed until the fine is paid.

After the announcement of the sentence, a few persons hissed, but the noise was instantly suppressed.

2.25   Petition against Blacklisting, 1843. Quoted in David A. Zonderman, *Aspirations and Anxieties: New England Workers and the Mechanized Factory System, 1815—1850* (New York: Oxford University Press, 1992), p. 160.

We, the undersigned, Females, dependent upon the labour of our hands for subsistence: having left the employment of the Middlesex Manufacturing Company on account of a violation on their part, of the agreement existing between the undersigned and said Company; are now suffering persecution from said Company, and are hunted from place to place that we may find no employment by which to earn a living.

Not being able to contend against our rich persecutors by bringing a suit at law for satisfaction, we are compelled to seek redress, or protection, from the powers which created said Company. . . .

We . . . quit working for said Company and the consequence to us is as follows. Some of us went to work for other companies, but these Companies soon received our names and we were immediately turned off. Some of us applied for work where hands were wanted; but were informed that they could employ none of "The turnouts from the Middlesex," and many who laboured with us have been obliged to leave Lowell and seek their bread, they know not where on account of the persecution carried on against them by the Middlesex Company; our names are upon all the Corporations in Lowell; that we may find no employment; we therefore pray, that you will, if consistent with your constitutional powers, Stay the hands of our persecutors; and if not, that some law may be enacted, which will prevent our Brothers, Sisters and Friends, suffering as we suffer, if ever they should resist injustice from Manufacturing Companies.

A BROADER REFORM AGENDA

The vision of the workers' organizations that emerged in the 1830s extended beyond the workplace to politics. Workers participated actively in the formation of Workingmen's Parties in some large cities. When such parties were active, workers sought enactment of a broad agenda of reforms, including the abolition of debtors' prisons and the creation of universal public schooling. Still, the entry of unions into the political field caused controversy among trade unionists, as the 1834 debate at the founding of National Trades Union illustrates (Document 2.26). Following the collapse of the NTU and the breakup of many unions in the post–1837 economic downturn, workers increasingly looked to politics rather than union organization for solutions to their problems. In the 1840s two initiatives took precedence. One was the land reform campaign launched by George Henry Evans and the National Reform Union in 1844 (Document 2.27). The other was the campaign to enact a ten-hour workday that spread from state to state in the 1840s promoted by anthems like the one excerpted in Document 2.28. What do these documents indicate about the aspirations and concerns of workers in this period?

2.26 The National Trades' Union and Politics, 1834. A report on the NTU convention printed in *The Man*, Sept. 6, 1834, and reprinted in Commons et al., eds., *Documentary History*, Vol. 6, pp. 211–16.

TRADES' UNION NATIONAL CONVENTION. The following is a very brief sketch of a debate on the word *politics*, which took place in the

National Convention the second day of its session; the following resolution, offered by Mr. Townsend, being under consideration:

RESOLVED, that a Committee be appointed to draft resolutions expressive of the views of the Convention on the social, civil, and political condition of the laboring classes of the country.

Mr. Schenck hoped that the word "political" in the resolution would be omitted. The proceedings of the Unions, he said, were watched, narrowly watched, and although he believed that in reality the term implied nothing improper, it was misunderstood by many, and might prove fatal to the interests of the Unions, by arraying against them the force of one or other of the political parties. He therefore moved that the word "political" be stricken out.

Mr. Townsend opposed the motion. He considered it bad policy for the working classes to allow the word "politics" to be used as a bugbear by the aristocracy. What, he asked, did politics mean, but the science of government? It was the right and the duty of the working classes, he contended, to view and review all the measures of public men and public bodies, and to test them by the lever of equal rights and the plumb rule of justice. If the measures of government would not bear this test, who were the sufferers? The useful laboring classes. It behooved them, therefore, not to allow themselves to be frightened from a proper attention to their interests by a bugbear of the aristocracy. . . .

Mr. Douglass thought, with the gentleman last up, that the word "politics" had been far too much used as a bugbear against the working men. The policy of every human being was to promote his own happiness; whatever measures, therefore, were calculated to promote the welfare and happiness of the mass were essentially the policy of the working classes. There was nothing in that doctrine that ought to excite alarm. Every good man was and ought to be so much of a politician as support measures calculated to increase the sum of human happiness. Why, as a whole, were the useful classes so degraded? The reason was obvious: the policy pursued by their legislators was not their own policy, not that policy calculated to promote their welfare. They had become degraded by bad legislation; they had got into difficulty by it, and how were they to get out but by legislating themselves out? They could only advance their interests by choosing such men for legislators as were identified with them. They belonged to no party; they were neither disciples of Jacksonism nor Clayism, Van Burenism nor Websterism, nor any other *ism* but *workeyism*. . . .

Mr. Schenck could subscribe entirely to the gentleman's definition of the word politics, but it was not so understood and acted upon by the Societies. He spoke from knowledge when he said it was almost impossible to retain some of them now. He would therefore wish that the Trades might first organize, and improve their condition. It could do no harm to leave the word out of the resolution. . . .

Mr. Labarthe (if we rightly understood him) thought that the Unions, for the present, at least, should confine their efforts to a reduction of the hours, and to maintaining the price of labor. He alluded to the formation of a Trades Union in Philadelphia [evidently the Mechanics' Union of Trade Associations] a few years ago, which afterwards became merged in the "Working Men's Party" in consequence of taking a part in politics, and that, he said, was now extinct, as well as the Union. He was in favor of striking out the word political.

Mr. Townsend said it was by no means his wish that the working classes of the Union should act with any political party. They hold the balance of power and could more easily obtain what they want by keeping aloof from party. It was only necessary for them to say what they want, and each party would be anxious to adopt their measures. If the word political in the resolution could be construed to favor [any] party, he would say strike it out. . . .

The President here read an extract from the call of the Convention, showing that its objects were "to consult on such measures as shall be most conducive to advance the moral and intellectual dignity of the laboring classes, sustain their pecuniary interest, succor the oppressed, and by all just means maintain the honor and respectability of the mechanical profession." No delegate elected under the call, he said, would transcend his authority by voting for the resolution, which was a legitimate subject for discussion.

Mr. English agreed that the subject matter of the resolution was within the power of the Convention, but the means to be used to effect their object might be various. The resolution proposed to appoint a committee to draft resolutions "on the social, civil, and political condition of the working classes," and an objection to striking out the word "political" had been urged, on the ground that it was intended to favor neither of the two political parties; but it had not been said that it was not intended to form a third party, which he thought would be equally inimical to the interests of the Unions. . . .

Mr. Townsend expressly disclaimed all intention of forming a political party. He thought the laboring classes could do more by maintaining the balance of power.

Mr. Ferral thought, from the shape the debate had assumed, that the Convention would be liable to the charge of being more acted upon by sound than sense. All were agreed as to advancing their moral and social condition, but thought this bugbear "political" was in the way. . . . If the Trades could form a perfect Union, by concert they would disseminate knowledge; therefore if the word political in the resolution was calculated to retard the formation of such a Union, he would strike it out, as he need not attempt to show that "social, civil, and intellectual" would embrace all that was necessary, though he was fully satisfied that the working classes would never effectually remedy the evils under which they were suffering until they carried their grievances to the polls, and make them known by a judicious selection of law makers. He moved, as an amendment, that "political" be stricken out and "intellectual" inserted in the resolution.

[handwritten margin note: education so they can have better political standing(?)]

The amendment having been seconded, the President remarked that the resolution with the proposed amendment, would embrace all that was necessary or desirable. Let the intellectual condition of the working classes be improved, and an improvement in their political condition would be the necessary consequence.

[The amendment was carried, and the resolution passed unanimously.]

2.27   A Plea for Land Reform, 1844. A report published in the *Working Man's Advocate*, July 6, 1844, and reprinted in Commons et al., eds., *Documentary History*, Vol. 7, pp. 293–305.

"TO THE PEOPLE OF THE UNITED STATES"

The National Reform Union of the City of New York, although in existence only a few weeks, has attained a perfect Organization. . . .

On the 13th of March last, at a public meeting of workingmen, a committee was appointed to inquire into the causes which produce in this Republic a depression of labor, and a social degradation of the laborer, very similar to that which prevails under the detestable governments of Europe.

At the next public meeting of the workingmen's Committee submitted the following Report, which was adopted unanimously nearly in its present form. Read it working men, you that would escape the fate that overwhelms your brother men in Europe. . . .

REPORT. Having made due inquiry into the facts, the Committee are satisfied that there is a much larger number of laboring people congregated in the towns than can find constant and profitable employment. Your committee do not think it necessary to enter into statistical details in order to prove a fact that is not disputed by anybody. The result of this oversupply of labor is a competition among the laborers, tending to reduce wages, even where employment is obtained, to a scale greatly below what is necessary for the comfortable subsistence of the working man, and the education of his family. It appears to your Committee, that as long as the supply of labor exceeds the demand, the natural laws which regulate prices, will render it very difficult, if not altogether impossible, to permanently improve the condition of the working people.

Our inquiries, therefore, were naturally directed to ascertain how far existing causes are likely to affect the supply and demand, of labor— whether those causes tend to lessen, or to increase the evil under which the working classes are now suffering.

First we find in our cities, and Factory Stations, an increasing population, the great majority of whom depend for a subsistence on Mechanical labor; and secondly we find the new born power of machinery throwing itself into the labor-market, with the most astounding effects—withering up all human competition with a sudden decisiveness that leaves no hope for the future. Indeed if we judge of the next half century by the half century just past, there will be, by the end of that time, little mechanical labor performed by human hands. . . .

This result—this triumph of machine labor, and ultimate prostration of human labor, cannot in the opinion of your committee, be averted. . . .

The question then recurs—the momentous question "Where lies our remedy? How shall we escape from an evil which it is impossible to avert?"

This question admits of an answer at once simple, satisfactory, and conclusive. Nature is not unjust. The Power who called forth those mechanical forces did not call them forth for our destruction. Our refuge is upon the soil, in all its freshness and fertility—our heritage is on the Public Domain, in all its wealth and infinite variety. This heritage once secure to us, the evil we complain of will become our greatest good. Machinery, from the formidable rival, will sink into the obedient instrument of our will—the master shall become our servant—the tyrant shall become our slave.

If we were circumstanced like the inhabitants of Europe, there would seem to be little hope of getting the laboring population out of the difficulties, and distress, in which they are at present involved. . . .

But in this Republic, all that the Creator designed for man's use, is ours—belongs, not to the Aristocracy, but to the People. The deep and interminable forest; the fertile and boundless prairie; the rich and inexhaustible mine—all—all belong to the People, or are held by the Government in trust for them. Here, indeed, is the natural and healthful field for man's labor. Let him apply to his Mother Earth, and she will not refuse to give him employment—neither will she withhold from him in due season the fulness of his reward. We are the inhabitants of a country which for boundless extent of territory, fertility of soil, and exhaustless resources of mineral wealth, stands unequalled by any nation, either of ancient or modern times. We live under a Constitution, so just and so equal, that it may well lay claim to a divine origin. As a People we are second to none, in enterprise, industry, and skill. Thus it is clear, that we are in possession of all the elements of individual and national prosperity. . . .

The first great object, then, is to assert and establish the right of the people to the soil; to be used by them in their own day, and transmitted—an inalienable heritage—to their posterity. The principles of justice, and the voice of expediency, or rather of necessity, demand that this fundamental principle shall be established as the paramount law, with the least possible delay.

That once effected, let an outlet be formed that will carry off our superabundant labor to the salubrious and fertile West. In those regions thousands, and tens of thousands, who are now languishing in hopeless poverty, will find a certain and a speedy independence. The labor market will be thus eased of the present distressing competition; and those who remain, as well as those who emigrate, will have the opportunity of realizing a comfortable living. . . .

But it may be said that all we have here laid down is sufficiently obvious to everybody. We believe that it is so, and we anticipate you in saying that the real question of difficulty is, how to achieve those rights, and realize those advantages, which every individual acknowledges to exist.

Your Committee can perceive but one way of accomplishing those objects, and that is by combination—by a determined and brotherly union of all citizens who believe the principles set forth to be just, in themselves, and necessary to the public welfare. We propose, therefore, that such Union be organized at once. It is our opinion that all citizens who desire to join the ranks of the National Reformers shall have an opportunity of doing so without delay. . . . Any man who would oppose the measure of justice for which we contend is not a Republican at all—he is a Monarchist, in soul, and we should treat him as such at the Ballot Box.

The labor of your committee ends here, but we cannot close without expressing our belief, that, if the working men lead the way, manfully, in this reform, they will be immediately joined by a great majority of the non-producing classes. Various motives of a personal nature will induce them to join us—not to say a word about that patriotism and love of justice which, we trust, belong alike to every class in this Republican Community. Signed:

Thomas A. Devyr, George H. Evans, John Commerford, [et al.]

2.28   A Ten-Hour Anthem, 1844. From *The Mechanic*, June 8, 1844, reprinted in Teresa Ann Murphy, *Ten Hours' Labor: Religion, Reform, and Gender in Early New England* (Ithaca: Cornell University Press, 1992), p. 164.

Now be the "ten hour" banner,
In every land unfurl'd
    And be the shout hosanna,
Re-echoed through the world.
        Till every isle and nation,
Till every tribe and tongue,
        Receive the great salvation,
And join the happy throng.

FROM SLAVERY TO FREEDOM

The debate over slavery divided white northern workers. Some, like the working men of Pittsburgh who drafted the statement excerpted in Document 2.29, saw slave labor as a danger to all free labor and staunchly advocated support of the new Republican party, which opposed slavery's extension in the West. Others, like the Irish editors of the *Boston Pilot*, believed that freedom for African Americans would undermine the fragile position of Irish laborers (Document 2.30). Once freedom did come as a result of the war, with the Emancipation Proclamation of 1863, and the enactment of the Thirteenth Amendment in 1865, whites sought to regulate black labor. As Document 2.31 shows, the Union Army issued careful instructions on the treatment of "contraband," even down to the wage rates the freed people were to be paid for various forms of labor. After the war the Freedmen's Bureau played a leading role in trying to shape a free black agrarian labor force in the South, drafting labor contracts between those freed by the war and their former masters (Document 2.32). What do these documents suggest about the ways in which the status of African Americans, whether enslaved or newly freed, served as a constant reference point for white Americans seeking to define the dimensions of free labor?

2.29   Workers' Anti-Slavery Statement, 1856. Address of the Working-Men of Pittsburgh to Their Fellow Working-Men of Pennsylvania, *New York Tribune*, October 31, 1856; Reprinted in Philip S. Foner and Herbert Shapiro, eds., *Northern Labor and Antislavery: A Documentary History* (Westport: Greenwood Press, 1994), pp. 242–43.

The Great Issue

Address of the Working-Men of Pittsburgh to Their Fellow Working-Men of Pennsylvania

The undersigned, Workingmen of the City of Pittsburgh, convinced that our interests as a class are seriously involved in the present political struggle, send greeting to you, our fellow workingmen of Pennsylvania asking you to aid in the protection of our common rights, now in great peril. . . .

In another section of our country, exists a practical aristocracy, owning Labor, and thereby independent of us. With them, Labor is servitude, and Freedom is only compatible with mastership. They despise us. They calls us "Greasy Mechanics," "Filthy Operatives," and "small Farmers doing their own drudgery," and "unfit to associate with a Southern gentleman's body servant,"—and, being gentlemen, no doubt believe what they say. The political power of that section is in their hands, and from the ignorant and depressed condition of our fellow-workingmen there—the "poor whites," as they call them. These aristocrats desire to extend this system over all the Territories of the nation. To extend it over the Territories is to give them supreme power in the government, and then they will extend it over us. Free workingmen, shall they do it? The present Presidential contest is to decide. . . .

2.30   Anti-black statement, Boston Irish, 1862. From *Boston Pilot* reprinted in *The Liberator*, August 22, 1862, reprinted in Foner and Shapiro, eds., *Northern Labor and Antislavery* (Westport: Greenwood Press, 1994), pp. 281–82.

What has the African done for America? To white toil this nation owes everything; but to black, *nothing*. . . . It is the whites that made and are to perpetuate this nation. The perpetuity of it may be measured by the circumstances of it chief props—its laborers in brain and hand. The condition of the negro—whether he be in dependence or misery—can have no effect whatever on the continuance of the Republic; neither himself nor his children can ever constitute a true part of the State. But such is not the case with the white laborer. He is a citizen. . . .

Therefore, by justice, and by patriotism, they [white workers] have the right and duty to resist this black current that is invading them, for it will injure their condition. So without violence, down with the Abolitionism, and away, from the certainty of injuring the white laborer, with the African!

Let no man employ a black while he can get a white laborer. He who prefers the black to white may yet find his own injured in the choice.

2.31   Orders Regarding Contraband, 1862. From the Headquarters of the 2nd Brigade of the South Carolina Expeditionary Corps to the Superintendent of Contrabands at Beaufort, South Carolina, March 1862, reproduced in Ira Berlin et al., eds., *Freedom: A Documentary History of Emancipation, 1861—67*, Vol. 3, (New York: Cambridge University Press, 1990), pp. 176–77.

Beaufort, SC. March [28?] 1862

Sir. I enclose to you a series of instructions for the proper regulation of the system of Management of the Department of Contraband negroes resident within this city.

You are instructed to retain within the city such number of contraband Negroes as are requisite for the ordinary labor at the Government works. The remainder you are directed to remove to the plantations for employment in the fields.

In detaining negroes for city duty you will be careful to give the preference to efficient refugees from the main land and the longest dwellers in the city. Orders permitting negroes to pass from this island to any other shall be issued only from your department on the requisition of the overseer of the plantation on which the applicant may reside. . . .

You are instructed to punish at your discretion all negroes absent beyond the time granted by their passes by sending them for penal servitude on public works. . . .

The rates of wages of negroes in government employ shall be as follows. First class mechanics from $9 to $12 per month, with one ration daily

Second class mechanics	$5 per month with one ration daily
Drivers of Gangs from	$9 to $12 per month, with one ration daily
First class laborers	$6 per month, with one ration daily
Second " "	$4 " " "

All persons in this command having negroes employed as servants or otherwise shall be required to report to your dept on the First and Fourteenth of every month, in writing, the names and ages of such servants, their masters names, the rate of pay they each receive, and to what day they were last paid.

The rates of wages of domestic servants shall be as follows
First class servants of either sex $6 per month and board
Second "   "   " $4 " "
Waiting boys & girls $3 " "
Ostler coachmen &c $4 " "

2.32   A Free Labor Contract, 1865. In Berlin et al., eds., *Freedom*, p. 341.

[Dathaw Island, S.C. February 27, 1865]
Article of agreement made & entered in to between W. T. Calkins and H. P. Kellam of Dathaw Island South Carolina party of the first part, and
   Bess Perry, Grace Perry, Will Mack, Rose Mack, Ellen Mack, Juno Mack, Isaac Jenkins, Hanah Jenkins, Lycynda Jenkins, Thomas Jenkins, Lydia Upright, Phebe Washington, Tamer Chism, Mol Chism, William Roach, Mariah Roach, Mary A Polite, Brutus Bronson, and Dorcas Bronson Inhabitants of Inlet Plantation Dathaw Island South Carolina party of the Second part withnesseth that each and every one of the Said party of the second agrees to Cultivate the land plant and attend properly three acres of Cotton and Pick Sort Gin mote and Sack the Same all the above work to be done in the proper time and in good order. They farther agree to plant one task of Corn each attend the same & gather the Corn blades to feed the Horses & mules to be used in the Cultivation of the above mention Cotton & Corn
   The Said party of the first part agrees to furnish to the party of the Second part the use of Horses or Mules Harnes & Ploughs Sufficient to do the team work in the Cultivation of the above mentioned Cotton & Corn
   The Said party of the Second part are to have one forth part of all the Corn they rase and the use of one & a half acres of land to plant with Corn Potatoes & other vegitables for their own benefit
   The contract is to remain in force until the first day of January 1866
   Given under our hands this 27th day of February 1865
W. T. Calkins
H. P. Kellam

[Endorsement] The within contract have been read and explained to the laborers whose [names] are endorsed upon them, and they have signified their intention to work for the season of 1865 on the terms proposed, C. F. William, Gen'l. Sup't.

POSTWAR HOPES FOR THE EMANCIPATION OF FREE LABOR

In the aftermath of the Civil War, as the country adapted to the end of slavery and its peacetime economy revived, workers' organizations proliferated. The National Labor Union, founded in 1866 and led by the iron molder William Sylvis, provided the most ambitious attempt yet to unite workers in a national union federation. As the excerpt of a William Sylvis speech on monopoly (Document 2.33) makes clear, the NLU's leaders saw themselves battling to preserve workers' independence against the encroachments of large new corporate entities such as railroads. Postwar labor agitation drew a great deal of momentum from the recently concluded battle against slavery, as the 1865 speech by abolitionist Wendell Phillips on the demand for an eight-hour workday makes clear (Document 2.34). The wartime triumph of "free labor" laid the ideological basis for the labor reform platform introduced by Massachusetts reformers in 1871, which is excerpted in Document 2.35. Free African American workers themselves moved enthusiastically to realize the advantages of organization after the war, as the address of George T. Downing to the Colored National Labor Convention shows (Document 2.36). Unfortunately, the end of Reconstruction in 1877 and the failure of white labor organizations to embrace black members soon betrayed the hopes expressed in Downing's 1869 vision. What do these documents suggest about the activists' visions of "free labor" after the Civil War?

2.33 Attacking Entrenched Privilege. William Sylvis's speech, "The Spirit of Monopoly," reproduced in James C. Sylvis, *The Life, Speeches, Labors, and Essays of William H. Sylvis* (Philadelphia: Claxton, Remsen, and Haffelfinger, 1872), pp. 417–18.

The American people, if they would profit by the experience of other countries, should wage unrelenting war against every species of monopoly. It is a remarkable fact, that a spirit of monopoly is invariably developed in proportion to the accumulation of wealth in all nations. Pride is the parent of selfishness, and prosperity is a sure tributary to that vanity which begets notions of superiority; for the estimate of mankind is measured by bank accounts, rent rolls, or broad acres; and "the more we have the more we want," is a truthful adage which exactly fits the craving instincts of avarice. . . .

This is all very well, so long as the laws of competition are kept inviolate, and an equal chance is offered to all for advancement. We claim that the road to wealth should be left open to all, and that those who are foremost in the race should place no obstructions in the path of those struggling on behind them. We want no special privileges, no favoritism, no legislation that singles out the few for fortune's bounty, while the many are suffered to toil on in cold neglect. We regard equal laws as the only safeguards that can be thrown around the people—the surest basis upon which social happiness can rest—the best guarantee against political inequality. We contend that, in the broad field of enterprise presented by this country, no possible contingency can arise which would warrant the bestowal of special privileges upon capital in either an individual or collective capacity; but, above all, none should be extended to a company which is denied to an individual; for it creates a combination of power which crushes private effort, breaks down wholesome competition, and absorbs all surrounding elements of prosperity.

2.34   Arguing for the Eight-Hour Day, 1865. Wendell Phillips, *Speeches, Lectures, and Writings*, Second Series (Boston: Lee & Shepard Publishers, 1891), pp. 140–41.

Where the government rests on the people, its administrators are bound to give time to the laborers to understand the theory of government. When shut up an excessive number of hours in labor, the workman comes out but the fag-end of a man, without brain to think such subjects. Now, therefore, it is a fair division to give him eight hours for labor, eight hours for sleep, and eight hours for his own,—his own to use as he pleases. [Applause.] I shall not be the first to say, "You shall not have it unless you come under bonds to use it well." It is none of my business to say what he shall do with what is his own. I shall not say to the millionaire, "We will defend you in the possession of your stocks and bonds, if you will use them well." I may argue with him, and shall, to use his wealth properly; but my first object shall be to give it to him, because it belongs to him. It has been argued that the negro would not work if his freedom was given to him. I have answered, his freedom belongs to him, and he is responsible for its use.

The present effort is to give the laborer more leisure, in order to make him more intelligent. Never, in history, has more leisure been secured to the working-classes, but greater intelligence has resulted therefrom. . . .

2.35   Labor Reform Platform, Massachusetts, 1871. A platform introduced by
Wendell Phillips and adopted unanimously at the Labor-Reform Convention,
Worcester, Mass., Sept. 4, 1871. Phillips, *Speeches, Lectures, and Writings,*
pp. 152–53.

We affirm, as a fundamental principle, that labor, the creator of wealth, is
entitled to all it creates. . . .
   Resolved—That we declare war with the wages system, which demoral-
ized alike the hirer and the hired, cheats both, and enslaves the workingman; war with the present system of finance, which robs labor, and gorges
capital, makes the rich richer, and the poor poorer, and turns a republic
into an aristocracy of capital; war with these lavish grants of the public
lands to speculating companies, and whenever in power, we pledge to use
every just and legal means to resume all such grants heretofore made; war
with the system of enriching capitalists by the creation of interest-bearing
debts. We demand that every facility, and all encouragement, shall be given
by law to co-operation in all branches of industry and trade, and that the
same aid be given to co-operative efforts that has heretofore been given to
railroads and other enterprises. We demand a ten-hour day for factory-
work, as a first step, and that eight hours be the working-day of all persons
thus employed hereafter. We demand that, whenever women are employed
at public expense to do the same kind and amount of work as men perform
they shall receive the same wages. We demand that all public debts be paid
at once in accordance with the terms of the contract, and that no more
debts be created. Viewing the contract importation of coolies as only
another form of the slave-trade, we demand that all contracts made relative thereto be void in this country and that no public ship, and no
steamship which receives public subsidy, shall aid in such importation.

2.36   Toward a World of Free Labor "Without Regard to Color," 1869.
Address of George T. Downing to the Colored National Labor Convention of
1869 in the *Proceedings of the Colored National Labor Convention Held in
Washington, D.C., December 6th, 7th, 8th, 9th, and 10th, 1869* (Washington,
D.C., New Era, 1870), pp. 3–4.

This convention bears the title, "National Labor Convention;" I desire
that it shall not falsify its name; that it be a "labor convention;" in a
word, that it shall labor, that it bring forth something. Much is expected
of it; the eyes of every intelligent laborer of the land, without regard to
color, are fixed on it; its doings will be eagerly caught up and canvassed by
laborers of Europe, now banding together to the end of causing labor to
be respected, and of enjoying its just rewards.
   The colored, as well as the white laborers of the United States, are not
satisfied as to the estimate that is placed on their labor, as to their opportunities, as to the remuneration for their labor, the call for this convention,

and the very general and highly intelligent response which I gaze on in you, my fellow delegates, attest. No other class of men would be satisfied under the circumstances; why should we be?

The colored man's struggle until now has been for naked existence, for the right to life and liberty; with the fifteenth amendment, henceforth his struggle will be in pursuit of happiness; in this instance; it is to turn his labor to the most effective account, to be respected therein; this is a great problem; it is racking the brains of the ablest economists; the most we can hope to effect, at this gathering, is a crude organization; the formation of a labor bureau to send out agents, to organize colored labor throughout the land, to effect union with laborers without regard to color.

Good has come out of Nazareth. Slavery, when it existed, shut out the light to the end of shutting out the right; it had, however, to have some light for its own purposes. It did not permit the educated white mechanic and laborer from the North and abroad to come within its darkened abode; to have done so would have jeopardised its existence; hence, it had to and did teach its subjects, the slaves, mechanical arts; they now have those arts as freemen. In the North, from selfish motives, from prejudice, to serve their then Southern master, they would not teach or encourage the colored man in mechanism; so that, whatever mechanical acquirements, with some exceptions, exist among colored men in the country, are to be found in the South. They are crying for organization. We desire Union with the white laborer for a common interest; it is the interest of both parties, that such a union should exist, with a fair, open and unconcealed intent; with no aim to destroy any organization, political or otherwise; with no thought of fostering dishonor, whether in the nation or in individuals; repudiating all attempts to weaken obligations engaged in openly, seriously, with a full knowledge of the same; with an intent to share honorably all obligations "as nominated in the bond." I think that I may say, in behalf of the delegates here assembled that they stand ready to extend an earnest hand of welcome to every effort, associated or otherwise, that looks to the dignity of labor, to its enjoyment of full remuneration and protection, and which shall manifest a spirit to be in harmony with capital in every instance, when capital shall be properly mindful of its true interest in harmonizing with labor.

3

WORKERS IN A MATURING INDUSTRIAL
SOCIETY, 1877–1914

Between 1877 and 1914 the United States became the world's leading industrial society. It was an era of free trade in people, goods, and capital. As people moved incessantly over the face of the globe crossing oceans and borders, international commerce flourished as never before and capitalists searched ceaselessly for the most profitable investment opportunities. The United States benefited more fully from those three interrelated processes than perhaps any other nation. If for much of the nineteenth century the United States had been a relatively underdeveloped economy, dependent on the importation of capital and technology from abroad, by the turn of the twentieth century the United States could boast of one of the most developed economies in the world. In those economic sectors that marked a modern, developed economy most clearly—coal and steel, petroleum-based enterprises, chemicals, food processing, electrical equipment (all of which required large capital investments and the use of new technologies)—the United States had few rivals. Its economy could boast some of the largest enterprises in the world and the first that truly established a system based on mass production, mass distribution, and mass consumption. Whereas the United States had once exported primarily agricultural products and raw materials, importing manufactured goods from abroad, by the end of the nineteenth century such American enterprises as Standard Oil, International Harvester, Singer Sewing Machine, and the G. Swift Packing Company not only exported their products abroad but established branch plants overseas. Where once the United States had built its canals and railroads with capital borrowed from foreign investors, its domestic economy now created enough surplus capital of its own for American investors to search eagerly for profits around the world.

The United States could not have built its dynamic economy without the labor of millions of people who came from every part of the North American continent and the world as well. Between 1870 and World War I nearly thirty million immigrants entered the country. They came from areas of the world to the east, west, and south of the United States. At first, the majority of immigrants continued to come from the north and west of Europe, mostly

Germans, Scandinavians, British, and Irish newcomers. Increasingly, after 1881, the great masses of immigrants originated in the south of Italy, the Austro-Hungarian Empire, and Tsarist Russia. In the 1860s and 1870s, substantial numbers of Chinese immigrants arrived on the West Coast to provide labor to build the first trans-Continental railroads, work in the hard-rock mining industry, and provide services (domestic labor and laundering) for the white middle and upper classes. After Congress closed entry to Chinese laborers (so-called Coolies) in the Chinese Exclusion Act of 1882 (reenacted in 1892 and 1902), Asian laborers arrived from Japan (until they were excluded by informal government action in 1908), and later the Philippines after it became a U.S. territorial possession in 1898. Throughout this period, Mexicans crossed the porous border between their nation and its neighbor to the north with regularity. Their labor proved absolutely essential to the railroads, the underground mining industries, and the beet-sugar ranches of the Southwest (and later to the citrus, fruit, and vegetable fields of California). In one of the least noted and least examined aspects of immigration to the United States, considerable numbers of eastern and southern Europeans immigrated initially to Canada and then migrated south. By the eve of World War I, nearly all the primary extractive and manufacturing industries of the country depended on the labor of immigrants and their children to fill the ranks of laborers and machine operators. And the majority of the residents of major metropolises and industrial cities consisted of immigrants and their children.

People born in the United States, particularly those at the bottom of the occupational and income ladder, moved almost as widely and as often. Although in the years between 1877 and 1914 the number of farms and acres brought under cultivation multiplied rapidly, millions of young people deserted farms and the countryside for work in mines, mills, and factories and a life in the city. Entire families of poor rural Southerners deserted their places of birth to work in the region's cotton-textile mills, which sought the labor of women and children as well as adult men, and which promised to respect the Southern racial code by reserving all respectable jobs for whites only. Some remained in the countryside to labor in forests or to dig phosphate and salt. Younger African Americans proved as mobile as white Southern poor folk or European immigrants but they seldom left the South. Instead, they deserted sharecropping to work as coal miners, forest and saw-mill hands, railroad roustabouts, longshoremen, and in a variety of casual, day-labor jobs. Both white and black farm boys also ran away to sea to serve in the merchant marine.

The result of all this human movement was the creation of one of the most heterogeneous labor forces in the world. It was also a labor force marked by ethnic and racial occupational hierarchies. Old-stock citizens and immigrants from the north and west of Europe, which by the late nineteenth century included the Irish, tended to dominate the ranks of supervisory and skilled employees. The newer immigrants from the south and east of Europe satisfied an almost insatiable demand for unskilled laborers willing to work and be paid by the day or hour, and their children flooded the ranks of the machine operators demanded by mass-production industry. Young women of Irish, German, Scandinavian, and domestic rural origins satisfied the demand for household domestic labor everywhere outside the South; in the South, African Americans cleaned the houses, cooked the meals, and washed the laundry of white families. In the cities, recently arrived immigrant men and women provided the labor for the less technologically advanced, highly competitive, and marginally profitable trades that continued to exist and grow in number: clothing production, artificial flower-making, candy manufacture, baking. These trades were marked by work sites characterized as sweatshops and by the commonality of household or tenement labor in which whole families, especially wives and young children, toiled in their homes. Millions of U.S.-born single, young men and armies of recent immigrants recruited by labor contractors, sometimes known as *padrones*, filled the ranks of migratory labor so necessary for seasonal, construction, and agricultural industries. And everywhere an almost unbridgeable wage and occupational gap separated white workers, whatever their place of origin, from Asian laborers concentrated in the West, Mexicans in the Southwest, and African Americans mostly in the South. However great the wage or status difference between a south Italian immigrant or Russian Jew (Hebrew was the term used in 1900) and a U.S.-born, English, Welsh, German, or Swedish worker, the chasm between the former and workers of color was even greater.

These millions of new and older workers were pouring into enterprises engaged in bringing science and technology into the labor process. Employers began to subject all forms of work to scientific study, firm managerial control, and redefinition. Almost everywhere old skills and forms of knowledge grew less valuable; newer skills, often the product of technological and managerial innovation, emerged; and capital in the guise of machinery replaced the strong backs and brawny muscles of unskilled day laborers. While the ranks of those workers defined as skilled rose in number and probably remained a constant proportion of the total labor force, the ranks of those characterized as unskilled steadily diminished and the number of those labeled semi-skilled (mostly machine operators) skyrocketed. Indeed, by 1914 the semi-skilled had become the numerically predominant core of the labor force. Formal education also grew in importance as a labor market qualification in an economy focused on the mass production and mass consumption of manufactured goods. Armies of clerks, bookkeepers, and salespeople had to track the production and distribution of the goods that flowed through the system. Other record-keepers had to track the work-time and output of laborers paid by the piece or the hour. These rapidly growing new occupations provided employment opportunities for the older-stock young white workers and the Americanized children of immigrants fortunate enough to complete secondary school. The ranks of white-collar wage and salary earners grew apace.

As skills rose and declined, job specifications changed, and work controls tightened, workers felt themselves under great pressure. In the last third of the nineteenth century, their real wages and earnings rose considerably, largely as a result of an era of secular deflation and the redistribution of labor from lower to higher wage sectors of the economy (actual wage rates barely changed at all, declining somewhat nominally but rising in real monetary value). Between 1897 and 1914, however, real wages and earnings advanced far more slowly, owing to rapid price inflation, surging immigration, and persistent domestic migration from farm to factory. Most galling to workers was that, however much or little their real earnings advanced, their employers, professionals, and the most advantaged employees and citizens seemed able to claim a disproportionate share of national income and wealth. The upper 1 percent of the population possessed one-fourth of the total wealth, and the top 5 percent owned one-half; the bottom two-thirds claimed only a tiny residual share of wealth. In a phrase made famous in the title of perhaps the most widely purchased and read book of the period, written by the reformer Henry George, economic progress produced greater poverty. George may have used the phrase "progress and poverty" metaphorically but in most working-class families it took the work of multiple wage-earners to satisfy a minimal health and decency standard for all its members.

New tensions at work and inadequate incomes were not the only factors that fostered discontent among many workers. Worse, perhaps, was that the typical worker rarely could expect to be employed regularly. Whether annual unemployment, as tracked by new state bureaus of labor and other agencies, was high or low, most workers experienced considerable bouts of unemployment nearly every year, and this at a time when unemployment insurance and other forms of public assistance did not exist. To compound discontent, the late nineteenth century experienced two major depressions (1873–77, 1893–97) and one minor depression (1883–85), at which times unemployment and need became common among working people. The more expansive and prosperous early twentieth century was not without its own business cycles, as the economy contracted between 1907 and 1909, and again between 1913 and 1915, on both occasions causing mass unemployment.

One obvious result of such worker discontent was industrial conflict and its by-product, violence. The era opened with 1877, "the year of violence," when a strike by railroad workers that began in West Virginia spread across the nation's railroads and precipitated a number of city-wide strikes, of which the most violent and threatening occurred in Pittsburgh, Baltimore, and St. Louis. In some places, the turmoil did not end until President Rutherford B. Hayes sent the regular U.S. Army to control the strikers and their sympathizers. For the remainder of this period industrial strikes swelled and receded in great waves, peaking in 1885–86, 1892–95, 1899–1905, and 1910–13, and ebbing at other times. Some of the later conflicts matched the 1877 railroad strike in participation rates, intensity, violence, and national impact. The Homestead steel strike of 1892, the Pullman strike and boycott of 1894, the bituminous coal strike of 1894, the Chicago teamsters' strike of 1905, and the Lawrence textile strike of 1912, are only a few such conflicts that fit the category of "the year of violence." More typical were the thousands of local strikes conducted by workers in the building trades, printing trades, metal trades, and clothing trades; where union discipline prevailed, violence proved the exception, and workers were as likely to win, or gain a compromise, as to lose. The intensity of the conflict and the level of violence usually had little to do with the ideology of the workers or the unions involved. More important was the relative strength and/or weakness of the union and employer in conflict. Where employers were relatively powerful and the unions by contrast weak, as in the urban public transit strikes that persisted throughout these years, violence was all too common especially because these strikes were fought on public streets where large crowds gathered easily. The union with jurisdiction over urban transit was a relatively moderate one; the unions in the garment trades, nearly all of which were left-wing, radical, and socialist by public pronouncement, engaged in overwhelmingly peaceful strikes against economically weak employers. Even the most radical labor organization of the era, the Industrial Workers of the World, led some of the more orderly mass strikes of the early twentieth century, newspaper reports to the contrary notwithstanding.

One clear pattern emerges from all the statistical and other data that we now have about the incidence of industrial conflict between 1877 and 1914. Over time, strikes more and more were called, regulated, and legitimated by established trade unions with written constitutions and formal procedures. The spontaneous strike conducted without formal organizational sanction or presence disappeared from common use. That should occasion no surprise for this was the era in which a modern labor movement came into being.

The Knights of Labor (K of L), which was founded in 1869, served as a bridge between what might be called the pre-modern, and distinctly localized labor organizations that preceded it, and the modern and more nationalized or international (meaning the United States and Canada) form of organization that followed it. Between 1885 and 1886, indeed nearly overnight, the Knights of Labor built the first truly mass national labor organization in United States history, with 750,000–850,000 members at its peak in every region of the nation and in most every industry and trade; many millions more of working people and their sympathizers enlisted in and later deserted the ranks of the K of L. Yet, it collapsed almost as rapidly as it rose, having lost more than half its peak membership by 1888 and entering its death throes by the depression of the 1890s (in fact, a slow and lingering death). The Knights failed for many reasons. Their leaders fought with each other; its membership was so diverse occupationally, regionally, ethnically, and even religiously, it was hard to maintain solidarity; its organizational structures and principles were rudimentary and contradictory; its goals were poorly defined and seldom shared in full by all members. Most importantly, however, the Knights failed primarily because employers resisted them so strenuously and effectively. In truth, employers simply had more power than their labor adversary and when they decided in the aftermath of labor triumphs in 1885 that the Knights had grown too powerful, business counterattacked and crushed its foe.

At precisely the same time that the Knights of Labor rose and fell, another labor organization appeared in the shadow of its larger competitor for the loyalty of workers. Established first as the Federation of Organized Trades and Labor Unions of the United States and Canada and in this guise experiencing a largely still birth, the parents tried again and in 1886 succeeded in creating the American Federation of Labor (AFL), which exists to this day as the far larger half of the AFL-CIO. Unlike the Knights, the AFL limited its membership and centered authority and power in the separate trade unions that chose to affiliate with it. At first, the AFL's founders, Adolph Strasser and Samuel Gompers, most notably, promised to represent and to organize all wage workers regardless of craft, nationality, race, or gender. In practice, however, the affiliates that came to dominate the AFL represented only the more highly skilled workers who had real bargaining power with employers owing to their irreplaceability. These unions succeeded by gaining control of their particular labor markets and monopolizing, in so far as they could, entry into them. They did so by restricting membership on the basis of race, nationality, gender, and, of course, skill. Their leaders showed scant interest in organizing the mass of unskilled and semi-skilled workers, who lacked labor market bargaining power, and they practiced a narrow form of unionism that some praised and many condemned as "business unionism." At first, Gompers, the longtime president of the AFL (1886–94, 1896–1925) used radical language, enunciated grandiose goals, and urged trade unionists to organize workers regardless of race, gender, nationality, or skill. But his words fell on the largely deaf ears of the craft unionists whose affiliates dominated and held effective power in the Federation.

Results proved the worth of the practices and policies preferred by the craft unionists. Between 1898 and 1904, the affiliates of the AFL built the first stable mass labor movement in the United States, amassing a membership of just under two million workers. Their stronger affiliates bargained collectively with employers, negotiated enforceable contracts, increased wages, won a measure of job security, and achieved the eight-hour day in several trades. The success of the craft unions, among other factors, led Gompers to temper his rhetoric, to abandon ambitious goals, and to temporize with the racists, sexists, and craft aristocrats in the Federation. By 1914 the AFL seemed to represent and to be controlled by the successful and the satisfied among trade unionists, those who praised the American system and compared capitalism to the goose that laid the golden egg.

The great mass of workers, however, remained unorganized and unable even to earn a living wage. Neglected by the craft unionists and the AFL, these more numerous laborers had their own defenders. Most committed to their cause were the American socialists who enjoyed their golden age between 1901 and 1914, a time of increasing membership, electoral gains, and candidates elected to local, state, and even federal office (two members of Congress between 1910 and 1918). The Socialists even amassed one-third of the voting delegates at AFL conventions by 1911 and controlled a number of the affiliates. They saw their political party in alliance with the trade unions as the twin edge of labor's sword.

Yet some socialists and other labor radicals worried that the AFL and the majority of its affiliates would never reject business unionism for a broader social movement unionism. They also believed that the established craft unions would continue to ignore the expanding ranks of less skilled workers and fail to organize employees in the most technologically advanced and mass-producing sectors of the economy. In the summer of 1905 these radicals met in Chicago to establish a radical labor alternative to the AFL and to craft unionism as a way of organization. Acting in response to an "Industrial Union Manifesto," the Chicago convention created the Industrial Workers of the World (IWW), or Wobblies. In the new organization's founding document, its drafters declared perpetual industrial war against capitalism; ridiculed the AFL as the American Separation of Labor; pledged to organize all workers regardless of skill, nationality, race, or gender into industrial unions rather than craft unions; and promised to create a new society in the shell of the old. After early growing pains and a number of internal splits between 1905 and 1908, the IWW evolved into the most radical labor organization in the nation. Between 1909 and 1913, it led mass strikes in McKees Rock, Pennsylvania; the piney woods of Louisiana; the Douglas Fir forests of the Pacific Northwest; Akron, Ohio; and most famously at Lawrence, Massachusetts, and Paterson, New Jersey. Journalists and scholars wrote about the rising tide of socialism and syndicalism (the Socialist Party of America [SPA] and the IWW), and public officials and conservative observers condemned the Wobblies as the most dangerous people in the United States. On the eve of World War I, then, masses of workers mobilized and fought against their employers and the established order.

IMMIGRANTS TO INDUSTRIAL SOCIETY

The documents in this section offer a glimpse into the heterogeneity of the labor force and the central role played by immigrants in the creation of an industrial economy. They also illustrate the irregularity of employment for many workers and the incredible mobility of the labor force. Document 3.1, a letter from a German immigrant, indicates that even skilled workers were at the mercy of an unregulated labor market. From his language can you determine what his beliefs and politics were? How typical do you think the life of the Irish itinerant, or hobo day laborer, as described in Document 3.2

was? Was he a victim of his own behavior or of forces beyond his control? What do you learn about labor markets in Document 3.3, a description of the experiences of a Russian immigrant? Compare his work pattern and attitude toward the job to that of the Irish worker in Document 3.2. Is the Chinese immigrant portrayed in Document 3.4 at all comparable to the Irish and Russian immigrants described in the preceding documents? In what ways is he similar or different? Document 3.5 offers an employer's perspective on the advantage of hiring Chinese laborers, while in Document 3.6, the reformer Henry George's analysis of employers' preferences for Chinese workers asserts that their low wages and more primitive living standards affected white workers detrimentally, undercutting their position in the labor market and harming their standard of living.

3.1   Letter from a Disaffected German Immigrant, 1883. Originally published in the *Chicagoer Arbeiter-Zeitung* February 6, 1883. Reprinted in Hartmut Keil and John B. Jentz, eds., *German Workers in Chicago: A Documentary of Working-Class Culture from 1850 to World War I* (Urbana: University of Illinois Press, 1988), pp. 50–51.

To the editorial staff of the "Arbeiter-Zeitung"!

In November of the year 1881, I was urged to travel to America by the slave trader, Jaburek. He made me the most gliterring promises. I am a meerschaum and amber worker by trade, and during my stay in Vienna I worked for four years in one of the largest Viennese factories, where I made a so-called good living.

Nevertheless, I let myself be deceived by the scoundrel and have been paying bitterly for it ever since. I was sent by the agent across the ocean on a steamship, and after a stormy twenty-two day trip, I arrived in New York where my distant fate awaited me. No one fetched me in New York, though Jaburek had promised me that someone would find me a job and a place to live as soon as I got there. But that was all part of the swindle. Jaburek just wanted to stick me with a 120 Mark ticket, and in this he succeeded. Like many of my comrades in suffering, I was lured here to compete with other workers. After three weeks I finally found work with Karl Weiss in New York, where I was supposed to make $13.00 a week. But my problems had only begun. Weiss was going to deduct one dollar a week, so that, as he put it, he could give me the money at the end of the year. I wouldn't hear of it and was let go. Here and there I found part-time work with masters in small shops and in this way just managed to eke out a living.

I was informed by Mr. Bensziger in New York that a Mr. Metzler had written him; he and a Mr. Rothschild wanted him to send meerschaum and amber cutters to Chicago. Travel costs were to be reimbursed and the salary was said to be good. At that time I was completely out of work. A few people from Vienna took me into their care and got together the money necessary for me to buy a train ticket to Chicago. I had already been warned about Mssrs. Metzler and Rothchild's foreman in New York. I didn't like him from the very start, and he acted hostilely toward me. He made trouble in order to get me to work for less and then offered me $10.00 a week. I demanded $12.00. He said the business turned little profit, which was new to me, since the owners were millionaires and the workers beggars. He finally gave me $12.00, but at the same time he wrote to New York for another worker. Eight days before Christmas I was let go. This clearly illustrates the capitalists' ruthlessness. I was thrown out on the pavement without a penny in my pocket, no friends, no relatives, starving and freezing. For eight full weeks I led a wretched existence, I would long since have put an end to all my misery and suffering.

The foreman spread another outrageous lie about me in the firm. Kempelmacher, that's the fool's name, said I had wanted $14.00 and that I had left of my own accord. At that point I went directly to the owners in order to tell them the truth and ask for work. But they believed that foreman instead of me, and calling me a liar, showed me the door. I had conducted myself properly and that's why this action was even more disgraceful. Metzler recently went to New York to recruit new cheap labor but came back empty-handed. Now he is going to write off to Vienna to inflict the same fate as mine on those who don't know any better. Publish these lines for this reason, Mr. Editor, so that my countrymen will not be swindled and driven into the arms of poverty as have been I and so many others.

Johann Rosinger

3.2   Struggles of an Irish Immigrant, ca. 1913. Interview of Sam Gray by P. A. Speek, for his report on "Life Histories of Twenty-Five Native and Foreign-born Unemployed Floating Laborers, 1913 and 1914," in *U.S. Commission on Industrial Relations: Unpublished Records of the Division of Research and Investigation*, R. Boehm, ed. (Frederick, MD.: University Publications of America, 1985), Reel 6.

Sam Gray

35 years, pretty husky man, although his face is rather thin and worn out looking. Irish. 12 years in the United States. A shipyard painter in England. Clerks in the shipping offices were agitating the people to go to America; they said that America was a better country with much higher wages than in England. He thinks that the clerks did this in the interest of the shipping companies. He believed at that time in the clerks' agitation, and he read the same in the newspapers. This is the reason he came to America.

He left his painting trade for the following reason: He felt its bad influence upon his health in England. When he came over he tried to continue the same trade here, but very soon he noticed the danger of white lead poison—"painter's colic." He quit the trade never to return again to it. He became a casual laborer, earning at first good wages on different jobs. He wrote to his parents in Ireland once every two months sending some money with each letter. But in the later years he fell down and it became more difficult to get jobs. . . .

His home is in Ireland. His mother and sister are living there. . . . He has no home, no relatives, and no friends in America. Other people call him a hobo, but he calls himself just a common laborer belonging to the ranks which are roaming over the country. He earns his living by laboring.

A year ago he was in Milwaukee. He came here [Chicago] on Nov. 1, having $35.00. Two weeks he "rested," drank with other "floaters" in the saloons—both whiskey and beer; went to shows, and courted the girls. After two weeks the money was gone. He started to look for work, during which time he was helped out by his temporary friends—other laborers, whom he knew, and who continued to come in from work with money. Once he went to the Catholic Sisters who gave him to eat, and once he was three days having nothing to eat whatever.

The first night he came to Milwaukee he slept in the Rescue Mission; paid $0.10 for a night, had a hot bath and had his clothes fumed which is a necessity when coming in from construction and all other camps. He looked for work all over the city; wanted a job in a factory . . . but could not get anything. . . . The Free Employment Office then shipped him out to an ice camp in Salem, Wis., 10 hours a day, pay $1.50 a day if he worked less than a month and $1.75 if he worked a month or over. He paid $4.00 for camp and board; 2 men slept in a bunk; bunks were two story high. They lived in an old house. The bedding was very dirty and lousy; 38 men slept in one room and the air was foul. Every morning the men complained of headaches and bad tastes in their mouths. The room was swept only once a week by "bullcooks," but never mopped; no cuspidors, no washing or bathing facilities. The board was good and the foreman was fair. Worked five weeks—the icehouse was filled. He had $20 and paid his way to Milwaukee where he "rested" one week. The Free Employment Office then shipped him to a railway construction camp in Medford, Wis., 10 hours a day; $1.75 per day; board was $4.00; two men in a bunk and bunks were two stories high; 22 men slept in a car. . . .

He could only stand to be with the foreman three weeks. In order to get his pay he was compelled to go to Stevens Point, 60 miles. He jumped a freight train and from there he jumped another freight to Minneapolis. He spent three days there for having a "little time." He then walked to Hudson, 16 miles from Minneapolis. He got work with a railway "steel gang;" 10 hours a day; $2 per day; $4.50 for board. . . . After six weeks he quit because he could not eat the grub. He "beat" his way back to Minneapolis. There he "rested" two weeks. After this his money was all gone. He jumped a freight to Milwaukee. He was here 3 days without work; his "friends" helped him out. . . . The State Free Employment Office then shipped him to a telephone gang in Mecqon, 14 miles from Milwaukee; 9 hours a day, pay $30 a month with sleeping place and board.

The work consisted in digging holes and raising poles. . . . The work was finished in one month. With $28 he came to Milwaukee and "blew it" in the first two weeks. The next job he got through the Free Employment Office to load wagons and cars with materials for a construction Co., 10 hours a day; 2 dollars per day. The job was finished in two weeks. During his next two weeks he tried to live on his money, $10, and to improve himself by not drinking and only using the money for meals and lodging and shows. The next two weeks he was still out of work. The sisters in the Catholic Hospital gave him a light meal every day. He slept in parks, barns, and last night with several other men slept in the police station.

He has no hopes for the immediate future. He has done everything to get out of the position of a casual laborer in America, but has always failed. This is the reason he has lost all hopes and even his belief in God.

3.3   Struggles of a Russian Immigrant, ca. 1913. Interview of George Madis by P. A. Speek, for his report on "Life Histories of Twenty-Five Native and Foreign-born Unemployed Floating Laborers, 1913 and 1914," in *U.S. Commission on Industrial Relations: Unpublished Reports*, R. Boehm, ed. (UPA, 1986), Reel 6.

George Madis
Thirty-one years of age. Five years of public school education in Russia. Five years in America. By trade a ship carpenter. Came to this country because he wanted to earn money. . . . He is single. He had had a girl in Russia, but could not marry her because he never had enough money for the establishment of a family.

After landing he was three months out of work. During all this time he was eagerly looking for work, but could not get any because he did not know enough English and did not know the proper ways of getting work. He did not suffer very much because he had saved a sum of money while he was working on ships. After three months when his saved money was gone, he, compelled by need, applied at once for a job at the docks (in New York) and found work as a deck hand; ten hours a day and thirty cents an hour. As the work was not steady—in some weeks he had work only two or three days-and as the work itself was very dirty and heavy, he could tolerate that job only a month. All that was left from his monthly earnings was a check for $5.30.

He applied to a private German employment office on 73rd St. E. between 1st and 2nd Aves. This office offered to him a job as a stair-builder for the price of $5.00. The office man told him that the pay was about $5.50 a day. He gave the office man his check, who refused to return thirty cents, which sum was quite vital for him, because he had in his pocket only five cents left. The job was in Newark, N.J. He walked from New York to Newark, expending his five cents for a ferry. When he arrived at the work place the boss told him that there was no place for him and that the job of which the office man had told him was already taken. Just when he was about to start away the boss told him he could start to work, which he did. The boss, in the evening, refused to advance him any money, but a German fellow-worker loaned him $1.50. When the next pay day came the boss paid him only $1.75 a day. Although the work was easy and the work day only eight hours, nevertheless he felt the employment office and probably the boss had cheated him. As he did not expect to find another job there, he continued the same job. After two weeks his pay was raised to two dollars a day, after four weeks to $2.50 and after five weeks, to $2.75. As after two more weeks no more raise was made, he quit the job, hoping to find a job for higher pay elsewhere.

He at once found another job on a house which was being built, eight hours and $3.00 a day. Worked three weeks on that job. Quit because the weather became cold and he wanted inside work.

After four days he found fitting work in an automobile factory, nine hours a day and $18.00 a week. After three weeks the pay was raised to $21 per week. He worked four months. He was then laid off because of the lack of work. (On the same job he had joined the union, paid three dollars as entrance fee and fifty cents each month as membership fees. He still continues to be a member.)

One and a half months out of work. He was all the time looking for work, mainly through want ads, but could not find any. He then paid his way to Buffalo. One and a half weeks out of work. Paid his way to Cleveland, Ohio. Five days out of work. He then found work as an automobile body builder, through want ads; ten hours a day and twenty-five cents an hour. After six weeks he quit because he wanted to earn more money. He at once found work in a ship-building plant. Ten hours and $3.50 a day. After three and a half months he was laid off because of lack of work. Three weeks were spent looking for work through want ads.

He then found work as a concrete framer; ten hours and thirty cents an hour. As the work was high and dangerous he quit after seven days.

Two weeks out of work. He then applied to a private employment office and paid $2.00 for a job in an automobile factory; ten hours a day and $18.00 a week. Worked seven months. Quit because he wanted higher wages. He had now saved about $300.

He at once found work in another automobile factory (body builder); ten hours and $3.50 a day. Worked five months. Quit because he felt very tired and worked out. Rested only three days—slept mostly. He then found work again in an automobile factory; nine hours and $5.75 a day. Worked ten months. Quit, because he wanted to go to Europe to see his relations and farmer friends there, and also because he wanted to go to Siberia to prospect for gold. He hoped to make a good strike there and to become a rich man. He suffered in Siberia great privations and was badly treated by other prospectors. He found there all but gold. He lost there all his money made in America, so that his home friends helped him out. The adventure lasted eleven months. Last April he returned again to America on the money loaned by his friends. . . .

He does not drink, but sometimes he sees the girls. Only in Europe he had a slight sexual disease.

He has no plans for his future—lives from day to day. Will only try to save money again.

Still [he thinks], all considered, especially American wage, the labor conditions in America are better than in any European country. For instance, the skill of a workingman is paid here, while in Europe all workingmen, skilled or unskilled, get almost the same wages—there is no free play for individual abilities.

3.4 Struggles of a Chinese Immigrant, ca. 1902. Interview with Lee Chew published in *The Independent* (1902). Reprinted in Hamilton Holt, ed., *The Life Stories of Undistinguished Americans* (New York: Routledge, 1990), pp. 178–81.

I worked on my father's farm till I was about sixteen years of age, when a man of our tribe came back from America and took ground as large as four city blocks and made a paradise of it. He put a large stone wall around and led some streams through and built a palace and summer house and about twenty other structures, with beautiful bridges over the streams and walks and roads. . . . The man had gone away from our village a poor boy. Now he returned with unlimited wealth. . . .

The wealth of this man filled my mind with the idea that I, too, would like to go to the country of the wizards and gain some of their wealth, and after a long time my father consented, and gave me his blessing, and my mother took leave of me with tears, while my grandfather laid his hand upon my head and told me to remember and live up to the admonitions of the Sages, to avoid gambling, bad women and men of evil minds, and so to govern my conduct that when I died my ancestors might rejoice to welcome me as a guest on high.

My father gave me $100, and I went to Hong Kong with five other boys from our place and we got steerage passage on a steamer, paying $50 each. . . . When I got to San Francisco, which was before the passage of the Exclusion act, I was half starved, because I was afraid to eat the provisions of the barbarians, but a few days' living in the Chinese quarter made me happy again. A man got me work as a house servant in an American family, and my start was the same as that of almost all the Chinese in this country.

The Chinese laundryman does not learn his trade in China; there are no laundries in China. The women there do the washing in tubs and have not washboards or flat irons. All the Chinese laundrymen here were taught in the first place by American women just as I was taught.

When I went to work for an American family I could not speak a word of English, and I did not know anything about housework. The family consisted of husband, wife, and two children. They were very good to me and paid me $3.50 a week, of which I could save $3.

I did not know how to do anything, and I did not understand what the lady said to me, but she showed me how to cook, wash, iron, sweep, dust, make beds, wash dishes, clean windows, paint and brass, polish the knives and forks, etc., by doing the things herself and then overseeing my efforts to imitate her. . . .

In six months I had learned how to do the work of our house quite well, and I was getting $5 a week and board, and putting away about $4.25 a week. . . .

I worked for two years as a servant, getting at the last $35 a month. I sent money home to comfort my parents, but though I dressed well and lived well and had pleasure, going quite often to the Chinese theater and to dinner parties in Chinatown, I saved. . . . So I had $410 at the end of two years, and I was now ready to start in business.

When I first opened a laundry it was in company with a partner, who had been in the business for some years. We went to a town about 500 miles inland, where a railroad was being built. We got a board shanty and worked for the men employed by the railroads. . . . When the railroad construction gang moved on we went with them. The men were rough and prejudiced against us, but not more so than in the big Eastern cities. It is only lately in New York that the Chinese have been able to discontinue putting wire screens in front of their windows, and at the present time the street boys are still breaking the windows of Chinese laundries all over the city, while the police seem to think it a joke.

We were three years with the railroad, and then went to the mines, where we made plenty of money in gold dust, but had hard time, for many of the miners were wild men who carried revolvers and after drinking would come in to our place to shoot and steal shirts, for which we had to pay. One of these men hit his head hard against a flat iron and all the miners came and broke up our laundry, chasing us out of town. They were going to hang us. We lost all our property and $365 in money, which members of the mob must have found.

I went home to China in 1897, but returned in 1898, and began a laundry business in Buffalo. But Chinese laundry business now is not as good as it was ten years ago. American cheap labor in the steam laundries has hurt it. So I determined to become a general merchant, and with this idea I came to New York and opened a shop in the Chinese quarter.

3.5   An Employer Compares Chinese and White Labor, 1877. U.S. Senate, *Report of the Joint Special Committee to Investigate Chinese Immigration,* 44th Cong., 2d Sess., Report No. 689 (Washington, D.C.: Government Printing Office, 1877), pp. 606–08.

Donald McLennan sworn and examined.
Question [by Mr. Bee]. You are connected with the Mission Woolen Mills, I believe.

Answer [by Donald McLennan]. I am. . . .

Q: What would be the effect upon your mills and all other manufacturing business here, if we should drive the Chinamen out of the country?

A: I think the effect would be very detrimental to the interests of the State [California]. . . . When I first started the Mission Mills I started with Chinese labor for the reason that I could not get white labor. I found them very intelligent, sober, and industrious, and ready to adapt themselves to anything and everything that turned up or whatever was required of them, so much so that I found they were equally as intelligent as the same type or class of labor of any nationality. They would readily do the most intricate and complicated work, and in fact learned it in one-third less time than any other class of white labor. They are very imitative and ready, very apt, and can do almost anything you show them how to do. I think they do it more carefully than a white person. . . .

Q: Originally you employed Chinese entirely?

A: Yes, sir; I used to employ probably six or eight hundred of them.

Q: What led you to the substitution of white labor in part?

A: We found really a scarcity of Chinese labor, and then there was a desire on our part to accommodate ourselves to the wishes of the public so far as employing white help. Furthermore, I think that we would employ a great many more white help than we are doing now if habits of industry were instilled into the minds of children in their homes, which is not the case here. Children are not taught any idea of industry at all. The consequence is, when they come into those establishments they are unruly; they will not obey any regulations we have in regard to how they shall conduct themselves or deport themselves in the business, and we are obliged to let them go. . . . I wish you to understand distinctly that it is not my wish at all ever to employ a Chinaman where a white man ought to be employed; but we must employ them as we . . . cannot get along without them; they are a necessity.

3.6   Henry George on Chinese labor, 1876. U.S. Senate, *Report of the Joint Special Committee to Investigate Chinese Immigration*, 44th Cong., 2d Sess., Report No. 689 (Washington, D.C.: Government Printing Office, 1877), pp. 275–76.

Henry George sworn and examined.

Question [by Mr. King]: Are you acquainted with the effect of Chinese employment on white labor on this coast?

Answer [by Henry George]: Yes, sir.

Q: State what in your opinion the effect is.

A: Year by year they [the Chinese] are getting into new trades. For instance, in mining, they are now going into deep mining. In the last two or three years they have been going into agriculture very extensively, besides the various trades, one after another, which they have gone into.

They seem capable of doing almost anything a white man can do in the way of labor. There is a Chinaman now running a printing-press in this city and running it very well. . . . I have seen them work at iron-work as machinists. . . .

Q: In your opinion do they prevent the immigration of white labor to this coast?

A: Undoubtedly they do by lowering the rate of wages. I think one way in which you can see how they prevent white immigration is that if you go all through this country, wherever you go you will eat food cooked by Chinese, you will be waited on by Chinamen. One of the most striking differences between the East and the West to a Californian who has lived here a long while is in going East, after getting on the Union Pacific and traveling a little while he finds the Chinamen succeeded by white girls. In all these places were it not for the Chinamen we would have white girls as they have in the East, and they would in due course become a permanent population. . . . The essential thing about Chinese laborer is that they are cheap laborers; that they work for a little less than the whites. Of course the employment of the Chinese must be more profitable to the employer than that of whites, or they would not be employed.

WORKING WOMEN AND CHILDREN

Women engaged in all sorts of paid labor, including such illicit forms of work as prostitution. Document 3.7 is a contract signed by an immigrant Chinese woman to serve as a prostitute. Can a woman, even a Chinese immigrant, contract voluntarily to serve as a prostitute? Why would the woman agree to the terms of such a contract? In the late nineteenth and early twentieth century, increasing numbers of women entered the paid labor market and worked outside the home. Document 3.8 explores the heated debate that arose among women as well as between male and female workers about the right of married women to work for wages outside the home. Why would women disagree among themselves on this issue? More common than married women entering the labor market was the experience of young single women who left their parental households, sought waged labor, and appeared to be "women adrift." Document 3.9 suggests how some reformers and institutions sought to protect the virtue and respectability of unattached women workers. In Document 3.10 a male worker laments the rising employment of women and children because it limits the employment opportunities and wages for men who must earn enough to support their families. The final document in this section (3.11) explains the employment of children in the textile mills of Fall River, MA, and the fact that they are hired as much by their parents as their employers.

3.7   A Chinese Woman's Indenture Agreement to Work as a Prostitute, 1873. Reprinted in Alexander McLeod, *Pigtails and Gold Dust* (Caldwell, Idaho: Caxton Printers, 1947), pp. 180–81.

An agreement to assist the woman, An Ho, because coming from China to San Francisco she became indebted to her mistress for passage. Ah Ho herself asks Mr. Yee Kwan to advance for her six hundred and thirty dollars, for which Ah Ho distinctly agrees to give her body to Mr. Yee for service of prostitution for a term of four years. There shall be no interest on the money. Ah Ho shall receive no wages. At the expiration of four years, Ah Ho shall be her own master. Mr. Yee Kwan shall not hinder or trouble her. If Ah Ho runs away before her time is out, her mistress shall find her and return her, and whatever expense is incurred in finding and returning her, Ah Ho shall pay. On this day of agreement Ah Ho, with her own hands, has received from Mr. Yee Kwan six hundred and thirty dollars. If Ah Ho shall be sick at any time for more than ten days, she shall make up by an extra month of service for every ten days' sickness. Now this agreement has proof—this paper received by Ah Ho is witness.
Tung Chee [October 1873]

3.8   Women Debate Work, 1879. Two women debate the merits of married women working in shoe shops in the *Lynn Record* (MA), 1879, as quoted in Mary H. Blewett, *We Will Rise in Our Might: Workingwomen's Voices from Nineteenth-century New England* (Ithaca: Cornell University Press, 1991), pp. 142–43.

MARRIED WOMEN IN THE SHOE SHOPS

[February 15, 1879]
Mr. Editor, I do not believe any woman, married or single, works for the fun of it in these times; neither do I believe most married women work in the shop because they are obliged to—that is to provide themselves with the actual necessaries of life. To be sure, some of them may have shiftless husbands, but I think the men would make greater exertions if the women were not so eager and willing to take a man's place. If married women had to pay board bills, washing bills, and then had to be denied all the comforts of home, with no one to look to for aid or support, they would be less content to sit quietly down and submit to reduction after reduction, but would be ready to join any honorable scheme which would bring relief.

Were times good, work and money plenty, why, then, if married women wanted to work out and neglect their homes, they could do so for all me. But so long as there are a surplus of laborers, with a scarcity of work, I shall

protest against the married woman question, even though I stand alone. . . .
—A. Stitcher

[February 22, 1879]
Mr. Editor,—Ah! my dear Stitcher. . . . You say: "So long as there are a surplus of laborers, with a scarcity of work, I shall protest against the married women question." And I reply:—So long as there are "a surplus of laborers with a scarcity of work" so long will your protest be of no avail. So long as there are "a surplus of laborers with a scarcity of work" so long will many married men find it impossible to support their families, and when the husband and father cannot provide for his wife and children, it is perfectly natural that the wife and mother should desire to work for her husband and her little ones, and we have no right to deny her that privilege.

My dear child, don't blame married women if the land of the free has become a land of slavery and oppression. Women are not to blame. . . .
—Americus

[March 1, 1879]
Mr. Editor,—For years I have been homeless, thrown here and there by circumstances, but have kept my eyes and ears open to all that has been going on around me; and many times I have been deeply pained at the utter selfishness manifested by a certain class of married women in the shops, till I have been thoroughly disgusted with them all. . . .

From statistical reports there is found to be sixty odd thousand more females than males in the state of Massachusetts, and it is safe to say three-fourths of them have to earn their own support. Now these can never have homes of their own unless they make them. No strong arm on which to lean can ever rightfully be theirs. In the face and eyes of this, can it be fair for them to have to compete with married women who have protectors, in the struggle for bread, besides all the other obstacles in their way?

It is no use, "Americus," since the days of Mother Eve women have been at the bottom of nearly every trouble: and . . . I think a foolish extravagance in dress and love of display on the part of women, has caused many a once honest man to turn thief, and has helped, if did not wholly, bring about this fearful crisis of distress and want. . . .
—A. Stitcher

3.9 Working Women in the 1880s. Excerpts from Carroll D. Wright, *The Working Girls of Boston* (Boston: Wright & Potter Printing Co., 1889), pp. 130–33.

Those employers who understand the power of moral forces, of human sympathy, of care for the welfare of their employees have seen the positive economic results of their broad-heartedness; positive and practical benefits are the actual outcome of an investment of this kind. We are not suggesting sentimentalism, but the application of the highest principles.

We would suggest that parents teach their children to respect all honest labor; the honest working girl engaged in honest labor should be respected by all honest minded people; she should be welcomed in the churches of the city, she should be drawn into the best associations where social and moral surroundings would aid her in cultivating her own self respect, and in which mutual assistance would be rendered; certainly it should not be possible to class her as the "forgotten woman;" her struggle is too heroic, her hardships too painful, her lot too dreary for Christian people to thoughtlessly pass her by.

One great lack in the lower grades of industry is the want of thorough training in technical knowledge, and of the capacity for close application; to secure these, there should be numerous institutions for free instruction in various branches of work. Such institutions already exist and are doing most excellent work; prominent among these are, sewing schools under the patronage of churches, the Chapel of the Evangelists, the Young Women's Christian Association, the North End Laundry, the Temporary Home for Working Women, the Training School for Nurses, the School of the Church of our Father, and several others; all such institutions should be generously supported and their number increased. These institutions together with evening schools can do much towards making the labor of the working girls far more efficient, thus bringing their economic conditions to a higher plane.

We would like to see established homes for working girls; these should be founded on the basis of such homes in London on the plan elaborated by John Shrimpton, Esq., of London. These homes are for the express purpose of accommodating young women engaged in business during the day the object being to furnish a respectable home during those trying periods of non-employment, and while looking for a new situation; it is during this time that the girl is most subject to temptation, and most liable to succumb to evil. Poor, out of work, and seeking employment day after day, then is the time she needs all the strength of the highest virtue; and the more attractive she is the greater must be her moral power. We have seen that the girls are employed on an average but 42.95 weeks in the year; this fact shows the necessity of the establishment of one or more such homes; these homes are not charity affairs in the general sense, but really excellent girl boarding houses where a girl out of employment can find a good home with good living, including use of dining and sitting rooms, and library, at a minimum cost, which cost is charged to her, if she has no means to pay, until such time as she finds a new situation; she is then allowed to remain in the home and pay off her indebtedness by installments, while the rate of her living is not increased. If she has been obliged to remain at the home so long that the indebtedness is a burden the matron of the home reports this fact to the proper officers, or to benevolent individuals, and she is aided. Of course no girl of bad character is allowed to remain in these homes. . . .

If people of wealth, in making provision for the distribution of that wealth by will, could be impressed with a knowledge of the amount of happiness they could bring to deserving people by remembering the generally weak institutions which are fighting bad conditions, they would, we feel certain, liberally endow such institutions, or provide the means for the establishment of new ones upon better and broader plans. It may be that the time has now come when, instead of leaving great sums to educational institutions, money can be made to tell more for the practical Christianity of the age by so placing it as to help relieve those who are obliged to make the contest of life with the barely elementary education furnished by the lowest grades of schools, the necessity of providing their own support too often obliging them to forsake the school for the shop.

3.10   A Male Critique of Women's Labor, 1884. From *John Swinton's Paper*, November 9, 1884.

The Impending Revolution: Women Underworking Men, Whom They Turn to Tramps

To the Editor:

In a certain establishment of this city (Cleveland, Oh.), over whose front window is the significant sign, "Economy Printing House," there are employed quite a little army of operatives, five-sixths of whom are women and boys.

There would be nothing to note in this but for the pertinent fact that the women and boys, by aid of machinery, do men's work for boy's pay. Of late years, there has been an everlasting cry for new avenues of industry for women. Well, they have found them; and as every woman displaces, for the most part, a skilled workman for half, and often at less than half pay, what is the result? Able-bodied and skilled men idle, and women doing their work for boys' pay. Where boys are employed, they are retained until knowledge of their craft entitles them to increase of salary, when they are thrown on the street for still cheaper boys, or half-pay women.

Right along this ruinous system is steadily on the increase. Wherever a half-price woman can thrust aside a better-paid workman she is employed, until our workshops begin to swarm with them, as the men they have supplanted are sinking into trampdom. . . .

Then what is to be the final result? Smart men will keep right on inventing labor-saving machines, requiring less and less of skilled labor, and bosses will be sure to hire boys and women, so long as they are to be had for half-pay. Again, we ask—What?

We can only see one ultimate settlement of the difficulty. As soon as a workman has provided his quota of boys and girls to do the work, let him be carted away to a sort of adult reformatory farm, where his labor would

keep him and support a ruck of high-paid officials or strangle him out of
the way.

W. Whitworth
Cleveland, Oh.

3.11 The Uses of Child Labor, 1883. From the testimony of Thomas
O'Donnell, an 11-year veteran of the Fall River, Massachusetts, textile mills who
had emigrated from Ramsbotham, England, as found in *U.S. Senate Report on
Capital and Labor*, Vol. 3 (1883). Reprinted in John A. Garraty, ed., *Labor and
Capital in the Gilded Age: Testimony Taken by the Senate Committee upon the
Relations Between Labor and Capital*, 1883 (Boston: Little, Brown, 1968),
pp. 33–36.

Sen. Blair: Are you a married man?
A: Yes, sir; I am a married man; have a wife and two children. I am not
very well educated. I went to work when I was young, and have been
working ever since in the cotton business; went to work when I was about
eight or nine years old. I was going to state how I live. My children get
along very well in summer time, on account of not having to buy fuel or
shoes or one thing and another. I earn $1.50 a day and can't afford to pay
a very big house rent. I pay $1.50 a week for rent, which comes to about
$6.00 a month. . . .
Q: Do you have work right along?
A: No, sir; since that strike we had down in Fall River about three years
ago I have not worked much more than half the time, and that has brought
my circumstances down very much.
Q: Why have you not worked more than half the time since then?
A: Well, at Fall River if a man has not got a boy to act as "back-boy" it is
very hard for him to get along. In a great many cases they discharge men
in that work and put in men who have boys. . . . Men who have boys of
their own capable enough to work in a mill, to earn $.30 or $.40 a day.
Q: Is the object of that to enable the boy to earn something for himself?
A: Well, no; the object is this: They are doing away with a great deal of
mule-spinning there and putting in ring-spinning, and for that reason it
takes a good deal of small help to run this ring work, and it throws the men
out of work because they are doing away with the mules and putting these
ring-frames in to take their places. For that reason they get all the small
help they can to run these ring-frames. There are so many men in the city
to work, and whoever has a boy can have work, and whoever has no boy
stands no chance. Probably he may have a few months of work in the summer time, but will be discharged in the fall. That is what leaves me in poor
circumstances. Our children, of course, are very often sickly from one
cause or another, on account of not having sufficient clothes, or shoes, or
food, or something. And also my woman; she never did work in a mill; she

was a housekeeper, and for that reason she can't help me to anything at
present, as many women do help their husbands down there, by working,
like themselves. My wife never did work in a mill, and that leaves me to
provide for the whole family. I have two children. . . .

Q: Is there anything else you wanted to say?

A: Nothing further, except that I would like some remedy to be got to
help us poor people down there in some way. Excepting the government
decides to do something with us we have a poor show. We are all, or mostly
all, in good health; that is, as far as the men who are at work go.

Q: You do not know anything but mule-spinning, I suppose?

A: I sometimes do something with pick and shovel. I have worked for a
man at that, because I am so put on. I am looking for work in a mill. The
way they do there is this:

There are about twelve or thirteen men that go into a mill every morning, and they have to stand their chance, looking for work. The man who
has a boy with him he stands the best chance, and then, if it is my turn or
a neighbor's turn who has no boy, if another man comes in who has a boy
he is taken right in, and we are left out. I said to the boss once it was my
turn to go in, and now you have taken on that man; what am I to do; I
have got two little boys at home, one of them three years and a half and
the other one year and a half old, and how am I to find something for them
to eat; I can't get my turn when I come here.

He said he could not do anything for me. I says, "Have I got to starve;
ain't I to have any work?" They are forcing these young boys into the mills
that should not be in mills at all; forcing them in because they are throwing the mules out and putting on ring-frames. They are doing everything
of that kind that they possibly can to crush down the poor people the poor
operatives there.

IMMIGRANTS, TENEMENTS, AND SWEATED LABOR

For many workers no clear demarcation separated home from work.
Especially for low-wage immigrant workers and their wives and children,
work in their own dingy apartments or in sweatshops located in residential
neighborhoods and buildings proved common. Document 3.12 describes
the types of homes occupied by working people in Cincinnati, residences
that differed considerably in quality depending upon the skills and earnings
of the owners or occupants. The next document (3.13) describes a typical
tenement flat in which an entire immigrant family worked together for
wages. Who, if anyone, was the exploiter or the boss in such a setting?
Document 3.14 portrays the character of work in a typical garment industry
sweatshop. Does the subject of this sketch seem exploited or dissatisfied with

her job? Compare the poet's response to sweatshop labor (Document 3.15) with that of the young woman worker in Document 3.14. Explain the difference in their reactions.

3.12 Working-Class Housing, 1883. Testimony of William H. Foster in *Report of the Committee of the Senate upon the Relations between Labor and Capital and Testimony Taken by the Committee,* Vol. 1 (Washington, D.C.: Government Printing Office, 1885), pp. 408–09.

Sen. George: Describe the ordinary average dwelling of the laborer in Cincinnati.

A: My landlord works in the same establishment that I do myself; he is a married man. He rents a $25 house. I do not know whether the house would be considered very fine here, but is a five-room house, with a bay window and a cellar; there is no yard, but there is a rather fine paved terrace in front. It is a very convenient place for anybody who has children; they can run up and down on their roller skates and have a good time. It is a five-room house, and I have one of the rooms, and the landlord occupies the rest with his wife and child.

Q: How many stories high is the house?

A: Three.

Q: What is the size of the rooms?

A: I am not a judge of measurement by sight, but the one I occupy is about 20 by 16. That is what I would call about the average residence of the first-class mechanics who are paid good wages.

Q: Now, give us the condition of a second-class.

A: Well, many mechanics, earning about $3 a day, will live in a house that will cost $16 a month a portion of a large tenement building generally, with three or four rooms to each flat. They may live with comparative comfort in such a building, but the rooms would be too small for me. I want room to swing a pair of clubs if I choose to.

Q: Then the next lower class.

A: The lower-class men—I have seen men so low that they had to shove a family of five or six children and themselves, and perhaps their parents, and do their cooking and all, in one room. They have a little trundle bed to put all the children in, and they shove it under their bed when not in use. . . . I know that when the smallpox ran through the city, the greatest proportion of people died out among those tenement buildings. Whether crowding into small rooms makes the people negligent of their personal cleanliness or not, I do not know, but I think it has that effect. I think also it has a tendency to make men who are forced to live under those conditions inclined to be intemperate in their habits. They find no comfort at home, living in one room, and if they can get a few cents they go and spend it in the saloon. . . . A man ought to have a room where he could go and sit down and read without his children climbing all over him and making a nuisance of the house. . . .

3.13   A Tenement Sweatshop, ca. 1890. Jacob Riis, *How the Other Half Lives* (Cambridge, Mass.: Harvard University Press, 1970 [orig. 1890]), pp. 81–83.

The bulk of the sweater's work is done in the tenements, which the law that regulates factory labor does not reach. To the factories themselves that are taking the place of the rear tenements in rapidly growing numbers, letting in bigger day-crowds than those the health officers banished, the tenement shops serve as a supplement through which the law is successfully evaded. Ten hours is the legal workday in the factories, and nine o'clock the closing hour at the latest. Forty-five minutes at least must be allowed for dinner, and children under sixteen must not be employed unless they can read and write English; none at all under fourteen. The very fact that such a law should stand on the statute book, shows how desperate the plight of these people. But the tenement has defeated its benevolent purpose. In it the child works unchallenged from the day he is old enough to pull a thread. There is no such thing as a dinner hour; men and women eat while they work, and the "day" is lengthened at both ends far into the night. Factory hands take their work with them at the close of the lawful day to eke out their scanty earnings by working overtime at home. Little chance on this ground for the campaign of education that alone can bring the needed relief; small wonder that there are whole settlements on this East Side where English is practically an unknown tongue, though the people be both willing and anxious to learn. "When shall we find time to learn?" asked one of them of me once. I owe him the answer yet.

Take the Second Avenue Elevated Railroad at Chatham Square and ride up half a mile through the sweaters' district. Every open window of the big tenements, that stand like a continuous brick wall on both sides of the way, gives you a glimpse of one of these shops as the train speeds by. Men and women bending over their machines, or ironing clothes at the window, half-naked. Proprieties do not count on the East Side; nothing counts that cannot be converted into hard cash. The road is like a big gangway through an endless workroom where vast multitudes are forever laboring. Morning, noon, or night, it makes no difference; the scene is always the same. At Rivington Street let us get off and continue our trip on foot. It is Sunday evening west of the Bowery. Here, under the rule of Mosaic law, the week of work is under full headway, its first day far spent. The hucksters' wagons are absent or stand idle at the curb; the saloons admit the thirsty crowds through the side door labelled "Family Entrance"; a tin sign in a store window announces that a "Sunday School" gathers in stray children of the new dispensation; but beyond these things there is little to suggest the Christian Sabbath. Men stagger along the sidewalk groaning under heavy burdens of unsewn garments, or enormous black bags stuffed full of finished coats and trousers. Let us follow one to his home and see how Sunday passes in a Ludlow Street tenement.

Up two flights of dark stairs, three, four, with new smells of cabbage, of onions, of frying fish, on every landing, whirring sewing machines behind closed doors betraying what goes on within, to the door that opens to admit the bundle and the man. A sweater, this, in a small way. Five men and a woman, two young girls, not fifteen, and a boy who says unasked that he is fifteen, and lies in saying it, are at the machines sewing knicker-bockers, "knee-pants" in the Ludlow Street dialect. The floor is littered ankle-deep with half-sewn garments. In the alcove, on a couch of many dozens of "pants" ready for the finisher, a barelegged baby with pinched face is asleep. A fence of piled-up clothing keeps him from rolling off on the floor. The faces, hands, and arms to the elbows of everyone in the room are black with the color of the cloth on which they are working. The boy and the woman alone look up at our entrance. The girls shoot side-long glances, but at a warning look from the man with the bundle they tread their machines more energetically than ever. The men do not appear to be aware even of the presence of a stranger.

3.14   Jewish Immigrant, ca. 1902. Interview with Sadie Frowne, published in *The Independent*, 1902. Reprinted in Holt, ed., *The Life Stories of Undistinguished Americans*, pp. 23–27.

So I went to work in Allen Street (Manhattan) in what they call a sweat-shop, making shirts by machine. I was new at the work and the foreman scolded me a great deal.

"Now then," he would say, "this place is not for you to be looking around in. Attend to your work. That is what you have to do."

I did not know at first that you must not look around and talk, and I made many mistakes with the sewing, so that I was often called a stupid animal. But I made $4 a week by working six days in the week. For there are two Sabbaths here—our own Sabbath, that comes on a Saturday, and the Christian Sabbath that comes on a Sunday. It is against our law to work on our own Sabbath, so we work on their Sabbath.

In Poland I and my father and mother used to go to the synagogue on the Sabbath, but here the women don't go to the synagogue much, though the men do. They are shut up working hard all the week long and when the Sabbath comes they like to sleep long in bed and afterward they must go out where they can breathe the air. . . .

Two years ago I came to Brownsville [Brooklyn], where so many of my people are, and where I have friends. I got work in a factory making underskirts—all sorts of cheap underskirts. . . . The factory is in the third story of a brick building. It is in a room twenty feet long and fourteen broad. There are fourteen machines in it. I and the daughter of the people with whom I live work two of these machines. The other operators are all men some young some old.

At first a few young men were rude. When they passed me they would touch my fair and talk about my eyes and my red cheeks, and make jokes. I cried and said that if they did not stop I would leave the place. The boss said that . . . no one must annoy me. . . .

I get up a half-past five o'clock every morning and make myself a cup of coffee on the oil stove. I eat a bit of bread and perhaps some fruit and then go to work. . . .

At seven o'clock we all sit down to our machines and the boss brings to each one the pile of work that he or she is to finish during the day, what they call in English their "stint." This pile is put down beside the machine and as soon as a skirt is done it is laid on the other side of the machine. Sometimes the work is not all finished by six o'clock and then the one who is behind must work overtime. Sometimes one is finished ahead of time and gets away at four or five o'clock, but generally we are not done till six o'clock.

The machines go like mad all day, because the faster you work the more money you get. Sometimes in my haste I get my finger caught and the needle goes right through it. It goes so quick, though, that it does not hurt much. I bind the finger with cotton and go on working. We all have accidents like that. . . .

All the time we are working the boss walks about examining the finished garments and making us do them over again if they are not just right. So we have to be carful as well as swift. But I am getting so good at the work that within a year I will be making $7 a week, and then I can save a least $3.50 a week. I have over $200 saved now. . . .

3.15   Poet of the Sweatshops. Excerpts of Morris Rosenfeld's poem, "The Sweatshop," in Itche Goldberg and Max Rosenfeld, eds., *Morris Rosenfeld: Selections from His Poetry and Prose* (New York: Yiddisher Kultur Farband, 1964), pp. 26–27.

The Sweatshop

So wild is the roar of the machines in the sweatshop,
 · I often forget I'm alive—in that din!
I'm drowned in the tide of the terrible tumult—
My ego is slain; I become a machine.
I work, and I work, without rhyme, without
         reason—
Produce, and produce, and produce without end.
For what? and for whom? I don't know, I don't wonder—
Since when can a whirling machine comprehend? . . .

The clock in the shop, even he toils forever:
He points, and he ticks, and he wakes us from
    dreams—
A long time ago someone taught me the meaning:
His pointing, his waking, are more than they seem.
I only remember a few things about it:
The clock wakes our senses, and sets us aglow,
And wakes something else—I've forgotten—don't
    ask me!
I'm just a machine, I don't know, I don't know! . . .

But once in a while, when I hear the clock ticking,
His pointing, his language, are not as before:
I feel that his pendulum lashes me, prods me
To work ever faster, to do more and more!
I hear the wild yell of the boss in his ticking,
I see a dark frown in the two pointing hands;
I shudder to think it; the clock is my master!
He calls me "Machine!" "Hurry up!" He commands.

KNIGHTS OF LABOR

The Knights of Labor, despite its meteoric rise and fall, represented the first true mass labor movement in the United States. It both echoed a past of Christian-influenced male fraternalism and foreshadowed a future of secular worker movements. Document 3.16 suggests how the Knights of Labor was influenced by the broader environment of fraternal societies, like the Masons, and by a form of Protestant Christianity. Document 3.17 describes how the Knights added more programmatic content to their ritualistic appeal to workers seeking fraternal brotherhood. It asserts a diluted labor theory of value, extols the virtues of cooperation over competition, lauds equal pay (an appeal to women workers), demands the eight-hour day, and places morality above wealth. Yet, Christianity remained an essential part of the Knights' message, as Document 3.18 hints. This document also reveals the confused conception of capitalism in what the Knights defined as a workingman's nation. Document 3.19 explains why the organization believed that political action and voting offered the best means to oust aristocrats and monopolists from power in order to create a moral capitalist society. Finally, Document 3.20 gives the testimony of a powerful employer, Jay Gould, whose resistance to the demands of the Knights of Labor precipitated the organization's rapid decline.

3.16 K. of L. Initiation Ritual, 1886. Excerpt from *The Knights of Labor Illustrated. "Adelphon Kruptos." The Full and Illustrated Ritual Including "Unwritten Work," and a Historical Sketch of the Order* (Chicago: Ezra A. Cook Publisher, 1886), p. 29.

The Master Workman gives one tap to seat the assembly. The Unknown Knight will, after the assembly is seated, proceed with the candidate to the Capitol, and report to the Master Workman.

Unknown Knight—Master Workman, our friend has taken the pledge of secrecy, obedience and mutual assistance.

Master Workman—That act covers our friend with the shield of our Order. Proceed with the candidate to the Base, there to receive the instructions of the Worthy Foreman.

Arrived at the base, the Unknown Knight introduces the candidate to the Worthy Foreman thus:

Unknown Knight—Worthy Foreman, by permission of this assembly of true Knights, and the command of the Master Workman, I present our friend for instruction.

Worthy Foreman—By labor is brought forth the kindly fruits of the earth in rich abundance for our sustenance and comfort; by labor are promoted health of body and strength of mind, and labor garners the priceless stores of wisdom and knowledge. It is the "Philosopher's Stone,"—everything it touches turns to wealth. "Labor is noble and holy." To defend it from degradation, to divest it of the evils to body, mind, and estate, which ignorance and greed have imposed; to rescue the toiler from the grasp of the selfish is a work worthy of the noblest and best of our race. You have been selected from among your associates for that exalted purpose. Are you willing to accept the responsibility, and, trusting in the support of the pledged true Knights, labor, with what ability you possess, for the triumph of these principles among men?

The candidate answers. If affirmatively, the Worthy Foreman will say to the candidate and the Unknown Knight:

Worthy Foreman—We will now proceed with our friend to the Master Workman.

And, accompanying them to the Master Workman, says:

Worthy Foreman—Master Workman, I present our friend as a fitting and worthy person to receive the honor of fellowship with this noble order.

3.17 The K. of L. Vision, 1886. Excerpt from the founding ceremony for a new assembly of the Knights of Labor from *The Knights of Labor Illustrated*, pp. 46–49.

Organizer—By the authority of the General Assembly of America, of the Order of the Knights of Labor, delegated to me this commission, I appear at this time for the purpose of founding and instructing a Local Assembly of the Order.

The alarming development and aggressiveness of great capitalists and corporations, unless checked, will inevitably lead to the pauperization and hopeless degradation of the toiling masses.

It is imperative if we desire to enjoy the full blessings of life, that a check be placed upon the unjust accumulation, and the power for evil of aggregated wealth.

This much-desired object can be accomplished only by the united efforts of those who obey the Divine injunction, "In the sweat of thy face, thou shall eat bread."

Therefor, you have been invited to join us in an organization that embraces within its folds every department of productive industry, whose aims are:

To make industrial and moral worth, not wealth, the true standard of individual and national greatness.

To secure to all workers the wealth they create, sufficient leisure in which to develop their intellectual, moral and social faculties; all of the benefits, recreation and pleasures of association, in a word to enable them to share the gains and honors of advancing civilization. . . .

To establish co-operative institutions such as will tend to supercede the wage system, by introduction of a co-operative industrial system.

To secure for both sexes equal pay for equal work.

To shorten the hours of labor by a general refusal to work for more than eight hours. . . .

Do you approve of those objects and all legitimate effort for the benefit of labor and the cause of humanity?

Response—We do.

Organizer—Are you willing to take a pledge of secrecy, obedience, and mutual assistance that will not interfere with any religious convictions you may entertain or your duty to your country?

Response—We are.

The organizer will then prepare or draft the Great Seal of Knighthood at the centre and when done resume the station, give three raps, form the members around the center, and say:

Organizer—Thus do I imprint the Great Seal of Knighthood at the center, and thereby dedicate this new Assembly to the service of Humanity. Let the memory of that symbol ever remind you of the duties and obligations you owe to the cause of labor.

3.18 Fusing the Religious and Secular; Capital and Labor, 1886. From *The Knights of Labor Illustrated*, p. 19.

This country is emphatically a working man's country. Our moral, social and political opportunities are such to make every citizen heir to an inheritance that millions of dollars could not buy. With an open bible before him, a common school in every neighborhood, a ballot in his hand, and the government working by, with and for him, against caste and titled aristocracy; with a Father Almighty in heaven and a Savior calling by his Holy Spirit, every workingman, however humble, is a capitalist, in the largest sense of the word.

3.19   Labor to the Polls, 1888. From *Labor Songs Dedicated to the Knights of Labor* (Chicago: J. D. Talmadge, 1888), p. 17.

To the Polls!

Tune: "To the Work."

To the polls! to the polls! ye are serving the right;
Let us follow the path that our fathers have trod;
With the light of their counsel our strength to renew,
Let us do with our might what our hands find to do.

Chorus:

Voting on, voting on,
voting on, voting on,
Voting on, voting on,
voting on, voting on,
Let us work, let us vote,
and watch, and trust,
And labor till victory comes.

To the polls! to the polls! let the hungry be fed,
To the banner of life let the weary be led;
In our ballot and banner our glory shall be,
While we herald the tidings,—*The People are free!*

Chorus: Voting on, etc.

To the polls! to the polls! there is labor for all,
For the kingdom of rapine and error shall fall,
And the rights of the people exalted shall be,
In the loud-swelling chorus—*The People are free!*

Chorus: Voting on, etc.

To the polls! to the polls! we will rally again
And we'll free our dear land from the bondsman and
Then the home of the faithful our dwelling shall be,
And we'll shout with the ransom'd—*The people are free!*

Chorus: Voting on, etc.

3.20   Jay Gould on Strikes, 1883. Testimony of Jay Gould, before the
Senate Committee on the Relations between Labor and Capital, Vol. 1, pp. 1084–85.

Sen. Blair: You have had considerable practical experience with labor, have
you not? . . . . What is your observation and opinion in regard to strikes,
their causes, and their results?
[Jay Gould]: Strikes, of course, come from various causes, but they generally
come from a class of dissatisfied men—the poorest part of your labor generally
are at the bottom of a strike. Your best men do not care how many hours they
work, or anything of that kind; they are looking to get higher up; either to own
a business of their own and control it, or to get higher up in the ranks. . . . Of
course there are only so many places to be filled, but there are a great many that
are looking after those places. There may be only one place to be filled, but
there may be five hundred nice, industrious fellows who are all working for it.
Q: That keeps them quiet?
A: Yes, sir. . . .
Q: Now, don't you think . . . their dissatisfaction may oftentimes be based
on the fact that they do not receive compensation enough to keep them
from suffering?
A: Is it not true that they get better pay here than in any other country?
That is why they come here, I believe. . . . And is it not true also that capital, if it gets better remuneration in some other country than it gets here, will
go there? You cannot transfer your house, but you can transfer your money;
and if labor is put up too high here, all the manufacturing will be done
abroad, because the capitalists will go where they can get cheaper labor. So
that when you sit down and try to get a panacea for a particular evil you run
against a great many obstacles that come in the way of putting it in practice,
and my observation has been that capital and labor, if let alone, generally
come together and mutually regulate their relations to each other. There are
some of these people who think they can regulate the whole of mankind, but
they generally get wrong ideas into the minds of the public.
Q: Notwithstanding the fact that labor is better paid in this country than
elsewhere, capital is also very much better paid in this country, and is likely
to be so, at least for the present, and capital, like labor, is coming here from
the older countries; and yet we find labor here dissatisfied to a great extent.
Is not that so?
A: I think not. I think there is a far greater satisfaction here among the
workingmen generally than anywhere else in the world, far greater than
among the laboring classes that I have seen abroad. I only speak of what I
have seen myself. . . .

AMERICAN FEDERATION OF LABOR

The AFL offered itself as an alternative to the Knights of Labor for those
workers who wanted more security and power on the job, higher wages, and

a less cutthroat, competitive economic system. Document 3.21 defines the purpose of the predecessor organization to the AFL, the Federation of Organized Trades and Labor Unions. It should enable readers to distinguish the goals and methods of the new organization from those of the K of L. Women workers appealed to the organization (Document 3.22) to listen to them and to treat them as well as men, and that they would prove to be equally loyal and active trade unionists. Frank Foster, an AFL spokesperson, responded positively to the women's appeal in Document 3.23. In Document 3.24, Samuel Gompers describes what the AFL and its affiliated trade unions wanted. He does so using radical rhetoric that condemns the super-rich and the greedy capitalists who were building a two-class society. But Gompers could also speak the language of moderation as he does in Document 3.25, when he explains why a modern industrial economy requires independent worker organization and collective bargaining. Document 3.26 analyzes why trade unionism is equally vital to women workers and the sort of unions most conducive to the organization of women.

3.21   Call to Launch the Federation of Organized Trades and Labor Unions, 1881. From the *Report of the First Annual Session of the Federation of Organized Trades and Labor Unions of the United States and Canada [FOTLU] Held in Pittsburgh, Pennsylvania, December 15, 16, 17, and 18, 1881* (New York: Federation of Organized Trades and Labor Unions, 1881), p. 6.

[Terre Haute, Indiana, Sept. 15, 1881]
To all Trades and Labor Unions of the United States and Canada:
Fellow Workingmen: The time has now arrived for a more perfect combination of Labor—one that will concentrate our forces so as to more successfully cope with concentrated capital.

We have numberless trades unions, trades assemblies or councils, and various other local, national and international labor unions, all engaged in the noble task of elevating and improving the condition of the working classes. But, great as has been the work done by these bodies, there is vastly more that can be done by a combination of all these organizations in a federation of trades. . . .

Only in such a body can proper action be taken to promote the general welfare of the industrial classes. There we can discuss and examine all questions affecting the national interests of each and every trade, and by a combination of forces secure that justice which isolated and separated trade and labor unions can never fully command.

A National Trades Union Congress can prepare labor measures and agree upon laws they desire passed by the Congress of the United States; and a Congressional Labor Committee . . . could be elected to urge and advance legislation at Washington on all such measures, and report to the various trades.

In addition to this, an annual congress of trades unions could organize a systematic agitation to propagate trade union principles, and to impress the necessity of protective trade and labor organizations, and to encourage the formation of such unions and their amalgamation in trades assemblies. Thus we could elevate trades unionism and obtain for the working classes that respect for their rights, and that reward for their services, to which they are justly entitled.

A federation of this character can be organized with a few simple rules and no salaried officers. The expenses of its management will be trivial and can be provided for by the Trades Union Congress.

Impressed with the necessity of such a federation, and the importance of an International Trades Union Congress to perfect the organization, we the undersigned . . . do hereby resolve to issue the following call:

That all international and national unions, trades assemblies or councils, and local trades or labor unions are hereby invited to send delegates to an International Trades Union Congress, to be held in Pittsburgh, Pa., on Tuesday, November 15, 1881. Each local union will be entitled to one delegate for one hundred members or less, and one additional delegate for each additional five hundred members or major part thereof; also, one delegate for each international or national union, and one delegate for each trades assembly or council.

[Signed by]

J. E. Coughlin, President National Tanners' and Curriers' Union [and 14 other leaders of trades unions and labor assemblies].

3.22 Women Beseech the FOTLU, 1883. A letter from Charlotte Smith of the Woman's Industrial League to the FOTLU, 1883. From the *Report of the Third Annual Session of the Federation of Organized Trades and Labor Unions of the United States and Canada Held in New York City, New York, August 21, 22, 23, and 24, 1883* (New York: Federation of Organized Trades and Labor Unions, 1883), p. 17.

Woman looks to labor organizations as the hope of her future. From them she expects both sympathy and assistance. She knows that laboring men understand better than any one else can the necessities of her position— the necessity that every person shall have an opportunity to do work which shall be paid for; for there is nothing else that will give true independence. Men work against the crushing power of capital; woman has not only that to contend with, but also the power of prejudice, and added to that the fact that she is not recognized in the scheme of government. What redress has she? We see no hope for her except in concerted and organized action. In order to effect this we frankly ask for the advice, assistance, and co-operation of labor organizations. . . . In every locality where large numbers of women are at work, they should be assisted to organize and take concerted action against all oppression; and also for the purpose of perfecting themselves in various crafts, so that their work may be more valuable. By doing this women will not only receive the direct benefit of better wages for their work, but there will be another and even a nobler result; it will attract greater attention to the subject of labor organizations, and bring about a wider recognition of their importance, and thus give these organizations more weight and power. It is not now necessary to discuss the question of woman's ability to perform arduous work. It has been asserted over and over again that woman cannot do the hard work of the world, and she has gone right on working eight, ten, even sixteen hours a day, in the face of these assertions. Has she not thus proved her right to be admitted to your ranks? We wish to call your attention to another fact which has recently been exemplified; that is, that women *do* stand the test of an emergency. Men associated with women in labor organizations know that when concerted action is necessary to maintain the position of the employed, women will stand by their colors even longer than men will. They have attested their nerve, courage, and energy in trying positions; and with these high qualities they can well bear the burden of work, even [if] they have not mere brute strength.

In conclusion, we would say that we believe that the working-men have more respect for women and for true womanhood than is to be found elsewhere in society. Therefore it is to labor organizations that we look for aid to carry forward our best interests in the future.

3.23   FOTLU's Frank Foster Replies to Working Women, 1883. From *the Report of the Third Annual Session of the Federation of Organized Trades and Labor Unions of the United States and Canada Held in New York City, New York, August 21, 22, 23, and 24, 1883*, p. 19.

To Working Girls and Women

The Federation of Trades and Labor Unions of the United States and Canada makes to you the following appeal: . . .

There is to-day, in the most civilized country on the face of the globe, a vast multitude of girls and women condemned to struggle for very existence. They are doubly handicapped by poverty and sex. Neither sentiment nor humanity counts in the race for gain. The weaker become the prey of the stronger when the labor marked is glutted, and keen competition disposes of the products of labor at the lowest market price. The toil of our seamstresses, shop girls, and factory operatives is exploited by hard taskmasters and soulless corporations. Thousands of tragedies are daily enacted, where virtue falls a victim to want, and shame springs from social needs. It is the mission of the labor movement to shield and protect those who cannot defend themselves. It is the creed of the labor movement that labor should be fairly paid for, that the laborer should be more than a passive factor in the contract that disposes of his labor. It is further the creed of the labor movement that equal amount of work should bring the same price, whether performed by man or woman. In other words, that the value to the purchaser, not the necessity of the seller, should fix the standard of a day's wages.

In the carrying out of this belief there is needed the hearty co-operation of all interested parties. The working-women of the land should array themselves under the banner of united labor. It is the hope of the Federated Trades to assist in bringing about this much needed result. Those who desire to form labor societies will be supplied with all necessary information, by applying to the Secretary, and will be either furnished with an organizer or directed to the proper source from which to obtain one.

We solicit your correspondence, and pledge you our support.

Fraternally,

Legislative Committee Federated Trades.

Frank K. Foster Secretary

3.24   Trade Unions the "Only Hope of Civilization," 1893. From Samuel Gompers, "What Does Labor Want?" An address before the International Labor Congress, Aug. 28, 1893, reprinted in Stuart Kaufman, ed., *The Samuel Gompers Papers, Volume 3: Unrest and Depression* (Urbana: University of Illinois Press, 1986), pp. 388–96.

An Address before the International Labor Congress
in Chicago [August 28, 1893]
WHAT DOES LABOR WANT?

Modern society, the most complex organization yet evolved by the human race, is based on one simple fact, the practical separation of the capitalistic class from the great mass of the industrious.

If this separation were only that resulting from a differentiation in the functions of directions of industrial operations and their execution in detail then that separation would be regarded as real, direct progress. But the separation between the capitalistic class and the laboring mass is not so much a difference in industrial rank as it is a difference in social status, placing the laborers in a position involving a degradation of mind and body.

This distinction, scarcely noticeable in the United States before the previous generation, rapidly became more and more marked, increasing day by day, until at length, it has widened into a veritable chasm; economic, social and moral. On each side of this seemingly impassable chasm, we see the hostile camps of rich and poor. On one side, a class in possession of all the tools and means of labor; on the other, an immense mass begging for the opportunity to labor. In the mansion, the soft notes betokening ease and security; in the tenement the stifled wail of drudgery and poverty. The arrogance of the rich ever mounting in proportion to the debasement of the poor.

From across the chasm we hear the old familiar drone of the priests of Mammon called "Political Economists." The words of the song they sing are stolen from the vocabulary of science, but the chant itself is the old barbaric lay. It tells us that the present absolute domination of wealth is the result of material and invariable laws and counsels the laborers, whom they regard as ignorant and misguided, to patiently submit to the natural operations of the immutable law of "supply and demand." The laborers reply. They say that the political economists never learned sufficient science to know the difference between the operation of a natural law and the law on petty larceny. The day is past when the laborers could be cajoled or humbugged by the sacred chickens of the augers or by the bogus laws of the political economists.

The laborers know that there are few historic facts capable of more complete demonstration than those showing when and how the capitalists gained possession of the tools and opportunities of labor. They know that the capitalists gained their industrial monopoly by the infamous abuse of arbitrary power on the part of royal and federal potentates. They know that by the exercise of this arbitrary power a well established system of industry was overthrown and absolute power was placed in the hands of the selfish incompetents. . . .

The laborers well know how baseless is the claim made by the political economists that the subsequent development of the capitalist class was spontaneous and natural, for they know that the capitalists not content with a monopoly of industry enabling them to increase the price of products at will and reduce the wages of labor to a bare subsistence also procured legislation forbidding the disfranchised and plundered workmen from organizing in their own defense.

The laborers will never forget that the coalition and conspiracy laws, directed by the capitalists against the journeymen who had sublime fidelity and heroic courage to defend their natural rights to organization, punished them with slavery, torture and death. In short, the laborers know that the capitalist class had its origin in force and fraud, that it has maintained and extended its brutal sway more or less directly through the agency of specified legislation, most ferocious and barbarous, but always in cynical disregard of all law save its own arbitrary will. . . .

The state of industrial anarchy produced by the capitalist system is first strongly illustrated in the existence of a class of wealthy social parasites; those who do no work, never did any work and never intend to work. This class of parasites devours incomes derived from many sources; from the stunted babies employed in the mills, mines and factories to the lessees of the gambling hells and the profits of fashionable brothels; from the lands which the labor of others has made valuable; from royalties on coal and other minerals beneath the surface and from rent of houses above the surface, the rent paying all cost of the houses many times over and the houses coming back to those who never paid for them. . . .

To-day modern society is beginning to regard the Trade Unions as the only hope of civilization; to regard them as the only power capable of evolving order out of the social chaos. But will the Sibyl's demand be regarded or heeded before it is too late? Let us hope so. The Trade Unions having a thorough knowledge of the origin and development of the capitalist class entertain no desire for revenge or retaliation. The Trade Unions have deprecated the malevolent and unjust spirit with which they have had to contend in their protests and struggles against the abuse of the capitalist system, yet while seeking justice have not permitted their movement to become acrid by the desire of revenge. Their methods were always conservative, their steps evolutionary.

One of the greatest impediments to a better appreciation by the capitalists of the devoted efforts of the Trade Unions to establish harmony in the industrial relations, has been the perverted view taken by the capitalists in regarding their capital as essentially if not absolutely their own, whereas, the Trade Unions taking a more comprehensive and purer view, regard all capitals large and small, as the fruits of labor's economies and discoveries, inventions and institutions of many generations of laborers and capitalists, of theoreticians and practitioners, practically as indivisible as a living man. . . .

What does labor want? It wants the earth and the fullness thereof. There is nothing too precious, there is nothing too beautiful, too lofty, too ennobling, unless it is within the scope and comprehension of labor's aspirations and wants. But to be more specific: The expressed demands of labor are first and foremost a reduction of the hours of daily labor to eight hours to-day, fewer to-morrow. . . .

The prosperity of a nation, the success of a people, the civilizing influence of our era, can always be measured by the comparative consuming power of a people.

If as it has often been said, cheap labor and long hours of toil are necessary to a country's prosperity, commercially and industrially, China should necessarily be at the height of civilization.

Millions of willing heads, hands and hearts are ready to frame and to fashion the fabrics and supply the necessities as well as the desires of the people. . . . The ordinary man may truly inquire why it is that the political economist answers our demand for work by saying that the law of supply and demand, from which they say there is no relief, regulates these conditions. Might we not say fails to regulate them?

The organized working men and women, the producers of the wealth of the world, declare that men, women and children with human brains and human hearts, should have a better consideration than inanimate and dormant things, usually known under the euphonious title of "Property." We maintain that it is both inhuman, barbaric and retrogressive to allow the members of the human family to suffer for want, while the very things that could and would contribute to their wants and comforts as well as to the advantage of the entire people, are allowed to decay.

We demand a reduction of the hours of labor which would give a due share of work and wages to the reserve army of labor and eliminate many of the worst abuses of the industrial system now filling our poor houses and jails. . . .

Labor demands the right to organize for self and mutual protection. The toilers want the abrogation of all laws discriminating against them in the exercise of those functions which make our organizations in the economic struggle a factor and not a farce.

That the lives and limbs of the wage-workers shall be regarded as sacred as those of all others of our fellow human beings; that an injury or destruction of either by reason of negligence or maliciousness of another, shall not leave him without redress simply because he is a wage worker. We demand equality before the law, in fact as well as in theory. . . .

Render our lives while working as safe and healthful as modern science demonstrates it is possible. Give us better homes is just as potent a cry today as when Dickens voiced the yearnings of the people of a generation ago.

Save our children in their infancy from being forced into the maelstrom of wage slavery. See to it that they are not dwarfed in body and mind or brought to a premature death by early drudgery. Give them the sunshine of the school and playground instead of the factory, the mine and the workshop.

We want more school houses and less jails; more books and less arsenals; more learning and less vice; more constant work and less crime; more leisure and less greed; more justice and less revenge; in fact, more of the opportunities to cultivate our better natures, to make manhood more noble, womanhood more beautiful and childhood more happy and bright.

These in brief are the primary demands made by the Trade Unions in the name of labor.

3.25   Gompers on Collective Bargaining, 1913. Testimony before the U.S. Commission on Industrial Relations from the *Final report and testimony, submitted to Congress by the Commission on Industrial Relations* (Washington, D.C.: Government Printing Office, 1916), pp. 718–21.

Mr. Thompson: Mr Gompers, will you tell us your views of the advantage of collective bargaining to the employees in your own way?

Mr. Gompers: To give anything like an intelligent answer to that question it is necessary to call attention to the industrial conditions, the industrial development of the last half century. . . . For many years, that is to say, the last 50 years, and attenuated in the last 30 years, there has been going on a great development in industry and a concentration of industry under the directions of partnerships and companies and corporations and trusts, so that, in many of the great basic industries, they are under the control and direction of a few persons or companies. Then . . . the development of the industry in the form of new devices implements, tools machines, and so on, has caused the industries to become divided and subdivided and specialized. That is, the division and subdivision and the specialization of many of these large basic industries has gone on to the extent that we seldom find one man being a practical mechanic who has the mastery in the production of any one given whole article. . . .

As a consequence of these two things, concentration of industry and the division and specialization and subdivision and specialization of the trades, the workman now no longer owns the tools which the workman of old possessed and with which the worker of old performed his labor. He has nothing to offer but his power to labor . . . in the modern industrial plant. To say that an individual workman can make a better bargain in such an industrial plan is to beg the question and is flying in the face of obvious facts. . . . To say, for instance that an individual workman can make a bargain for his labor power, for his employment with the United States Steel Corporation better than can an organization of workmen—that is, workmen associated and in agreement making an effort to reach a collective bargain for the labor of themselves and in association—is obviously a mistake. I am trying to put it mildly. . . .

Those who have property may find their own way of protecting it. I am speaking for those who work, the great mass of the people of our country, and I speak for some perhaps who would not have me speak for them, but I will speak for them nevertheless. . . .

3.26   On the Formation of Women's Union Locals, 1915. Alice Henry argues that women should organize separate locals. Reprinted in Rosalyn Baxandall et al., eds., *America's Working Women* (New York: Vintage Books, 1976), pp. 170–71.

THE TRADE UNION WOMAN

The commonest complaint of all is that women members of a trade union do not attend their meetings. It is indeed a very serious difficulty to cope with, and the reasons for this poor attendance and want of interest in union affairs have to be fairly faced.

At first glance it seems curious that the meetings of a mixed local composed of both men and girls, should have for the girls even less attraction than meetings of their own sex only. But so it is. A business meeting of a local affords none of the lively social intercourse of a gathering for pleasure or even of a class for instruction. The men, mostly the older men, run the meeting and often are the meeting. Their influence may be out of all proportion to their numbers. It is they who decide the place where the local shall meet and the hour at which members shall assemble. The place is therefore often over a saloon, to which many girls naturally and rightly object. Sometimes it is even in a disreputable district. The girls may prefer that the meeting should begin shortly after closing time so that they do not need to go home and return, or have to loiter about for two or three hours. They like meetings to be over early. The men mostly name eight o'clock as the time of beginning, but business very often will not start much before nine. Then, too, the men feel that they have come together to talk, and talk they do while they allow the real business to drag. Of course, the girls are not interested in long discussions on matters they do not understand and in which they have no part and naturally they stay away, and so make matters worse, for the men feel they are doing their best for the interests of the union, resent the women's indifference, and are more sure than ever that women do not make good unionists.

Among the remedies proposed for this unsatisfactory state of affairs is compulsory attendance at a certain number of meetings per year under penalty of a fine or even losing of the card. (A very drastic measure this last and risky, unless the trade has the closed shop.)

Where the conditions of the trade permit it by far the best plan is to have the women organized in separate locals. The meetings of women and girls only draw better attendances, give far more opportunity for all the members to take part in the business, and beyond all question form the finest training ground for the women leaders who in considerable numbers are needed so badly in the woman's side of the trade-union movement today.

Those trade-union women who advocate mixed locals for every trade which embraces both men and women are of two types. Some are mature, perhaps elderly women, who have been trade unionists all their lives, who have grown up in the same locals with men, who have in the long years passed through and left behind their period of probation and training, and to whose presence and active cooperation the men have become accustomed. These women are able to express their views in public, can put or discuss a motion or take the chair as readily as their brothers. The other type is represented by those individual women or girls in whom exceptional ability takes the place of experience, and who appreciate the educational advantages of working along with experienced trade-union leaders. I have in my mind at this moment one girl over whose face comes all the rapture of the keen student as she explains how much she has learnt from working with men in their meetings. She ardently advocates mixed locals for all. For the born captain the plea is sound. Always she is quick enough to profit by the men's experience, by their ways of managing conferences and balancing advantages and losses.

But with the average girl today the plan does not work. The mixed local does not, as a general rule, offer the best training-class for new girl recruits, in which they may obtain their training in collective bargaining or cooperative effort. . . . Many of the discussions that go on are quite above the girls' heads. And even when a young girl has something to say and wishes to say it, want of practice and timidity often keep her silent. It is to be regretted, too, that some trade-union men are far from realizing either the girls' ends in their daily work or their difficulties in meetings, and lecture, reprove or bully, where they ought to listen and persuade.

The girls, as a rule, are not only happier in their own women's local, but they have the interest of running the meetings themselves. They choose their own hall and fix their own time of meeting. Their officers are of their own selecting and taken from among themselves. The rank and file, too, get the splendid training that is conferred when persons actually and not merely nominally work together for a common end. Their introduction to the great problems of labor is through their practical understanding and handling of those problems as they encounter them in the everyday difficulties of the shop and the factory and as dealt with when they come up before the union meeting or have to be settled in bargaining with an employer.

BLACK WORKERS AND UNIONS

As African Americans increasingly turned to wage labor to support themselves and their families, they behaved similarly to their white brothers and sisters. They joined unions of their own creation or the AFL affiliates that would accept them as members, and they participated in strikes. For most of this period, however, the relationship between African Americans and the labor movement remained, at best, difficult. Documents 3.27 and 3.28 describe the strike actions of African American waterfront workers in Savannah, Georgia, who had formed their own all-black union. The letters included in Document 3.29 discuss the Caucasian-only membership policy of the International Association of Machinists (IAM), and the AFL's decision to deny affiliation to the IAM unless it eliminated its whites-only rule. In Document 3.30, a white worker defends the IAM's traditional racial exclusivity. A black worker responds in Document 3.31 by condemning whites-only union practices. And in Document 3.32 a white Alabama coal miner explains why his union should include African Americans and why the two races must join together. In fact, his union, the United Mine Workers of America (UMW), probably included more African American members than any other trade union of the era.

3.27   Black Longshoremen State Demands, 1891. *Savannah Morning News,* September 29, 1891, p. 2.

Special Notice

We the LABOR AND PROTECTIVE ASSOCIATION, give notice that we don't want war with any one, but we want an increase of wages and be sure we will not work for the same price. We want 20 cents for wharf hands, 25 cents for ship's hands, 30 cents for headers. We have twelve committees to wait on the agent that we have to communicate with, and no other arrangement can be made except through the committees. They can be got at any time to wait on the gentlemen. We have been engaged in singing and praying all day and expect to continue until we get good or bad news. If it be a month it is all the same to us. We have 4,000 men, and we have the labor, and you have got the money and the guns and the ammunition so we will take God for our ammunition. That is all the war we want. We want to keep peace.

3.28   White Press Views a Black Longshoremen's Strike, 1891. *Savannah Morning News*, September 29, 1891, p. 8.

One Thousand Men Out: The Colored Wharf Laborers'
Strike Inaugurated

The wharf laborers' strike went into effect yesterday morning. Over 1,000 men are out. There is a complete tie-up at the Central railroad wharves. Between 800 and 900 men are out.... The only disturbance that occurred was at the Baltimore wharves. As the non-union hands who had been unloading the steamship *Allegheny* left the yard at 6 o'clock last night there were met by a crowd of strikers who began cursing and abusing them. They started to run and all of them managed to escape but four.

The strikers did not go near the wharves yesterday morning, but held a meeting instead at Odd Fellows' hall on Duffy street. The hall was well filled with the strikers. The speeches were of a temperate tone, and the leaders cautioned the men to avoid any violence, saying that if they adopted a dignified course they would have the sympathy of the community behind them, and would probably carry their point. The nasty action at the Baltimore wharf indicates that all the strikers are not in accord with their leaders.

The strike has been systematically conducted. The laying of the plans has been going on for weeks and a determination was arrived at to head off the corporations from securing help in the country. The union has in its treasury, it is said, over $5,000, and circulars announcing the intention to strike, together with the grievances and appeal to the colored people to remain away from the city were printed and scattered broadcast through the country districts by agents. The pulpit was also appealed to, and the agents managed to get the preachers to talk of the intended strike and beg their people to remain at home and not be induced by any promise of the railroad companies to take the place of strikers....

The strikers have held daily meetings for several days, ... attended by immense crowds. Their meeting there Sunday lasted almost all the forenoon and people living in the vicinity say the whole neighborhood was black with colored people. They have been holding meetings there at nights for some time in preparation for the strike and the colored military companies have been doing a great deal of drilling there....

3.29   IAM Leaders Ask about Race Exclusion, 1893. Philip S. Foner and Ronald L. Lewis, eds., *The Black Worker during the Era of the American*

Federation of Labor and the Railroad Brotherhoods, Vol. 4 (Philadelphia: Temple University Press, 1979), pp. 53–54.

JAMES O'CONNELL TO SAMUEL GOMPERS, NOVEMBER 1, 1893
James O'Connell, Grand Master Machinist
International Assn. of Machinists
Richmond, Virginia

Dear Sir:
I take this opportunity of addressing you on a subject that is of great interest to both of us in the matter of bringing more closely together the Labor Organizations of this country, and harmonizing any differences that may exist among them. As you are fully aware of the action taken by our Conventions on that portion of our Constitution which has the word "white" in it, it has been a bone of contention among our members for sometime, and at the Indianapolis Convention we adopted a resolution to take a referendum vote as to taking the word "white" out of our Constitution. This matter I will lay before our Organization about the middle of this month, and knowing that on several occasions you have said if it were not for that portion of our Constitution there would be no rival Organization of the machinist craft in this country, and that the I.M.U. would at once become an organization of the past; now any assurance that you can give me on this matter will add a great deal towards helping us to bring this matter to a speedy conclusion, and also a successful one to all concerned.

There is no reason in the world, that I know of, why we should have two Organizations of the same craft in this country, or in fact of any other country. Our Organization is advancing rapidly under the present condition of affairs in this country, and have prospects of still greater growth; and with these facts in view I address you this letter for the purpose of having you give me your ideas as to what would be the result if we had this word taken out of our Constitution.

An early reply to this letter would be very acceptable.
Believe me,
Yours Respectfully & Fraternally,
James O'Connell,
[G.M.M., A.F. of L. Archives, Incoming Correspondence]

JAMES DUNCAN TO W. S. DAVIS, APRIL 1, 1895
W. S. Davis
International Association of Machinists

Dear Sir:
(As) long as you have the word "white" establishing the color line as a part of your constitution either your action must be changed or your lodges and your national body must stand debarred from all affiliation with us.

I believe yours is the only national union, that at present, has the color line as distinctly formed, while at the same time many crafts refused to admit a colored man without having such provision in their constitutions the matter being left absolutely with the local unions as whether or not they admit colored applicants.

James Duncan,

Acting President of the A.F. of L.

3.30   A White Worker Defends Racial Exclusion, 1895. Letter from J. Best to *Machinists' Journal,* April 1895. Reprinted in Foner and Lewis, *The Black Worker,* Vol. 4, pp. 53–54.

THIS WORD WHITE

We ought to remember all these things when the Convention takes place, instruct our delegates to that effect, make an effort to keep politics, religion, and petty grievances out of the Convention, not strike the word "white" out of our constitution, and so on.

Brothers, have you ever read attentively the many articles published in our Journal about this word "white," and especially the one in the last issue, in which a brother says himself that there were to his knowledge only five Negro machinists in the South, and still he proposes to give the "colored" a partial membership, restrictions which are not practicable, but unjust. If you admit the negro you must admit him like the rest of us or not all. Our craft, which heretofore was a white man's calling exclusively, will cease to be; it will become flooded with negroes to such an extent that there will be shops where a white man will be driven out and have no chance whatever.

The negro don't need us now, nor will he ever benefit us even if we make him a brother. Only think of it. Not that he ain't as good a man as many whites, no, but it is not good for us, as he is a born competitor with us, and we will command still less pay than we are getting now. We want our craft elevated, if not above the level of the best paid craft of the United States, then at the same height; but we cannot do it by admitting the negro. Progress will stop, there will be a split in our order, and if this occurs, the end will be near at hand, and some one will try and start something else until everything bursts again on the same rocky question. Now is the time, however, to meditate over such matters, and by instructing the delegates when they go to the convention it will save a good deal of trouble to decide it.

J. Best

Philadelphia, Pa.

February 5, 1895

3.31   A Black Newspaper Reports Gompers's Statements Against Discrimination, 1893. "Nothing but Prejudice," *The Freeman* (Indianapolis), May 27, 1893. Reprinted in Foner and Lewis, *The Black Worker,* Vol. 4, p. 52.

NOTHING BUT PREJUDICE

President Samuel Gompers of the American Federation of Labor talked to the International Association of Machinists in Indianapolis recently asking them to extend the privileges and protection of their organization to the colored man. This association and the plasterers' union are about the only organizations which exclude the Negro. Mr. Gompers did not, however, succeed in his object. When asked what reason was assigned by the machinists for still closing their doors to the colored man: "Now," he said, "they have answered that this would be a step toward social equality. It's nothing of the kind. We don't expect them to go any further, but certainly if a Negro is good enough to work alongside of the white man, he ought to be admitted to the trade unions. Then from another standpoint it is advisable to admit them: If we don't they bid against us, and competition in labor is the very thing that labor organizations are agitating against.

The machinists say there are so few colored men among them that it is not worth while to bother about them. As I said in my address yesterday, if there are none then this article in their by-laws denying them admission is altogether unnecessary, while if there are colored men, the article is brutal and inhuman. They will see the effect of this too. My talk to the association could have had no effect upon them during this session, as they had already disposed of the question before I arrived. I am told they did this on purpose to anticipate my endeavors. There is another association of machinists which admits the colored man and is in the federation of labor. It was my desire to unite the two organizations, but it cannot be done as long as this association persists in its determination to draw the color line. It is nothing but prejudice that keeps them out."

3.32   A White Miner Advocates on Behalf of Blacks, 1916. *Birmingham Labor Advocate,* August 5, 1916, p. 1.

Editor, *Labor Advocate,*

At the outset I want to inform you that I am a White Man, and a miner of twenty-five years experience, and have worked in many mines and with many Negro miners, and the Negro, whatever might be said of him, is loyal to the core. He is one whom you can rely upon at all times when he says he is with you.

As I afore said, I know conditions in Alabama. The white miner is treated bad enough, but the Negro as a general thing simply catches "hell" in the big way. He is, in many instances, treated worse than a convict by the superintendents as the companies uphold them in all their wickedness. . . .

The Negro has not got a chance in Alabama's coal fields, and never will come into his rights as a man and a citizen; not until some leading white man with the moral courage goes into the different mining districts and meets their preachers and proves to them the absolute necessity of the union. This should be done not only in self-defense, but for the sake of humanity as the Negro is worthy of being saved from the industrial and moral death that he is dying, and his blood will be required at our hands.

The Negro miner is in the South to stay and there is no way on earth to get rid of him; and again, I do not believe we honest Southerners would get rid of him if we could. Therefore, there is only one way for us to better our condition and that way is by bettering the Negro's condition for it is a fact that we cannot rise and leave him in the ditch. . . .

I am converted to the truth that in order to save the industrial life of the white man in this Southland not in the coal fields but in every other avenue of industry, we must lay aside prejudice and face the situation like white men with back bone and lift him out of the damnable industrial pit and make him a man, and thus by saving him we will save ourselves, our wives, and children. . . .

[Signed]

A White Miner

RADICAL ALTERNATIVES

The final two documents in this chapter (3.33 and 3.34) discuss radical alternatives to the style of unionism practiced by most affiliates of the AFL. In the first document, Eugene V. Debs, formerly a prominent labor leader of the railroad crafts and founder of the American Railway Union (ARU), but at the time he wrote the document the nation's most prominent socialist leader, argues for the amalgamation of socialism and unionism. The next document, the Industrial Union Manifesto that called the founding convention of the IWW, describes why modern mass-production industry has made craft unionism anachronistic and why industrial unionism is the necessary form of worker organization. It also promises no compromise with capitalism.

3.33 American Socialism's Vision, 1904. From Eugene V. Debs, *Unionism and Socialism: A Plea for Both* (Terre Haute, Ind.: Standard Publishing Company, 1904), pp. 29, 30, 43–44.

It is our conviction that no workingman can clearly understand what socialism means without becoming and remaining a socialist. It is simply impossible for him to be anything else and the only reason that all work-ingmen are not socialists is that they do not know what it means. . . .

Socialism is first of all a political movement of the working class, clearly defined and uncompromising, which aims at the overthrow of the prevail-ing capitalist system by the exercise of the public powers, supplanting the existing capitalist class government with socialist administration—that is to say, changing a republic in name to a republic in fact. . . .

In the capitalist system the soul has no business. It cannot produce profit by any process of capitalist calculation.

The working hand is what is needed for the capitalist's tool and so the human must be reduced to a hand.

No head, no heart, no soul—simply a hand.

A thousand hands to one brain—the hands of workingmen, the brain of the capitalist.

A thousand dumb animals in human form—a thousand slaves in the fet-ters of ignorance, their heads having run to hands—all these owned and worked and fleeced by one stock-demanding, profit-mongering capitalist.

This is capitalism!

A thousand hands to one head is the abnormal development of the cap-italist system.

A thousand workingmen turned into hands, to develop and gorge and decorate one capitalist paunch!

This brutal order of things must be overthrown. The human race was not born to degeneracy.

A thousand heads have grown for every thousand pairs of hands; a thou-sand hearts throb in testimony of the unity of heads and hands and a thou-sand souls, though crushed and mangled, burn in protest and are pledged to redeem a thousand men.

Heads and hands, hearts and souls, are the heritage of all. . . .

Co-operative industry in which all shall work together in harmony as the basis of a new social order, a richer civilization, a real republic. That is the demand.

The end of class struggles and class rule, of master and slave, of ignorance and vice, of poverty and shame, of cruelty and crime—the birth of freedom, the dawn of brotherhood, the beginning of MAN. That is the demand.

This is socialism!

3.34   An "Industrial Union Manifesto," 1905. From *The Founding convention of the IWW; Proceedings* (New York: Merit Publishers, 1969 [orig. 1905]), pp. 3–6.

MANIFESTO

Social relations and groupings only reflect mechanical and industrial condi-tions. The great facts of present industry are the displacement of human skill by machines and the increase of capitalist power through concentration in the possession of the tools with which wealth is produced and distributed.

Because of these facts trade divisions among laborers and competition among capitalists are alike disappearing. Class divisions grow ever more fixed and class antagonisms more sharp. Trade lines have been swallowed up in a common servitude of all workers to the machines which they tend. . . .

The worker, wholly separated from the land and the tools, with his skill of craftsmenship rendered useless, is sunk in the uniform mass of wage slaves. He sees his power of resistance broken by craft divisions, perpetuated from out-grown industrial stages. His wages constantly grow less as his hours grow longer and monopolized prices grow higher. . . . Laborers are no longer classified by differences in trade skill, but the employer assigns them according to the machines to which they are attached. These divisions, far from representing differences in skill or interests among the laborers, are imposed by the employers that workers may be pitted against one another and spurred to greater exertion in the shop, and that all resistance to capitalist tyranny may be weakened by artificial distinctions. . . .

Separation of craft from craft renders industrial and financial solidarity impossible.

Union men scab upon union men; hatred of worker for worker is engendered, and the workers are delivered helpless and disintegrated into the hands of the capitalists.

Craft jealousy leads to the attempt to create trade monopolies.

Prohibitive initiation fees are established that force men to become scabs against their will. Men whom manliness or circumstances have driven from one trade are thereby fined when they seek to transfer membership to the union of a new craft.

Craft divisions foster political ignorance among the workers, thus dividing their class at the ballot box, as well as in the shop, mine and factory.

Craft unions may be and have been used to assist employers in the establishment of monopolies and the raising of prices. One set of workers are thus used to make harder the conditions of life of another body of laborers.

Craft divisions hinder the growth of class consciousness of the workers, foster the idea of harmony of interests between employing exploiter and employed slave. They permit the association of the misleaders of the workers with the capitalists in the Civic Federations, where plans are made for the perpetuation of capitalism, and the permanent enslavement of the workers through the wage system.

Previous efforts for the betterment of the working class have proven abortive because limited in scope and disconnected in action.

Universal economic evils afflicting the working class can be eradicated only by a universal working class movement. Such a movement of the working class is impossible while separate craft and wage agreements are made favoring the employer against other crafts in the same industry, and while energies are wasted in fruitless jurisdiction struggles which serve only to further the personal aggrandizement of union officials.

A movement to fulfill these conditions must consist of one great industrial union embracing all industries,—providing for craft autonomy locally, industrial autonomy internationally, and working class unity generally.

It must be founded on the class struggle, and its general administration must be conducted in harmony with the recognition of the irrepressible conflict between the capitalist class and the working class.

It should be established as the economic organization of the working class, without affiliation with any political party.

All power should rest in a collective membership.

Local, national and general administration, including union labels, buttons, badges, transfer cards, initiation fees, and per capita tax should be uniform throughout.

All members must hold membership in the local, national or international union covering the industry in which they are employed, but transfers of membership between unions, local, national or international, should be universal.

Workingmen bringing union cards from industrial unions in foreign countries should be freely, admitted into the organization.

The general administration should issue a publication representing the entire union and its principles which should reach all members in every industry at regular intervals.

A *central defense fund,* to which all members contribute equally, should be established and maintained.

All workers, therefore, who agree with the principles herein set forth, will meet in convention at Chicago the 27th day of June, 1905, for the purpose of forming an economic organization of the working class along the lines marked out in this Manifesto.

Adopted at Chicago, January 2, 3 and 4, 1905.

A. G. SWING, A. M. SIMONS, . . . GEO. ESTES, WM. D. HAYWOOD, MOTHER JONES, . . . CHAS. H. MOYER . . . WILLIAM ERNEST TRAUTMANN . . . EUGENE V. DEBS . . . THOS. J. HAGERTY . . . CHAS. O. SHERMAN, FRANK BOHN [et al.]

4

WARS, DEPRESSION, AND THE
STRUGGLE FOR INDUSTRIAL DEMOCRACY,
1914–1947

The years bounded by the two world wars constitute a watershed in U.S. labor history, a time of profound changes in almost every feature of working-class life. During these years, the structure of the economy was transformed by consolidation of a mass production economy and the emergence of its mass consumption counterpart. The composition of the U.S. working class was altered by dramatic changes in the racial composition of the industrial labor force. Paradoxically, these years also saw corporate industrial capitalism plunge from the zenith of its vast cultural and economic power in the 1920s to the nadir of its political influence and credibility in the 1930s. The Great Depression of the 1930s exacted an enormous human toll on working-class America and the frail community institutions upon which workers had traditionally relied during periods of economic hardship. The scale of the economic collapse was so vast that it triggered the sea change in American economic and labor policy ushered in by Franklin D. Roosevelt's New Deal. Together with the political and social dynamics unleashed by U.S. participation in two world wars, the New Deal laid the basis for a policy of state intervention in the economy, a policy that directly benefited workers and their efforts to organize unions. Taking advantage of changing federal policy toward labor, union organizers orchestrated the most dramatic labor upsurge in American history during the 1930s, a departure best symbolized by the launching of the Committee for Industrial Organization (CIO) in 1935. By the end of World War II, roughly one-third of all U.S. workers were in unions, New Deal liberalism occupied the center ground of American politics, and working-class America was poised to experience a period of unprecedented stability, prosperity, and rising expectations. It would not be too much to say that the interwar years covered in this chapter led to the emancipation of working-class Americans from decades of economic uncertainty, political marginalization, and callous or paternalistic treatment at the hands of employers.

Few of these changes could have been anticipated when the United States plunged into World War I in 1917. That war occurred at a moment of profound importance for American workers. The progressive movement that had been gathering momentum during the decade prior to the war had shaped President Woodrow Wilson's reform-minded approach to labor policy. Wilson embraced the progressives' demand that "industrial democracy" should replace the autocratic and oppressive practices of U.S. employers. This shift was welcome news for the AFL, which was in the process of trying to fight off the radical IWW by turning increasingly toward organizing mass production workers. During the war, the Wilson administration implemented reforms that strengthened the AFL (best illustrated by the creation of the National War Labor Board in 1918) even while it repressed the IWW. Workers responded to wartime reforms by organizing in large numbers. But their gains were short-lived. In 1919 and the decade that followed, employers drove labor organizations out of most of the industries where they had made headway during the war and Wilsonian progressivism collapsed under the wave of political reaction that swept the country once the armistice was signed.

With organized labor in retreat after World War I, it was corporate America that exerted the greatest influence over working-class life. During these years, corporate industrial capitalism instituted vast changes in the structure of the U.S. economy. The establishment of Henry Ford's famous Highland Park assembly line in 1913 is perhaps the best-known milepost marking the emergence of the mass production economy. Lesser-known changes occurred almost simultaneously with Ford's introduction of the assembly line. The more efficient open hearth process far outstripped the Bessemer process in steel production. Factories increasingly converted to electric-powered machinery between 1912 and 1929 and electricity became the dominant power source in industrial facilities. Chemical and electrical manufacturing industries soared, spurred especially by the defense demands of World War I. And the theories of such labor efficiency consultants as Frederick Winslow Taylor and Elton Mayo helped employers who sought to maximize the output of their workers.

The changes in manufacturing in turn influenced consumption patterns, providing the basis for an emerging mass-consumption economy in the 1920s. Radios, refrigerators, and automobiles led the way as that decade's hottest consumer items. Radio production alone rose from $15 million in 1920 to $338 million in 1929. Nearly 2.8 million cars rolled off assembly lines in 1929 alone, and gasoline production quadrupled over the course of the 1920s in a desperate effort to keep up with rising consumer demand. Changing patterns of credit contributed to the consumption boom of the 1920s. Beginning in 1919, the General Motors Acceptance Corporation provided potential buyers with loans to help them buy GM cars. When they could afford them, most workers bought items such as radios and refrigerators on installment plans. Although not all working-class Americans enjoyed the fruits of the boom of the 1920s, the emergence of a mass-consumption economy for many workers dramatically transformed their daily leisure and living patterns, and perhaps even their desires.

Nothing better symbolized business ascendancy during the post-World War I years than the emergence of what historians have come to call welfare capitalism, a series of policies designed by employers to gain the loyalty of their workers and to obviate the need for union organization. Large employers offered recreational programs, paid vacations, and profit-sharing plans to gain their employees' fealty. They also created company unions, promising a watered-down version of industrial democracy through management-dominated instrumentalities.

As the changing economy altered the horizons of working-class life in the interwar years, large forces changed the demographic composition of the U.S. working class. Immigration to the United States from Europe surged both before and just after World War I. But that immigration was nearly shut off completely by postwar legislative initiatives that culminated in the passage of the Johnson-Reed Immigration Act of 1924. That act established a quota system that discriminated against potential immigrants from southern and eastern Europe. No longer replenished by waves of new immigrants from their native lands, immigrant neighborhoods and cultures became increasingly Americanized in the interwar years.

As European immigrants and their children became more Americanized, the character of the U.S. working class was being altered by two vast northward migrations. One of these migrations saw millions of black sharecroppers and tenant farmers flee the increasingly tenuous cotton culture and oppressive social conditions of the American South for jobs in the urban North and West. During the wartime boom years of 1916–18 and 1941–45, this persistent population movement became the surging flood of humanity that historians refer to as the Great Migration. Although black migrants were scarcely welcomed by white northern workers and their unions (indeed, the racial tensions that had persistently divided the U.S. working class worsened in the early years of this migration), blacks still found opportunities to substantially improve their lives in urban industrial America.

Seeking the same sort of opportunities, a second population movement gathered momentum in the years around World War I when labor was scarce in the United States. That movement saw hundreds of thousands of Mexican workers head north across the border for jobs in agriculture, food processing, mining, steel, and a host of other industries. Doubly marked by their native tongue and darker complexions, Mexican workers, too, encountered discrimination. But like American blacks, they often found ways to fight back against the worst instances of exploitations, wringing enough from their labor to compensate for the loneliness and indignity that so often characterized their working lives in *el Norte*.

Black and Latino workers were among those hardest hit by the onset of the Great Depression in 1929— a depression unlike any ever experienced in the United States. Between 1929 and 1933 the size of the economy was cut in half. Jobless rates rose as high as 25 percent. And underemployment rates (those who could not find full-time work) rose just as high. Workers' credit unions, church-based relief programs, and fraternal societies were overwhelmed by the misery unleashed in the first years after the stock market crash of October 1929. By 1933, the nation's banking structure was near total collapse and tent colonies of jobless, homeless migrants could be found on the outskirts of virtually all American cities. These conditions paved the way for the election of Franklin D. Roosevelt in 1932 and for the unfolding of his New Deal.

The New Deal promised to rescue the "Common Man" from despair, although little agreement existed among Roosevelt's advisors on just how this ought to be done. Some advocated supply-centered policies that would empower business leaders to reorganize the various sectors of the economy to manage competition and promote greater efficiency. Others urged policies designed to stimulate a demand-centered recovery by raising workers' wages and encouraging their organization in unions. Roosevelt initially vacillated between these competing impulses, but between 1935 and 1938 he signed legislation oriented much more to the latter impulse than to the former. Foremost among these laws was the National Labor Relations (or Wagner) Act of 1935, which unambiguously legalized the rights of industrial workers to join unions and bargain collectively. That same year he signed the Social Security Act, which simultaneously created a national retirement system paid for by joint contributions from employees and employers and funded state-administered unemployment insurance and welfare programs. Roosevelt signed the Fair Labor Standards Act in 1938, which finally abolished child labor and set a national minimum wage, goals long sought by labor reformers.

The new departure in federal labor policy presided over by the Roosevelt administration cleared the way for a massive upsurge in union organization. Acting on their own, without government aid, unions had been unsuccessful in organizing the open shops of America's mass production industries. But the New Deal era saw the law shift in a direction that favored unions. First, the 1932 Norris-LaGuardia Act limited the use of injunctions against unions. Then Section 7a of the National Industrial Recovery Act of 1933 encouraged workers to engage in collective bargaining. Finally, the NLRA of 1935 established the National Labor Relations Board, banned employer-dominated company unions from engaging in collective bargaining, and outlawed a variety of anti-union tactics.

In response, labor organizers began to build a powerful movement to organize the mass production industries. Initially that movement was fostered by factions within the AFL, closely linked to John L. Lewis of the United Mine Workers of America and Sidney Hillman of the Amalgamated Clothing Workers of America. When Lewis, Hillman, and their allies were unable to persuade the AFL's leadership to endorse a full-scale policy of industrial organization, they acted on their own. In 1935 they formed the Committee on Industrial Organization (CIO). When the AFL objected to the CIO's activities, the AFL and CIO leaders severed their ties in 1938.

CIO unions soon won contracts in the historically open-shop auto, steel, and rubber industries, marking a turning point in U.S. union history.

Nonetheless it was not until World War II that organized labor's gains under the New Deal were consolidated. The war ended unemployment and ushered in a period of working-class prosperity, bringing an end to more than a decade of deprivation. During the war, federal policies also helped unions grow, as the government encouraged collective bargaining in return for the unions' promises to avoid strikes during the war's duration (promises that elicited no small amount of controversy in labor's ranks). African Americans and women saw their job opportunities vastly improve during the war, even though racial and gender discrimination persisted among employers and white and male workers alike.

By the end of the war, industrial workers had seen a surprising transformation of their lives over a scant four decades. Historically beleaguered unions were now entrenched in basic industries. Orderly grievance procedures had replaced the employers' whim in governing the workplaces of basic industry. A social insurance system had given a semblance of stability to working-class life that had never known that blessing. And through their unions workers possessed more political power than they had ever exercised before.

WORKERS IN THE ERA OF THE GREAT WAR

U.S. entry into World War I in 1917 held contradictory consequences for workers. On the one hand, wartime hysteria provided a cover for labor repression. In Document 4.1, two victims of the Bisbee deportation of 1917 recall what happened when a band of super-patriot vigilantes swooped down on this Arizona copper mining community, rounded up anyone suspected of being an IWW member, loaded them onto cattle cars, and sent them into the New Mexico desert. On the other hand, wartime labor shortages provided workers with new opportunities to exert their power on the shop floors of war-related factories, as one General Electric worker's testimony in 1918 makes clear (Document 4.2). The spread of 3,000 strikes during the first six months of the war forced the Wilson administration to create a National War Labor Board, whose principles validated the ideal of industrial democracy and supported many of labor's most important demands (Document 4.3). The war also opened up new opportunities for working women, as labor writer Florence Thorne observed in 1917 (Document 4.4). And although they were rarely granted just treatment, African American workers were quick to invoke their patriotism to reinforce their claims for just treatment from both employers and unions, as the letter from a black trade unionist to the head of the all-white Brotherhood of Railway & Steamship Clerks union illustrates (Document 4.5). What do these documents suggest about the impact the war had on workers' expectations for justice in the workplace?

4.1   Two Workers Recall the Bisbee Deportation, 1917. Excerpts from a hearing before the President's Mediation Commission, November 2, 1917, Bisbee, Arizona, pp. 80–81, 115–16, in Melvyn Dubofsky, ed., *Papers of the President's Mediation Commission, 1917–1918* (Frederick, Md.: University Publications of America, 1985), Reel 2.

Charles Ward was called, and testified before the Commission as follows. Mr. [Felix] Frankfurter [Secretary of the President's Mediation Commission]: Mr. Ward, you were working in the mines here?
By Mr. Ward: I am a blacksmith; I was working at the Higgins Mine Company up the Gulch here.
By Mr. Frankfurter: In which of the labor organizations were you?
By Mr. Ward: In two of them; the Industrial Workers [IWW], and this one I belong to ten years, and the other one [the IWW] about a month.
By Secretary [of Labor William B.] Wilson: The International Brotherhood of Blacksmiths and Helpers, and you also had a Red Card [membership in the IWW]?
By Mr. Ward: About a month.
By Secretary Wilson: Why did you join it?
By Mr. Ward: Well, the miners wanted me to take out a card with them and I was in a mining camp.
By Secretary Wilson: Do you believe, or did you believe when you joined them, in the principles of the IWW?
By Mr. Ward: I didn't get to know much about them in a month, you know.
By Secretary Wilson: Did you join it because you thought they represented the union in the mines?
By Mr. Ward: Yes.
By Secretary Wilson: Is that the sole reason?
By Mr. Ward: Yes. . . .
By Mr. Frankfurter: When the strike broke out did you go out?
By Mr. Ward: This place up here, the miners stayed away and of course they didn't want no blacksmith on the job when there was nothing doing in the mines. . . .
By Mr. Frankfurter: On the morning of the twelfth, what happened to you?
By Mr. Ward: I was down there by the depot and they told me to get in line with the rest of them.
By Secretary Wilson: What did they say to you when they told you to get in line with the rest of them?
By Mr. Ward: That is all. . . . They never asked me if I was at work.

[Testimony of Thomas N. English]
By Mr. Frankfurter: What is your full name?
By Mr. English: Thomas N. English.

By Mr. Frankfurter: Were you working in the mines here when the strike broke out?

By Mr. English: Yes, sir. . . .

By Mr. Frankfurter: Were you deported?

By Mr. English: I was.

By Mr. Frankfurter: Tell the Commission how it happened.

By Mr. English: Well, on the morning of the twelfth, about 7 o'clock in the morning, somebody knocked on the door and I told them to come in, and they asked me if I was working and, I said, no sir, and they said, "well, come out of there right away and dress; we want you," and I said "what's this for" and they said "get in line with the rest of them." That was all of the information I could get. There was another man rooming with me by the name of Swanson, and they made him get out at the same time and they taken us down to the line and then into the Ball Park and I was loaded into a stock car about 11 o'clock in the morning. [Ward, English and other suspected Wobblies or IWW sympathizers were then shipped out into the desert.]

4.2 Women Fight Piece Rate Cut at General Electric, 1917. Transcript of Proceedings, Casefile 231; August 23, 1918, pp. 1191–98, in Melvyn Dubofsky, ed. *Papers of the National War Labor Board, 1918–1919* (Frederick, Md.: University Publications of America, 1984), Reel 15.

Q: Your full name is Elizabeth Gillespie?

A: Yes, sir.

Q: You have worked for the General Electric Company how long?

A: Well, in all, about six or seven years.

Q: Now, what do you say as to the cuts [in piece rates]? Please tell us your story on the cuts.

A: Well . . . my story on cuts is this, in a few words; it has always been cuts ever since I have been acquainted with the job—it has been cuts.

Q: Nibbling at the wages?

A: Yes, nibbling. A year ago—a year ago, I think it is a year ago last May, they tried a general cut, and the girls struck, refused to work. . . . I guess . . . between 250 and 300 girls.

Q: What was done at that time?

A: I guess the foreman passed around a paper . . . that they were going to cut the job 25 percent. . . . The girls went on strike. They refused to work, and took off their aprons and were walking out when they met the foremen and the foreman advised them that he would look into the matter, which he did . . . and finally he decided it would be better not to cut it at the present time. That was a year ago last May. . . . Then everything ran along quite smoothly until the introduction of a price cutter. . . .

Q: Go ahead. What happened when he came?

A: Well, he hung around for two or three days, and we really did not know what he was for a little while, but we finally found out he was a price setter—a price cutter we call him. . . . So when the girls found out for sure what he was, why they got very excited, and, well, they started what I would call a rough house, and it was some rough house. I under- stand . . . that the foreman . . . asked him to go out of the building, because he couldn't do a thing with the women while he stayed there. . . . He [disappeared] in about fifteen minutes. . . . [H]e hasn't been back since. But a little later on they introduced a lady. They brought one lady off the floor. They sent for her, and she went over to the office and she refused to take the job, and she told me herself that she asked them what would be in it for her and they told her there that would be up to herself. She said, "Do you mean to say that the more jobs I cut, the big- ger my pay will be?" And they told her that was about how it was. The lady . . . has left long ago, and finally they found a woman who did take the job. . . .

Q: Now . . . were you girls unionized?

A: No, sir . . .

Q: Go ahead. . . .

A: They introduced this lady on the floor, and she went down among the girls and finally she selected one and sat there with her with a stop watch and a pad of paper and pencil and the girl refused to work. She got up and walked away, and she tried another one, and the other one done the same thing. And she complained about it, but it did not do any good. The girls decided that the weren't going to have anybody standing back of them. The job has been cut so much—the girls were making about $12 [per week] at that time—and they told me they had to make $12 to live honestly. . . .

I told [the foreman] that . . . if they did not take the price setter off the floor, that the girls were going to go out, and the girls had not been work- ing all the while this was going on. They were already on strike. . . . We were sent for to go over and see Mr. Fish [the plant superintendent]. . . . The result of our interview with Mr. Fish was that he promised us if we went back to work and created harmony . . . he would guarantee us that work wouldn't be interfered with for one year. . . .

4.3   NWLB Principles, 1918. *Report of the Secretary of the National War Labor Board to the Secretary of Labor for the Twelve Months Ending May 31, 1919* (Washington, D.C.: Government Printing Office, 1919), pp. 121–23.

Principles and Policies to Govern Relations Between Workers and Employers in War Industries for the Duration of the War

RIGHT TO ORGANIZE

The right of workers to organize in trade-unions and to bargain collectively through chosen representatives is recognized and affirmed. The right shall not be denied, abridged, or interfered with by employers in any manner whatsoever. . . .

EXISTING CONDITIONS

In establishments were the union shop exists the same shall continue, and the union standards as to wages, hours of labor, and other conditions of employment shall be maintained. . . .

WOMEN IN INDUSTRY

If it shall be become necessary to employ women on work ordinarily performed by men, they must be allowed equal pay for equal work and must not be allotted tasks disproportionate to their strength. . . .

HOURS OF LABOR

The basic eight-hour day is recognized as applying in all cases in which existing law requires it. In all other cases the question . . . shall be settled with due regard to governmental necessities and the welfare, health, and proper comfort of the workers.

MAXIMUM PRODUCTION

The maximum production of all war industries should be maintained. . . .

MOBILIZATION OF LABOR

. . . [Government] agencies shall be given opportunity to aid in the distribution of labor as necessity demands.

CUSTOM OF LOCALITIES

In fixing wages, hours, and conditions of labor, regard should always be given to the . . . conditions prevailing in the localities affected.

THE LIVING WAGE

1. The right of all workers, including common laborers, to a living is hereby declared.

2. In fixing wages, minimum rates of pay shall be established which will insure subsistence of the worker and his family in health and reasonable comfort.

4.4 Women and Wartime Opportunity, 1917. Excerpt from Florence Thorne, "The Trend Toward Equality," *American Federationist* (February 1917), pp. 120–21.

The extraordinary necessity arising out of the European war has brought with it extraordinary opportunity. Women have made a magnificent response to their countries' needs. They have made heroic sacrifices and rendered the service of patriots at home, and at work. They have given up their dear ones. In all countries the war has withdrawn men from work in many industries and service in transportation and communication. Wherever the work was of such a nature that the demands upon physical strength were moderate, women have replaced men as workers either entirely or in preponderant proportions. We know that the women of France, England, and Germany have made a whole-hearted response and have proven their right to participate equally with men in the thought and the life of the world. When the happenings in other countries are disclosed, without doubt we shall learn that they responded in a way equally splendid. Able-bodied men are needed on the battlefield. Yet the fate of the war depends upon the ability of the nations to organize and mobilize industrial resources. The demand for soldiers withdrew men from industry and commerce. But the women of warring countries took up the service which their fathers, husbands and brothers were compelled to leave.

Conventional theory of women's life excludes them from the larger aspects and movements of life and work. In theory women live a protected home life. In reality many earn their own livelihood and provide for those dependent upon them. Conventional, social and moral traditions deny women the advantages and opportunities accorded to men workers while obligations and restrictions fall more rigorously upon women than upon men. Laws, customs, and duties are determined by men and made obligatory upon women. In but few countries are women citizens, and in no country do they as yet have industrial equality with men. Upon working women this inequality falls most heavily. With the whole force of society against them organization is difficult.

A change has been slowly gaining direction and force, known as the woman movement. Women are learning that freedom will not be given them but that they must achieve freedom. Experience is teaching them that men will never voluntarily recognize equality of ability in work regardless of sex distinction. . . .

The war has given women an opportunity to escape from a world of conventions and fictions into the realities of work, where recognition of truths is fundamental. The very natures of these women have been transformed by the change. They can not and will not return to the old existence. . . .

4.5   African American Workers Demand Justice, 1919. Letter to J. J. Forrester, Grand President, Brotherhood of Railway & Steamship Clerks, from John H. Dailey and Oliver Johnson, Freight Handlers Union, #16700, September 14, 1919, demanding help from the union for black freight handlers whose officers have been fired by their railroad employer. From U.S. Railroad Administration Records, Record Group 14, Entry 86, Box 35, Casefile, 878, National Archives, Washington, D.C.

Dear Sir,
At our . . . meeting, Sept. 14, 1919, which convened 3 o'clock P.M., for a general discussion of the welfare of the above organization [Freight Handlers Union, #16700], wherein it was decided that you be duly notified of the exact circumstances and unjust dealings against us as laborers organized under the auspices of the constitution of the A.F. of L. Frankly we have been before withholding many discriminations and details, of which, according to the law and the constitution of the A.F. of L., subjecting us to be guided and protected under. To begin with, we have put

up fight after fight, petition for rights, grievances, sought time after time in conference by our committees with the agents to reach some justice to our demands for what the A.F. of L. guarantees those organized under its government, and must report the whole a miserable failure. Now we began this organization . . . June 1919. . . . All before then was calm. But ever since it was known that we had determined unionism . . . we are forced to be subject of prejudice, such is aimed chiefly against the officers the Secretary John Dailey and Pres. Oliver Johnson, with premeditated desire to break up our organization by force, to crush the leadership, in hopes to stampede the rest of the body in a miserable wreck.

We have a right to organize, and we demand the executive officers of the A. F. of L. to now take proper steps to defend us in defending this principle, to apply to you for relief which the world owes labor in National Justice to obliterate such humiliation to men who have stood by this Government in its critical hours and times. . . . Now we respect our [supervisor], his position and official duty, but we want to understand what is our use of being organized if we have no rights to our demand as others are entitled to. We want to know why . . . we have got to take such treatment. . . .

We are tired of such men who seem to think we are ignorant . . . and here let you know plainly that our circumstances . . . have become intolerable, and unbearable, as we are worse off than before organized. Plainly giving evidence that on account of color and being organized we are denounced on every side on every occasion by agent. For how are we to ever get our demand of right against might and [still] be told to work as agent desires us or sees fit to advantage of his work [?] We demand you will consider these statements, and if we are entitled to the compromise offered by the A.F. of L. concerning working conditions, treatment and principle, someone be selected to be sent here and curtail this condition; a man who is not afraid to tell us the truth and tell the agent what is right or wrong. . . .
John H. Dailey, Sec'y
Oliver Johnson, Pres.
P.S. Answer immediately.

POST-WAR BACKLASH

Following World War I, employers unleashed a ferocious backlash against unions. In a desperate and largely unsuccessful attempt to defend their wartime gains, more workers went on strike in 1919 than ever before in U.S. history. The crucial loss occurred in the steel industry. In Document 4.6, William Z. Foster, the chief organizer of the steel strike of 1919, recalls the kinds of vigilante activity that broke the back of the walkout in western Pennsylvania. Employers often relied upon professional strikebreakers, such as those who advertised their services in Document 4.7, to help them eradicate unions after the war. Employers also exploited racial and ethnic cleavages among workers to break unions. Document 4.8 shows a leaflet circulated by some steel employers urging native-born workers not to stand shoulder-to-shoulder with immigrants during the steel strike. Document 4.9 illustrates the desperate effort by the Chicago Federation of Labor to cool racial tensions following the explosive Chicago race riot of July 1919. Once unions had been broken in the postwar strike wave, employers established open shops under what they called the "American Plan." Humorist Finley Peter Dunne's fictional character Mr. Dooley was among those who saw through the employers' high-minded defense of the rights of their workers to be non-union (Document 4.10). What do these documents suggest about the power imbalance that existed between unions and employers once World War I ended?

4.6   Repression of the Steel Strike, 1919. From William Z. Foster, *The Great Steel Strike and its Lessons* (New York: B. W. Huebsch, Inc., 1920), pp. 187–98.

The Johnstown strike was so complete that for eight weeks the great Cambria Steel Co., despite strenuous efforts, could not put a single department of its enormous mills into operation. Every trick was used to break the strike. The Back-to-Work organization [sponsored and financed by companies] labored ceaselessly, holding meetings and writing and telephoning the workers to coax or intimidate them back to their jobs. Droves of scabs were brought in from outside points. But to no effect; the workers held fast. Then the company embarked upon the usual Pennsylvania policy of terrorism.

I, personally, was the first to feel its weight. I was billed to speak in the Johnstown on November 7. Upon alighting from the train I was met by two newspaper men who advised me to quit the town at once, stating that the business men and company officials had held a meeting the night before and organized a "Citizens' Committee," which was to break the strike by applying "Duquesne tactics." Beginning with myself, all the organizers were to be driven from the city. Disregarding this warning, I started for the Labor Temple; but was again warned by the newspapermen, and finally stopped on the street by city detectives, who told me that it would be at the risk of my life to take a step nearer the meeting place. I demanded protection, but it was not forthcoming. I was told to leave.

In the meantime, Secretary Conboy arriving upon the scene, the two of us started to the Mayor's office to protest, when suddenly, in broad daylight, at a main street corner in the heart of the city, a mob of about forty men rushed us. Shouldering me away from Mr. Conboy, they stuck guns against my ribs and took me to the depot. While there they made a cowardly attempt to force me to sign a Back-To-Work card, which meant to write myself down a scab. Later I was put aboard an eastbound train. Several of the mob accompanied me to Conemaugh, a few miles out. The same night this "Citizens' Committee," with several hundred more, surrounded the organizers in their hotel and gave them twenty-four hours time to leave town. The city authorities refused to stir to defend them, and the following day organizers T. J. Conboy, Frank Hall, Frank Butterworth, and Frank Kurowsky were compelled to go. Domenick Gelotte, a local organizer of the miners, refused to depart and was promptly arrested. Up to this time the strike had been perfectly peaceful. The shut-down was so thorough that not even a picket line was necessary.

The mob perpetrating these outrages (duly praised by the newspapers as examples of 100 per cent. Americanism) was led by W. R. Lunk, secretary of the Y. M. C. A., and H. L. Tredennick, president of the chamber of commerce. This pair freely stated that the strike could never be broken by peaceful means, and that they were prepared to apply the necessary violence, which they did. Of course, they were never arrested. Had they been workers and engaged in a similar escapade against business men, they would have been lucky to get off with twenty years imprisonment apiece.

4.7 Professional Strikebreakers Solicit Business, 1917–20. Excerpts from evidence gathered during the investigation by the U.S. Senate's Subcommittee of the Committee on Education and Labor, *Hearings, Violations of Free Speech and Assembly and Interference with Rights of Labor.* 74th Cong., 2d Sess., 1936, pp. 70, 71. Reprinted in Leon Litwack, *The American Labor Movement* (Englewood Cliffs, N.J.: Prentice Hall, 1962), pp. 94–95.

O'NEIL SECRET SERVICE
Detroit, Mich., January 15, 1917.

DEAR SIR: We have just passed through a year of great prosperity. What will this year bring? The present outlook is for a year more prosperous than its predecessor, but this is an ominous outlook for a year full of strife and struggles between capital and labor.

In the last year labor organizations made more headway in organizing in the city of Detroit than had been done in any ten previous years; and a grand final effort will be made to swing many more workers into the ranks of labor unions to prepare for a general strike which is contemplated for May 1917.

Are you, a representative manufacturer of the city of Detroit, going to allow your shop to be organized? You owe it to your concern and the other manufacturers of this city to do your part in suppressing the proposed unionization of your employees. Possibly you do not fully realize, being in an open-shop town, just what union domination means. If not, ask some manufacturer of Chicago or San Francisco where for a number of years the manufacturers were dominated by the unions and their hirelings.

If you act now, you can do your part in helping to combat this proposed strike and reduce the efforts of the labor agitators to a minimum of results. Preparedness against labor agitators is an absolute business necessity at this time. Allow us to call upon you and tell you how we can assist you in keeping your plant free from agitators.

Thanking you for an interview, we remain,

Yours for service,

E. I. McCOLLISTER,

General Manager.

FOSTER SERVICE,

New York, July 30, 1920.

Mr._____,

_____Co., New York City.

Dear Sir: Your letter of July 28 is received. With reference to your inquiry about my experience and what I am prepared to do in case of disturbance, etc.:

First. I will say that if we are employed before any union or organization is formed by the employees, there will be no strike and no disturbance. This does not say that there will be no unions formed, but it does say that we will control the activities of the union and direct its policies, provided we are allowed a free hand by our clients.

Second. If a union is already formed and no strike is on or expected to be declared within thirty to sixty days, although we are not in the same position as we would be in the above case, we could—and I believe with success—carry on an intrigue which would result in factions, disagreement, resignations of officers, and general decrease in the membership; and if a strike were called, we would be in a position to furnish information, etc., of contemplated assaults.

If a strike is already on, I am not so sure of being of much material assistance, because the bars are up against all newcomers and everyone looks upon you with an eye of suspicion. Of course, it is possible that we might be of some material assistance, but the percentage is too high against us to be encouraging to our clients. Of course, if we were just looking for your money and nothing else, we would not be so particular in setting forth our limits.

Every one of our investigators is of high caliber and is made to feel that he is part of the business and permanently in our employ as long as he is faithful in the performance of his duty. Their success means our success and that of our clients.

As to experience, I will say I have rubbed elbows with all classes of society, do not "carry a chip on my shoulder," and believe in the motto that "molasses instead of vinegar" in many cases brings results. This does not necessarily say that we would dodge danger or desert our post in time of danger. Far from it. An experience of seventeen years in my present field has taught me that you must give the other fellow credit for being as clever as yourself, if you want to be a success.

A conference with me will cost you nothing, if you are in the city, and you can then judge for yourself whether it is desirable to retain us.
Yours truly,
ROBERT J. FOSTER.

4.8   Anti-Immigrant Sentiment, 1919. Leaflet, "Wake Up Americans" from William Z. Foster, *The Great Steel Strike*, p. 199.

WAKE UP AMERICANS! !

ITALIAN LABORERS, organized under the American Federation of Labor are going to strike Monday and are threatening workmen who want to continue working.

These foreigners have been told by labor agitators that if they would join the union they would get Americans' jobs.

They are being encouraged by ITALIAN MER-CHANTS, who are in sympathy with them.

ARE YOU GOING TO SLEEP AND LET MOB RULE THREATEN THE PEACE OF OUR TOWN?

4.9   Chicago Federation of Labor Pleads for Racial Calm, 1919. "Proclamation Concerning the Race Riots by the Chicago Federation of Labor," *The New Majority*, August 4, 1919, p. 1.

PROCLAMATION
Concerning the Race Riots by the Chicago Federation of Labor

The profiteering meat packers of Chicago are responsible for the race riots that have disgraced this city. It is the outcome of their deliberate attempt to disrupt the union labor movement in the stockyards. . . . These same meat packers can solve the problem if they will put a stop to the trouble, but it can be done only in one way. . . . The packers know that way. They have been told what it is and they are doing nothing about it.

Ever since organized labor first started to unite the stockyards employes, the packers have fought with every weapon at their command these efforts of workers. Discriminating against union men, they have fired them and hired nonunion men in their places. In recent years their principal recruiting points for nonunion workers have been in the south, and nonunion colored workers have been brought here in great numbers just as they are being brought here now by the railroads—or were up to the outbreak of the race riots. . . .

Organized labor has no quarrel with the colored worker. Workers, white and black, are fighting the same battle. . . .

4.10 Lampooning the Logic of the Open Shop, 1920. Finley Peter Dunne's character, "Mr. Dooley," comments on the Open Shop, Literary Digest, LXVII (November 27, 1920), p. 19. Quoted in Litwack, *The American Labor Movement*, p. 77.

"What's all this that's in the papers about the open shop?" asked Mr. Hennessey.

"Why, don't ye know?" said Mr. Dooley. "Really, I'm surprized at yer ignorance, Hinnissey. What is th' open shop? Sure, 'tis where they kape the doors open to accommodate th' constant stream av' min comin' in t' take jobs cheaper than th' min what has th' jobs. 'Tis like this, Hinnissey: Suppose wan av these freeborn citizens is workin' in an open shop f'r th' princely wage av wan large iron dollar a day av tin hour. Along comes anither son-av-gun and he sez t' th' boss, 'Oi think Oi could handle th' job nicely f'r ninety cints. 'Sure,' sez th' boss, and th' wan dollar man gets out into th' crool woruld t' exercise hiz inalienable roights as a freeborn American citizen an' scab on some other poor devil. An' so it goes on, Hinnissey. An' who gits th' benefit? Thrue, it saves th' boss money, but he don't care no more f'r money thin he does f'r his right eye. It's all princi-ple wid him. He hates t' see men robbed av their indipindence. They must have their indipindence, regardless av anything else."

"But," said Mr. Hennessey, "those open-shop min ye menshun say they are f'r unions if properly conducted."

"Shure," said Mr. Dooley, "if properly conducted. An' there we are: an' how would they have them conducted? No strikes, no rules, no contracts, no scales, hardly iny wages, an' dam' few mimbers."

WORKERS AND UNIONS IN THE 1920S

The 1920s saw large employers inaugurate the era of welfare capitalism, in which they attempted to gain their workers' loyalty through company-furnished benefits. Welfare capitalism sought to promote the kind of identi-fication with the company fostered by the report of the Bethlehem Steel Company on employee policies as reproduced in Document 4.11. Is it pos-sible to ascertain from the company's report what proportion of its hourly employees actually benefited from its welfare policies? Do the benefits, as specified in the report, appear to apply equally to all hourly-rated employees? Although the 1920s ushered in a period of economic advancement for a large cross section of workers, wage earners did not share in jazz-age prosperity to the same extent as their employers or the middle class did. Document 4.12 illustrates the differing income and spending patterns among different classes of workers and professionals at the end of the 1920s. Where are these differences most pronounced and what do they indicate about differences in everyday life experiences? Working-class families increasingly sent women into the workplace in the 1920s in order for the family to buy what it considered necessary to sustain its desired standard of living. In their intensive study of Middletown (Muncie, Indiana) workers in the 1920s, sociologists Robert and Helen Lynd uncovered some of the reasons why working-class women went out to work for wages (Document 4.13). Meanwhile, as unions fell increasingly on the defensive in the 1920s, those labor reformers who hoped to revive their militancy became frustrated. In Document 4.14, union reformer John Brophy describes what happened in 1926 when he decided to challenge the reelection of the autocratic incumbent president of the United Mine Workers, John L. Lewis. Can one reconcile the character of Lewis as depicted by Brophy with his later role as the leader of the forces trying to reform the AFL's craft structure in the 1930s?

4.11   Welfare Capitalism in the 1920s. "Ten Years Progress in Human Relations," Bethlehem Steel Company, Bethlehem, PA, 1928. Reprinted with the permission of the Hagley Museum and Library.

The Human Side of Our Business

EMPLOYEES AT THREE of the Bethlehem plants joined with the management ten years ago in laying the foundation of a new kind of structure in American industry. Employees in other plants have since built wisely and firmly upon this foundation. The cooperative efforts of all have brought the undertaking to a success which fully justifies the faith of its pioneers.

This structure is built not of steel and brick and mortar. Its cornerstone is men. Its pillars and walls are the human relations that exist today between Bethlehem and its employees, that join together the activities and agencies which make this a business of men, not merely of machines.

It was ten years ago that the Bethlehem Plan of Employee Representation was inaugurated in Bethlehem's plants. In that period the principles adopted in the formulation of this Plan have grown into a broad, enlightened policy covering all the human relations properly involved in an industrial company of more than 70,000 employees.

The same ten years have witnessed significant changes generally in the attitude of employers and employees toward each other and toward their mutual responsibility for the success of their joint efforts. It has come to be realized on the part of the management that industry depends for its success largely upon human beings. This applies not only to the quality and quantity of production: it is true also of the market for industry's products which requires the continuing purchasing power of those who work for wages. On the part of the employees this new attitude is reflected in a more intimate knowledge of their company and its objectives, in a better understanding of their part in production and distribution and in a willingness to play fair with employers who treat them fairly and justly as friends and partners as well as fellow workers.

. . . It is fitting at this time to review the progress which has been made in this eventful decade and to pay a deserving tribute to the men whose cooperation has achieved such notable success.

Faith in Each Other
Keynote of Employee Representation

IN THE TEN years since the Bethlehem Plan of Employee Representation began to operate, 1,601 employees have served as elected spokesmen of their fellow employees in meetings with management representatives to discuss and decide matters of common interest. To a very large degree these men together with the management have been responsible for the development and successful conduct of all those activities and agencies which are conveniently grouped as Bethlehem's human relations.

It is true, of course, that means of acquiring a stock ownership in the company and aid buying a home have little directly to do with the peaceful adjustment of wage schedules and working conditions. Nevertheless, the fact is that employee representation is responsible for both. You cannot have either without a solid basis of understanding between management and employees. Employee representation in Bethlehem plants and yards has been carried on since its beginning in such a fine spirit of good faith, good will and fair play on the part of both officials and employees that sincerity has become the keynote of every phase of their relationship.

Consequently, out of what was frankly regarded ten years ago as an experiment in dealing with employees on a democratic basis in matters affecting their wages and working conditions there has developed a whole program of mutually beneficial activities jointly operated for the most part and steadily gaining in interest. The enthusiastic support with which these other activities have been carried on constitutes an eloquent tribute to the men who have made employee representation a practical working success. . . .

The widespread interest of employees in the Plan could not better be demonstrated than by their participation in the annual elections for representatives. Each year more than 800 men are elected representatives by secret ballot among all the employees generally one representative for each 200 employees. Ten years ago a little less than 60 percent of the employees participated in the first elections. This percentage, however, has progressively increased. Since 1924 more than 90 per cent of the employees have cast ballots annually for representatives. This is a far higher percentage of active voters than ordinarily participates in national, state and city elections.

Usually about half of those elected for a given year have had previous experience as employee representatives. It is interesting to note, too, that there are now serving for this year 18 men who have been elected every year and have served continuously since the Plan was established at their respective plants.

In terms of subjects and cases taken up and settled under this Plan in the ten years since its inauguration, the record is one of unusual interest. In all 5183 major cases have been considered, not to mention the thousands of cases informally settled from day to day between the foreman and the representative of which no mention is made here. More than 8400 were settled in favor of the employees. Of the remainder, 800 were settled in the company's favor, 680 were compromised and 322 were withdrawn by the employees. . . .

Monthly meetings are held by the plant managers with the employees' representatives in their respective plants, but a most far-reaching development of the Plan is the annual conference in which the old and the new representatives meet with the President and other executive officers of the company to review the progress of the business and to consider pending questions and the future outlook of the company and its employees.

There is no question which cannot be raised and discussed at these conferences and the management is pledged to state frankly its position and to cooperate in so far as conditions will permit in carrying out constructive suggestions.

A Steady Job at Fair Wages

FAR MORE IMPORTANT than anything else in the relations between employers and employees are two essential needs which must he recognized as fundamental-a steady job and good wages. Rates of pay mean nothing without an opportunity to work, nor is seasonal or periodical employment at any wage, however high, satisfactory to meet every-day needs. Food, clothing, shelter and other requirements of a man and his family know no seasonal limits. Uninterrupted employment at fair wages enables men to plan their current expenses against a definite income and to provide in advance for savings and investment.

Employment Policy

This is the policy of Bethlehem Steel Corporation:

First, to provide in so far as it is possible steady jobs for its employees, and,

Second, to enable its employees to earn wages as high as can be paid consistent with sound management, safe-guarding the investment in the company and the general economic conditions of the country.

Real progress has been made in both directions in the last ten years. Regularity of jobs has been sought by as even an allocation of work as possible among different plants and by a fair division of work in those plants.

Each plant has a carefully administered employment department. Its function is not only to secure men as they are needed but, even more important, from the standpoint of stability of the working force, to supervise the employment of men generally so that they may fit in where they are best suited for the work. In other words, dissatisfied or misplaced workers in one job are frequently enabled to secure work in some other department and thus continue as Bethlehem employees. For the most part new men are obtained from local applicants in the community in which the plant is located. Bethlehem has practically ceased getting men recruited and sent in from distant points.

Lower Labor Turnover

This policy has resulted in recent years in a marked decrease in what is known as "labor turnover" which has always meant a direct loss to industry. Last year the turnover was only 55% as against 151% ten years ago. Such a remarkable improvement in employment stability is an index of the effectiveness of the company's labor and employment policy; it also illustrates how the elimination of a wasteful practice through modern management methods works to the mutual advantage of employer and employee.

Progress Toward Stability

Another measure of stability of employment is the extent to which the payroll fluctuates above or below the average payroll for the year. Bethlehem has made substantial progress in this respect. . . . In 1921 the payroll fluctuated all the way from 54% above the average to 33% below it but since then there has been a yearly leveling out of working time. During the last two years the high and low point of employment varied only 12% from the average.

This improvement toward which forward-looking management has been devoting a great deal of attention has tended to eliminate one of the greatest evils of industrial activity, that is, unemployment and uncertainty of jobs. The resulting regularity of work benefits not only the employee and the company but also the community at large.

High Earnings Encouraged

Not only have average hourly earnings increased due partly to the shortened working day, but average total earnings have also increased in recent years.

How employees have profited through improved manufacturing methods and greater efficiency is indicated by the increase in average earnings of employees while labor costs per ton of ingots produced has been reduced. An important factor in this connection is that practically one-half of all employees of Bethlehem Steel Corporation are on some form of incentive payment such as bonus, piece work, tonnage or premium where they are paid for what they produce rather than for time served.

Safety At Work

NEXT TO A steady job at fair wages and a voice in determining the regulations under which they shall work, employees have the right to expect industry to make every reasonable provision for their physical well-being while they are at work. That means good safe physical working conditions; practical safeguards for their lives and health and expert as well as kindly medical and surgical attention in the event of injury. . . .

In Bethlehem plants these are essentially cooperative activities. Better understanding of the economical as well as the human waste due to accidents has brought about a steady reduction in this loss. Both management and employees have shown their ability and willingness to accomplish substantial results in this field of joint responsibility. Recently these efforts have been stimulated by the gold award accident prevention contest of 1928.

In this contest three prizes of $1,000, $500 and $250 in gold are awarded each quarter to the three groups of employees which make the greatest reduction in lost time due to accidents. For purposes of the contest all the employees are divided into 11 groups.

Marked improvement in accident prevention was effected by the employees during the first quarter of the year. The Corporation as a whole improved its best previous record by 17.8%. The steel plants alone bettered their safety record by 44%. . . .

Medical Care

It is recognized of course that despite all precautions mechanical and human, accidents may occur. Bethlehem provides a highly efficient surgical and medical staff for the treatment of injured employees without cost to them and for the physical examination of applicants for employment. Not only scientific skill and experience are required of these physicians but also sympathetic and kindly treatment and the men are thereby encouraged to report to the doctor in every minor accident in order to avoid serious after-effects.

Lasting Benefits to Employees and Their Families

Bethlehem's interest in its employees extends beyond those everyday needs which relate particularly to the job itself. The Company's policy of human relations aims to be of lasting benefit to the employees and their families as well as to the Company. That does not mean a meddlesome interference with one's private affairs. On the contrary, Bethlehem seeks to put at a man's own disposal such opportunities as will enable him by his own efforts to become a substantial self-sustaining member of the community not only during the active years of his life but also through his declining years.

No Bethlehem employee need want for the means to attain such a position. Moreover the response on the part of the employees to these opportunities is steadily increasing. Briefly, the Bethlehem policy is this:

1. To assist employees to practice a wholesome thrift by saving part of their earnings.

2. To help them acquire a home of their own in the community in which they live and work.

3. To enable them to provide against the needs of old age while they are still young enough to store up a reserve for that purpose.

4. To aid them to acquire an interest in the business through stock ownership and thereby share in the profits of their own making.

The success which has attended this policy is another indication of the practical results of the operation of the Plan of Employee Representation. It takes mutual confidence on the part of management and employees to enable them to work out satisfactorily such a system as Bethlehem now provides for savings and stock ownership, hone aid, relief and pensions. Employee Representation laid the foundation ten years ago for the successful administration of these features of Bethlehem's employee relations.

Home Ownership Aid

Bethlehem encourages its employees to purchase homes within their means. At some of the plants large numbers of houses have been built and offered for sale for what they cost to build. Near other plants where it has not been practical to build homes, employees have been aided in financing homes which they want to build or buy. Ordinarily the employee pays down 10 per cent cash and Bethlehem cooperates with the local bank or trust company in carrying a second mortgage paid off monthly by the employee as rent. The first mortgage is usually taken by a local trust company.

In the five years since this practice was adopted the company has built 370 new and separate houses for sale at cost to employees at an average price of $4,500. These houses contain from four to eight rooms, are constructed in many different styles and are surrounded by yards, pavements and concrete roads. The company has assisted 4,537 employees to build or buy homes valued at $18,380,000. No data is available to show the number of employees who own their own homes but of the employee representatives who represent a cross section of the whole body of employees nearly half are home owners.

Pension Plan

Next to the ownership of a home the family and community interests are best served by provision against dependent old age. Bethlehem's Pension Plan gives every member of the organization some protection in this respect. The Plan does not contemplate that the pension will in itself provide a living wage but that combined with the savings of a retired employee it will help him to live more comfortably. The Pension Plan therefore is directly related to the company's policy of encouraging its employees and assisting them to practice thrift.

Prior to January 1, 1928 various retirement systems were in operation in the Bethlehem plants. Under the Pension Plan now in effect, however, uniform pension provisions apply to the whole organization. An employee may be pensioned at the age of 65 after 25 years of service.

Since the Plan became effective 1486 employees have been pensioned, $1,970,532 has been paid out to retired employees and 1040 employees are now on the pension rolls.

Relief Plan

Means are also provided to relieve the financial needs of employees who become physically disabled by sickness or by accidents for which they do not receive compensation under the workmen's compensation laws and likewise for the relief of widows and dependents of employees in the event of death. This is accomplished through the Relief Plan. Employees are grouped in three classes under this Plan according to their annual earnings, monthly contributions being $1.00, $1.50 and $9.00. Death benefits are paid in amounts of $500, $1,000 and $1,500, and disability benefits in amounts of $10.00, $11.00 and $19.00 weekly according to the class of participation. The period for which disability benefits are paid depends upon the employee's years of service and varies from 13 weeks for two years service or less to 208 weeks for twenty years service or more. Since the plan was adopted on June 1, 1926, $1,604,797.49 has been paid to employees and their dependents. The entire cost of organization and administration is assumed by the Company, so that all employee contributions are available for distribution in benefits.

4.12   Consumption Trends, ca. 1931. *Recent Social Trends in the United States: Report of the President's Research Committee on Social Trends, Vol. II* (New York: McGraw-Hill, 1933), pp. 895–96.

Estimates of annual expenditures for various income & social levels in the San Francisco Bay region, November 1931:

Item	Wage earner, family of five	Clerk, family of five	Professional, family of four
Total	$1,631.81	$2,175.19	$6,085.36
Food	507.84	677.64	891.12
Clothing	225.87	339.97	672.19
Husband	61.22	95.32	194.64
Wife	64.37	111.36	320.73
Boy, 11 years	45.13	54.21	79.42
Girl, 5 years	29.43	43.19	77.40
Boy, 2 years	25.72	35.89	—
Rent	336.00	396.00	1,380.94
House operation	199.30	262.69	923.84
Fuel, light, heat	80.42	90.86	192.00
Replacement, furniture	52.68	79.21	229.15
Other items	66.20	92.62	502.69
Miscellaneous	362.80	498.89	2,217.27

Fuel percentages are somewhat low in comparison with most other sections of the country.

The details of the miscellaneous expenditures for the three levels are:

Item	Wage earner, family of five	Clerk, family of five	Clerk, family of four
Savings	—	—	$360.00
Life insurance	$65.00	$130.00	260.00
Medical and dental care	75.00	75.00	275.00
Church and charity	18.00	18.00	110.00
Gifts	22.50	22.50	112.50
Organization dues	—	—	36.00
Entertaining guests at home	22.52	22.60	116.60
Theatre and concerts	6.00	12.00	34.00
Movies	22.56	22.56	11.28
Other commercial amusements	10.00	10.00	20.00
Radio upkeep	6.00	7.00	8.00
Excursions	15.00	—	—
Vacation	—	52.38	125.00
Automobile	—	—	416.27
Carfare	45.00	60.00	40.00
School supplies	5.00	5.00	5.00
Daily paper	9.00	9.00	13.80
Periodicals and books	2.00	4.00	22.00
Music lessons	—	—	96.00
Tobacco	13.00	18.00	54.00
Haircut and shaving	23.68	27.46	36.12
Cosmetics	2.54	3.39	5.70
Incidentals	—	—	60.00
Total	362.80	498.89	2,217.27

4.13   Why Married Women Work for Wages, ca. 1928. Excerpts from Robert S. and Helen M. Lynd, *Middletown; A Study in American Culture* (New York: Harcourt Brace, 1956 [orig. 1929]), pp. 25–30.

These married women workers, according to the Census distribution, go largely into working class occupations. Only one of forty business class women interviewed had worked for money during the previous five years (1920-24), and she in work of a semi-artistic nature. Of the fifty-five wives out of a sample of 124 working class families who had worked at some time during the previous five years (1920-24), twenty-four pointed to their husbands' unemployment as a major reason for their working, six to money needed for their children's education, five to debt, four spoke of "always needing extra money," or "It takes the work of two to keep a family nowadays," three of needing to help out with "so many children"; the other answers were scattered: "Just decided I'd like to try factory work. I was tired of housekeeping and had a baby old enough [five months] to be left"; "I needed clothes"; "I wanted spending money of my own"; "Other women could and I felt like I ought to"; and "The mister was sick and I had to."

The cases of a few representative women will make more specific the complex of factors involved in the wife's working:

In one family, characteristic of a large number of those in which the mother works, a woman of forty-five, mother of four children aged eighteen, sixteen, fifteen, and twelve, had worked fifteen months during the previous five years at two different factories. At the first she worked ten hours a day for $15.15 a week, stopping work because of a layoff; at the second nine and a half hours a day for approximately the same wages, stopping because her health "gave out." She went into factory work because "We always seemed to have a doctor's bill around. The mister had an operation and I wanted to help pay that bill. Then he got back to work and was laid off again. He was out of work nine months last year. The children needed clothes and I had to do it." But although the mother did what she could at home after her day at the factory and washed and ironed on Sundays, the oldest daughter had to leave high school and give up going to the Girl Reserves to look after the children. "I made a big mistake in leaving them. The youngest got to running away from home with other girls. Then was the time I should have been home with her."

Another type of situation, less frequent than the above, appears in a family of five—a woman of forty-six, her husband of forty-nine, a farmer prior to 1920 and now employed fairly steadily at semi-skilled machine shop work, and their three boys of nineteen, thirteen, and ten. The oldest boy is in the small local college and the mother works continuously at factory work in order that all three boys may go through high school and college, "so that they can get along easier than their father." In a recent stretch of family unemployment the boy borrowed $125 to keep on at his schooling, both parents going on his note. The family manages by all buckling to the common job: husband and boys have taken over much of the housework; the boy of ten has dinner ready when the family gets home at noon.

In some more prosperous families securing a higher standard of living as well as education for her children leads the mother to work. One mother of two high school boys, a woman of forty-two, the wife of a pipe-fitter, goes outside her home to do cleaning in one of the city's public institutions six days a week. "I began to work during the war," she said, "when every one else did; we had to meet payments on our house and everything else was getting so high. The mister objected at first, but now he don't mind. I'd rather keep on working so my boys can play football and basketball and have spending money their father can't give them. We've built our own home, a nice brown and white bungalow, by a building and loan like every one else does. We have it almost all paid off and it's worth about $6,000. No, I don't lose out with my neighbors because I work; some of them have jobs and those who don't envy us who do. I have felt better since I worked than ever before in my life. I get up at five-thirty. My husband takes his dinner and the boys buy theirs uptown and I cook supper. We have an electric washing machine, electric iron, and vacuum sweeper. I don't even have to ask my husband any more because I buy these things with my own money. I bought an icebox last year—a big one that holds 125 pounds; most of the time I don't fill it, but we have our folks visit us from back East and then I do. We own a $1,200 Studebaker with a nice California top, semi-enclosed. Last summer we all spent our vacation going back to Pennsylvania—taking in Niagara Falls on the way. The two boys want to go to college, and I want them to. I graduated from high school myself, but I feel if I can't give my boys a little more all my work will have been useless."

This increasing employment of married women, which at the last Census involved nearly a thousand wives from the upwards of nine thousand families then in Middletown, must be viewed as a process of readjustment jammed in among the other changes occurring in the home and other sectors of Middletown life. Fifty-six per cent of the 124 working class wives interviewed had not worked for money during the five years 1920-24, while 75 per cent of 102 of their mothers on whom data was secured had not worked for money during their entire married lives. These figures undoubtedly dwarf the extent of the shift, as the interviews took place in most cases during the day and therefore included few women continuously employed away from home at the time. Of the twenty-five mothers of the 1890 period who worked for pay, all but one worked either at home, e.g., taking in washing, or at work such as sewing and cleaning that took them away from home only occasionally, while thirty of the fifty-five present-day wives who had worked had worked in factories or other places necessitating absence from home all day and every day. These women, two-thirds of them reared in a farm or village environment in which family life centered about the wife and mother in the home, must now attempt to integrate with these early habits the diverse business of being a wife and mother in a city culture where from time to time their best energies are expended for eight and a half to ten hours a day in extraneous work away from home.

Thus, from one point of view the section of Middletown's population that gets its living by working for money is becoming larger; to a greater extent than thirty-five years ago women share this activity with men.

4.14 A Losing Battle for Democracy in the United Mine Workers, 1926. Excerpt from John Brophy, *A Miner's Life* (Madison & Milwaukee: University of Wisconsin Press, 1964), pp. 212–18. Reprinted by permission of the University of Wisconsin Press.

By the beginning of 1926, there was little room for argument that [John L. Lewis's] policy . . . had been a disastrous failure. . . .

In order to hold his power against the discontent of the miners, Lewis became increasingly ruthless in crushing union democracy. "Provisionalism" became the rule. Lewis had the power to impose a "provisional" government on any district, if it got into financial trouble, or if its leadership was troublesome to him. Provisional administrations became permanent, so that Lewis could use them to dominate the international board and perpetuate himself in power. Fortunately, District 2 was one of the best managed and most solvent in the union, so he could not use that particular weapon against me.

Slowly but inexorably, I was driven to the conclusion that Lewis's power had to be challenged by a candidate for the presidency of the UMW who would offer a constructive program for rebuilding the union. . . .

In August, 1926, I announced my candidacy, pledging myself to organization of the unorganized fields, advocacy of nationalization of the mines, and support for a labor party. Local unions sent in enough nominations to ensure that my fellow candidates and I would appear on the ballot. I then issued an open letter to the membership, printed in a four-page leaflet under the caption, *Save the Union*. I pointed out that entire districts—West Virginia, Maryland, Tennessee, Alabama, Colorado—had been destroyed, and others were crumbling away because of the do-nothing policy of the international administration. Local and district strikes, effective twenty years before, were no longer effective, because of the increasing prevalence of large corporations controlling many mines in many districts. The cause of the union's decline was the shortsighted policy of allowing operators to sign up for part of their holdings. Our desertion of the non-union fields in 1922 had cost us 100,000 members, and more were being lost every year. The policy of trying only to hold onto what we already had meant that we would soon be unable to hold onto anything. Aggressive and active field organizers, armed with a hopeful and constructive program, could still bring the non-union fields into the union fold. Nothing could be done by a gang of political gumshoers, miscalled organizers, who sat around hotel lobbies waiting for something to happen.

I rejected flatly all proposals for wage reductions—this would change nothing in the industry, except to drive the miners' standard of living to even more intolerable levels. Wage cuts were taking place everywhere, however, and could not be stopped by futile proclamations about "no backward step." If we failed to push forward, we must inevitably fall back. Nationalization would give us a concrete and practical alternative to the anarchy and futility of private operation. It would be a threat we could use to get better government controls over wasteful practices, even before we could win our full program. A labor party was necessary to cut the union loose from dependence on reactionary politicians like Hoover and Coolidge, and to get justice for labor in the courts and legislatures.

Throughout the campaign, I stressed the necessity of restoring democracy to the union by the reinstatement of Alex Howat (who had been expelled by Lewis on flimsy charges), by the curbing of provisionalism, and by the conduct of honest elections. I disavowed any personal grudges, but asked only that there be a full and fair discussion of the real problems of the union.

I need hardly say that I got nothing of the sort out of Lewis. He made no effort to discuss my platform, or even to refute my charges as to his failure. I was charged with dualism, disruption, trafficking with outsiders of various kinds, from Communists to capitalists, and lots more. My effort to get the administration and membership to face the facts of the decline in union strength was pictured as undermining the union and an attempt to destroy morale. Lewis and company radiated optimism, while I was denounced as a "prophet of doom and gloom," if I may borrow that phrase from a later, but similar, situation.

I had two or three hundred dollars to spend on printing and postage, most of which went to mail out copies of my open letter. My campaign committee consisted, for the most part, of Powers Hapgood, Anita, and me, sitting around a table sending out the open letter. Copies were sent to all local unions, but since I did not know anybody in most of them, I had to send the material to the local secretaries, many of whom were Lewis men and who no doubt loyally consigned my letters to the wastebasket. . . .

Lewis outdid himself in a speech at the AFL convention in October, in which he charged that my campaign was part of a "Bolshevik plot" to take over American labor, and pictured himself as Horatius at the bridge, valiantly fighting off alien hordes. I denounced this display as a smokescreen, raised to hide Lewis's unwillingness to debate issues. Lewis's charge got more publicity than my answer; a sensational lie is better "news" than anything so humdrum as truth.

In December, the tellers in the international office announced that Lewis had won, by a vote of about 170,000 to 60,000. Nobody was surprised by the outcome, but I was a little surprised that they had admitted to that large a vote for me.

The constitution provided that the tellers' report be published, with figures for each local union. At the international convention in February,

1927, I demanded that this be done, but it was May before I received the accounting. Reading the report, I could see the reason for the delay: it would take time to cook the figures that thoroughly. . . .

I was able to check the actual vote sent in to the national office from five locals in District 5 and compare it with the national report. The actual vote was: Lewis, 487, Brophy, 685. The reported vote was: Lewis, 1,478; Brophy, 158. Thus in only five locals, Lewis was given 986 stolen votes and I was robbed of 477. I secured affidavits from officers of these locals, but evidence had no effect on the international board, which rubber-stamped the report of Lewis's tellers.

Nobody can ever prove who won the election of 1926, because the evidence can never be secured. Those reports that were not falsified in the locals were taken care of by agents of the international office. But the vote-stealing is so obvious and flagrant in the official report itself that the inference that Lewis would not have won without stealing votes is a defensible one.

I took the position that my running mates and I had been elected, and sent a letter to the international board, pointing out the prima facie evidence of fraud in the report and demanding an impartial investigation. The board refused to act; for them the election was over. . . .

My protest got publicity in some of the radical and labor papers not under Lewis's spell, such as the *Illinois Miner* and some members of Federated Press. A few newspapers in coal towns printed something about the matter, but it was no time for "rocking the boat." Lewis had built up a reputation as a "conservative labor statesman," and, if any-thing, the general press gave him the benefit of the doubt.

All I could do was to try to keep alive the "Save the Union" program, even though I now held no official post in the union, and was soon to lose even my membership, as Lewis moved to eliminate me altogether.

Immigrants from Mexico

The number of Mexican workers who crossed the border into the United States in search of employment began to grow in the years around World War I. Mexicans were often misled when they were promised good work and decent wages by labor contractors (*padrones*), a phenomenon described in the *canción* (song) reproduced in Document 4.15. Although they encountered significant discrimination, Mexican workers took advantage of the opportunities they found in America, as the excerpt of an interview with migrant Pedro Villamil suggests (Document 4.16). Mexicans also launched organizing initiatives of their own. In 1928, Mexicans organized a strike in the California cantaloupe fields, putting forward the demands detailed in

Document 4.17. Mexicans also launched an unsuccessful effort to unite Mexican workers in the United States under the rubric of one umbrella organization, the manifesto of which is published in Document 4.18. In most cases Mexican laborers were unable to fend off aggressive efforts by employers to break their organizations through threats of deportation (see Document 4.19) or even violence. What do these documents suggest about what Mexican laborers sought and what they found in the United States?

4.15 "Los Engachados," [The Hooked Ones], ca. 1920s. Manuel Gamio, *Mexican Immigration to the United States: A Study of Human Migration and Adjustment* (Chicago: University of Chicago Press, 1930), pp. 84–86.

The Immigrants
(Los Enganchados—"The Hooked Ones")

On the 28th day of February,
That important day
When we left El Paso,
They took us out as contract labor.

When we left El Paso
At two in the morning,
I asked the boss contractor
If we were going to Louisiana.

We arrived at Laguna
Without any hope.
I asked the boss
If we were going to Oklahoma.

Along the line of the Katy
There goes a very fast train.
It runs a hundred miles and hour
And then they don't give it all the steam.

And he who doesn't want to believe it,
Just let him get on board.
Just let him get on board at night;
He will see where he gets to.

We arrived on the first day
And on the second began to work.
With our picks in our hands
We set out tramping.

Some unloaded rails
And others unloaded ties,
And others of my companions
Threw out thousands of curses.

Those who knew the work
Went repairing the jack
With sledge hammers and shovels,
Throwing earth up the track.

Eight crowbars lined up,
We followed disgusted;
To shouts and signs
We remained indifferent.

Said Don José Maria
With his hell's mouth,
"It would be better to be in Kansas
Where the government would maintain us."

Said Jesus, "El Coyote,"
As if he wanted to weep,
"It would be better to be in Juarez
Even if we were without work."

These words were composed
By a poor Mexican
To spread the word about
The American system.

Chicago, Ill.

4.16 Interview with Mexican immigrant Pedro Villamil, native of Durango, Mexico, in Manuel Gamio, *The Mexican Immigrant* (New York: Arno Press and *The New York Times,* 1969 [orig. 1931]), pp. 69–71. Reprinted with permission by the University of Chicago Press.

I came to the United States for the first time in 1918 together with my brother Guadalupe. We didn't have any trouble in crossing the border having gone under contract to go and work on the tracks in the state of Nebraska. We were there about eight months working in several railroad camps until we were able to save some money and then we went to Kansas City.

We left Durango because work was very scarce and we were told one could get good money in the United States and there was work for whoever wanted it.

In Kansas City, I took charge of a pool room and didn't do anything else but watch the table and collect for them. My brother took charge of caring for a hotel. There I began a love affair with a very pretty American girl and lived with her a long time, about two years. At the end of that time my brother and I decided to take a trip to Ciudad Juarez and we sent money to an aunt we had in Durango, the only who was left of our family, so that she could come to be with us.

We joined our aunt here in Ciudad Juarez and with a little money which she brought and another little bit we had we bought this little house which we have here. Although it isn't worth much, it is ours.

We live here in this city of Juarez for more than six months, but we worked in El Paso, Texas, my brother, my aunt and I. My aunt worked as a maid in a hotel, my brother and I in a foundry as laborers.

I fell in love here in Ciudad Juarez with a girl to whom I became engaged, for she likes me a lot. After the six months which I have told you we spent here, we went back north, working at different things, sometimes on the railroad, other times in the beet fields, and we even go almost to the Canadian border. We were up there a couple of years and then came back to Ciudad Juarez, staying here two months. I kept on being the sweetheart of the same girls. Later we returned to Kansas City. From there I wrote to my sweetheart and she to me until finally we decided that I should go back to Ciudad Juarez and marry her. . . .

I didn't find the life in the interior of the United States hard. It all depends on one's keeping wide awake, knowing how to work and in saving. One can have a good time there; there are good dances and one can make good money. Only he who is dumb doesn't get along. . . .

I don't feel the change very much in moving from place to place since I come back to this city every two years.

4.17   Mexican Workers' Cantaloupe Strike, 1928. Excerpts from *Mexicans in California: Report of Governor C. C. Young's Fact Finding Committee* (Sacramento: California State Printing Office, 1930), pp. 135–39.

THE STRIKE OF THE MEXICAN CANTALOUPE PICKERS

The following is an exact copy of the statement of wages and working conditions requested by the union and delivered to the principle cantaloupe growers during the first week in May, 1928:

[May 3, 1928]
TO WHOM IT MAY CONCERN:
Hereby, we make to your acknowledgment, that on the 22d day of April, of the year 1928, was formed the board of directors of the Union of United Workers of Imperial Valley, State of California. . . .

In accordance with the bad occasions that we've had in the past years it makes us necessary of a better understanding of our business among the Mexican people residing as strangers in the United States. We want to keep on cooperating with our hand of labor, but we claim a more liberal wages, enough to cover our most urgent necessities of the actual situations, and we hereby propose to you gentlemen the points of our wishes.

During the year we scarcely work 185 days, of which we acquire the sum of $555 in which we couldn't meet our expenses of alimentation, clothing, house rent, medicine, automobile, and other small exigents.

As you understand, with this amount above stated, we live in the most unhonorable and miserable way, in our concept. For instance, you know that the picking season of cantaloupes is at hand, and we make to your acknowledgment that the prices we are asking for are very reasonable according to justice of the companies and we union laborers.

We hereby note the prices in accordance with all the laborers and were approved convenient, and we hereby await the approval of the honorable companies. The fact is that in the past years in cases like the present, they have demonstrated their willing attitude as we've said before in our sacrifices, in complements of our labors, for such reason we wish that the prices we ask for will be approved.

Therefore, we ask your valuable moral and material influence to our petition before the companies. For the above anticipated, this union retires, giving you many thanks for the present.

Yours truly,
(signed) Roman Mireles,
[et al.]

Prices that we wish the companies to pay, starting with the early crop: The least price of cantaloupes is:

Standard crates—$0.15 per crate
Flat crates———$0.17 1/2 per flat

All empty crates must be distributed all over the fields by the companies own account, and the full crates must be hauled by the pickers, at the same time the company or farmers must furnish such as horses, wagons, or trucks, to be at hand, and the packing sheds must be built in the fields.

The companies must furnish picking sacks and enough ice.

In the final picking season, the *least* re-collection must be at least two crates to the acre.

Prices on Honey Dew per crate is 8 cents.

Prices on casaba per crate—Able conditions for the hauling of said crop.

4.18 Mexican Workers Organize, 1928. Excerpts from *Mexicans in California: Report of Governor C. C. Young's Fact Finding Committee,* pp. 124–26.

On January 9, 1928, the Central Committee of the Confederation of Mexican Labor Unions issued a Manifesto setting forth principles of the Confederation and inviting all Mexican societies and unorganized Mexican laborers to attend the first convention of the Confederation. Since this manifesto describes the philosophy, aspirations, and purposes of the Mexican labor movement in California an exact copy of it, published in English by the Central Committee, is reproduced below:

MANIFESTO

From the active Group of the Federation of Mexican Laborer's Union in the United States
Fellow Countrymen:

In view of the difficult situation which confronts approximately a million

Mexican laborers residing in the United States, the active group which directs the work of the Federation of Mexican Laborer's Unions which have just been founded in the city of Los Angeles, has decided to publish this Manifesto in order to make known its fundamental principles and the point of view it has taken toward a successful accomplishment of the work it has initiated.

It is undisputable that the numerous Mexican Colonies in the United States are composed almost in their whole of working men, proletarians that so far have lived in the utmost disorganization, helpless and ignorant of the world wide Social movement, which works entirely within the law for their improvement.

Social unity is indispensable for the prosperity of the laboring classes, promoting their defense, stimulating remunerative salaries and the constant betterment of the proletarian.

This added to the conditions which prevail among Mexican labor that has come into the United States to lend its work and effort, along with the fact that he is a foreigner, which deprives him of the full protection that is given to the natives and in the present circumstances is compelled to work at a minimum wage which is not only harmful to himself, but also to the organized American workman.

All this at the present makes necessary an organization capable of uniting as a whole the Mexican laboring classes in the United States. On the other hand it must be understood that this movement aim is not to agitate. . . . All that is desired is to equalize Mexican labor to American labor and to obtain for them what the Law justly allows them. . . .

For the carrying out of these ideas and to form a general plan of activities, a convention will he held in the city of Los Angeles to which all the Mexican Societies established in the United States no matter what their principles and also the unorganized labor are invited to attend, that they may join this movement for their own welfare conscious that the effort that they put on this work shall transform the present concept of the Mexican laborer in the United States.

And so that it will not be supposed that the movement in question is harmful, the Active Group makes known its fundamental principles. . . .

1. To organize all Mexican workers in the U.S. in Unions according to Sindical principles.

2. To establish a solid pact with the American and the Mexican working men that any difficulty in the future may be solved mutually.

3. To establish likewise solid relations with the organized Labor of Mexico (Confederación Regional Obrera Mexicana) and to try to stop the immigration of unorganized Labor into the U. S. which is harmful to the working men of both Countries.

4. To do away with the exploitation of . . . Mexican victims in the so called employment Agencies, and to get the unions to constitute their own employment department. . . .

5. To constitute provision offices with the exclusive object of illustrating to Mexican laborers who for the first time come to the U.S. as well as to

those who already reside here, all that is referent to working systems, job revenues, contract, forms, interpretations, translations from English to Spanish or vice-versa. . . .

6. To keep Mexican laborers from being exploited in the so called commissary stores that still exist in some regions of the U.S., by substituting in their place cooperative stores. . . .

7. To study and resolve in accord with the Mexican government the best systems of repatriation so that those wishing to go back will form agricultural cooperatives. . . .

8. Negotiate with the Mexican Government so that the immigration of Mexican Labor into the U.S. may be regulated. . . .

4.19 Employers' Respond to Mexican Workers' Demands, 1928. Excerpts from *Mexicans in California: Report of Governor C. C. Young's Fact Finding Committee*, pp. 144–45.

MEXICANS: WORKERS LOOK OUT!

Federal officers of the United States are watching the working conditions in the Imperial Valley.

You know that the Imperial Valley growers have expended thousands of dollars for their cause. They have sent representatives to Washington in order to fight legislation which might prevent you from entering this country. Many of you, who are now in the Imperial Valley, would have to return to your country with little chance of coming back to the United States, were it not for the valley growers and shippers who have spent their time and money in your behalf.

Remember this. If you fail to cooperate, the same men who have given their time and money to get you in this country and to protect you here, the same men will turn against you. They will use their funds and their influence to have you brought back to your country and your chances of seeing the Unites States again will be rather remote. Remember this carefully before cooperating with those who are working solely for their own interests and who enrich themselves at your expense. They have nothing to lose. You lose everything and gain nothing.

ATTENTION MEXICAN WORKERS:

The organization of the Imperial alley Growers and Shippers of Melons offers you a regular wage scale which you pay to organizers who defraud you and who are not interested in your personal wellbeing. Remember the sufferings you had to endure several years ago. You were then persuaded to enter an organization which seized your money and deprived you of your profits.

At the present time the Imperial valley planters have mobilized, all through Arizona, New Mexico and Texas, thousands of Mexican laborers who are ready to come to the Imperial Valley at short notice and who will seize your work. The railway company is prepared to bring these workers to the valley within twenty-four hours. . . .

This information is furnished you by experts who are interested in your welfare, while the paid organizers merely try to defraud you and to have you included in their lists.

Many of you have prospects of obtaining work. Accept it at once. Tomorrow may be too late.

THE GREAT MIGRATION

African American sharecroppers and tenant farmers began fleeing the poverty and repression of the cotton South in large numbers during the World War I years. As they moved northward, they encountered both new opportunities and the hostility of white workers. In the aftermath of the Chicago Race Riot of 1919, the Chicago Commission on Race Relations conducted an in-depth study of the conditions faced by African American workers in the city, excerpts of which appear in Document 4.20. What does the document suggest about the treatment accorded to black workers by unions and employers in Chicago?

4.20   Reaction to the Great Migration in Chicago. Excerpts from the Chicago Commission on Race Relations, *The Negro in Chicago: A Study of Race Relations and a Race Riot* (Chicago: University of Chicago Press, 1922), pp. 605–29.

Several important industries have not opened their doors to Negroes except as janitors and porters. Among these are the traction companies, elevated and surface, the State Street department stores, and the taxicab companies. Employers in these establishments express the belief that the public would object to Negroes.

Attention has been called to the waste involved in the limitations of Negroes in industry. Men with college training are forced to work as waiters and porters, and young women college graduates are frequently forced to work as ushers in theaters and as ladies' maids. This condition helps to account for the ease with which 1,500 Negro girls with more than average schooling were recruited in less than two months for the mail-order houses.

Through working together friendliness between white and Negro workers has been increased, according to prevalent views. Information concerning relations was secured from all the 137 plants studied. Two reported that race friction was a disturbing factor in the plants. Minor instances of friction have occurred, but it appeared that as a rule the workers reflected the attitude of the management. The setting up of partitions separating the races developed an antagonistic sentiment, and in some instances this antagonism was removed when the partitions were taken down. Of 101 establishments visited eighteen, or 11 per cent, with 2,623 Negroes, maintained separate accommodations. This constituted a continuous source of dissatisfaction for Negro workers, who felt themselves "Jim Crowed." In the remaining 89 per cent, employing 19,714 Negroes among more than 100,000 whites, all accommodations were used in common by both races. . . .

Clashing interests have manifested themselves conspicuously in the relations between union labor organizations and Negro workers, and this antagonism has been carried over into the relations of whites and Negroes generally. The efforts of union labor to promote its cause have built up a body of sentiment not easy to oppose by workers unsympathetic toward the labor movement. Circumstances have frequently made Negroes strike breakers, and thus centered upon them as a racial group all the bitterness of the unionist toward strike breakers as a class.

On the other hand, Negroes have often expressed themselves as having little faith in the union labor movement because the unions have manifested prejudices against permitting them to share equal benefits of membership; and again they have gained their first opportunity in a new industry frequently through the desire of a strike-bound employer to keep his plant running when his white employees have walked out.

From its beginning the American Federation of Labor has declared a uniform policy of non-racial discrimination, but this policy has not been carried out in practice by all its constituent or affiliated bodies. . . .

The general exclusion policy of the railway brotherhoods and several unions of the Railway Department of the American Federation of Labor has created a feeling of bitterness among Negroes, many of whom are employed in branches of the railway service. . . .

The Commission obtained information from local unions in Chicago with a membership of 294,437, of whom 12,106 were Negroes. . . . Wherever and whenever Negroes are admitted on an equal basis and given a square deal, the feeling inside the union is nearly always harmonious. Examples . . . are the Amalgamated Meat Cutters and Butcher Workmen of the World, Hodcarriers, Flat Janitors, and Ladies' Garment Workers. In some of these organizations Negroes hold office. . . .

Unions . . . admitting Negroes to subordinate locals, are few in number, apparently because Negroes strongly resent this form of affiliation. . . .

. . . In addition to the eight internationals which exclude the Negro by constitutional provision, there are other locals which are known to reject Negro applicants. The Machinists' Union, for example, although complying in its constitution with the American Federation of Labor policy of no racial discrimination, still effectually bars the Negro by a provision in its secret ritual. With the Machinists' Union must be grouped such unions as the Amalgamated Sheet Metal Workers' International Alliance, the Electrical Workers, and the Plumbers and Steam Fitters.

Some Negro leaders, in view of these practices, have been strong in their advocacy of non-affiliation with union organizations, holding that the employers, after all, offer for Negroes the fairer terms, and that they have, in fact, given Negroes their first opportunity in industry. However, certain other Negroes have taken advantage of the rift between employers and labor unions to exploit Negro laborers. They have played upon racial sentiment to establish separate unions for Negroes, both in lines of work where they are admitted to the general unions and in lines of work where they are excluded. This type of leadership has been irresponsible and dangerous; it has made ridiculously generous promises, and has addressed its appeal to the less intelligent classes of Negro workers. Its literature has in turn provoked extreme bitterness among labor union members and officials, who have mistakenly accepted it as representative of the sentiment of all Negro workers.

Interviews with Negro workers outside of the unions reveal an attitude of indifference or suspicion which is attributed by both white and Negro labor leaders and union men to the following reasons: (1) the usual treatment of Negroes by white men, (2) traditional treatment of Negroes by white men, (3) influence of racial leaders who oppose unionism, (4) influence of employers' propaganda against unionism. Many of them, it was learned, have a distorted view of the purposes and principles of unionism, and many others, while sympathetic with the movement, object to the practices of the locals. An experience frequently referred to was the waiters' strike in 1911, when Negro union men walked out with white union men and were replaced by white girls, while the white union men returned to their jobs; since that time Negro waiters have been out of the more desirable hotel jobs.

The explanations by labor leaders of the practices of local unions are to the effect that while the general public race prejudice might be expected in organizations of white workingmen, the unions, as a group, are fairer to the Negro than other groups; that unions are blamed for conditions which are really due to general public opinion. . . . These union officials believe that the unions will eventually be the most powerful agencies in the removal of race prejudice.

DEPRESSION

The onset of the Great Depression brought severe misery to untold millions of Americans. In Document 4.21 one of those who hit the road and rode the rails in the vain search for work recalls his experiences. Joblessness disrupted even stable, working-class families. An excerpt from Edmund Wilson's reporting on the depression, *An American Earthquake,* gives a glimpse of the despair of one unemployed Italian immigrant worker (Document 4.22). Nonetheless, as writer Louis Adamic concluded, joblessness did not tend to radicalize most workers (Document 4.23). Why do you suppose this might have been true? Indeed, researcher Alfred Winslow Jones's interviews with depression-era workers confirmed for him their essential conservatism (Document 4.24). Yet, as the depression deepened, workers looked increasingly to their government for help. Ironically, the more the government promised to address the concerns of the "common man," the more workers expected of government leaders. Document 4.25 shows how one black sharecropper framed his demands for federal help in the 1930s. And Document 4.26 shows that even those families that received relief from the New Deal's Works Progress Administration (WPA) did not simply meekly accept aid, they demanded fair treatment as well. E. W. Bakke found that unemployed workers also developed ways to manipulate the relief system to gain the maximum benefits from it (Document 4.27). What, if anything, do these last documents indicate about the changing attitudes of workers toward the state?

4.21   A Hobo's Life, 1930s. Louis Banks interviewed in Studs Terkel, *Hard Times: An Oral History of the Great Depression* (New York: Pantheon, 1970), pp. 40–43. Reprinted by permission of Danadio & Olsen, Inc. Copyright 1970, 1974 by Studs Terkel.

From a bed at a Veteran's Hospital, he talks feverishly; the words pour out. . . . "My family had a little old farm, cotton, McGehee, Arkansas. I came to Chicago, I was a little bitty boy, I used to prize-fight. When the big boys got through, they put us on there."

I got to be fourteen years old, I went to work on the Great Lakes at $41.50 a month. I thought: Someday I'm gonna be a great chef. Rough times, though. It was the year 1929. . . . 1929 was pretty hard. I hoboed, I bummed, I begged for a nickel to get somethin' to eat. Go get a job, oh, at the foundry there. They didn't hire me because I didn't belong to the right kind of race. 'Nother time I went into Saginaw, it was two white fellas and myself made three. The fella there hired the two men and didn't hire me. I was back out on the streets. That hurt me pretty bad, the race part.

When I was hoboing, I would lay on the side of the tracks and wait until I could see the train comin'. I would always carry a bottle of water in my pocket and a piece of tape or rag to keep it from bustin' and put a piece of bread in my pocket, so I wouldn't starve on the way. I would ride all day all night long in the hot sun. . . .

Black and white, it didn't make any difference who you were, 'cause everybody was poor. All friendly, sleep in a jungle. We used to take a big pot and cook food, cabbage, meat and beans all together. We all set together, we made a tent. Twenty-five or thirty would be out on the side of the rail, white and colored. They didn't have no mothers or sisters, they have no home, they were dirty, they had overalls on, they didn't have no food, they didn't have anything.

Sometimes we sent one hobo to walk, to see if there were any jobs open. He'd come back and say: Detroit, no jobs. He'd say: they're hirin' in New York City. So we went to New York City. Sometimes ten or fifteen of us be on the train. And I'd hear one of 'em holler. He'd fall off, he'd get killed. He was tryin' to get off the train, he thought he was gettin' home there. He heard a sound. (Imitates train whistle, a low, long, mournful sound.)

And then I saw a railroad police, a white police. They call him Texas Slim. He shoots you off all trains. We come out of Lima, Ohio . . . Lima Slim, he would kill you if he catch you on any train. Sheep train or any kind of merchandise train. He would shoot you off, he wouldn't ask you to get off. . . .

I knocked on people's doors. They'd say, "What do you want? I'll call the police." And they'd put you in jail for vag. They'd make you milk cows, thirty or ninety days. Up in Wisconsin, they'd do the same thing. Alabama, they'd do the same thing. California, anywhere you'd go. Always in jail, and I never did nothin'. . . .

I had fifteen or twenty jobs. Each job I would have it would be so hard. From six o'clock in the morning till seven o'clock at night. I was fixin' the meat, cookin', washin' dishes and cleaning up. Just like you threw the ball at one end and run down and catch it on the other. You're jack of all trade, you're doin' it all. White chefs were gettin' $40 a week, but I was gettin' $21 for doin' what they were doin' and everything else. The poor people had it rough. The rich people was livin' off the poor. . . .

Work on the WPA, earn $27.50. We just dig a ditch and cover it back up. You thought you was rich. You could buy a suit of clothes. Before that, you wanted money, you didn't have any. No clothes for the kids. My little niece and my little kids had to have hand-down clothes. Couldn't steal. If you did, you went to the penitentiary. You had to shoot pool, walk all day and all night, the best you could make was $15. I raised up all my kids during the Depression. Scuffled . . . a hard way to go.

4.22   The Despair of the Jobless. A report on the Dimicelis, Italian immigrants, from Edmund Wilson, "A Bad Day in Brooklyn," *American Earthquake: A Documentary of the Jazz Age, the Great Depression, and the New Deal* (New York: Anchor Books, 1964), pp. 288–91. Copyright 1958 by Edmund Wilson. Copyright renewed 1986 by Miranda Wilson. Reprinted by permission of Farrar, Straus and Giroux, LLC.

The Sicilian Dimicelis live in one of the clapboarded buildings above a grocery store [off Flushing Avenue in Brooklyn]. They had to move there from a better-class apartment when Mr. Dimiceli was earning so little. . . . The Dimicelis' flat is extremely clean, and it is furnished with an unexpected vividness that contrasts with the discolored streets of Flushing. The walls of every room are decorated with bright religious prints in green, blue and red—the Bleeding Heart and the Holy Family, the Virgin with flowers in her arms that presides above the bed in the bedroom, the Last Supper over the kitchen table. The whole apartment, in fact, has the brightness and the clear outlines of one of those simple prints: bedroom walls in green, kitchen oilcloth in blue and white squares, kitchen curtains in green and white, kitchen table and sink smooth white, and three yellow canaries in yellow cages.

The Dimicelis themselves are clear, vivid and handsome, too. The mother and daughter have just been out to the hospital, and they are wearing clean dresses in plain colors, black stockings and polished shoes. The black-eyed daughter is dressed in white, and the mother, with her black hair smoked gray, in blue. Mrs. Dimiceli is a small woman with a quick, attractive, fine-boned face, in which irony, sadness, pride and calm succeed each other in swift responses.

Mr. Dimiceli himself is recognizable, not primarily as a Sicilian, but as a type that, with the development of engineering, has become familiar all over the world. He is tall and thin with strong dark eyes, which themselves give the impression of lenses, behind the lenses of rimless spectacles, strong black hair brushed back and parted in the middle, and long efficient tool-like fingers.

When Mr. Dimiceli was still a young man, he left Sicily and went to France, and he worked there for thirteen years as a skilled machinist in automobile plants. Several years before the War, he came back to his native Palermo and went into business as an electrical contractor. Electricity was at that time still more or less of a novelty in Sicily, and Mr. Dimiceli got a good many commissions wiring Sicilian towns. Then the War broke out, and he had to serve. He went through the whole four years and a half as sergeant of horse artillery. There is a picture of him with a kepi, a Caruso mustache and a whole rainbow of campaign ribbons. During the War, he had Mrs. Dimiceli sell all his electrical equipment so that the family would have something to live on in case anything happened to him.

When the War was over and he came home to Palermo, he could not get his business back: it bad been captured during his absence by new electrical contractors. He decided that there were better opportunities in America than in Europe, so he brought the family over and found a job with a company on Long Island that made automobile parts. He got to be shop superintendent and worked there until the fall of '29, when the company sold the patent on a piston it had been making to another firm in Cleveland, and sent all its big machines out there. They laid off about three hundred men and among them Mr. Dimiceli: they gave him a recommendation which said that he was "a very reliable man, and only the fact we are reducing our production forces us to part with him." The few men they still kept on were the ones who had been with them longest. Mr. Dimiceli, however, got another job the next month with the Otis Elevator Company, but as the demand for elevators was also falling off, the Otis people, also, last spring, had to lay off their newest men.

After that, Mr. Dimiceli went out every day looking for work, but all he was able to find were odd jobs at the rate of one or two days a month. Sometimes the best he could do was to make a dollar a day driving a truck. At last Mrs. Dimiceli had to begin to look for work herself, and she succeeded from time to time in getting from $7 to $12 a week finishing dresses for a Brooklyn dressmaker. The youngest son also turned to working and earned $5 a week as a delivery boy. The eldest son was married and had a child and only made $20 a week as a presser, so that he couldn't help them out. The family had come down in the world, and as time went on, they couldn't see how they were even going to be able to stick where they were. They already owed three months' rent on their new and inferior apartment, and it was only the fact that the landlord was an Italian and a friend of theirs which made it possible for them to stay on there.

Mr. Dimiceli was a man in his fifties, who had once been a successful contractor in Palermo, whose career had been broken up by the War and who now spent every day going the rounds of the factories in Brooklyn and Jersey and not being able to get any of them to give him even the lowest paid job. Wednesday night, when he came home, he was nervous and gloomy, but the family didn't notice it particularly because he was like that every night. He would come back and read the paper, and sometimes just lie down on the bed without talking. Nobody had any suspicion of what he was going to do. The family were down listening to the radio in the apartment of the woman below when the youngest boy, who was coming up, heard a shot from their own apartment. He found his father sitting in the kitchen with his head all covered with blood. He had turned on the gas in the stove, but had evidently been afraid that that wouldn't be quick enough. They took him at once to the hospital, and the doctors couldn't tell the family whether he was going to live or die; but now he is at home and recovering.

Mrs. Dimiceli says that the Italians who come to the United States and go in for racketeering have wonderful opportunities, but that it is no place for a skilled machinist.

4.23 Impact of the Depression on Workers, 1931. Diary Entry, December 31, 1931, in Louis Adamic, *My America 1928–1938* (New York: Da Capo Press, 1976 [orig. 1938]), pp. 298-99. Copyright 1938 by Louis Adamic; renewed 1966 by Stena Adamic. Reprinted by permission of HarperCollins Publishers Inc.

From My Diary

LITTLE MAN, WHAT NOW?

December 15, 1931.—Economically the most severely affected by this crisis—which, however, is *much* more than an economic crisis—are, of course, the ordinary, most numerous folk: the factory workers, the many kinds of unskilled laborers, and petty clerks: the anonymous mass, which some of our current "revolutionary intellectuals" think Marx had in mind when he wrote the words "proletariat" and "revolution." But I believe that if Marx saw this "proletariat" in America today he would see precious few who might encourage him in his idea (if I understand him all right) that the impetus for the great change toward a new collectivist social order would come directly from this class.

A good many American "proletarians" have been living from hand to mouth in so-called good times; now that they have lost their jobs millions of them are completely down—and I think that is where, alas! many or even most of them are going to stay. Many, I believe, are mainly done for as positive human material. No movement, no "revolution," can save them. I think I know workers as men, as functioning organisms [I have long been one of them], and I have seen hundreds of them lately, talked with scores of them, watched their gait and movements, observed the postures of those few who got into the bread lines; and I have a definite feeling that millions of them, now that they are unemployed, are licked as men, as "proletarians," or whatever positive they ever have or could have been. They are licked by the chaos of America, by the machine, by industrialism; by regimentation on the one hand and by their futile, frustrated individualist psychology on the other. It is horrible to say this, but it is true—millions now unemployed are mainly or completely paralyzed, impotent, "washed up," doomed never again to be part of the vital, constructive economic processes of the country. They are caught in the Depression, which is grinding them down, destroying whatever spirit they may still have possessed before they lost their last job, and—for complex reasons—they cannot rise above it, see beyond it, fight it.

These people—not all, of course, but many, perhaps most of them, millions of them—seem to me the residue, the unsuccessful leftovers from the struggle in America on the part of the working-people during the last few decades to become middle-class, to get on socially and economically. Essentially, they are as individualistic as those who have more or less succeeded in the struggle. Or maybe even more so: for they, it seems to me, are much more hopeless, because, failing so drastically as individualists, they have lost something from their makeup as men, as cooperative human beings.

They have been unwilling "proletarians" all their lives—industrial slaves, wage slaves. And here I want to make this point: Wage slavery has had a dire effect on their characters as men, on their manhood, especially on those who are, say, forty or over. For ten, fifteen, twenty years these proletarian individualists of America, possessed by the prevalent psychology of the country, have been competing with one another in the labor market. Always they have been looking for immediate advantages, no matter at whose immediate or long-range expense. There was little or no class-consciousness. No *social* consciousness whatever. 'Rah for Number One! To the devil with labor unions, which were mostly graft schemes on the part of the leaders, who, also looking out for Number One, had frequently betrayed the workers. The thing to do was to earn money, to work, hold one's nose above the water, watch for a chance to improve one's individual lot—and, to keep one's little job, one had to compromise right and left; compromise with one's manhood and human dignity, betray one's class, act against one's own best feelings and instincts. As a worker, a man had to go around and humiliate himself, peddle his brawn, his hands, as though they were not a part of him, but articles he had picked up somewhere. Always he—this factory hand, this common laborer, this petty clerk—was afraid he might lose his job, and then his wife and kids would suffer and reproach him. Always he feared somebody was going to step on him; and often somebody did step on him, and he had to take it, for he was without say-so or comeback. Always he looked for a chance to escape from the low-down working-class and get on, get up in the world, become a foreman, a boss, a business man, an insurance agent, an exploiter of others, and do to others what had been done to him; but there was always some one else trying at the same time to squeeze himself through the same hole through which he had been aiming to escape, and so he stayed where he was—a worker, a balked individualist, his ego a pathetic affair which he kept from collapse by puffing himself up in various artificial ways, but in his essential being really a victim of the profound and complex basic socio-economic-political incongruity and chaos of American life. . . .

And all this wanting, but being unable, to become something better had an evil, degenerating effect on the worker's character, on his manhood, his mind. This was true of many a native, as well as foreign-born, "proletarian" now unemployed. He had little, if any, self-respect even when he worked: how could he when he usually had no idea when he might get the boot? He lacked pride in his job, because it involved, or called for, no skill. Now caught in the Depression, jobless, his family wanting, he is in many cases bewildered to the point of all-around ineffectiveness. In many cases, when one talks with him, there appears a faint symptom of disbalance in his mind, a faint nervous jerkiness in his movements and manner. No wonder. He cannot make head or tail of the situation in which he painfully finds himself; in fact, is afraid to really think of it, lest he be overwhelmed entirely. . . .

4.24 Not-So-Turbulent Workers, ca. 1930s. Interviews of rubber workers William Benson and James Hunt in Alfred Winslow Jones, *Life, Liberty, and Property: A Story of Conflict and a Measurement of Conflicting Rights* (Philadelphia: J. B. Lippincott Company, 1941), pp. 161–65, 172–76.

A white rubber worker, *William Benson,* talked to us. . . . Benson is not a member of any labor organization. . . . Benson comes from a town of 2,500 inhabitants in Alabama, and has lived in Akron for the last twenty-one of his forty-four years. For twenty years he has worked for the same company. Like Hunt, he is one of the highest paid of the rubber workers, earning about $1,600 a year at curing tires. "To live up to an average standard of living" he would like $500 more a year. In a joking sort of way, he is very proud of the fact that his wife used to be a school-teacher. They have one child, a boy of nineteen, who is a student at Akron University. His own education stopped after two years of high school. His car is paid for, but the house he owns (it would be worth $40 a month if it were rented) carries a mortgage. The family are Baptists and go to church every Sunday. . . .

"Yes, my job is pretty good—or at least it was pretty good. Nowadays you really have to make enough during the good months to be able to put something away for the months when they cut you down to three or four days a week. Fifteen years ago a man made ten to fifteen tires in eight hours. Now today one man makes sixty tires in six hours. The speed-up in production has made a lot of unemployment. The union? I don't think they do much about it. I joined the union in the beginning when everybody was rushing into it, and went to one meeting. All they talked about was striking. I dropped out right away. I don't believe in strikes. I won't belong to a union again unless there is an arbitration board to settle disputes, controlled by the government.

"I suppose if I had stayed in the South I would be a Democrat. Here I am a Republican. I'm not satisfied with the New Deal. I think too much power has been given to Roosevelt. He has held things up all along by bucking the business men. Some people say he will run for a third term, but I don't think he should. I certainly wouldn't vote for him. How about the W.P.A.? Well, I think it has ruined a good many men. A lot of them don't try to get anything else. For example, my wife's cousin had a chance to move to a farm and work for the owner. They would get all their food and clothing furnished, their rent free, and have a small amount of cash every month. He wouldn't take it. He'd rather stay on W.P.A."

James Hunt

Some of the rubber workers—picked at random—sat with us in their living rooms and told us at some length about their lives and their ideas. *James Hunt* was one. He was home from a six-hour stretch at "building tires," had washed up and put on a clean blue shirt and stretched out his six feet in an armchair. He spoke slowly and in the relaxed way of men who have done their day's work and are glad to talk. His wife was getting supper and talking to the children in the kitchen while we carried on our conversation in the living room. . . .

"All my spare time I devote to the union—to meetings and activities. That's my social enjoyment. I want to see the union eventually a sound and steady organization. I'm not at all satisfied with it the way it works at present. It's just an infant yet and needs a lot of instructing and correcting. Don't get me wrong. I'm a hundred per cent for unions and I think we are twice as well off since the union was organized, but I want to see more honest and sound-thinking men in the union, and see it made even better.

Since the union was organized we have had more freedom, security, dependability, and stability in wages. The union has sprung up as a sort of social change in the face of the present fast speed-up system. In the beginning the union grew so fast that it was just 'follow the flag.' Anybody and everybody just jumped in and went along. Socialism has crept in and I'm no Socialist so I greatly disapprove of that. I want to see the majority rule in a union as well as in our government, but that is not true in either at present. Unions must get some educated men to lead and direct them and do some weeding out as in any organization. We are getting more active members now than ever before and this is necessary in order to make the union more active and stable. We must build a constructive organization instead of a destructive one.

"In all this the government must try to keep up instead of lagging behind and even pulling back. The big trouble with the New Deal is that a few people run the country instead of the majority like they should. Although I have been non-partisan all my life, I am hanging on to the principles of the New Deal, but I really know that it won't solve our problems.

"At least I don't expect it will solve my problems. I am a lot better off than most, but Akron has been a disappointment to me financially. I have less now than when I came here. But as I said before, I would not be any better off any place else, so why blame Akron?

"Every worker should make more than just living expenses, but the average one certainly does not. There ought to be a limit on how much the rich can earn and on the profits of any factory or corporation. There ought also to be a minimum for everybody. There is no sense in one man making a dollar an hour and another working twice as hard and making fifty cents. But I don't contend that everyone should make equal wages for that would be wrong, too."

The talk ended with more ideas about religion. Hunt did not reject any of its doctrines, but showed an active dislike for it in all of its organized forms. Churches were for him nothing but another manifestation of the authority and power against which he had always set himself.

4.25   A Sharecropper's Plea, 1935. Letter from a black sharecropper, Marion, Arkansas, Feb. 3, 1935, in Robert S. McElvaine, *Down and Out in the Great Depression: Letters from the "Forgotten Man"* (Chapel Hill: University of North Carolina Press, 1983), p. 82.

                                                        Marion Ark
                                                        Feb 3, 1935

Pres Roosevelt
of Washington DC
Dear sir if every eny body need you we poor peoples need you here at marion we are all sufing mody bad the drauf [drought] come and cut off

the corn and white peoples took all the cotton and wont give us a day work at in the marion cort House mrs miller and mrs nomen and mr mace ant doing nottien for the poor negores at all wont give them no work and just robing the Govement and mr abry Kooser is roobing all the negroes on the farm he wont furnish the peoples untell the last of April and he wont furnish nothen but a little somtom to eat and don't car how large your family is he just you 2 sack of flour and one sack of meal and 8 lbs of lard for weeks if you got 13 in family that is what he give don't even gave a rag of clothen and shoes. and all of his peoples that is got large family has made from 11 to 17 bales of cotton and come out in deat over 300 hirndraw dellers in dat.

you aught send a man around one his farm just talk with his negores and see how they is suffen and that money all the otheres white men has pay thay negroes he did not gives his negroes but 5 dollers and mad them sine on the second day of this month and told all that dident sine to give him his house and move please send a man here one orbry Kooser plase at marion ark and don't send the letter back here he will have every negro on his place put in jail please come here at marion ark and helpe the poor negros and stop them peoples at the cort house frome Robing the govment don't send this back here do these white peoples will kill all the negroes in marion some of us have been here one this man place fore 10 to 17 years and all over 3 hundrew dollars in deat yet

[Anonymous]

4.26 Relief Worker's Protest, 1935. Letter from an angry wife of a WPA worker, November 21, 1935, in McElvaine, *Down and Out in the Great Depression*, pp. 188–89.

Kalamazoo Mich.
Nov. 21 1935

Harry Hopkins:—
Washington D.C.

Dear Sir:—I am writing to you concerning the W. P. A.. . . . We are completely out of coal and how can he [her husband] work without no food or clothes. I don't see how times are going to get better if men have to work for so low wages and food stuffs so high and rent has raised. The government put out clothing and sheets and pillow cases blankets & etc but how many got them and those that did had to fight to get them and they never gave us any clothes at all and now that we are asking for a little help till he gets started they wont help us.

It was simply a graft the things were put places they weren't supposed to be and the poor people went half starved as there were three grown up's in our family and they gave us $3.50 a week to live on my son had to go through a physical exam and Dr told him he hadn't the proper food But still President Roosevelt says he doesnt want any one to starve why keep them going on existing I think Mr Roosevelt means all right but it is others that put out these cheap projects it just keeps him down everybody should work with him instead against him I am going to register and believe me my vote will be placed right as I think he means for this money to be put to a better advantage. Instead of a man trying to keep up a home on $13.00 a week and go out and grub stumps without the necessary food.

There sure must be a way figured out that a poor man can live instead of being half starved when there is so much money in this country and a poor man is the one that does the work and gets nothing in return.

Well anyway I would like for President Roosevelt to know what is being done to the people he is putting this money out for.

This W.P.A. already has lead a man with a family to crime he cant live on $13.00 or no one else can he got busy the other evening and brought home some extra money. poor people are human and it sure isnt his fault he is poor just because some have hoged it.

This is just a letter to let you know what is going on in Kalamazoo what people must endure for a very little food.

Yours Truly

W.P.A. Workers Wife.

4.27   The Unemployed, 1930s. Excerpts from E. W. Bakke, *The Unemployed Worker,* (New Haven: Yale University Press, 1940), pp. 377–79. Reprinted with permission from Yale University Press.

Said one sheet-metal worker:

Experience shows that it pays to holler. "The wheel that does the squeaking gets the grease" is exchanged for—now what would you change it for? Did you ever hear of any saying opposite? Folks don't have enough experience like that to invent sayings for it.

During the time that Mr. Thompson was on the F.E.R.A. Mrs. Thompson said she tried to skimp and save and plan as best I could to make the $12 a week do for us. It was an insult asking a family with two growing boys to live on that. The social worker came and asked how I was getting along. I said we were just "getting by," trying to show her that I was careful, but she seemed to think that because we were "getting by" we were getting along wonderful. Our clothes began to wear out and the blankets were in shreds. There was an Italian family downstairs and they always seemed to have nice clothes even though they were getting a charity order and not working at all. Then reading the papers I found out we could get more, so what did I do? I called up the Charities Department and told them that if we didn't get some milk and other things we were going to steal them. I kept the kids home from school two days and called up the principal and told him the kids weren't coming to school until they had clothes enough to keep them warm. The next day the social worker came up and they sent clothes and blankets and shoes so that they covered the whole floor here. It was more than we needed. Then the city gave us a $3 order and sent milk. It didn't pay to plan and save; the social worker didn't give you any credit. If I had known all along what I found out the last year, we could have been living wonderful for the last four years. What you got to do is use up what you got and make a big holler for more. Then they give you what you ought to have.

INDUSTRIAL UNION UPSURGE

Following the passage of the Wagner Act in 1935, momentum began to build for the launching of an industrial union drive in the mass manufacturing sector. When the AFL fell short of endorsing an industrial union drive at its 1935 convention, a minority of union officials led by John L. Lewis announced that they would launch such an effort nonetheless (Document 4.28). Lewis and his allies launched the Committee on Industrial Organization (CIO) to implement this vision. In early 1937 the CIO experienced its first huge win as union activists affiliated with the CIO's United Automobile Workers union staged a successful sitdown strike, occupying General Motors' crucial Fisher Body works in Flint, Michigan, until the company agreed to sign a contract with the union. In Document 4.29 sit-down striker Bob Stinson remembers that struggle, while Document 4.30 provides an excerpt of the historic 1937 GM-UAW contract won during the strike. How could the winning of such a brief, bare-bones contract have caused Stinson to feel such a sense of accomplishment? The CIO, unlike the AFL, worked hard to recruit black workers to its ranks. This effort was immeasurably aided by the formation of the National Negro Congress in 1936, which allied itself firmly with the CIO. Document 4.31 provides a brief report on the founding of the NNC. Document 4.32 shows how NNC leaders such as John P. Davis aided the efforts of the CIO's Steel Worker Organizing Committee (SWOC). What do these documents indicate about the spirit unleashed among industrial workers by the CIO?

4.28   Toward the CIO, 1935. "Minority Report of Resolutions Committee on Organization Policies," from the *Report of the Proceedings of the Fifty-Fifth Annual Convention of The American Federation of Labor Held at Atlantic City, New Jersey 7–19 October 1935* (Washington, D.C.: Judd & Detweiler, 1935), pp. 523–24.

Minority Report of Resolutions Committee on Organization Policies

During the fifty-five years the American Federation of Labor has existed its declared purpose has been to organize the unorganized industrial workers of the nation. . . .

We refuse to accept existing conditions as evidence that the organization policies of the American Federation of Labor have been successful. The fact that after fifty-five years of activity and effort we have enrolled under the banner of the American Federation of Labor approximately three and one-half millions of members of the thirty-nine millions of organizable workers is a condition that speaks for itself.

We declare the time has arrived when common sense demands the organization policies of the American Federation of Labor must be molded to meet present day needs. In the great mass production industries and those in which the workers are composite mechanics, specialized and engaged upon classes of work which do not fully qualify them for craft union membership, industrial organization is the only solution. Continuous employment, economic security and the ability to protect the individual worker depends upon organization upon industrial lines.

In those industries where the work performed by a majority of the workers is of such nature that it might fall within the jurisdictional claim of more than one craft union, or no established craft union, it is declared that industrial organization is the only form that will be acceptable to the workers or adequately meet their needs. Jurisdictional claims over small groups of workers in these industries prevent organization by breeding a fear that when once organized the workers in these plants will be separated, unity of action and their economic power destroyed by requiring various groups to transfer to National and International Unions organized upon craft lines.

To successfully organize the workers in industrial establishments where conditions outlined herein obtain there must be a clear declaration by the American Federation of Labor. It must recognize the right of these work-ers to organize into industrial unions and be granted unrestricted charters which guaranteed the right to accept into membership all workers employed in the industry or establishment without fear of being compelled to destroy unity of action through recognition of jurisdictional claims made by national or International Unions.

It is not the intention of this declaration of policy to permit the taking away from National or International craft unions any part of their present membership, or potential membership in establishments where the domi-nant factor is skilled craftsmen coming under a proper definition of the jurisdiction of such National or International Unions. However, it is the declared purpose to provide for the organization of workers in mass pro-duction and other industries upon industrial and plant lines, regardless of claims based upon the question of jurisdiction.

The Executive Council of the American Federation of Labor is expressly directed and instructed to issue unrestricted charters to organizations formed in accordance with the policy herein enunciated. The Executive Council is also instructed to enter upon an aggressive organization campaign in those industries in which the great mass of the workers are not now organized, issue unrestricted charters to workers organized into independent unions, company-dominated unions and those organizations now affiliated with associations not recognized by the American Federation of Labor as bona-fide labor organizations.

Submitted by:
Charles P. Howard,
David Dubinsky,
Frank B. Powers,
John L. Lewis,
A. A. Myrup,
J. C. Lewis.

4.29   Remembering the Flint Sit-Down Strike, 1937. Sit-down striker Bob Stinson interviewed in Terkel, *Hard Times,* pp. 188–89. Reprinted by permission of Donadio & Olsen, Inc. Copyright 1970, 1974 by Studs Terkel.

It took about five minutes to shut the line down. The foreman was pretty well astonished. (Laughs.)

The boys pulled the switches and asked all the women who was in Cut-and-Sew to go home. They informed the supervisors they could stay, if they stayed in their office. They told the plant police they could do their job as long as they didn't interfere with the workers.

We had guys patrol the plant, see that nobody got involved in anything they shouldn't. If anybody got careless with company property—such as sitting on an automobile cushion without putting burlap over it—he was talked to. You couldn't paint a sign on the wall or anything like that. You used bare springs for a bed. 'Cause if you slept on a finished cushion, it was no longer a new cushion.

Governor [Frank] Murphy said he hoped to God he would never have to use National Guard against people. But if there was damage to property, he would do so. This was right down our alley, because we invited him to the plant and see how well we were taking care of the place.

They'd assign roles to you. When some of the guys at headquarters wanted to tell some of the guys in the plant what was cookin', I carried the message. I was a scavenger, too.

The merchants cooperated. There'd be apples, bushels of potatoes, crates of oranges that was beginnin' to spoil. Some of our members were also little farmers, they come up with a couple of baskets of junk.

The soup kitchen was outside the plant. The women handled all the cooking, outside of one chef who came from New York. He had anywhere from ten to twenty women washing dishes and peeling potatoes in the strike kitchen. Mostly stews, pretty good meals. They were put in containers and hoisted up through the window. The boys in there had their own plates and cups and saucers. . . .

We had a ladies' auxiliary. They'd visit the homes of the guys that was in the plant. They would find out if there was any shortage of coal or food. Then they'd maneuver around amongst themselves until they found some place to get a ton of coal. Some of them even put the arm on Consumer Power if there was a possibility of having her power shut off.

Some of [the wives] would have foremen come to their homes: "Sorry, your husband was a very good operator. But if he don't get out of the plant and away from the union, he'll never again have a job at General Motors." If this woman was the least bit scared, she'd come down and cry on her husband's shoulder. He'd more than likely get a little disturbed, get a hold of his strike captain. . . . Maybe we'd send a couple of women out there. Sometimes you just had to let 'em go. Because if you kept them in there, they'd worry so damn much over it, that'd start ruinin' the morale of the rest of the guys.

Morale was very high at the time. It started out kinda ugly because the guys were afraid they put their foot in it and all they was gonna do is lose their jobs. But as time went on, they begin to realize they could win this darn thing, 'cause we had a lot of outside people comin' in showin' their sympathy.

Time after time, people would come driving by the plant slowly. They might pull up at the curb and roll down the window and say, "How you guys doin'?" Our guys would be lookin' out the windows, they'd be singin' songs and hollerin'. Just generally keeping themselves alive.

Sometimes a guy'd come up to you on the street and say, "How the guys doin'?" You say, "They're doin' all right." Then he'd give ya a song and dance: "I hear the boys at Chevrolet are gonna get run out tonight." I'd say, "Hogwash." He'd end with sayin': "Well, I wish you guys the best of luck because, God damn, when I worked there it was a mess." The guy'd turn around and walk away. . . .

The men sat in there for forty-four days. Governor Murphy—I get emotional over him (laughs)—was trying to get both sides to meet on some common ground. I think he lost many a good night's sleep. We wouldn't use force. Mr. Knudsen was head of General Motors and, of course, there was John L. Lewis. . . .

John L. was as close to a Shakespearean actor as any I've ever listened. He could get up there and damn all the adversaries—he had more command of language. He made a speech that if they shoot the boys out at the plant, they'd have to shoot him first.

There were a half a dozen false starts at settlement. Finally, we got the word: THE THING IS SETTLED. My God, you had to send about three people, one right after the other, down to some of those plants because the guys didn't believe it. Finally, when they did get it, they marched out of the plants with the flag flyin' and all that stuff.

You'd see some guys comin' out of there with whiskers as long as Santa Claus. They made a rule they wasn't gonna shave until the strike was over.

Oh, it was just like—you've gone through the Armistice delirium, haven't you? Everybody was runnin' around shaking everybody by the hand, sayin', "Jesus, you look strange, you got a beard on you now." (Laughs.) Women kissin' their husbands. There was a lotta drunks on the streets that night.

When Mr. Knudsen put his name to a piece of paper and says that General Motors recognizes the UAW—CIO—until that moment, we were non-people, we didn't even exist. (Laughs.) That was the big one. (His eyes are moist.)

4.30 General Motors-United Automobile Worker Agreement, February 11, 1937. From *Monthly Labor Review*, XLIV (March 1937), pp. 669–70.

AGREEMENT ENTERED INTO ON THIS 11TH DAY OF FEBRUARY 1937, BETWEEN THE GENERAL MOTORS CORPORATION (HEREINAFTER REFERRED TO AS THE "CORPORATION"), AND THE INTERNATIONAL UNION, UNITED AUTOMOBILE WORKERS OF AMERICA (HEREINAFTER REFERRED TO AS THE "UNION")

1. The Corporation hereby recognizes the Union as the collective bargaining agency for those employees of the Corporation who are members of the Union. The Corporation recognizes and will not interfere with the right of its employees to be members of the Union. There shall be no discrimination, interference, restraint, or coercion by the Corporation or any of its agents against any employees because of membership in the Union.

2. The Corporation and the Union agree to commence collective bargaining negotiations on February 16 with regard to the issues specified in the letter of January 4, 1937, from the Union to the Corporation, for the purpose of entering into a collective bargaining agreement, or agreements, covering such issues, looking to a final and complete settlement of all matters in dispute.

3. The Union agrees to forthwith terminate the present strike against the Corporation, and to evacuate all plants now occupied by strikers.

4. The Corporation agrees that all of its plants, which are on strike or otherwise idle shall resume operations as rapidly as possible.

5. It is understood that all employees now on strike or otherwise idle will return to their usual work when called and that no discrimination shall be made or prejudices exercised by the Corporation against any employee because of his former affiliation with, or activities in, the Union or the present strike.

6. The Union agrees that pending the negotiations referred to in paragraph 2, there shall be no strikes called, or any other interruption to or interference with production, by the Union or its members.

7. During the existence of the collective bargaining agreement contemplated pursuant to paragraph 2, all opportunities to achieve a satisfactory settlement of any grievance or the enforcement of any demands by negotiation shall be exhausted, before there shall be any strikes or other interruption to or interference with production by the Union or its members. There shall be no attempts to intimidate or coerce any employee by the Union and there shall not be any solicitation or signing up of members by the Union on the premises of the company. This is not to preclude individual discussion.

8. After the evacuation of its plants and the termination of the strike the Corporation agrees to consent to the entry of orders, dismissing the injunction proceedings which have been started by the Corporation against the Union, or any of its members, or officers or any of its locals, including these pending in Flint, Mich., and in Cleveland, Ohio, and subject to the approval of the courts to discontinue all contempt proceedings which it has instituted thereunder.

4.31   The National Negro Congress is Launched, 1936. From Herbert Newton, "The National Negro Congress (U.S.A.)," *The Negro Worker* VI (May-June 1936): pp. 22–25.

Frederick Douglass, that fearless organizer of the anti-slavery forces in pre-Civil War days, in the U.S.A., would have leaped with joy had he lived to attend the National Negro Congress, held in Chicago February 14-16.

Over 900 delegates attended the Congress. They came from all over the country and from all walks of life. The report of the Credentials Committee based on the first day of delegates' arrival showed an incomplete total of 763 delegates. Of this number 214 came from various civic organizations, 8 from trade unions; 76 from churches of various religious organizations, 70 from fraternities, 44 from various political organizations and . . . newspapers. These delegates were sent by 551 organizations and directly represented 3,322,093 people or a quarter of the Negro population in the U.S. To a certain extent the Congress assumed an international character as shown by the presence of representatives from Ethiopia, South Africa and the Chinese Soviets. . . .

A three day discussion in which utmost democracy prevailed, gave an accurate picture of the conditions, struggles and determination of the American Negro. Sharecroppers and tenant farmers from Alabama, longshoremen from the West Coast, coal miners from Kentucky and Pennsylvania steel workers from Georgia and Illinois, together with professionals, intellectuals churchmen and small traders worked out a programme for swinging into action the whole Negro peoples with their white brothers. . . .

The trade union representation to the Congress, while small in comparison to the representation from civic organizations was its most vital force. Of tremendous significance, for example, in view of the Congress' anti-imperialist war stand, is the solidarity of the Italian Local 270 of the Amalgamated Clothing Workers of America and in voting full support and in sending delegates.

Equally important is the election of A. Phillip Randolph as the Congress leader. Randolph, formerly a water boy on a road gang, and now President of the Brotherhood of Sleeping Car Porters, has successfully led his national Negro Union in a victorious 10-year battle against the Pullman company, a battle as glorious as any that grace the pages of the history of the American trade union movement. . . .

John P. Davis, fiery young Negro intellectual, was elected Executive Secretary Randolph's assistant. Davis is proof of the rapidly growing cleavage in Negro leadership. . . . None can say whether these progressives [like Davis] will go the entire distance in the liberation struggle. But now, working in close contact with tried and experienced working class leaders such as James Ford, A. W. Berry, and Harry Haywood, they make considerable contributions to the immediate struggles of the Negro people.

It was Davis, for example, who was most effective in having a motion passed to endorse Randolph's American Federation of Labor (AF of L) resolution which is aimed at smashing trade union colour bars. It was Davis, again who raised his voice for the proposals, successfully passed, to launch a nation-wide drive in cooperation with the AF of L for the organization of Negro workers into trade unions, and to start by the organization of the most exploited strata,-laundry and domestic workers—as the dramatic focal point for the organization of all Negro labour. . . .

4.32 National Negro Congress supports SWOC, 1936. Memorandum from John P. Davis to All Local Councils, July 10, 1936, Adolph Germer Papers, Reel 3, Library of Congress, Manuscript Division.

July 10, 1936

Memorandum   Confidential
From: John P. Davis, National Secretary [of the National Negro Congress]
To: All Local Councils [of the National Negro Congress]
Subject: Organizing Drive of the Steel Workers Organizing Committee

I have just returned from Cleveland, Ohio, and Pittsburgh, Pa., where I had conferences with officials of the Steel Workers Organizing Committee formed by the Committee for Industrial Organization. . . . I am submitting for your action a proposed plan for cooperation with the Steel Workers Organizing Committee in their efforts to organize Negro steel workers.

Negro workers constitute roughly 15 percent of all workers employed in the steel industry. . . . Most of the Negro workers are employed in unskilled occupations, at so-called "Negro jobs." They are given heavy, dirty work as laborers in the rolling mills and blast furnaces. Regardless of their skill they seldom receive an opportunity for advancement.

Large proportions of the total number of Negro steel workers live in company-owned towns, notorious for their squalor, vice conditions, and for company spy systems used to deter workers from engaging in union activity. The company unions maintained in the industry furnish no means of adjusting grievances of the workers or of improving the status of steel workers.

Employers in the steel industry have maintained a studied policy with regard to Negro workers. In order to maintain the open shop they have kept a certain percentage of Negro workers employed. These workers have been used to buttress the resistance of the employers to attempts at unionization in the past. The Negro workers have been kept on a subsistence level in constant fear of loss of employment. They have become indoctrinated with the belief that unionization will mean loss of employment.

To maintain the open shop employers may be expected to discharge Negro workers known to be union members. As well they will make use of every possible method to intimidate Negro workers. Company thugs will beat Negro organizers. Negro community leaders will be enlisted to advise Negroes against joining unions. Already in the steel towns of Homestead and Clairton emissaries of the company have gone the rounds of Negro steel workers' homes telling their wives to keep their husband out of the union if they want them to remain employed. Already attempts to influence press, church, and other agencies in the Negro community have been begun. As well in a period of strikes, the employers may be expected to provoke and incite disturbances between Negro and white workers.

Thus the organization of Negro workers, the maintenance of friendly relations between Negro and white workers, the winning of the families of the workers to the cause of the union and the winning of the church, press, and other forms of organizational life among Negroes in steel communities becomes a paramount issue to the success of the organization drive of the Steel Workers Organizing Committee. . . .

It is of utmost importance to stress the need for cooperation of every local council of the National Negro Congress in a steel community with local officials of the Steel Workers Organizing Committee. Negro Congress labor committees must at once begin to establish leadership among Negro steel workers and urge them to join the union. . . .

WORLD WAR II

World War II brought an end to unemployment and produced labor shortages in some vital war industries. In Document 4.33, Pennsylvania miner Gabe

Ferrence suggests how workers coped with the strains of the wartime labor environment. In return for their agreements not to strike, unions gained important concessions from the government, including support for maintenance-of-membership clauses in defense contracts (which ensured that covered workers would remain union members and pay dues for the duration of a contract). Nonetheless there was dissent in labor's ranks over the unions' decision to offer a "no-strike pledge," as the debate that took place at the 1943 Michigan CIO convention indicates (Document 4.34). Which argument seems most persuasive? Unauthorized "wildcat" strikes proliferated during the war despite the "no-strike pledge." Several of the most prominent of those strikes were triggered not by management mistreatment of union members, but by white workers' protests against the introduction of African Americans into their workplaces. Newspaper coverage of the 1942 Hudson Motors walkout illustrates the dynamics of a "hate strike" (Document 4.35). Yet blacks gained greater opportunities to earn high wages and join the ranks of organized labor during the war. Even in the deep South wartime conditions were favorable enough to encourage black workers to try to overcome white employers' intimidation against the formation of unions. Document 4.36 excerpts the NLRB's investigation of the plight of black woodworkers from Fort Gibson, Mississippi, in 1944. What do Documents 4.35 and 4.36 suggest about the contested nature of black gains during the war? Women workers also found working conditions in war industries often less than hospitable, as Document 4.37 makes clear. Yet, following the war, Gladys Dickason believed that working women had achieved a degree of progress in both the workplace and the union that was unimaginable before the war (Document 4.38). What do these two documents suggest about the impact the war on women?

4.33 Coal Miners at War. Interview with Gabe Ferrence (1994), in Thomas Dublin, *When the Mines Closed: Stories of Struggles in Hard Times* (Ithaca: Cornell University Press, 1998), pp. 170–71. Reprinted with permission of Cornell University Press.

[During World War II there were lots of opportunities.] Francis Montgomery, one of the big superintendents of Lansford, knew my father was a hoisting engineer and fireman years ago; he asked me if I wanted a job hoisting engineer. I was running shovel on the stripping and I didn't want to take the job. He wanted me 'cause I guess some of their hoisting engineers probably had to go away during World War II. He knew I was available so he wanted me to get to be a hoisting engineer.

[During the war] we were busy. Many a time I ran the machine without an oiler because they didn't have anybody. They'd see a hobo walking on the road, they'd say, "Hey, you want a job?" Sometimes I had school teachers for oilers during their summer vacation, because they were needed. Some of them taught me in high school, such as Warren Ulshafer and James Vaiana, [from] Nesquehoning, and Andy Kalen, a football coach from Coaldale.

I figured if the boys were in the jungles laying in the mud and freezing in bad weather and everything, why can't I run this machine and grease it myself? So I did many a time. The contractor saved money because he wasn't paying two men, but I only got my regular shovel runner salary. "I would shut the machine down for an hour or so and I'd grease it myself". I did something for my war effort, can't say that I was just a slacker or something like that. I helped the production of coal, which was needed for industries all over the world. A lot of coal was going over to Germany and foreign countries for the troops to have for their fuel. I worked for Fauzio Brothers all during World War II and loaded thousands of tons of coal.

4.34   Michigan CIO Convention Debates No-Strike Pledge, 1943. Excerpt from *Proceedings of Sixth Annual Convention of the Michigan CIO*, June 30, 1943, pp. 136–45. [Taken from http://historymatters.gmu.edu/d/5147].

Delegate Reynolds (Dodge Local No. 3): Mr. Chairman, I rise to support the resolution [to recommend that the CIO revoke its no-strike pledge]. I believe that we of labor should stay on the side of labor. . . . I don't believe we should strike these plants unless we absolutely have to. You can take the Chrysler workers. Chrysler workers are underpaid. We have our contract. We have been trying to get a contract for some six or seven months out of the War Labor Board and what do we get. We get just a plain run around! When we had a three-day stoppage, the War Labor Board promised us that they would get the Chrysler contract out of the red tape that it is meshed down in Washington inside of two weeks. Here it is going into another five or six weeks and we still have not a contract. . . . The corporation that I work for knows only one language and that is the language of strike, and there isn't any one in this convention that can say they can deal with the Chrysler Corporation on any other terms. The only language they understand is the language of strike, and I say, let's give it to them. [Boos and applause]

Delegate Paul Weber (American Newspaper Guild): Brother President, I am speaking against the resolution. . . . It seems to me that no better argument against this resolution can be made than the address of Brother Reynolds who stated that he had gone on strike in the Chrysler plant, that is men were still on the street, and the total net result of that has been that the case had been taken to the War Labor Board. I would like also to make this point,—that when you strike in a war industry, you do not damage the management. Unfortunately, that is true. I think Chrysler exemplified that fact. The company has a contract with the government for X number of guns and they don't care whether you make those guns in six weeks or eight weeks. The only one hurt is the future of the labor movement and the capacity of the armed forces that defend us all. And on those grounds I am opposed to the resolution. [Applause and cheers]

Delegate John Cole (Local 50, UAWA): Mr. Chairman . . . Our Local 50 is going along with this [resolution] a thousand per cent due to the fact we don't want dictation. You are going to be dictated to. Let's not be dictated to by Phil Murray and Green. . . . Don't lose your individuality. Don't give it up. A no-strike pledge at this time is going to do one thing, going to let us down, we are going to be jockeyed into position by pressure groups and run along to their way of doing. Don't let this happen in the labor movement here. Let this entire group go as fighting for the individual . . .

Delegate Washington (Local 600, UAWA): I represent approximately 90,000 workers, [Boos] the majority of whom are against striking at this time because we recognize that it is important that the people who are fighting in South Africa, North Africa, Guadalcanal, need the things which we make. I also feel that as a member of the International Union of Auto Workers, the majority of whom have already gone on record as against striking at this time, do not feel that such a resolution should be supported. . . . We are hurting ourselves. We are taking things away from our boys who are on the battle lines the products of labor that they need to protect themselves and win this war. And I want to urge all of you who are Americans, who are with the allied nations, who are sincere in wanting to see this war won that you vote down this resolution and continue to give your support to the Administration. [Applause and Cheers]

Delegate Lucas: Brother Chairman and Brothers and Sisters: In the first place this resolution does not revoke the no-strike pledge. It is only a question of certain policy and advising with the National CIO as to how we feel on this particular question. And what group has a better right to advise with the National CIO than the Michigan CIO? . . . Now I have become convinced that the giving of the no-strike pledge was the biggest mistake that labor has ever made. [Applause and boos] You have only to look into your own particular plant and see what your conditions, your collective bargaining set up is. Are the managements bargaining in these plants? [Voices: No]

I certainly don't think they are. When it comes to question of giving labor its just due, it seems that the administration seems to not be able to find any money to do anything with but when it comes to the question of building plants for corporations who have already more than they need, they can find billions of dollars to do that with. Is that giving labor a square deal? I don't think so. My personal sentiments are on this question that the no-strike pledge should be revoked here and now. [Applause and boos and time called]

Delegate Boatin: Surely we have grievances. Surely the manufacturers create numerous grievances for us, and why? And who in particular are these manufacturers? In the majority of cases the manufacturers [who] create numerous grievances are the ones who are not interested in winning the war. They create these grievances, they help to create these grievances and refuse to negotiate primarily because they want us to go on strike, so we can have a negotiated peace, so Hitler can continue in war and so we can have Hitlerism in this country. A strike would be against our men who are on the battlefields, against the entire labor movement, against the very war we are fighting. The revocation of the no-strike pledge will not solve the problem. Brother Reynolds indicated that it did not solve their problem. Strikes will not establish democracy in the world.

4.35   Wildcat Hate Strike, 1942. Report of a Racist Wildcat Strike at Hudson Motors, Detroit *News,* June 19, 1942, pp. 1, 4. Reprinted with permission from the *Detroit News.*

Walkout Ends in Gun Plant: Schedule Is Normal at Hudson Plant

Production was normal again in the Naval Ordinance (Hudson) Arsenal at 23500 Mound road today, a Navy spokesman said, after UAW-CIO officials ended a brief walkout this morning in one building.

"Production, is 100 per cent," Capt. A. S. Wotherspoon, chief inspector of ordnance at the arsenal, said. . . .

A wildcat strike halted production most of Thursday at the plant, manufacturing, vitally-needed guns for the Navy. The workers struck in protest over employment of Negroes, members of the UAW-CIO on production jobs, officials said.

UNION PLEA EFFECTIVE

When the day shift went into the plant today, Richard T. Frankensteen and Melvin Bishop, UAW regional directors; Al Germaine president of Hudson Local 154, UAW, and Leo Lamonte, an organizer called the workers together and urged that work be resumed. Frankensteen said later that the men went back to work except in one building where about 100 employees stopped work. After UAW officials addressed this group, pointing out that the "guns are needed to beat the Japs" and that their actions were injuring the union, they returned to the jobs, he said.

Frankensteen said that he did not expect further trouble today at the plant but that he and other officials were remaining to make sure. By nightfall there will be 33 Negroes employed in the plant, he said. "It looks like the Klan is responsible for this," Frankensteen said. "There were some Black Legion members at the Hudson plant, and we have had trouble with the Klan before in other plants on the Negro question. The overwhelming majority of the workers are 100 per cent American, however, and when we told them what a strike meant in terms of aiding the enemy, they went back to work."

Frankensteen denied that any employee had walked out of the plant, although observers at the gates reported some of the day shift went in at 7 a. m. and left at 8 a. m. Frankensteen said those coming out at 8 o'clock were the second crew from the night shift. Earlier, R. J. Thomas, UAW-CIO president, threatened to pull the charter of the local union unless the strike ended. He said he believed some Ku Klux Klan members were promoting the walkout, but he said officials of the local had done everything in their power to end the strike and were not involved in the Klan charges.

The strike started Thursday morning when some 1,800 of the arsenal's 11,000 workers walked out. They protested against the management placing two Negro production workers in each of the arsenal's four main buildings.

The white workers at first moved the Negroes' benches to another end of the building, but the management ordered guards to replace the benches. At that point the men walked out.

THOMAS FLIES BACK

Thomas and Frankensteen flew back from Washington in a Navy bomber to order the men back to work, and Frankensteen was at the plant this morning when the shift was scheduled to come to work.

A Navy spokesman admitted the arsenal had difficulty maintaining an even flow of production during the afternoon and midnight shifts Thursday because of the strike.

Asked why the Navy had not acceded to the striking workers' request that the eight Negroes be placed in one building, instead of spread throughout the plant, the spokesman said:

"The Negroes protested against segregation. We expected trouble. This is just a test of strength on a serious problem we may run into at some other plants."

ORDERS CARRIED OUT

Secretary Knox, in a telegram to Capt. Wotherspoon, demanded immediate resumption of work.

A spokesman for the union local to which the striking workers belong said the unit's fair employment practice committee had attempted throughout Thursday to get the men back to work. After citing the group's protest against the Negroes, Capt. Wotherspoon said:

"We have orders not to discriminate against any race or creed and we are used to carrying out orders here."

4.36   Overcoming Racial Intimidation in Mississippi, 1944. Casefile 15-C-1020, National Labor Relations Board Records, National Archives, Washington, D.C.

Excerpt from Official Report of Proceedings before the National Labor Relations Board, Case No. 15-C-1020, November 26–28, 1945.

Q. By Mr. [Stanley D.] Kane [on behalf of the NLRB]: What is your full name?

A. Howard Leon Thomas. . . .

Q. And what was your occupation during August, September, October, and November, 1944?

A. Representative of the CIO Woodworkers; International Woodworkers, CIO. . . .

Q. And, Mr. Thomas, during that period, did you seek to organize the employees of the Port Gibson Veneer & Box Company, the respondent in this case?

A. I did. . . .

Q. And how often during that period did you come to Port Gibson?

A. An average of twice a month. . . .

Q. Did you on one occasion hold a meeting at a ball park in Port Gibson?

A. On several occasions.

Q. Did you hold a meeting at which the Sheriff of this county appeared?

A. I did. . . .

Q. Mr. Thomas, will you tell us what happened at this meeting when the sheriff came?

A. Well, I was in the ball park just across the street here; had quite a number of people there, and I notice the Sheriff, and I told him, I says, "Sheriff, come on in. This is a CIO meeting." He says, "Yes, you have done enough. You're just stirring these people up with the intention of getting their money, and you fellows will be gone. You're just disturbing good people for nothing". . . . He made the statement, "Go ahead with your meeting. If I had my way about it I would run you out of town." . . .

Q. Now, who all was there?

A. I don't know them by name.

Q. I mean, just practically all colored employees; practically all colored, weren't they?

A. Yes, they were practically all colored.

Q. Was that a public meeting. . . . or was it purely a Union meeting?

A. It was for the mill people. Any mill labor; anybody working in the mill could come. . . .

Q. Did the Sheriff . . . tell you why he was there?

A. He did not.

Certification of Representatives, December 1, 1944, Case No. 15-R-1241 On November 22, 1944, an election was conducted in the above matter . . . and in accordance with the Rules and Regulations of the Board. It appears from a tally of the ballots that a collective bargaining representative has been selected, since of the approximately 277 eligible voters, 218 cast valid votes, of which 199 were for the Union, and 19 against. . . . It is hereby certified that the International Woodworkers of America, Affiliated with the Congress of Industrial Organizations, has been designated and selected by a majority of all production and maintenance employees of the Port Gibson Veneer and Box Company, Port Gibson, Mississippi. . . .

By direction of the Board:

John E. Lawyer

Chief, Order Section

4.37   Rosie the Riveter, 1943–44. Letters about the dangers of war work, in Gerald Markowitz and David Rosner, "Slaves of the Depression": *Workers' Letters about Life on the Job* (Ithaca: Cornell University Press, 1987), pp. 214–15. Reprinted with permission from Cornell University Press.

Des Moines, Iowa, April 15, 1943

Dear Sir:

I have a problem of labor: I would like very much to have you help me out. I work for the Monarch Machine & Stamping Co. 1 day that is 8 hrs. I quit because I was afraid of my machine as they put three new people who never saw a press in their lives. They gave us a 5 minute rest period which isn't long enough to go to the rest room and back. Then we work fast and steady until we went home. Just a 1/2 hour out for lunch: I really didn't know which one was going to take my fingers off the man putting up steel plates or the press. I made $3.20 that night. I had 3 cents taken out for Social Security and 30 cents out for gloves that would leave me a check of $2.87. At least that is the way I had it figured out. When I went to get my check they told me I didn't have any thing coming. They told me because I had quit I had to pay for my own examination. They say they have a First Aid. It is nothing but a dirty box above the wash bowl. The top and bandage were all dirty and they didn't have any thing to wash out the cuts on your hands. I ask them what we would do if we ever got hurt and they said they would take care of us and pay our Dr. bill. I said just like you pay for the examination and my wages? Sir I really think I should have some thing for that days work. Its not the idea that I don't like to work hard. I do but I don't want to be treated like the people in Germany are. We are suppose to be a free country. But to work for places and people like that it doesn't seem that way. I am sorry to have to write you a letter like this but I want what's coming to me and so do other people. We are all trying to do what we can for our country but if we lose our hands then we are no good to our selves or our country. Hoping to hear from you soon.

M. L. L.

Wheeling, West Virginia, December 30, 1944

Mr. and Mrs. President Roosevelt:

Am writing to both of you as what I have to say is very important to the world of tomorrow. I know you are all very busy but you are the only one I can run to as a mother.

I have a daughter 23, very well educated, but when this war took her husband she thought she could do something for him and her country and she went into a defense plant. He has been overseas 2 years 4 months. One day I was called to the hospital; my daughter lost two fingers—index and middle finger. She just got over the second operation of these fingers and her health is broken. But she isn't the only girl; there were 5 girls in one week that worked at the Wheeling Corrugating in Wheeling that lost fingers. They make their help work without guards and tongs and bad presses. The girls are some day going to be mothers and do house work. How can they do this without fingers? I taught my daughter how to take care of a home before going out into the world and because some people want to make money these girls have to lose some part of their body. Yes, they have Government inspectors in but the Wheeling Steel can buy them over and have them on their side. They make these girls work in damp places, even stand in water. What do you think our future mothers are going to be like? I am not speaking for my daughter alone but for the other girls.

The C.I.O. tries to do every thing they can but the Wheeling runs Wheeling and round about town. I do think they should give these girls artificial fingers as being a mother means dresses to make and button up, and nearly everything means you need your fingers in the home to make good mothers and to rear good citizens. So Mr. and Mrs. Roosevelt that is why I am writing this letter to you as I have faith in you and know you both will understand. But after these girls are hurt they try to put them back on presses; they can't get jobs elsewhere. What can they do without fingers? So if you will give this a little of your attention I will be so thankful.
MRS. U. S.

4.38   Postwar Outlook for Working Women, 1947. Gladys Dickason, "Women in Labor Unions," *Annals of the American Academy of Political and Social Science*, Vol. 251 (May 1947), pp. 70–78.

In Alabama recently a farmer's wife, who was also a shirtmaker in a small-town clothing factory, visited the Governor of the state with a union delegation to report a case of mob violence against union organizers. After hearing her story, the Governor ordered an investigation and issued a statement emphasizing that union members possessed the same rights under the law as other people.

This woman in the office of the Governor of her state epitomizes the progress that working women have made through union organization. We have come a long way. . . .

The spectacular increase in women membership in unions during the war can undoubtedly be ascribed to the type of jobs they entered, yet in the decade before the war, the number of women union members tripled under the labor legislation of the first two Roosevelt administrations which put collective bargaining on a firmer basis. This, in turn made possible the new organizational policy adopted by the American labor movement in the later thirties, that of organizing workers on an industrial instead of a craft basis. As a result large numbers of unskilled, semi-skilled and white-collar workers were unionized, and it was to these groups that the majority of women workers largely belonged.

Traditional prejudices about the abilities and status of women have played a part in retarding the organization of women workers. Among the unions themselves there has been in the past some distrust of women's loyalty as union members and a tendency to look upon them as an unstable and unreliable factor in the union—a "blithering liability" as one male unionist put it.

On the side of society there has been an idea that the participation of women in union activities, and especially in strikes, was unfeminine and improper. Striking women garment workers in 1924 were arrested and sent to jail after being called "low women, a disgrace to their sex." Official government guarantees, after 1932, of the right to organize helped to remove the stigma of "disorderly" and "unfeminine" conduct from the union activities of women.

In the past some unions have had restrictions barring women from membership. Today all CIO unions and most AFL unions admit women without regard to skill, color or creed. . . .

The unions having the largest number of women members in 1945 included the United Automobile Workers of America, CIO with 280,000 women members, constituting 28 per cent of its total membership; the United Electrical Radio and Machine Workers of America, CIO with 280,000 women members, or 40 per cent of its total membership; the International Ladies' Garment Workers' Union, AFL, with 225,000 members, or 75 per cent of its membership; the Amalgamated Clothing Workers of America, CIO, with 200,000 women members, or 66 cent of its total membership; and Textile Workers Union of America, CIO, with 180,000 women members, making up 40 per cent of its total membership. . . .

The entrance of large numbers of women into industry during the war and the endorsement by the National War Labor Board of the principle of equal pay for equal work have given impetus to the efforts of unions to secure equal clauses in union contracts. . . .

The importance of union membership to women is by no means limited to the economic sphere. Unions promote the political education and community activities of women workers in a number of ways, both direct and indirect.

Women attending union meetings, discussing the concrete problem of whether management can afford to give them a raise, are led on into talking and thinking about such matters as the future of their industry, the relation of their industry to other industries, whether there will be a depression in 1947, what causes depressions, and so on, until they find themselves discussing and analyzing the fundamental social and economic problems of our time.

Through union activity women get to know their community and its problems as they could do in no other way. They become acquainted with fellow workers from different sections of the community and of different social, religious, and nationality groups. Seeing each other at union meetings, working together on union committees, they learn to know each other as people and to understand each other's problems. This helps to break down social barriers and racial and religious prejudices.

Working-class women do not as a rule belong to the Red Cross, women's clubs, and similar community organizations to which leisured middle-class women belong, unless the union provides an opportunity for them to participate. During the war unions secured for their women members a chance to work with the Red Cross, the United Service Organizations, civilian defense agencies, and similar groups. . . . The working girls, who were often self-distrustful because they lacked social and administrative experience, discovered that when put to the test they could acquit themselves as successfully as anybody else. In a number of cases the union women were made chairmen of their local units.

Women union members have taken an active part in the work of the CIO Political Action Committee and in the political activities of AFL and independent unions. They have helped to get out the vote, talked to their neighbors, studied the legislative records of their congressmen and representatives and enlisted support behind candidates with a good record on progressive legislation. These activities have not only made them more alert citizens but have added to their general self-confidence and self-respect. . . .

Many unions have expanded their educational programs in order to encourage women members' participation in union activities. The United Automobile Workers during the war established a Women's Bureau in its War Policy Division, and in 1944 held a national conference of women members. Some of the recommendations made at this conference were subsequently incorporated in model contract clauses and recommended to local unions for inclusion in their collective bargaining demands. This union is also training women as union officers through its Leadership Training Course, which educates members for administrative posts in the union.

Women members may be found in nearly all administrative union positions except that of national or international president, though they are not, as a rule, represented in proportion to their numbers in the union. This discrepancy arises partly from the fact that there are more men union members in highly skilled jobs and partly from the fact that women workers simply have less spare time to devote to union activities than have men. . . .

From what has been said, it is evident that the trade union movement, during the past several decades, has played an important part in the progress women have made toward full participation in the country's political, economic, and social life. It has done so primarily by working toward the achievement of full participation of all working people—men and women—in our society. What it has done for the male worker in giving him a greater degree of security, a greater measure of self-respect and confidence, a feeling of belonging, it has done similarly for the woman worker. But it has meant even more for the woman worker because of her special problems.

The labor movement has recognized these special problems and has helped solve them, as described above, by collective bargaining, legislative, and community activities. But the great contribution of the trade unions is in their concern for and protection of *all* workers, regardless of race, color, creed or sex. By increasing the economic protection and equality for all workers, it is making a great contribution toward the special problems of women, just as it has contributed toward the special problems of other groups.

5

THE ERA OF THE POSTWAR SOCIAL
CONTRACT, 1947–1973

The quarter century after World War II proved to be the most prosperous period in U.S. history. For most of that period the U.S. economy dominated world markets and its rising productivity raised the income of most citizens. The car in every garage and chicken in every pot that Herbert Hoover had promised voters on the eve of the Great Depression became by the 1960s sometimes more than one car in a multiple-car garage and a beef steak on every grill. Public policies and rising incomes created a suburban nation in which a majority of families and individuals, including most better-paid workers, owned their residences.

Mass immigration having ended more than 20 years earlier, the labor force consisted of far fewer foreign-born workers whose primary language was not English. World War II, which conscripted more than ten million men of working age, hastened the Americanization and acculturation of servicemen and women. Ethnic and religious differences still separated groups of working people from each other but with nothing like the force of such factors in the recent past. Far more divisive were racial tensions. Beginning with the World War II years and persisting without let-up in the immediate post-war decades, both blacks and whites left the farms and cities of the South for better jobs to the north and west. They brought with them Southern culture and mores, especially sharp racial identities and the color line. What had once been seen as a peculiarly Southern problem turned into a truly national problem, one that reverberated among workers and their organizations. Far sharper than the distinction between Protestant, Catholic, and Jew, which the religious sociologist Will Herberg declared to be post-war society's defining characteristic, was the split between a white nation and its black minority counterpart (or in the Southwest, the split between white and brown, Anglo and Mexican).

Three books written for popular audiences by the economist John Kenneth Galbraith best capture the spirit of the new age of prosperity. The first published in 1952, *American Capitalism: A Theory of Countervailing Power,* asserts that the United States had achieved relative economic stability (defining depressions and business cycles as a relic of a less knowledgeable past) through a system in which big business, big agriculture, big labor, and big government regulated and restrained each other. The visible hands of the leaders of powerful institutions replaced Adam Smith's invisible hand of the marketplace to create economic equilibrium, job security, and rising incomes. The second Galbraith book, published in 1958, *The Affluent Society,* provided the era with its name. In it, Galbraith described a society fueled by consumption of private goods, one in which the magnificence of private affluence stood in contrast to public squalor. Finally, the third book in the trilogy, *The New Industrial Society* (1967), saw American capitalism and affluence as the "end of history." A new class of technocrats who occupied the planning positions in major corporations and government (including the military) along with their junior partners in the trade unions created a "technostructure" in which they eliminated economic cycles, administered industrial relations harmoniously, and controlled the future. For Galbraith, all modern societies were fated to evolve in the pattern set by the United States.

A measure of reality underlay Galbraith's three-part portrait. Between 1947 and 1973, workers never seemed to have it so good. Despite a few hiccups in the economy, price stability and employment security proved to be the norm. Thus whenever prices rose more than expected or unemployment increased, Galbraith's technocratic private and public planners acted to ameliorate conditions. Real earnings and incomes more than doubled for most workers in this period; for their children a secondary school diploma became common currency; and ever-increasing numbers of working-class sons and daughters could plan on attending institutions of higher education in which they obtained two- or four-year degrees.

Much of the prosperity and stability for working people flowed from the strength and size of the labor movement. At the end of World War II and again in the midst of the Korean War, trade unionists represented one-third of the civilian, non-agricultural labor force, the highest union density ever attained. AFL affiliates had long histories of union power, collective bargaining, and enforceable contracts in the building, printing, and trucking trades, where many employers were relatively small and weak. In the 1950s the CIO unions bargained collectively with some of the largest and most powerful corporations in the nation, especially in the automobile, steel, rubber, and electrical industries. If most corporate leaders would have preferred a union-free environment, they respected the power of their union adversaries and also realized that they could no longer rely on the support of government officials or the courts when they were locked in industrial combat. So they negotiated firmly with the union leaders across the bargaining table, paying their workers generously in order to obtain a freer hand in regulating the workplace. *Fortune* magazine characterized the contract negotiated between General Motors and the United Automobile Workers in 1950, "the treaty of Detroit." It was a treaty that promised industrial peace for five years, guaranteed workers annual productivity wage increases on top of negotiated increases, offered protection against price inflation through cost-of-living-adjustments (COLAs), provided generous paid vacations, and improved substantially health and retirement benefits. In subsequent negotiations between the union and the automobile companies, workers won not only improved wages and benefits but also obtained Supplementary Unemployment Benefits (SUB), a back-door means for the union leaders to win a guaranteed annual wage for their members. SUB enabled automobile workers and also steel workers to survive cyclical layoffs in those industries without surrendering their customary income. The contracts negotiated by such relatively powerful unions as the UAW and the United Steel Workers had a ripple effect. Other unionized industries followed their template in order to keep their employees content. Industrial relations specialists described such developments as "pattern bargaining." Even non-union enterprises reacted to what happened in the unionized sector of the economy. Such successful non-union enterprises as IBM, Eastman Kodak, Sears Roebuck, and others kept unions at bay and their employees satisfied by providing their own version of the benefits negotiated by the UAW and the USW. They offered their own more informal versions of job seniority; developed avenues through which workers could express and resolve their work-related grievances; and tendered health and retirement benefits as generous, or more so, than those won by union workers.

With unions representing nearly a third of the labor force throughout the late 1940s, 1950s, and into the 1960s, politicians paid close attention to the desires of union members. Unionists and their family members voted more heavily than non-union working people. And many unions, especially those associated with the CIO, were more active politically than ever before. By and large, unions worked through and within the Democratic party. In Michigan, the CIO and the Democratic party were practically indistinguishable; the same was true in Chicago and many other places. If most unions and their members preferred Democrats, the two major parties competed with each other for the union vote. As a result, during the Eisenhower Republican presidency (1953–61) as well as during the Democratic administrations of Harry S. Truman, John F. Kennedy, and Lyndon B. Johnson, Congress increased the minimum wage and brought more workers under its aegis; improved social security benefits and also widened the ranks covered by federal pensions; and made unemployment benefits more generous.

Between the gains negotiated by their unions and the benefits funded by government, workers achieved remarkable advances in real income, a measure of economic security, and the promise of a decent retirement. It was the combination of a productive private economy in which unions wielded real power and a national government committed to creating a floor beneath which none could fall that fueled the age of high mass-consumption. Even a poorly paid, Bronx, New York worker, who seldom had enough discretionary income to enjoy a night on the town with his wife and family, boasted to a *New York Times* reporter in the 1950s that nowhere else in the world did workers have as many goods and as much choice as in the United States.

However, all was not roses for workers and unions. Even at the peak of their power, unions suffered from internal divisions and external attack. The cold war which raged internationally between the United States and its Allies and the Soviet Union and its friends echoed within the labor movement. Several CIO unions had been built and led by communists and AFL leaders had frequently charged the entire CIO with being under communist influence. As the Cold War heated up in 1948 and 1949, internal dissension and conflict intensified within CIO and its affiliates. Anti-reds fought reds in the UAW, with the anti-communist bloc led by Walter Reuther gaining control of the union after a bitter battle. As the CIO began to move against alleged communist-led affiliates, some former communist union leaders such as Joseph Curran of the National Maritime Union and Michael Quill of the Transport Workers repudiated communism. Within the United Electrical Workers Union and the International Longshoremen's and Warehousemen's Union, the left-wing leadership refused to repudiate communism or the Soviet Union. So, in 1949–50, the CIO expelled the electrical workers union, the longshoremen, and seven smaller affiliates for serving the interests of a political party and a foreign nation before those of its members and the labor movement.

If the CIO had long been associated with left-wing causes and communism, several AFL affiliates had their own traditions of corruption and gangsterism. In fact, such links between union leaders and communism or corruption enabled anti-union employers and politicians to engage in more effective forms of public relations and propaganda. If unions grew too powerful and monopolized the labor force, their enemies maintained, labor bosses would exploit their members for the benefit of crooks and foreign ideologies. Such charges reiterated regularly stoked the congressional campaign to modify the National Labor Relations Act (Wagner Act) of 1935 and to achieve success in 1947 with the passage of the Taft-Hartley Act. Taft-Hartley restored to employers many of the rights that they had used before 1937 to combat unions, and it denied workers and unions some of the most effective weapons of industrial combat. Neither the CIO's expulsion of its left-wing unions nor the AFL's suspension from membership of such corrupt unions as the International Longshoremen's Association, the Brotherhood of Teamsters, and the Bakery and Confectionary Workers' union, saved labor from congressional investigation or public condemnation. In the 1950s a select Senate investigating committee led by Senator John McClellan of Arkansas with Robert F. Kennedy as its chief counsel proved crime and corruption rampant in the labor movement, focusing most closely on Dave Beck and his associates in the Teamsters' union. The committee's findings led to the Landrum-Griffen Act of 1959, which further subjected trade unions to federal regulation and outlawed several union practices.

The rising criticism of trade unionism in the media and in government caused the leaders of a labor movement divided since 1936 to seek reconciliation. With the deaths of the long-time AFL and CIO presidents, William Green and Philip Murray, occurring in rapid order in 1953, their successors began peace talks that culminated in 1955 with the official merger of the CIO and the AFL into the AFL-CIO, with the latter federation gaining the bulk of the offices and power in the reunited movement, befitting its far larger membership. Formed ostensibly to foster a more powerful and dynamic labor movement, the AFL-CIO was, in reality, a defensive reaction to trade unionism's diminishing appeal and increasingly negative public face.

The reunification of the labor movement coincided with a host of forces, some barely perceptible in the 1950s, that foreshadowed the subsequent decline of trade unionism. Throughout the 1950s and 1960s the powerful national corporations that recognized and bargained with unions sought new means to limit union power. Never really reconciled to negotiating with representatives of their employees, these enterprises opened more and more plants in non-union sectors of the South and West. When they could not run away from unions or had little choice other than to recognize unions in their new plants, corporate leaders turned to technology to weaken labor power. A specter haunted the land in the 1950s: automation. Using capital to replace labor, new and better machines to increase per capita productivity, employers shrank the labor force in automobiles, steel, electrical goods, on the waterfront, in tire production, and in one mass-production industry after another. If automation did not enable corporations to eliminate unions, it did make it easier for them to negotiate hard bargains.

A partly unintended consequence of the union gains of the post-war era and the stability they brought to industrial relations was the growth of a gap between union members and leaders. Guaranteed annual wage increases, insured against the pain of cyclical unemployment, defended against arbitrary discipline or discharge by shop-floor superiors, protected against the costs of illness, and assured of a decent retirement, workers became separated from their unions. Seldom called on to strike and absent by choice from most local union meetings, members practiced what Walter Reuther condemned as "slot-machine unionism"; in return for their union dues, members expected to hit the jackpot. The widening estrangement between union members and their leaders increased the audience for critics of the labor movement and enabled more sophisticated employers to wean their employees away from union loyalty.

Other factors also fostered the estrangement. Many of the industrial unions in mass-production industry had more African American members than ever and yet leadership remained overwhelmingly white. Moreover, white workers seemed to control the most desirable, skilled, and highly paid jobs in industry. Unions had done much, perhaps more than any other comparable institution, to improve life for African American workers but in the highly charged environment created by the civil rights revolution that emerged in the 1950s and exploded in the 1960s, many African American workers were no longer content with what they perceived to be an intolerably slow pace of change. They wanted better jobs and higher pay, now! They wanted union office and power today, not in the distant future. The result was internecine conflict in many unions with a large African American membership, including the creation of schismatic and revolutionary black workers' organizations on the one hand, and efforts by union officials to combat them on the other.

A similar sort of estrangement developed in the 1960s between older, established union leaders who cut their hair short, wore business suits, used tobacco, and drank alcohol, and younger workers, who let their hair grow long, preferred jeans and t-shirts, listened to rock, and smoked marijuana. The cultural conflicts that rent society also played themselves out inside the trade unions. Union officials and younger workers seemed to speak different languages and worship different gods.

The war in southeast Asia which split the nation apart in the 1960s was also echoed in the trade unions. At first, most labor leaders, long-willing recruits in the war against "international communism," heartily supported the U.S. war in Vietnam. Yet, as resistance to the war grew among the general populace and within the Democratic party, comparable divisions began to emerge in the labor movement. Most "official" labor leaders continued to act as cold warriors and support the war. But rifts began to develop in the labor movement as Reuther, William Wimpinsinger (an emerging leader in the Machinists' union), Jerry Wurf of the fast-growing American Federation of State, County, and Municipal Employees (AFSCME), and several leaders of the clothing trades' unions joined the antiwar coalition. When the advocates of peace gained control of the Democratic party in 1972 and nominated George McGovern for president, George Meany and most of the other leaders of the AFL-CIO refused to go along with the party. Instead their silence implicitly provided political support to Richard Nixon and the Republican party. The labor movement became increasingly isolated politically and white workers, including many union members, drifted away from their former loyalties to the Roosevelt-New Deal Democratic party.

One bright hope loomed on the trade union scene. During the affluent decades, public employment had grown rapidly as the government built a welfare state and expanded education from kindergarten to college in order to cope with the children of the baby boom. In several large cities, New York City most especially in 1958, and at the federal level in 1962 under an executive order issued by President Kennedy, public employees gained the right to unionize and to bargain collectively. In response, all sorts of public employees, including clerks, mid-level managers, scientists, technicians, police, firefighters, and especially teachers, joined unions. Among the greatest beneficiaries of this surge of unionism were the American Federation of State, County, and Municipal Employees, the American Federation of Government Employees (AFGE), the American

Federation of Teachers (AFT), and the National Education Association (NEA). These public employee unions brought large numbers of women and minorities into the labor movement, making many labor leaders more sensitive to the concerns of women and non-whites. Their unions led the movement to remove the wage gap between men and women by seeking to redefine traditional definitions of skill and fighting for the principle of "comparable worth" in order to raise the wages and salaries of those doing traditionally women's jobs. They also pushed for affirmative action in order to provide more opportunities for qualified women and minority workers.

Union success in public employment was not matched in the rapidly expanding private white-collar and high-technology sectors. Most private technical, managerial, and service workers remained non-union. Because those sectors proved to be the fastest growing portion of the labor market, overall union density declined as the 1960s passed into the 1970s. In the banking and financial services and the innovative technology enterprises, employers proved successful in combating unions, practicing some of the same methods as IBM, Eastman Kodak, and Sears.

Few, however, were aware that as the 1970s opened, the era of affluence was at its end. Or that deindustrialization would wipe out jobs and communities in a wide swath of the country from Buffalo, Camden, and Pittsburgh on the northeastern end across the upper Midwest almost to the Mississippi River. With whole industries going under as competition in the world market intensified and with union density steadily declining, the age of ever-rising real wages and earnings would cease. The "Other America," that foreign nation that Michael Harrington identified in 1962 in which poverty and need still existed and where even many full-time workers did not earn enough to support themselves and their dependents, would come to incorporate a larger share of working-class Americans.

LABOR'S COLD WAR

The first two documents in this section show how the United Electrical Workers of America (UE) defended itself against charges by the CIO that the UE served the interests of both a non-union institution (the Communist Party, USA) and a foreign nation, the Soviet Union. Document 5.3, by contrast, provides the rationale for the CIO's expulsion and condemnation of such left-led unions as the UE. What do these arguments suggest about the impact of the Cold War on organized labor?

5.1   UE Resolution Against CIO, 1949. United Electrical, Radio & Machine Workers of America (UE), *Fourteenth Convention Proceeding*, Hotel Hollenden, Cleveland, Ohio, September 19–23, 1949, pp. 103–5.

RESOLUTION AGAINST RAIDING AND DICTATORSHIP IN THE CIO

From the beginning of April, 1948, until the end of July, 1949, the National Office of the CIO, the CIO Auto Workers, the United Steelworkers and the CIO Communications Workers of America have attempted to raid 456 UE shops. In 418 cases these efforts were defeated. Thirty-eight raids conducted in collusion with employers were successful, to the great injury of the workers in these shops.

More than a decade ago the workers of the mass production industries of America organized industrial unions through which they could fight to improve their wages and working conditions and gain greater security in their jobs. To strengthen themselves in carrying out these same objectives, the workers of our own and other great industries formed a federation of autonomous unions, the Congress of Industrial Organizations. Millions of workers joined the industrial unions of the CIO to advance their economic welfare.

The UE made its contribution to this growth by organizing 600,000 workers in the electrical and machine industry. . . . Gradually over the years, individuals in the top leadership of CIO and some of its affiliated unions have sought to pervert the original purpose and organization function of the CIO. They have sought to transform CIO from an instrumentality and servant of the unions and their membership to a dictatorship over unions and members alike.

These efforts came to a head some two years ago when this same group used the CIO executive board to decree that the CIO should henceforward subordinate itself to the political interests of the Democratic Party leadership. That decree meant that partisan politics should from that time forward take precedence over the economic interests of the membership of CIO unions.

This group has made it clear that it is not concerned with whether or not any CIO union takes action to advance the economic interests of its membership. But it does demand absolute and complete conformity on all matters of politics as a condition for remaining in the CIO.

This policy of subordinating the interests of the members of CIO unions to the political dictates of the CIO leadership is defended on the false ground that it represents the will of the majority. . . .

The UE and other CIO unions have fought against these efforts to pervert the purpose and function of the CIO. . . .

It will be the policy of the UE to strengthen itself by all possible means to protect and advance the interests of its membership. The UE will carry on an unremitting drive to organize the unorganized, and to bring into its ranks all workers in the industries covered by our Union. As we have always done, we will continue to work and cooperate with all unions who share our objectives.

5.2   A UE Delegate Unloads on the CIO, 1949. United Electrical, Radio & Machine Workers of America (UE), *Fourteenth Convention Proceedings*, Hotel Hollenden, Cleveland, Ohio, September 19–23, 1949, pp. 126–27.

DELEGATE ROBERT HANNIGAN (Local 262): Now, I heard so much at this convention and eight other conventions in the past eight years of all of the communists in the UE that are running this organization. I am a little sick and tired. I am an Irish Catholic from Boston and I am not a member of the Communist Party and I am not a paid member of the UE staff. (*Applause and shouts*)

I believe in the policies adopted in the past by the conventions and by the officers of this union for one reason, because they are an honest effort to improve the conditions of the workers that pay guys like me and paid people like you.

I have put a lot in my stomach for nine years, you know, and I have got a lot of things I could talk about. I don't want to take up the time of the delegates here to talk about them for one reason, previous speakers have spoken about the democracy of the CIO in Massachusetts. . . . There is no democracy in the State CIO in Massachusetts and there won't be any democracy in the National CIO if we continue or if we hope to adopt the policies of [the UE's anticommunist faction]. . . .

Reference must be made to Section 6 of the majority report. . . . It reads as follows: "The President of the CIO should give the UE assurance that CIO officers, regional directors, organizers, agents and employees will in no way interfere with the right of the UE members to run their union in accordance with their own wishes. He should give further assurance that UE will not in any way be interfered with by the national CIO in its right to designate its representative to the Executive Board of the CIO. . . ."

Here is the part I like—here is the part Hannigan from Boston likes: "In the event the Executive Board does not receive these assurances from the President of the CIO, this Convention authorizes the Board to withhold per capita tax to the CIO for such time as it deems necessary for the protection of the interests of the UE."

The part I like is that if the National CIO expects this union to sell its soul and follow their policies, I don't want to sleep in the same bed because I don't want to become contaminated. (*Applause*)

5.3 The CIO's Purge of the Left-Led Unions, 1950. "Report of the Committee on Resolutions." In the *1950 Proceedings of the Twelfth Constitutional Convention of the Congress of Industrial Organizations*. Chicago, Illinois, November 20–24, 1950, pp. 477–81.

NOW, THEREFORE BE IT RESOLVED

The CIO in convention assembled hereby ratifies, approves and confirms and adopts as the action of this convention in conformance with the provisions of Article III, Section 6 of our Constitution, the action of the CIO Executive Board in expelling from the CIO and canceling the certificates of affiliation of the American Communications Association

Food, Tobacco, Agricultural & Allied Workers Union of America
International Fishermen & Allied Workers of America
International Fur & Leather Workers Union
International Longshoremen's & Warehousemen's Union
International Union of Mine, Mill & Smelter Workers
National Union of Marine Cooks & Stewards
United Office & Professional Workers of America
United Public Workers of America

AND, BE IT FURTHER RESOLVED,

The CIO commends President Murray, the Executive Board and its Committees which conducted the hearings, on the fair and careful manner in which they carried out the mandate of the last Constitutional Convention. The CIO notes with satisfaction that each of the charged unions was given a full and fair hearing after notice, and was accorded every opportunity to introduce documentary evidence and to present testimony, to file briefs and supplementary material, and to cross-examine opposing witnesses. The CIO particularly commends the Committees for their careful and meticulous weighing of the evidence, and for their detailed and dispassionate reports to the Executive Board.

The CIO further notes that although the Committees concluded that the policies of the named international unions were directed toward the achievement of the purposes of the Communist Party rather than those of the CIO, the Committees also recognized that the rank and file members of the unions are not Communists but loyal American trade unionists who had been deceived and misled by leadership disloyal to them and to America.

NOW, THEREFORE, BE IT FURTHER RESOLVED,

The CIO urges the members of the expelled unions who are loyal to the principles of American democracy and of democratic unionism to return to the CIO and participate in building in CIO powerful industrial unions to protect and promote their trade union and democratic interests. Hundreds of thousands of workers have already done so.

The CIO declares that it will continue its fight against Communism until the last adherent of that vicious totalitarian ideology is rooted out of the trade union movement.

COMMITTEE SECRETARY CURRAN: Your committee recommends adoption of this resolution.

. . . The motion was seconded.

PRESIDENT MURRAY: You have heard the motion. It is to adopt the report of the committee, and in accordance with the provision of the Constitution you will again be required to stand.

Those favoring the report of the committee will stand.

Those opposed to committees report will stand.

The resolution has been adopted by more than two-thirds of the delegates accredited to this convention; in fact, by the unanimous vote of the delegates accredited to this convention. And the unions stand expelled. That is that.

EMBOURGEOISEMENT IN THE 1950S?

In the 1950s numerous observers of workers and their labor movement, including many within the trades unions, remarked about how middle-class workers had become in their consumption patterns and everyday behavior. Samuel Lubell portrays in Document 5.4 the evolution of trade unionists between the 1930s and 1950s from class warriors to contented citizens. Harvey Swados, however, in Document 5.5 tosses cold water on Lubell's portrayal of workers as just another group of contented middle-class citizens. According to Swados, why haven't workers become embourgeoisified? In Document 5.6 Mira Komarovsky describes how hard workers struggled to become part of a mass-consumer society, how such desires drove husbands and wives both to work for wages, and how the desire to consume created tensions in low wage-earning families.

5.4 "We Don't Have Any Really Big Issues Left," 1951. Excerpt from Samuel Lubell, *The Future of American Politics* (New York: Harper, 1952), pp. 174–76. Copyright 1951, 1952 by Samuel Lubell. Reprinted by permission of HarperCollins Publishers, Inc.

The same photographs of Franklin Roosevelt and Frank Murphy hung on the wall but it was hard to believe that it was the same place. When I first visited Chrysler Local Seven of the United Automobile Workers a few days after Roosevelt's third term victory, the scene was one of belligerent activity. Bulletin boards bristled with photographs of police clubbing strikers and of tear gas riotings. When the union's educational director heard that I was analyzing the election for the *Saturday Evening Post,* he stiffened suspiciously and seemed about to have me thrown out. Then, he began boasting freely of how class conscious the auto workers were and how ready they were to vote Roosevelt a fourth or a fifth term. He wore a lumber jacket. With his feet on his desk and a buzzer by his hand, he looked the very picture of newly arrived power.

Returning eight years later, after Truman's victory, the whole atmosphere of the local had changed. The strike photographs had come down from the bulletin boards and had been replaced by idyllic snapshots of the union's annual outings and sporting events. An honor roll listed fifty-nine union members who had been killed in the war. Nearby stood a cabinet filled with loving cups and other trophies won in city-wide UAW tournaments. The "class-conscious" educational director was gone—ousted in the UAW-wide fight against Communists which Walter Reuther led. On their desks, the new officers had propped the slogan, "UAW Americanism for Us." They were wearing green jackets and green silk legion caps.

In 1940 the flavor of the local was one of street barricades and sit-down strikes; eight years later it was almost like a lodge hall.

Not only Chrysler Seven but the whole American labor movement has undergone a striking transformation. The change may not be as sharp as the contrast between my two visits to Chrysler Seven suggests. Still, the dynamic near-revolutionary surge, which doubled union membership from 1935 to 1938 and which brought such industrial giants as General Motors and U.S. Steel to the bargaining table, is now gone. The labor dynamo has slowed down. . . .

Some union leaders, like Reuther, still talk of trade unionism as the revolutionary force of our times through which society is to be remade. But the inner mechanics of Reuther's own union have come to resemble more closely the momentum of a bureaucracy than the trampling of a new social movement. Once strikes flared in the auto industry at the drop of an unkind word by a foreman. Much of that militancy reflected the bitter factional rivalry for power within the UAW and the grudging refusal of employers to concede full union recognition. Both these minor wars have been settled, not alone in autos but in all of the mass production industries. With their leadership stabilized, the unions have become a disciplining and stabilizing force upon their own membership. With union recognition no longer in dispute, the grievance machinery which has been set up in the various industries has acquired a status all its own, with an established body of precedents accepted as binding by both labor and management.

In the giant industries, custom—a new kind of common law—has become the final umpire in more and more of the disputes between workers and management.

Nor are Reuther's dynamic public utterances supported by such actions as his signing in 1950 a five-year contract with General Motors. The five year contract was a hedge against expected depression. But, as one astute observer in Detroit remarked, "When Reuther agreed to stabilize working conditions and wages for so long a period, he removed the major incentive for militant political action from one immense segment of his union."

The threat of inflation after Korea sparked the labor dynamo with a new fighting cause—to keep wages rising with living costs; apart from this though, the urgent sense of grievance, so evident in the late 1930's, is gone. In the summer of 1951 one union leader complained to me at being asked to draft the platform for a state CIO. "Ten or fifteen years ago I would have welcomed the assignment," he remarked. "There were so many things I was mad about. But what can I agitate for now? We don't have any really big issues left."

5.5   The Persistence of Discontent, 1957. Harvey Swados, "The Myth of the Happy Worker," *The Nation* (August 17, 1957). Reprinted in Swados, *A Radical's America* (Boston: Little, Brown, 1962), pp. 110–120. Reprinted with permission from the August 17, 1957 issue of *The Nation*. For subscription information call 800.333.8536. Portions of each week's *Nation* magazine can be accessed at www.thenation.com.

With the personnel man and the union leader, both of whom presumably see the worker from day to day, growing so far away from him, it is hardly to be wondered at that the middle class in general, and articulate middle-class intellectuals in particular, see the worker vaguely, as through a cloud. One gets the impression that when they do consider him, they operate from one of two unspoken assumptions: (1) The worker has died out like the passenger pigeon, or is dying out, or becoming accultured, like the Navajo. (2) If he is still around, he is just like the rest of us—fat, satisfied, smug, a little restless, but hardly distinguishable from his fellow TV-viewers of the middle class. . . .

But there is one thing that the worker doesn't do like the middle class: he works like a worker. The steel-mill puddler does not yet sort memos, the coal miner does not yet sit in conferences, the cotton mill-hand does not yet sip martinis from his lunchbox. The worker's attitude toward his work is generally compounded of hatred, shame, and resignation. . . .

The average automobile worker gets a little better than two dollars an hour. As such he is one of the best-paid factory workers in the country. After twenty years of militant struggle led by the union that I believe to be one of the finest and most democratic labor organizations in the United States, he is earning less than the starting salaries offered to inexperienced and often semiliterate college graduates without dependents. After compulsory deductions for taxes, social security, old-age insurance and union dues, and optional deductions for hospitalization and assorted charities, his pay check for forty hours of work is going to be closer to seventy than to eighty dollars a week. Does this make him middle-class as to income? Does it rate with the weekly take of a dentist, an accountant, a salesman, a draftsman, a journalist? Surely it would be more to the point to ask how a family man can get by in the Fifties on that kind of income. I know how he does it, and I should think the answers would be a little disconcerting to those who wax glib on the satisfactory status of the "formerly" underprivileged.

For one thing, he works a lot longer than forty hours a week—when he can. Since no automobile company is as yet in a position to guarantee its workers anything like fifty weeks of steady forty-hour pay checks, the autoworker knows he has to make it while he can. During peak production periods he therefore puts in nine, ten, eleven, and often twelve hours a day on the assembly line for weeks on end. And that's not all. If he has dependents, as like as not he also holds down a "spare-time" job. I have worked on the line with men who doubled as mechanics, repairmen, salesmen, contractors, builders, farmers, cabdrivers, lumberyard workers, countermen. I would guess that there are many more of these than show up in the official statistics: often a man will work for less if he can be paid under the counter with tax-free dollars.

Nor is that all. The factory worker with dependents cannot carry the debt load he now shoulders—the middle-class debt load, if you like, of nagging payments on car, washer, dryer, TV, clothing, house itself—without family help. Even if he puts in fifty, sixty, or seventy hours a week at one or two jobs, he has to count on his wife's pay check, or his son's, his daughter's, his brother-in-law's; or on his mother's social security, or his father's veteran's pension. The working-class family today is not typically held together by the male wage-earner, but by multiple wage-earners often of several generations who club together to get the things they want and need—or are pressured into believing they must have. It is at best a precarious arrangement; as for its toll on the physical organism and the psyche, that is a question perhaps worthy of further investigation by those who currently pronounce themselves bored with Utopia Unlimited in the Fat Fifties. . . .

The plain truth is that factory work is degrading. It is degrading to any man who ever dreams of doing something worth while with his life; and it is about time we faced the fact. . . . Almost without exception, the men with whom I worked on the assembly line last year felt like trapped animals. Depending on their age and personal circumstances, they were either resigned to their fate, furiously angry at *themselves* for what they were doing, or desperately hunting other work that would pay as well and in addition offer some variety, some prospect of change and betterment. They were sick of being pushed around by harried foremen (themselves more pitied than hated), sick of working like blinkered donkeys, sick of being dependent for their livelihood on a maniacal production-merchandising setup, sick of working in a place where there was no spot to relax during the twelve-minute rest period. (Someday—let us hope—we will marvel that production was still so worshiped in the Fifties that new factories could be built with every splendid facility for the storage and movement of essential parts, but with no place for a resting worker to sit down for a moment but on a fireplug, the edge of a packing case, or the sputum- and oil-stained stairway of a toilet.) The older men stay put and wait for their vacations. But since the assembly line demands young blood (you will have a hard time getting hired if you are over thirty-five), the factory in which I worked was warm with new faces every day; labor turnover was so fantastic and absenteeism so rampant, with the young men knocking off a day or two every week to hunt up other jobs, that the company was forced to overhire in order to have sufficient workers on hand at the starting siren. . . .

5.6 Working Hard to Get Ahead, ca. 1960. An interview by Mira Komarovsky in *Blue Collar Marriage* (New York: Random House, 1962), pp. 66–67. From *Blue-Collar Marriage* by Mira Komarovsky, copyright 1962, 1964 by Random House, Inc. Used by permission of Random House, Inc.

"I guess we want to get things in a hurry," confessed a 19-year-old wife of a factory worker and a mother of a 2-year-old child. She works in a plastics factory, clearing $30 a week. She and her husband came from poor Southern families. When they married three years ago, they "had to start from scratch." They "didn't get a single wedding gift," and didn't have a dish or a fork or a chair. "You go into a store and you nearly go crazy with all the things you want to buy." They had to buy everything "on time," the living room set, the beds, the dinette set, the baby's crib and the car. In addition, they have had doctor's bills. The little girl needed braces on her legs, costing $50. The husband did not want her to work, but they realized that they needed her $30 a week to pay the bills.

This woman gets up at 6:00 A.M. to make breakfast for her husband and to put up his lunch. She wakes him up at 6:15. Then she goes back to sleep because their little girl stays up late at night and sleeps late in the morning. Getting up again at 8:00, she rushes through her housework, cleaning, washing and ironing; then she prepares dinner and leaves it to be warmed by her husband at night. At 3:30 she leaves for work. A neighbor looks after the little girl for half an hour or so before her husband returns to take over. He takes care of the child, giving her her bath and her supper. The wife returns home at 10:30. Her husband calls for her in the car, with the neighbor looking after the child. They go to sleep at about 11:00; once in a while they watch a late T.V. show and are sleepy the next morning.

The best time of the week is Saturday. They take the child along and spend the day in the stores. Her husband "isn't the kind who enjoys going out with the fellows . . . he is a homebody." Apart from her sister's family they know no couples in the community. Shopping appears to be their main recreation. "We have never seen such beautiful things as we see here in the stores. One time we had two hundred dollars and spent it like crazy. We got a bedspread and curtains for the living room and a tricycle for the girl. It's all the things that we need, but I guess we are in too great a hurry to get them." She expects to stop working when they get what they need and can live on her husband's salary, but she will miss work. "There is so much commotion and yelling in the house in the morning. When I get to the factory I work alone in the room and it's restful. It's the only time I get a chance to think straight. Then during the breaks and at lunch I talk to the girls and I like that too."

AFL-CIO

The following five documents suggest how the reunited labor movement planned to meet the needs of workers. Document 5.7 explains why it was necessary for the AFL and CIO to unite in 1955 in order to better serve unions and their members. In the next document (5.8), George Meany, the president of the united AFL-CIO, sings the praises of Cold War ideology, asserting how the organization will promote stability and freedom around the world. By contrast, in Document 5.9, Walter Reuther, an AFL-CIO vice president and head of its Industrial Union Department (IUD), lays out a far more ambitious agenda for the reunited labor movement with its primary focus on domestic matters. How do you account for the different visions held by Meany and Reuther concerning the role of a reunited labor movement? Which vision do you consider more representative of the labor movement in the age of Eisenhower? Document 5.10 illustrates how the AFL-CIO attempted to deal with a problem that had plagued many former AFL affiliates—union corruption—by criticizing and expelling the International Brotherhood of Teamsters from membership. In the 1950s new technologies that fell under the rubric of automation began to eliminate jobs in several mass-production industries. In response, Reuther explains (Document 5.11) why the nation, its government, corporations, and unions must deal with automation in a productive and socially beneficial way.

5.7 Era of Labor Unity, 1955. Preamble of the Constitution of American Federation of Labor and Congress of Industrial Organizations, 1955. Reprinted in *The Industrial and Labor Relations Review* (1955), p. 347.

Preamble

The establishment of this Federation through the merger of the American Federation of Labor and the Congress of Industrial Organizations is an expression of the hopes and aspirations of the working people of America.

We seek the fulfillment of these hopes and aspirations through democratic processes within the framework of our constitutional government and consistent with our institutions and traditions.

At the collective bargaining table, in the community, in the exercise of the rights and responsibilities of citizenship, we shall responsibly serve the interests of all the American people.

We pledge ourselves to the more effective organization of working men and women; to the securing to them of full recognition and enjoyment of the rights to which they are justly entitled; to the achievement of ever higher standards of living and working conditions; to the attainment of security for all the people; to the enjoyment of the leisure which their skills make possible; and to the strengthening and extension of our way of life and the fundamental freedoms which are the basis of our democratic society.

We shall combat resolutely the forces which seek to undermine the democratic institutions of our nation and to enslave the human soul. We shall strive always to win full respect for the dignity of the human individual whom our unions serve.

Grateful for the fine traditions of our past, confident of meeting the challenge of the future, we proclaim this constitution.

5.8 Securing the "Benefits of Freedom," 1955. George Meany on the "Merger and the National Welfare," *Industrial and Labor Relations Review* (1955), pp. 349–51.

On December 5, 1955, the largest trade union center in the world came into existence through the merger of the AFL and CIO. After some twenty years of division, the AFL and CIO have found an honorable and dignified basis for unity. . . .

The merged organization holds forth greater promise to the wage earners of America—both organized and unorganized. For trade unionists, the united labor movement means an end to the divisive forces which existed solely because there were two separate organizations. . . . Now and in the future, affiliates of the new organization can direct their funds into a genuine trade union channel: organizing the *un*-organized. . . .

The newly formed trade union center will be in a position, as a consequence of unity, to contribute realistically toward the establishment and maintenance of industrial peace. American management and American labor have developed, down through the years, many more areas of agreement than of disagreement. We both are firmly convinced that democracy is a guarantor of individual freedom, that economic freedom is assured in the free enterprise system, and we oppose tyranny in any totalitarian form. Our disagreements have arisen largely because of continued misunderstanding of trade unionism. Yet, here too, the basic fact remains that men of good will in labor and management have reached collective bargaining agreements year in and year out far more often than they have disagreed. . . .

By promoting economic stability here and at home, therefore, the merged AFL-CIO will make its greatest contribution to the well-being not alone of our fellow citizens but of free people everywhere. We can demonstrate to the world the benefits of freedom and thereby turn the minds of men and women away from the sinister forces which now threatening the enslavement of the free world. Certainly there is no greater contribution which any group of American can make to their fellow countrymen.

5.9 No Mere "Status Quo Unionism," 1955. Walter P. Reuther, "Labor's New Unity," *Industrial and Labor Relations Review* (1955), p. 352.

The realization of our long-cherished dream of honorable, principled labor unity is both a great challenge and a glorious opportunity. What we do with that opportunity, the way we meet that challenge, will in great measure determine the shape and the destiny of the American labor movement for all time.

We of the CIO are rightly proud of our record of fighting for economic, social, and political progress. To the very best of our ability, we have rejected every temptation to act in a narrow, selfish fashion. Rather we have approached the collective bargaining table and lobbied in Congress and the several legislatures, conscious always that we must make progress with, and never at the expense of, the community. Thus we have never considered our problems as unrelated to the needs of the broad community, but rather as symptomatic of the hopes and aspirations of free people in a difficult and trying time in history.

The CIO sees no value in merger if the only achievement is a bigger and more powerful labor movement. We do not want status quo unionism—a labor movement of stagnation. We want numerical growth, of course, but also growth in stature, dedication, and service to our members, their families, and to our nation. This we shall achieve by organizing the millions of workers who are not organized; by fighting against discrimination and racial intolerance, against reaction and corruption and communism; by fighting for the schools, homes, hospitals, and roads our nation needs; by working to bring economic and social justice and freedom to all men everywhere.

This we shall achieve if we use our greater power and resources to build a more effective labor movement and, thus, a better America.

It is in this spirit that we regard merger; in the spirit and the belief that this is the new beginning for organized labor.

We recognize well that no document, no constitution, no book of resolutions will automatically achieve the kind of labor movement we want and must have. These are but the tools at hand.

It is up to us to breathe life and inspiration into these documents. It is up to us to use these tools with dedication, with high resolve, with sweat, and with a real sense of human values.

If we are worthy of the trust which has been placed in us, we will not fail. We must not fail.

5.10 Facing Teamster Corruption, 1957. *Proceedings of the Second Constitutional Convention of the AFL-CIO.* Volume I, Daily Proceedings, Atlantic City, New Jersey, December 5–12, 1957; Use of Official Union Position for Personal Profit and Advantage—President Beck and Vice President Hoffa (Supp. Report, pp. 80–89).

The Committee found that President Beck had in many ways used his official union position for his own substantial personal profit and advantage, many times at the expense of the Teamsters Union. Included in these activities were loans for $200,000 from the Fruehauf Trailer Company after President Beck, as Chairman of the International Brotherhood's Finance Committee, had loaned $1,500,000 of Teamsters' Funds to that Company; a whole series of dealings with Nathan Shefferman by virtue of which Beck and his relatives received substantial sums of money and Shefferman and his relatives received substantial sums of Teamsters Union money; and control of the investment of Teamsters Union funds in such a manner as to advance the private business interests of Beck, members of his family and his associates.

The Committee found that typical of this latter category was a transaction by which President Beck, as a trustee of a memorial fund for the widow of a Teamster official, enriched himself out of the investment of the trust in a mortgage.

Vice President Hoffa similarly used his official union position, the Committee found, for personal profit and advantage, frequently to the direct detriment of the membership of the Teamsters Union. Typical of the findings with respect to Vice President Hoffa was the finding of the Committee with respect to Test Fleet Corporation. Test Fleet Corporation was established for the benefit of Vice President Hoffa and Bert Brennan by Commercial Carriers, a trucking company whose employees were represented by the Teamsters Union. Shortly after Vice President Hoffa terminated a strike of the employees of Commercial Carriers, Commercial Carriers established Test Fleet as a corporation, transferred trucks which it already owned to Test Fleet and leased back those same trucks from Test Fleet. Test Fleet, whose stock was held in the names of Brennan's and Hoffa's wives, had no employees and did no business other than to receive rentals from Commercial Carriers. The total investment of Hoffa and Brennan in Test Fleet was, at most,

$4,000 and they expended no actual effort or direction in the company's business. But, over a period of years, Commercial Carriers paid enough money to Test Fleet so that Brennan and Hoffa derived $125,000 in income from it.

Similar use of union position for personal advantage was demonstrated by Hoffa's borrowing $18,000 from eleven different Teamster business agents and at least $20,000 from employers under contract with the Teamsters Union. The final item found by the Ethical Practices Committee in this category was Vice President Hoffa's relationship with a real estate promoter whose subdivision was "sponsored" by the Teamsters Union at a time when Hoffa secretly held an option to participate in the profits of the enterprise and had borrowed $25,000 from the promoter.

COMMITTEE CHAIRMAN ROSE: Mr. President and fellow delegates, I want to begin by saying that I consider myself a friend of the Teamsters and that every member of our Committee considers himself a friend of the Teamsters. I believe that every delegate at this Convention considers himself a friend of the Teamsters.

Many of us have received benefits from the cooperation of the Teamsters' organization. I can tell you that right now, at this very minute, my Union is conducting a strike in Louisville, Kentucky, and we are getting splendid cooperation from the Teamsters local organization and its officers.

Because—and precisely because—we know the great role that the Teamsters Union can perform in cooperation with the entire trade union movement, precisely because we know the great record of the Teamsters and the contribution which they can make to the labor movement, we want to see a fraternal, clean Teamsters organization as part of the labor movement. . . .

Let me turn now to an appeal to the Teamsters. Don't waste time; act quickly. Restore the good name of the Teamsters Union, because involved in this appeal and in this proceeding today is not only the fate of 1,400,000 members of the Teamsters Union—involved also is the fate of 15 million organized workers and the fate of 30 million unorganized workers. Involved also is our whole democratic way of life, because in the struggles that are now going on in the world all democracy will be judged by the kind of labor movement we possess. We here this morning are about to make a historic decision on which will depend not only the fate of the organized workers and unorganized workers, but also the good name of our democracy and the role we can play in the events of the world.

The organized labor movement in every single modern civilized country stands in the forefront in fighting for social betterment. They are not merely an economic group, confirmed to their own economic interests. The labor movement is a moral force, must be a moral force, and it needs the cooperation and the good will of people outside the ranks of the organized labor movement in order to prevail. . . .

This is a very historic decision that we are to make this morning. It is a decision of morality versus cynicism and of honesty versus corruption. It is because of this that I urge you, on behalf of our Committee, to adopt our Committee's report.

5.11 The Response to Automation, 1960. Walter P. Reuther Congressional Testimony in Morris Philipson, ed., *Automation: Implications for the Future* (New York: Vintage, 1962), pp. 275–76.

It could mean the elimination of slums, the regeneration of depressed areas and the redevelopment of neglected areas in our cities.

It could give us the means to provide effective assistance to other countries which need help in building up their economies—help which may make the difference between survival or failure of freedom in those lands.

Automation and technological advance have put all these highly desirable goals within our reach. They have done something more. They have made it not merely desirable, hut absolutely essential that we reach them.

A 5 per cent growth rate or better can be achieved simply by generating sufficient demand to make full use of our productive resources and provide employment for those who are able and willing to work. This is a major responsibility of government. . . . If we fail to create the necessary demand, we fail to solve the unemployment problem.

That is a very real threat, which automation greatly intensifies.

Automation makes possible a 5 per cent growth rate, provided we develop economic policies which will generate sufficient private and public demand to make use of an additional 5 per cent of goods and services each year.

If we fail to do so, automation will not mean growing prosperity, but growing unemployment—as it has done, for the most part, during the past seven years.

This is the problem we must solve.

Our enemies believe we cannot solve it. When Premier Khrushchev says, "We will bury you" he means simply that he believes our economic system will fail to solve the problem of distribution. He believes that we will continue to fail, as we have in the past seven years, to match or approach the rate of growth achieved in the Soviet Union. He believes it is only a matter of time until Soviet production surpasses ours, and the Communists are able to take world leadership away from us, not by military might but by economic power alone.

If we fail to make proper use of the opportunities which automation offers us, Premier Khrushchev's prophecy could very well come true.

It is our task to prove him wrong.

WORKING WOMEN

Women, especially married women, began to enter the waged labor market in ever larger numbers beginning in the 1950s and their number increased rapidly thereafter. The following three documents describe aspects of that significant change. Document 5.12 explores the tensions created by the desire of married women to work for wages outside the home. Pauline Newman, a long-time union leader and reformer, in Document 5.13 explains that women work for the same reason as men, to earn enough to support themselves at a reasonable level of comfort, or, if married, to provide their families with an adequate standard of living. Document 5.14 shows the persistence of domestic labor as a major source of female employment, and also the bitter racial edge it assumed in the 1950s, as domestic laborers became overwhelmingly women of color. Do any aspects of these documents remind you of previous debates and discussions concerning the role of waged labor in women's lives and desires?

5.12 Tensions over Women's Waged Work, ca. 1960. An interview by Mira Komarovsky in Blue Collar Marriage (New York: Random House, 1962), pp. 70–71. From *Blue-Collar Marriage* by Mira Komarovsky, copyright 1962, 1964 by Random House, Inc. Used by permission of Random House, Inc.

"He doesn't want me to work at all," said the wife. Her husband nodded. "He's against it, but I got to do it because we got to have enough money to eat and dress and it isn't just the rent and the food we have to have. It's to keep on going and to get places. He works harder than most people and I work real hard too. But we still have to have more money coming in. We want to have another baby in a year or two and we have to save up for that too. We want to start him in his business and not be stuck this way for the rest of our lives. But he doesn't like me to work at all. He thinks kids should have their own mothers around. He thinks nobody can love them the way we can. He ain't proud about my working like some men are, no sirree. It's just that he thinks the kids really need us." At that the husband said firmly: "That's right. It's just like she says. If I can get the work the way I've been doing, you'll never have to go out and work again." "But, hon, I like to go out and do some work sometimes. It's nice for a change, and I like to think I'm bringing in some money too. We could buy our house sooner and get you set up sooner if we could just get some more money quicker." "If you feel that way about it," said the man, "We'll borrow money." But the wife countered that she doesn't believe in borrowing if they can possibly make it themselves.

5.13   Why Women Work for Wages, 1952. Pauline M. Newman, "Why Women Work," *Bulletin of the New York Women's Trade Union League* (March 1952), p. 2.

All through my working life I used to hear men say: "After all, why *should* women earn as much as we do since they have no financial responsibility, they are just working for 'pin money' anyway." I recall hearing this bit of wisdom in the shop, on the picket line, at union meetings, at minimum wage board hearings, and in personal conversations. I heard it from rich men, poor men, conservatives, liberals, employers, and union leaders. But some of us knew better. We knew from personal experience and observation that the overwhelming majority of women who work do so for exactly the same reasons as men do—*to support themselves and their dependents.* We knew then and we know now that women work because of economic necessity. That was our contention then and it is now. . . .

The cost of living being what it is today, it is not surprising that . . . 75% of . . . women use 75 cents or more of every dollar for just daily living. And this does not include savings for a rainy day. Furthermore, if their children are to receive an education, or, if they wish to own a home, or to acquire the mechanical contrivances to reduce housework to a minimum, if in short they are to enjoy an American standard of living, women of the family must work outside their home to supplement the earnings of a husband or father. These are the real reasons why women work. Their participation in our industrial world is of vital importance not only to themselves and their families but to our national economy as well.

5.14   "No Crystal Stair" for a Domestic Worker. Mary Yelling interviews Aletha Vaughn in Susan Tucker, *Telling Memories Among Southern Women: Domestic Workers and Their Employers in the Segregated South* (Baton Rouge & London: Louisiana State University Press, 1988), pp. 206–10. Copyright 1988 by Susan Tucker. Used by permission of Schocken Books, a division of Random House, Inc.

I myself, I always worked. I always worked all the time. Even when I was real little, I did a lot of work at home because I was the oldest of nine.

When I was eleven years old, I went to working out. My mother was working for some people, and she got sick, and I had to go in her place. I was eleven years old. And I've worked ever since. But I've had enough domestic work. The bad point is when you resent the person you're working for, for being, I guess you would call it, prejudiced and cruel and wanting to be superior to you. Just because you're working for 'em as an individual, they don't see that they're not any more than you are. They treat you like some type of animal instead of a person.

In fact, the animals get treated better than the servants. Plenty of 'em let the cat sleep in the bed with 'em! And then they'd be afraid you'd sit on the cat. And then they were afraid of you! Me I was told if you lie down with dogs, you get up with fleas. Not them.

But you could prepare their foods for 'em, and they trusted you. I could have felt the same way they felt, but I wasn't raised to be evil, so I'd just go on and do my work. A lot of time I felt like spitting in their food, but I didn't. I would just go on and say: "Well, they'll get theirs. This is their heaven, I suppose."

'Cause I don't see how anybody could see the Lord, the way they act. It's true! They even had separate bathrooms! Oh no, you didn't go in the bathrooms they went in. They had separate bathrooms and everything for you—everywhere, in those days. They would build a outhouse and put a bathroom outside before you could use the bathroom that you cleaned inside. They didn't want any stains in their bathrooms! It's just been in recent years, they've started letting people go in their bathrooms. And they had certain dishes you could eat out of. You ate out of certain dishes, and your particular plate and fork and spoon went in a certain place.

I don't know I just don't understand the whites' superiority to start with. That's why there is so much turmoil now, because everybody's suppose to have equal rights and just the white folks can't take that.

See, white people they don't have any interest in nothing but your work. They will butter you up, work fire out of you, and work you to death if you listen to the junk they say. They'll tell you they love you and be so nice and bribe you.

And with all white folks, the servant ate in the kitchen, and you had to wait until they got through eating, and what's left, you got some of it. That's the way that works.

And I've seen people of today like that. You get something that's left, or they'll serve themselves certain things and tell you to get a bologna sandwich. You done worked all day, and now they get the hot meal. "It's plenty of iced tea and bologna and a little ice cream," they'll tell you. And I wouldn't eat. I'd go home and eat. And maybe that's why my health is bad, because someone could act funny about food and I wouldn't touch it. . . .

But well, if they'd treat people better, really I don't mind domestic work. Work is just work, but just how you be treated and then how you be paid. They were unfair with the pay, and they probably would hire a white girl now and pay her $3.00 or $4.00 per hour just to baby-sit and want to pay you $1.75.

I know I've resented a lot of things they've done. But I had to work, so I did the work. But now I wouldn't do it no more if I had to eat lizards for a meal. I've learned better. It don't take all that to survive. Oh, the white man really had the black folks fooled. They had 'em fooled a long time. Some of 'em still fooled. And those old people, I try to explain to 'em so they will know better.

Explain that they don't have to call that young lady Miz So-and-so to eat, 'cause the same hand feeds her feeds you. And until we realize that, we're forever be taking some kind of old fare from these white folks.

RACE AND CIVIL RIGHTS

The civil rights revolution that blossomed in the 1950s and reached fruition in the 1960s had a great impact on the labor movement. In Document 5.15 we can see the impact of the new militancy on African American workers and why they became more militant than their white brothers and sisters. A black Alabaman and union leader describes in Document 5.16 his understanding of the dynamics of the Montgomery bus boycott. Martin Luther King, Jr., argues in Document 5.17 that African Americans and trade unions need each other and must work together to promote political, economic, and social equality. King also suggests in Document 5.18, his letter to Cesar Chavez, the leader of agricultural workers in California, why African American and Mexican American workers share a common cause. Document 5.19 describes how the civil rights movement influenced Mexican American and Mexican (Chicano and Chicana) workers in the West to demand the right to unionize and to bargain collectively. Finally, Document 5.20, a black worker's memory of the Memphis sanitation workers' strike of 1968 during which King was assassinated, shows the persistent link between civil rights and unionism. Based on these documents, assess the overall impact of the civil rights movement on the labor movement as well the contribution of trade unionism, if any, to the triumph of civil rights.

5.15 Labor and the Black Worker, ca. 1970. From Thomas Brooks, "Black Upsurge in the Unions," *Dissent* (Mar.-Apr. 1970), pp. 124–33. Reprinted with permission.

White workers, true, are often resentful of the change; they don't react politely to being called "Honkie," and the surfacing of subterranean racism is not unknown. I have a leaflet before me, distributed by the National Socialist White People's [Nazi] party at a Harvester plant, which says, among other things: "Not content to take our jobs away, these Black savages have beaten our kids in school, terrorized our women on the street and run us out of our own neighborhoods where we grew up and raised our families." There's no denying some think like this, but in fact few heed the call of this hate sheet. The membership of the NSWPP is probably smaller than that of HRUM at Harvester (Harvester Revolutionary Union Movement), and both are tiny indeed.

Polarization has occurred, but blue-collar Wallaceism is a response to developments outside the plant or the union. The Flint UAW local that endorsed Wallace (and later rescinded the endorsement) did not go on to adopt resolutions favoring the exclusion of black workers from the plant or the union. A black UAW representative who was elected a shop steward in that same local . . . [said] that several of his strongest white supporters wore Wallace buttons during the 1968 Presidential campaign. When Sexton asked if they were still friends and supporters, he said, "Hell, yes." There will be more "two Irishmen against two blacks" contests within our unions, but if blue-collar Wallaceism grows it will be because of social and economic developments outside the unions and not because of hotly fought elections. If this is not the case, then the unions are indeed in a bad way.

I don't believe they are. One would let it go at that if it were not for the deplorable tendency among academics, New Leftists, and others to see all elections which blacks lose as stolen. It happens—but not as often as some think. By and large, most union officers continue in office because they do a job, and not because of their ethnic origin or color. These factors play a role, but ordinarily not to the exclusion of all others. Human passions being what they are, one ought to add a cautionary note. The unions have not been hit as hard by black militancy as have the churches, the poverty programs, and the universities. When and if they are, there may well be an intensification of racial hostilities. (My feeling that this won't happen is based on two things. First, it hasn't happened although there are more black trade unionists than black parishioners in the churches under attack or black students in assaulted universities. Second, white workers just aren't loaded with the guilt feelings of white ministers and other middle-class types who are, for good or bad, vulnerable to supermilitancy.)

What will the impact be of increasing black representation in the unions? Progress, of course, but first allow me some skepticism. I am sure that some of the black youngsters now entering building-trades apprenticeships will end up running local unions—or become contractors. The building trades may swing a little as a result, but I doubt very much that the inherently conservative character of those unions will change. Black craftsmen will find, as white craftsmen did before them, that a tight rein on jobs, on entry and craft structure pays off. And they too will want buildings built, a feeling shared with the dominant real estate interests of every city. More blacks, perhaps, will add weight to the discernible sea change already underway among building tradesmen, away from the Republican party to the Democrats. Beyond this, one's hopes ought not rise. . . .

Nonetheless, greater black participation in the unions will reinvigorate social unionism. Many white workers, especially those in powerful unions and in well-organized industries, are content to leave job questions to the unions, while seeking solutions to social and economic problems elsewhere. This, as much as anything, explains blue-collar Wallaceism and conservative voting of young of home-owning workers on local tax-supported issues. Black workers are no more exempt from the pulls of class solidarity in the plant—and the pride of home-ownership—than white workers. But, on balance, they do want more government action along a broader front than their blue-collar white fellows. Black workers live in communities with drastic problems that cry out for radical solutions. And they are going to use all the resources at their command to get answers to their problem Local union leadership is a power base, and if that base can be mobilized for action to solve community problems black labor leaders are going to act. It'll be worth watching.

5.16 Labor and Civil Rights, 1956. E. D. Nixon speaks on the Montgomery Bus Boycott, March 28, 1956, in Joseph F. Wilson, *Tearing Down the Color Bar: A Documentary History and Analysis of the Brotherhood of Sleeping Car Porters* (New York: Columbia University Press, 1989), pp. 253–58. Reprinted with permission from Professor Wilson, Brooklyn College.

Thank you, Brother [A. Philip] Randolph . . . other members and friends. I'm very happy to be here this afternoon to bring you greetings from Montgomery, Alabama, the cradle of the Confederate that has stood still for a long, long time, prior to December the first, but is now being rocked by 50,000 Negroes in Montgomery. [*applause*] I bring you greetings from the Brotherhood of Sleeping Car Porters in Montgomery, and I'd like to say first that I'm proud that I am a member of the Brotherhood of Sleeping Car Porters. It's been thirty years ago that I first heard Brother Randolph make a speech. It was in St. Louis, Missouri. He made two statements in that speech that I didn't believe at that time, but I lived to see it come true. At that time, I was drawing $67.50 a month and he made a statement. He said, "If you'll stick with me, the day will soon come and I'll have you making a hundred and fifty dollars a month." I said, "I'm going to get my dollar, but I don't believe it." [*laughter*] And the next statement he made, he said, "Mark my words, the day will soon come when the leadership will come from the bottom of the deck." I've lived to see that day. I know and you know that had it not been for the Brotherhood of Sleeping Car Porters, that I never would have been the type of man I am today. I've learned organization through the method of organization from the Brotherhood of Sleeping Car Porters, and it built courage and given understanding, so when it's all said and done, I am grateful for what the Brotherhood of Sleeping Car Porters has done for me. Now, coming back to Montgomery. In Montgomery, Alabama today, even though it might be raining down there, but I'm here to tell you that there are 50,000 people down there, and the majority of those people are walking and hustling a ride to work, because of their belief in American democracy. We had any number of problems. We have over a period of years—we have met with the city commissioners and the Montgomery—the manager of the Montgomery bus line, with no result. During the year of 1955 there were three women who were arrested from time to time for refusing to give their seat to a white man. Now, the last incident was December the first. One Mrs. Rosa L. Parks, who was a passenger on the Montgomery City Line, who refused to get up and give her seat to a white gentleman who was standing. She was pulled off of the bus, arrested, put in jail, fingerprinted, mugged, tried in a city court and fined ten dollars and costs for a total of fourteen dollars. Now, the Negroes in Montgomery felt that this was just too much, that we couldn't take any more. We called all the members of all organizations, religious organizations, fraternities and clubs, whatnot, and on December the second, we met and discussed what action we would take to eliminate these conditions. It was brought out in that meeting that we turned out—get out a few leaflets or throwaways, and asked everybody to attend a meeting, a mass meeting, Monday night at the Holt Street Baptist Church. It so happened that the *Montgomery Advertiser* got a hold of one of those leaflets some time Saturday. They came out Sunday with a two-page spread in the *Montgomery Advertiser* on the front page, giving us about $500,000 worth of advertising that we never would have been able to buy and pay for in a lifetime. And because of this advertisement, we were able to reach any number of people that we never would have reached. Consequently, in the meeting that night, we had more than four thousand people in and around the church, and another two and a half thousand up and down the street parked in automobiles that couldn't get close enough to get to the church. In that, we passed resolutions in that meeting that we would protest the situation that exists on the bus, which was passed on by the people. We had recommendations, we took it up with the city official and they turned it down, and the people began to walk. That began on the fifth of December, and up to now there are people who are still walking, those that don't catch a ride. . . . We had to start out to organize a transportation system. We got 300 people to put their cars in a pool. . . . My friends, this thing is serious. It's really serious, because of the fact that the white man has went along over a period of years and he has built up a strong belief within himself that the South is supposed to be controlled by the white man, and Negroes is supposed to accept whatever the white man give them or do like the white man says. Well, they forget about one thing. When they start to make the statement, they say that outside interference or Communists or so forth, I want to say here, there's definitely no Communists in it, and number two, there's no outside interference there. But the white man there refuse to give the Negro credit for being intelligent in himself and able to think and act for himself. . . . But the Negroes in Montgomery is tired of the iron shoes of segregation on their neck. They're ready to fight for it, they're ready to die for it if necessary. But one thing that we have taught them through these eighteen weeks is that it definitely must not be any violence. We don't want any violence in this thing. We are using passive resistance for it, love, truth, and we expect to keep it that way. Regardless of what happens, we expect to stay on the firing line. . . . So, my friends, here's our fight in Montgomery. The Negroes in Montgomery is tired of being kicked around, is tired of being Jim-Crowed on the Montgomery City Line or any other form of transportation, as far as that's concerned. They have made it up in their mind that they're going to fight it until the court says that they don't have to do it. But to do that, we're going to have to have money, and the money is for the things mentioned—court costs and to pay these people who are in the office, buy gas and oil and take care of the expense of these people's cars to get these people to and fro from work. We've been getting contributions from all over the state. Sometimes it's large, sometimes it's small, but somehow we've been able to keep moving. So I say to you here, there are two things that you can do. I still believe in prayer, and had not I believed in it, I wouldn't have come here. So one thing, you can pray for us, and the next thing, that you can put your hand in your pocket and make a contribution. Whether it's large or small, the Montgomery Improvement Association will be eternally grateful. Thank you very kindly. [*applause*]

5.17   Martin Luther King, Jr. Addresses the AFL-CIO, 1961. From *Hotel* (February 12, 1962), pp. 4, 6.

We are confronted by powerful forces telling us to rely on the good will and understanding of those who profit by exploiting us. They deplore our discontent, they resent our will to organize, so that we may guarantee that humanity will prevail and equality will be exacted. They are shocked that action organizations, sit-ins, civil disobedience, and protests are becoming our everyday tools, just as strikes, demonstrations and union organization became yours to insure that bargaining power genuinely existed on both sides of the table.

We want to rely on upon the good will of those who oppose us. Indeed, we have brought forward the method of nonviolence to give an example of unilateral good will in an effort to evoke it in those who have not yet felt it in their hearts. But we know that if we are not simultaneously organizing our strength we will have no means to move forward. If we do not advance, the crushing burden of centuries of neglect and economic deprivation will destroy our will, our spirits, and our hopes. In this way, labor's historical tradition of moving forward to create vital people as consumers and citizens has become our own tradition, and for the same reasons.

This unity of purpose is not an historical coincidence. Negroes are almost entirely a working people. There are pitifully few Negro millionaires and few Negro employers. Our needs are identical with labor's needs: decent wages, fair working conditions, livable housing, old age security, health and welfare measures, conditions in which families can grow, have education for their children and respect in their community. That is why Negroes support labor's demands and fight laws which curb labor. That is why the labor-hater and the labor-baiter is virtually always a twin-headed creature spewing anti-Negro epithets from one mouth and anti-labor propaganda from the other mouth.

The duality of interests of labor and Negroes makes any crisis which lacerates you a crisis from which we bleed. . . .

To say that we are friends would be an empty platitude if we fail to behave as friends and honestly look to weaknesses in our relationship. Unfortunately, there are weaknesses. Labor has not adequately used its great power, its vision and resources to advance Negro rights. Undeniably, it has done more than other forces in American society to this end. Aid from real friends in labor has often come when the flames of struggle heighten. But Negroes are a solid component within the labor movement and a reliable bulwark for labor's whole program, and should expect more from it exactly as a member of a family expects more from his relatives than from his neighbors.

Labor, which made impatience for long-delayed justice for itself a vital motive force, cannot lack understanding of the Negro's impatience. It cannot speak, with the reactionaries' calm indifference, of progress around some obscure corner not yet possible even to see. There is a maxim in the law—justice too long delayed, is justice denied. When a Negro leader who has a reputation of purity and honesty which has benefitted the whole labor movement criticizes it, his motives should not be reviled nor his earnestness rebuked. Instead, the possibility that he is revealing a weakness in the labor movement which it can ill afford, should receive thoughtful examination. A man who has dedicated his long and faultless life to the labor movement cannot be raising questions harmful to it any more than a lifelong devoted parent can become the enemy of his child. The report of a committee may smother with legal constructions a list of complaints and dispose of it for the day. But if it buries a far larger truth it has disposed of nothing and made justice more elusive.

Discrimination does exist in the labor movement. It is true that organized labor has taken significant steps to remove the yoke of discrimination from its own body. But in spite of this, some unions, governed by the racist ethos, have contributed to the degraded economic status of the Negro. Negroes have been barred from membership in certain unions, and denied apprenticeship training and vocational education. In every section of the country one can find local unions existing as a serious obstacle when the Negro seeks jobs or upgrading in employment. Labor must honestly admit these conditions, and design the battle plan which will defeat and eliminate them. In this way, labor would be unearthing the big truth and utilizing its strength against the bleakness of injustice in the spirit of its finest traditions. . . .

Your conduct should and can set an example for others, as you have done in other crusades for justice. You should root out vigorously every manifestation of discrimination so that some . . . labor bodies . . . may not besmirch the positive accomplishments of labor. . . .

The political strength you are going to need . . . can be multiplied if you tap the vast reservoir of Negro political power. Negroes, if given the vote, will vote liberal and labor because they need the same liberal legislation labor needs. . . .

The two most dynamic and cohesive liberal forces in the country are the labor movement and the Negro freedom movement. Together we can be architects of democracy in a South now rapidly industrializing. Together we can retool the political structure of the South. . . . Together, we can bring about the day when there will be no separate identification of Negroes and labor. . . .

When that day comes, the fears of insecurity and the doubts clouding our future will be transformed into radiant confidence, into glowing excitement to reach creative goals and into an abiding moral balance where the brotherhood of man will be undergirded by a secure and expanding prosperity for all.

Yes, this will be the day when all of God's children, black men and white men, Jews and Gentiles, Protestants and Catholics, will be able to join hands all over this nation and sing in the words of the old Negro spiritual: "Free At Last, Free At Last. Thank God Almighty. We Are Free At Last."

5.18   Martin Luther King, Jr. and Cesar Chavez, 1968. Telegram from King to Chavez reprinted in *El Macriado*, on Monday, April 15, 1968, p. 4.

Cesar Chavez Director UFWOC Delano, Cal.

I am deeply moved by your courage in fasting as your personal sacrifice for justice through non-violence. Your past and present commitment is eloquent testimony to the constructive power of non-violent action and the destructive impotence of violent reprisal. You stand today as a living example of the Ghandian tradition with its great force for social progress and its healing spiritual powers. My colleagues and I commend you for your bravery, salute you for your indefatigable work against poverty and injustice, and pray for your health and continuing service as one of the outstanding men of America. The plight of your people and ours is so grave that we all desperately need the inspiring example of effective leadership you have given.

Dr. Martin Luther King, Jr.

President, Southern Christian Leadership Conference

5.19   Farm Workers Want Unions, 1969. Excerpts of testimony before the California Legislature. California Legislature, Assembly Committee on Agriculture, *Joint Interim Hearings of the Assembly Committee on Agriculture and the Assembly Committee on Labor Relations*, November 12–14, 1969, pp. 89–95.

MR. [David] GARCIA [on behalf of the United Farm Workers]: I would like to present a few people here who would like to present their part of the story. Mrs. Maria Seville and Ramon Espinosa, our translator.

ASSEMBLYMAN [William M.] KETCHUM [Chairman, California State Assembly Committee on Agriculture]: If they will sit down and identify themselves . . .

MARIA SEVILLE: (She speaks in Spanish)

TRANSLATOR: She's asking if you are here to take away the unions?

ASSEMBLYMAN KETCHUM: Absolutely not. There isn't a member of this committee who would deny anyone the right to join any organization he wants to. The answer is no.

MRS. SEVILLE (translation): Why don't you want the union for the farm workers?

ASSEMBLYMAN KETCHUM: I don't think anyone here has said that. . . . All we're trying to establish is whether guidelines for elections, collective bargaining, etc., should take place on the national level or the state level.

MRS. SEVILLE (translation): I want a more or less federal law. . . . that will not prohibit the strike or boycott during the harvest season. . . .

ASSEMBLYMAN KETCHUM: Fine. . . . I appreciate your coming.

TRANSLATOR: Now, we would like to call Ramon Garcia Espinosa.

ASSEMBLYMAN KETCHUM: Fine. . . .

TRANSLATOR: Ramon Espinosa . . . says that he gets many problems from the rancher. . . . He has so many problems with the ranchers. . . . He says the only way he can help his problems is with the union. . . .

ASSEMBLYMAN KETCHUM: Thank you very much, Mr. Espinosa. How many more are there?

Mr. ZAMORA: My name is Pedro Zamora.

TRANSLATOR: Mr. Zamora is a farm worker. He says that he was working, doing the boxes, and he was fired because he was helping in the strike. He says that's why he wants to join the union—because that way he will be protected against injustice by the grower.

ASSEMBLYMAN KETCHUM: Does he think the rule for this union, whatever union it might be, would be better on a national level or state level?

TRANSLATOR: He says he wants unions. He doesn't know much of the law. He can barely read or speak his own language, but he wants the union.

ASSEMBLYMAN KETCHUM: Thank you. . . . We have a . . . Mr. Pablo Lopez. . . .

PABLO LOPEZ: I can't speak too much good English, so I prefer speak Spanish.

ASSEMBLYMAN KETCHUM: Don't worry about that. . . .

PABLO LOPEZ [as translated by Gilbert Padilla]: My name is Pablo Lopez, and I am a member of the United Farm Workers Organizing Committee. I live in Richgrove, California, with my wife and four children. My children are American citizens; I am not an American citizen, but I will become one this year so I will be able to vote. This year I was elected an officer of the committee, and I have noticed the urge of everybody to become citizens of the United States so that we can . . . share the justice of this nation. . . .

5.20 The 1968 Memphis Sanitation Strike. Taylor Rodgers interviewed in Michael Keith Honey, *Black Workers Remember: An Oral History of Segregation, Unionism, and the Freedom Struggle* (Berkeley: University of California Press, 1999), pp. 294–300. Reprinted by permission of Mike Honey, Harry Bridges Endowed Chair of Labor Studies, University of Washington, Tacoma.

I . . . got a job with the city [of Memphis] in 1958, at the Sanitation Department. There wasn't too much opportunity for a black man at that time. Really wasn't no other jobs hardly to be found. I was at the point were I had to take what I could get. That was the situation with most of the men. . . .

I was workin' on the trucks. Now you see all these garbage cans on the street. Back then, everybody had a 50-gallon drum in the backyard. We had to go in those backyards with tubs. You carried those tubs on your head and shoulders. Most of those tubs were leakin' and that stuff was fallin' all over you. You got home you had to take your clothes off at the door 'cause you didn't want to bring all that filth in the house. We didn't have no decent place to eat your lunch. You didn't have no place to use the restroom. Conditions was just terrible. We didn't have no say about nothin.' Whatever they said, that's what you had to do; right, wrong, indifferent. Anything that you did that the supervisor didn't like, he'd fire you, whatever. You didn't have no recourse, no way of getting back at him. We just got tired of all that.

Most of the supervisors were white people. All the better jobs the whites had. . . . They didn't have to do too much of nothin' . . . The men workin' was 99 percent black. About 1966, I believe it was, we pulled a work stoppage. But we were on the picket line for about an hour . . . because they put an injunction on us. . . . We was making about $1.04 an hour. You could work a forty-hour week and be eligible for welfare. We didn't have no benefits, no safety. So we kept meeting, and we kept talking. . . .

We finally got to a point where we had lots of followers. We had talked with the city, we had tried to get . . . some recognition . . . and we always got turned down. We just finally got tired of it.

We had some guys that worked over on . . . a packer where you put your garbage. One rainy day [in 1968] they were up in there and something triggered that thing off, and it just crushed them. . . . Thirteen hundred men decided that they was tired and wasn't gonna take no more . . . and withdrew their services from the city. That was hard for us to do. All of us had families. We didn't know what . . . was gonna happen. . . . But we hung in there. . . .

It got a little rough. That's when Reverend Lawson got Dr. King involved. When Dr. King came in, he made some speeches and things, and that built the morale back up . . . and made the men more up and ready to keep on pushing to get something done. . . .

After King was killed, all over the country everybody was puttin' pressure, the president, everybody else was puttin' pressure on [Memphis

Mayor] Henry Loeb for lettin' this kind of thing happen. So . . . we finally got a contract, an agreement signed.

VIETNAM WAR AND COUNTERCULTURE

The long war that the United States fought in southeast Asia caused tensions and rifts throughout society, including within the labor movement, as Cold War verities collapsed. At first, the leaders of the labor movement remained true to the Cold War ideology that they had adopted in the late 1940s. Document 5.21 shows how the AFL-CIO applied Cold War ideology to the conflict in Vietnam and why it supported government actions there. The next document (5.22) indicates how the AFL-CIO provided a platform for a liberal academic to defend Cold War principles. In Document 5.23, a radio commentator sponsored by the AFL-CIO explores the positive as well as the negative aspects of the young people's counterculture that flowered during the 1960s. A left-wing trade unionist explains in Document 5.24 the sources and reasons for rising militancy and protest by younger workers. Walter Reuther's letter (Document 5.25) offers concrete evidence of the growing breach in the ranks of organized labor caused by the war in Vietnam. Do these documents suggest a labor movement increasingly out-of-touch with large segments of its membership or one that faithfully reflected the fractured character of its constituency?

5.21   Defending the Vietnam War as a Liberal Effort, 1969. Editorial, "To Win the Peace" *AFL-CIO News* (November 22, 1969), p. 4.

The gathering of over 250,000 mostly young, white middle-class Americans in Washington to demonstrate for "peace now" reflects more than anything else a lack of understanding of a strategy first enunciated by Pres. John F. Kennedy. . . .

It is difficult to believe that the college-trained youths that predominated on the monument grounds do not understand the nature of the Communist thrust and the strategy developed to meet it. In their cries for "relevancy" they must surely know that peace has no relevancy without freedom. They must surely understand what happened in Czechoslovakia.

A few weeks ago the Citizens Committee for Peace and Freedom in Viet Nam, whose organizing chairman is former Sen. Paul H. Douglas, reported on the findings of a special commission it had set up to visit Southeast Asia and Paris and report back on the existing situation. They said in part:

"An American policy of gradual disengagement is feasible, provided the withdrawal of U.S. forces is closely geared to demonstrated improvement in South Vietnamese capabilities and is not forced prematurely by war-weary American opinion."

Among the commission's recommendations were free elections, opposition to an "imposed" coalition government, reciprocal troop withdrawals. The group said the United States should urge "that the Vietnamese government broaden its base among non-Communist elements of the population and that it seek new support in the countryside."

The committee strongly opposed to risking a general war in Asia, notes that "we do not seek a military victory in Viet Nam; we seek to deny military victory to the enemy. We do not seek to win the war; we seek to win the peace."

Its latest appraisal is that "we are in a desperate race between the natural impatience of the American people and their education to the true situation. . . . It is ironical that at the very time when the prospect for peace with freedom is rising in Viet Nam, confidence in a successful outcome is at its lowest ebb here at home."

5.22 A Liberal Objects to the Anti-War Critique, 1969. Editorial, John P. Roche, "Support for Defense of Viet Nam Based on Firm Liberal Tenets," *AFL-CIO News* (November 22, 1969), p. 4.

[A]fter I spoke at our high school Oct. 15, in support of U.S. policy in Southeast Asia, my daughter asked me if it was true that I was "conservative." Since I am supporting the Republic of Viet Nam on almost precisely the same basis that, 30 years ago, I supported the Spanish Republic, I found this rather amusing. . . .

In my judgment, American support for the defense of Berlin, Israel, and Viet Nam is founded on the same principle—and it is a liberal principle. Historically speaking, isolationism is the bench mark of the American conservative.

But we live with the "corruption of the word."

The result is that any individual who opposes the evangelical fervor of true believers (on matters foreign or domestic), or insists that a university is not a zoo, is simply written off as a "conservative."

5.23 Assessing the Counter Culture, 1967. This is excerpted from the nightly broadcasts of an ABC commentator sponsored by the AFL-CIO, and printed in its newspaper. Edward P. Morgan, "Youthful Turbulence May Hide Sober if Clumsy Soul-Searching," *AFL-CIO* News, (January 14, 1967), p. 5.

When I was a boy in the Golden West the only long-hairs I ever saw, below the age of senility, were members of the House of David baseball team. Today girls wear the stretch pants and the boys sport unshorn locks but when the twain meet it is hard to tell which is Samson and which is Delilah. And more confusing still, sometimes neither is either. . . .

There is a warped aspect in this scene, including the stark, provocative video picture, because the focus is on the nut, the beatnik, the bizarre. So, suddenly the nation, especially its harassed middle-aged citizenry, finds itself generalizing with pompous shock about the lawlessness of the entire younger generation on the basis of a few sensational snapshots of the depredations of some youngsters who may be delinquent but who really are more lost than young.

Generalizations are inevitable on such a subject but I believe we are neglecting some valid generalizations on the plus side of the picture. The downright wild ones are, surely, a tiny minority of the crop. Nor does it follow that every young man or women who does something maddening to his elders is mad. I daresay there is more sober—if sometimes clumsy— soul-searching among the population bracketed by the ages 15 to 25 than ever before in America.

If this is true—and mail from and personal contact with students indicates to me that it is—it represents one of the most exciting turns in the maturing of the United States . . . . But it also holds a large measure of pain for everybody concerned.

This does not mean that treacherous, unsponsored trips to the wild blue yonder via LSD should be encouraged or condoned. They should not. It does not mean that the Medal of Honor should be bestowed on the fellow who tears up his draft card, with or without the benefit of news cameras. . . .

Exponents of the New Left, leaders of campus protest movements and their fellows seem at times to love anarchy more than they love peace. It is not impossible, however, that a little transitional anarchy is necessary to breed respect for a lawful society. What many of us fail to realize, however, is this: much of this younger turbulence is conscientious protest against what appears to be a pretty lawless society. . . .

5.24 Defending Youthful Rebels, 1968. Excerpts of UE General Secretary-Treasurer James J. Matles's lecture to a class for shop stewards held at Latrobe, Pennsylvania, November 1968. Reprinted as "The Young Worker Challenges the Union Establishment," in *UE News,* December 2, 1968, pp. 6–7.

The labor movement is faced with the most serious challenge since the 1930's. It comes from the young, the blacks and the other minorities. . . .

We have been witnessing a growing rebellion among students in the universities and colleges. They are challenging the *status quo* and the Establishment. They are doing this not because they are economically deprived or because they don't know where their next meal is coming from. Most of these young people in the leading universities and colleges come from well-to-do and middle-class families who are paying for their education.

These young men and women have reached an ideological conviction that there is something basically wrong with our society and our system. As we watch TV and read the newspapers and see this revolt spreading, the question is being asked—how about the working-class youth in the shops? Why don't they participate with the students in this revolt?

The answer to this question is simple. The young people in the shops are involved in a revolt of their own, which is growing day by day. It is not based on ideology. It is not political in character. It expresses itself today solely in economic terms, but as it develops it is bound to have far-reaching political consequences.

The young worker doesn't give a damn for the company's shop rules and he drives the foreman crazy. He comes to work when he feels like it and quits his job at the drop of a hat without knowing where his next day's pay will come from.

Young workers are storming membership meetings and voting down a constantly growing number of settlements negotiated by their union leaders. They are the most militant fighters on the picket lines. They spark the work stoppages in the shops in protest against grievances and contract violations by management, while the union leadership wrings its hands and runs around publicly denouncing the stoppages as wildcat, unauthorized and illegal. These young workers are in revolt against the company Establishment in the shop and they are challenging the union Establishment as well. . . .

He considers the union contract as a straitjacket instead of a source of security and protection. He sees a better job on the floor and he wants it, but the seniority clause in the contract is against him. He is ready to dump seniority and to scuttle other basic contractual working conditions that union men and women struck, fought and bled for. Even though this is not going to do a thing to solve his problems, like a drowning man he grabs at any straw in the hope of saving himself.

When he starts raising hell with the shop steward or local officer in the shop, what answers does he get? We usually tell him that he doesn't know how bad things were when we started 30 years ago. But he doesn't give a damn how bad things were because they are plenty bad for him right now.

We try to impress him with the fact that he doesn't really appreciate the great sacrifices that we have made in order to get where we are, but he is bored and wants to know not what we did yesterday, but what we are going to do today to get him out of the fix he is in right now. We then begin giving him some of the "Father knows best" stuff about his poor judgment. He is told that when we were his age we didn't go into hock to the tune of several thousands of dollars; that it took us ten years before we got some of the things that he got in one swoop.

It is at this point that we are losing him altogether.

All he sees is the company bragging about how good it is, and the union patting itself on the back about its past accomplishments—a couple of smug defenders of *status quo*. He sees no reason at all why America, the richest country in the world, can't give him a job that will provide him with all the necessities and some of the luxuries of life, and what's wrong with that? . . .

5.25   Labor Protests the War, 1970. Walter P. Reuther telegram to Richard Nixon following the invasion of Cambodia and the shooting of student protestors at Kent State University on May 4, 1970. Reprinted after Reuther's subsequent death in an aircraft accident as "His Last Message: A Call for Peace," in *UAW Solidarity* (June 1970), p. 23.

On behalf of the UAW, I wish to convey to you our deep concern and distress over your action authorizing the use of United States forces and material in a broadening of the war in Indochina.

Your decision to invade the territory of Cambodia can only increase the enormity of the tragedy in which our nation is already deeply and unfortunately involved in that region.

Your action must stand as a repudiation of your oft repeated pledge to bring this tragic war to an end and not to escalate it.

Widening the war at this point in time once again merely re-enforces the bankruptcy of our policy of force and violence in Vietnam.

Your action taken without the consultation or authorization by the Congress has created a serious Constitutional crisis at a time when there is growing division in our nation. . . .

However this dangerous adventure turns out militarily, America has already suffered a moral defeat beyond measure among the people of the world.

You pledged to bring America together. Yet by your action you have driven the wedge of division deeper and you have dangerously alienated millions of young Americans. The bitter fruits of this growing alienation and frustration among America's youth have been harvested on the campus of Kent State University where the lives of four students involved only in an emotional protest against the war were ended by the needless and inexcusable use of military force.

At no time in the history of our free society have so many troops been sent to so many campuses to suppress the voice of protest by so many young Americans.

With the exception of a small minority, the American people, including our young people, reject violence in all its forms as morally repugnant and counterproductive. The problem, Mr. President, is that we cannot successfully preach nonviolence at home while we escalate mass violence abroad.

It is your responsibility to lead us out of the Southeast Asian War—to peace at home and abroad. We must mobilize for peace rather than for wider theaters of war in order to turn our resources and the hearts, hands and minds of our people to the fulfillment of America's unfinished agenda at home.

NEW MILITANCY

The never-ending war in Vietnam and the failure of the civil rights movement to succeed as well economically as it did politically fueled a new radicalism in sectors of the labor movement, especially among African American
workers. Documents 5.26 and 5.27 give voice to African American militants
in the UAW, which had larger numbers of black workers than most unions
and one of the better union records on civil rights. The two documents provide a sense of the radical critique of the UAW offered by the League of
Revolutionary Black Workers, which included groups like the Dodge
Revolutionary Union Movement (DRUM) and the Ford Revolutionary
Union Movement (FRUM). In Document 5.28, the UAW leadership
responds to criticism by African American militants. The leaders plead for
brotherhood, cooperation, and solidarity in order to benefit all workers and
citizens alike. Which documents do you find more reflective of the position
and needs of African American workers in the automobile industry? The final
document in this section (5.29) explains why many younger white automobile workers were also discontent and unhappy with how their union
performed.

5.26 Labor's Burning House, 1971. Excerpts of the General Policy Statement
of the League of Revolutionary Black Workers, 1971, from *Inner-City Voice*, 3
(February 1971), 10–12, reprinted in Philip S. Foner and Ronald L. Lewis,
Black Workers: A Documentary History from Colonial Times to the Present
(Philadelphia: Temple University Press, 1989), pp. 652–58.

The labor movement as represented by United Mine Workers, Steel
Workers, UAW, AFL-CIO, etc. are all the antithesis of the freedom of
black people, in particular, and the world, in general. For the most part, at
this stage, white labor must be viewed as an enemy because of the position
it holds in working hand in glove with the imperialists.

The UAW and AFL-CIO, as well as other major unions, support imper-
ialist, fascist wars in Vietnam. Labor supports strong legislation against
"crime in the streets," but says nothing about organized crime or the
crimes against the people of Vietnam, etc. Nor do they protest the past and
current crimes against black people. Aside from white labor's political
stance, they are at best, pressure groups to obtain bourgeois rights. They
request wage increases, living allowances, etc., but say nothing about
worker control of plants, production and the state. Such bourgeois
demands exemplify a desire to live in this burning house. . . .

It is without question that white labor will be forced to shift gears.
Currently, however, the liberation struggle of blacks is moving at a quickening

pace. It is our contention that the key to black liberation lies with the black workers. . . .

Black workers are toiling under more and more severe working conditions while black children and wives go hungry because of the low wages, inflationary prices, and increased taxes. They exist as the most oppressed and exploited section of the proletariat and have the power to bring all of industry to a screeching halt. Their only hope can be seen through open class war and the potential of carrying out a Black General Strike which would bring the entire U.S. productive capacity and its monopoly capitalist owners to their demise.

5.27 Uprooting "Snakeism," 1969. The League of Revolutionary Black Workers' statement following a 1969 protest action, reprinted in James A. Geschwender, *Class, Race, and Worker Insurgency: The League of Revolutionary Black Workers* (New York: Cambridge University Press, 1977) pp. 97–98.

U.A.W. Runs from black workers

Once again the League of Revolutionary Black Workers has made its presence felt, and a good feeling it is for the Black community to be assured that at least one black organization is fearless when it comes to confronting the U.A.W.'s racism and its suppressive structure.

On Saturday, November 8, 1969, the U.A.W.'s national delegation convened in Cobo Hall for a two-day session to propose raising the dues of its rank and file membership. This convention was aborted in a very premature stage because of the delegation's knowledge and fear of the demonstration that was to take place the next day, Sunday, November 9th.

This demonstration was highly publicized in advance to the convention by the League of Revolutionary Black Workers (consisting of many well-known groups:

DRUM, FRUM, ELRUM, UPRUM, MARUM, JARUM, and other worker based groups).

Aware of the fact that if the convention was still in session on the day of protest, and afraid to be confronted with the questions and issues that the Black worker demands answers for, point-ducking Walter Reuther and his racist delegation hurriedly adjourned and slid back into their plush snakeholes.

Although the U.A.W.'s cowardly run left many black workers angrier than they were when they showed, the demonstration can hardly be called anything but a more startling success than was anticipated. It was successful for a number of reasons:

1. It made black workers more conscious of the fact that if their many grievances are ever to be answered they will have to answer them themselves.
2. It made the entire Black community aware of the fact the power to determine its own destiny is repelled by one of the most Black-built and Black-supported political machines in this country.

3. It showed Black workers the potential of their strength once it has been harnessed in a united war against U.A.W. suppression.

4. It left Walter Reuther trembling with the knowledge that if he constantly refuses to deal with the needs of the Black worker, the League of Revolutionary Black Workers will deal him out.

Black workers are now doing what they have always done on any job, standing up. And as long as Walter Reuther and his flunkies flee to their suburban holes, the League of Revolutionary Black Workers will use the shovel they keep in hand, and they will dig, dig and dig until the snakeism practiced by the U.A.W. is uprooted and beat to death.

5.28   The UAW's Response to Black Radicalism, 1969. Reprinted in Geschwender, *Class, Race, and Worker Insurgency*, pp. 110–13.

March 10, 1969

Greetings:

These are difficult and trying times—times that test the common sense of the American people and their commitment to democratic values.

As a nation and a people, we face deep crisis on many fronts—education, housing, health care, transportation, air and water pollution. Our major cities face financial crisis and most serious is the crisis in race relations for this is a crisis of the human spirit, of man's relationship with his fellow man.

The UAW came into being in the 1930's in a period of great economic crisis in our nation. To win recognition and the right to help shape their own destiny in the plants, the auto workers had to fight to overcome the opposition of wealthy and powerful corporations. We succeeded because we were united—black and white, foreign born and American born workers, skilled and production workers—dedicated to the achievement of common goals in a common bond of solidarity and brotherhood and true to a common belief in the worth and dignity of every person.

The UAW has from its very beginning fought for equal rights and equal opportunities for all people regardless of race, creed and color. We work for these principles in the plants, in the community and in the nation for as a matter of justice and morality every person must be judged by the quality of his character and not by the color of his skin.

We in the UAW believe there can be no separate answers. No white answers. No black answers. We believe there can only be common answers which we must find together in our common humanity.

We believe that the violence of extremism—whether white or black—can only create more bitterness, more misunderstanding, more division. . . .

A group now exists in a few plants where UAW represents the workers which calls itself a black revolutionary movement and whose goals are the complete separation of the races in the shop and the destruction of our Union through the tactics of violence, fear and intimidation. . . .

This group of extremists and racial separatists has sought to spread terror in the plants among both black and white workers and to undermine the unity and solidarity among all the workers, which are essential if the UAW members are to continue to make economic and social progress for themselves and their families.

They have sought to intimidate local union leaders who have been democratically elected to serve all the workers.

The weapons of fear, violence and intimidation have been used in the past in attempts to divide and weaken our Union. We have had to struggle against company goons, company police, gangsters, the underworld and the communists in order to survive and grow strong. But we did survive and we did grow strong—because we were together.

The UAW has a legal and moral responsibility to represent all workers in plants in which we have been democratically chosen by the workers as their collective bargaining agent. We are determined to carry out these responsibilities and we condemn all efforts of racial division and separatism both in the plants and in our society.

The UAW will continue to fight all forms of discrimination and will provide the fullest protection to workers who have legitimate grievances.

The UAW, however, will not protect workers who resort to violence and intimidation with the conscious purpose of dividing our Union along racial lines; for these workers would undermine our Union, the principles upon which our Union was founded and put in jeopardy the jobs which our members hold. . . .

Through the democratic procedures of our Union, the workers elect their union leaders.

In the Dodge and Eldon Avenue plants, black workers are solidly in the leadership of those UAW locals. At the Dodge plant in Hamtramck (UAW Local 3), four out of the six full-time officials are black and 56 percent of the elected stewards in the shop are black. At Eldon Axle (Local 961), 65 percent of all elected stewards and committeemen in the local are black. Both black and white workers have shared in and helped make possible the historic progress accomplished by the UAW.

The establishment of black organizations to influence the destiny of black people in American society is a sound concept. Separatism, dividing society, instilling fear and hatred, using violence and intimidation, however, are divisive, harmful to the workers and their welfare and damaging to the basic democratic values of society.

The UAW throughout its history has taken its stand firmly in support of the struggle for justice, for equal rights and equal opportunity to all people. UAW leaders and members have been in the vanguard of the legislative fight for civil rights. We have marched in Detroit, in Washington, D.C., Selma, Alabama, Jackson, Mississippi, Memphis, Tennessee, for justice and equity.

We have been in the leadership in the crusade against poverty. We have worked to help provide housing for low income families, to improve police—community relations, to establish community unions, to create job training programs and preapprenticeship programs for the disadvantaged, to improve our educational system particularly in the inner-city area, to insure equal rights and equal opportunity in the factories and also to bring to fruition the freedom, the self-respect, the dignity and the good life to all people which a democratic society can provide.

The UAW has built its progress in behalf of its members and their families and the community-at-large on the principles of human brotherhood and solidarity.

"Brotherhood," not "hatred," is the cornerstone on which to build a society in which each person lives and works in dignity and security with his neighbor. We in the UAW believe in brotherhood and in Union solidarity. We shall continue to dedicate ourselves and our efforts to the cause of justice and human brotherhood.

We call upon all UAW members to unite in this spirit. This is a time when men and women of good will must reject hatred and violence and must stand together for only as we join together can we build a better tomorrow for ourselves and our children.

Sincerely and fraternally,

The UAW International Executive Board

5.29 The Lordstown Rebellion, 1971. An interview with Gary Bryner, President, UAW Local 1112, Lordstown, Ohio, in Studs Terkel, *Working: People Talk About What They Do All Day and How They Feel About What They Do* (New York: Pantheon Books, 1974), pp. 187–94. Reprinted by permission of Donadio & Olson, Inc. Copyright 1970, 1974 by Studs Terkel.

Someone said Lordstown is the Woodstock of the *workingman*. There are young people who have the mod look, long hair, big Afros, beads, young gals. The average age is around twenty-five—which makes a guy thirty over the hill. I'm a young union president but I'm an old man in my plant.

Sixty-six, when they opened the complex for hiring, there was no Vega in mind. We built a B body, Impalas and Capris and wagons and whatnot— the big family car. . . .

When the plant first opened, it wasn't young people they drew from. It was people who had been in the community, who gave up jobs to come to GM because it was new. It was an attractive thing back in '66 to be one of the first thousand hired. I was twenty-three. I thought of it as security. I'm the 136th in a plant of seventy-eight hundred. You got the best jobs. You had the most seniority. A lot of the tradesmen hired had ten years of it, maintenance men, pipe fitters, millwrights, plumbers.

After so many hundreds were hired other people didn't want to come in and work the second shift or take lesser paying jobs, because they had already established themselves somewhere else. So that's when kids got hired right out of high school. This was in early '67. There was a drastic turnover in our plant. A guy would come in and work a week or two on his vacation, quit, and go back to the job he had. Standing in line, repetitively doing a job, not being able to get away, this wasn't for them. The young people were perfect—management thought. They were—boom!—dropped into it. But they wouldn't put up with it either.

That was '67. You go on to '68, '69, and they had sped up the line. They had started out at sixty cars an hour. Then they went on to a model 6, two models. We had a Pontiac, what is it called?—Firebird. And a B body on the same line. That presented difficulties. On top of it, '72 is not '66. There was a lot of employment then. Now there isn't. The turnover is almost nil. People get a job, they keep it because there's no place else.

I don't give a shit what anybody says it was boring, monotonous work, I was an inspector and I didn't actually shoot the screws or tighten the bolts or anything like that. A guy could be there eight hours and there was some other body doing the same job over and over, all day long, all week long, all year long. Years. If you thought about it, you'd go stir. People are unique animals. They are able to adjust. Jesus Christ! Can you imagine squeezing the trigger of a gun while it's spotted so many times? You count the spots, the same count, the same job, job after job after job. It's got to drive a guy nuts. . . .

In '70 came the Vega. They were fighting foreign imports. They were going to make a small compact that gets good milage. In the B body you had a much roomier car to work on, Guys could get in and out of it easily. Some guys could almost stand inside, stoop. With the Vega, a much smaller car, they were going from sixty an hour to a hundred an hour. They picked up an additional two thousand people.

When they started up with Vega we had what we call Paragraph 78 disputes. Management says, On every job you should do this much. . . . They use time, stopwatches. They say, It takes so many seconds or hundreds of seconds to walk from here to there. We know it takes so many seconds to shoot a screw. We know the gun turns so fast, the screw's so long, the hole's so deep. Our argument has always been: That's mechanical: that's not human. . . .

The workers said: We perspire, we sweat, we have hangovers, we have upset stomachs, we have feelings and emotions, and we're not about to be placed in a category of a machine. When you talk about that watch, you talk about it for a minute. We talk about a lifetime. We're gonna do what's normal and we're gonna tell you what's normal. We'll negotiate from there. We're not gonna start on a watch-time basis that has no feelings.

When they took the unimates on we were building sixty an hour. When we came back to work, with the unimates we were building a hundred cars an hour. A unimate is a welding robot. It looks just like a praying mantis. It goes from spot to spot to spot. It releases that thing and it jumps back into position, ready for the next car. They go by them about 110 an hour. They never tire, they never sweat, they never complain, they never miss work. Of course, they don't buy cars. I guess General Motors doesn't understand that argument. . . .

If the guys didn't stand up and fight, they'd become robots too. They're interested in being able to smoke a cigarette, bullshit a little bit with the guy next to them, open a book, look at something, just daydream if nothing else. You can't do that if you become a machine.

Thirty-five, thirty-six seconds to do your job—that includes the walking, the picking up of the parts, the assembly. Go to the next job, with never a letup, never a second to stand and think. . . .

In some parts of the plant cars pass a guy at 120 an hour. The main line goes at 101.6. They got the most modern dip system in paint. They got all the technological improvements. They got unimates. But one thing went wrong. (Chuckles.) They didn't have the human factor. We been telling them since we've been here: We have a say in how hard we're going to work. They didn't believe us. Young people didn't vocalize themselves before. We're putting human before property value and profits. . . .

The guys are not happy here. They don't come home thinking, Boy. I did a great job today and I can't wait to get back tomorrow. That's not the feeling at all, I don't think he thinks a blasted thing about the plant until he comes back. He's not concerned at all if the product's good, bad, or indifferent.

Their idea is not to run the plant. I don't think they'd know what to do with it. They don't want to tell the company what to do, but simply have something to say about what *they're* going to do. They just want to be treated with dignity. That's not asking a hell of a lot. . . .

PUBLIC EMPLOYEE UNIONISM

Perhaps the most significant development for organized labor in the 1960s was the surge in unionism among public employees. In 1962 President John F. Kennedy issued an executive order (Document 5.30) that some described as a Magna Carta for federal employees. Afterward, membership in the American Federation of Government Employees and the postal workers' unions grew rapidly. Document 5.31 explains why public employees, teachers especially, deserve the right to unionize and to bargain collectively. The song lyrics included in Document 5.32 hint at the new consciousness emerging among public employees. In Document 5.33, Senator Strom Thurmond of South Carolina enunciates the traditional rejoinder to public employee unionism and why such unionism is not in the general interest. How might the public employee unionists have responded to Thurmond's argument?

5.30   Federal Employees Unionizing "Freely and Without Fear," 1962. Executive Order 10988 issued by John F. Kennedy, January 17, 1962.

Employee-Management Cooperation in the Federal Service

WHEREAS participation of employees in the formulation and implementation of personnel policies affecting them contributes to effective conduct of public business; and

WHEREAS the efficient administration of the Government and the well-being of employees require that orderly and constructive relationships be maintained between employee organizations and management officials; and

WHEREAS subject to law and the paramount requirements of the public service, employee-management relations within the Federal service should be improved by providing employees an opportunity for greater participation in the formulation and implementation of policies and procedures affecting the conditions of their employment; and

WHEREAS effective employee-management cooperation in the public service requires a clear statement of the respective rights and obligations of employee organizations and agency management:

NOW, THEREFORE, by virtue of the authority vested in me by the Constitution of the United States, by section 1753 of the Revised Statutes (5 U.S.C. 631), and as President of the United States, I hereby direct that the following policies shall govern officers and agencies of the executive branch of the Government in all dealings with Federal employees and organizations representing such employees.

SECTION 1. (a) Employees of the Federal Government shall have, and shall be protected in the exercise of, the right, freely and without fear of penalty or reprisal, to form, join and assist any employee organization or to refrain from any such activity. Except as hereinafter expressly provided, the freedom of such employees to assist any employee organization shall be recognized as extending to participation in the management of the organization and acting for the organization in the capacity of an organization representative, including presentation of its views to officials of the executive branch, the Congress or other appropriate authority. The head of each executive department and agency (hereinafter referred to as "agency") shall take such action, consistent with law, as may be required in order to assist that employees in the agency are apprised of the rights described in this section, and that no interference, restraint, coercion or discrimination is practiced within such agency to encourage or discourage membership in any employee organization.

(b) The rights described in this section do not extend to participation in the management of an employee organization, or acting as a representative of any such organization, where such participation or activity would result in a conflict of interest or otherwise be incompatible with law or with the official duties of an employee.

SEC. 2. When used in this order, the term "employee organization" means any lawful association, labor organization, federation, council, or brotherhood having as a primary purpose the improvement of working conditions among Federal employees or any craft, trade or industrial union whose membership includes both Federal employees and employees of private organizations; but such term shall not include any organization (1) which asserts the right to strike against the Government of the United States or any agency thereof, or to assist or participate in any such strike, or which imposes a duty or obligation to conduct, assist or participate in any such strike, or (2) which advocates the overthrow of the constitutional form of Government in the United States, or (3) which discriminates with regard to the terms or conditions of membership because of race, color, creed or national origin. . . .

SEC. 16. This order . . . shall not apply to the Federal Bureau of Investigation, the Central Intelligence Agency, or any other agency, or to any office, bureau or entity within an agency, primarily performing intelligence, investigative, or security functions if the head of the agency determines that the provisions of this order cannot be applied in a manner consistent with national security requirements and considerations. When he deems it necessary in the national interest, and subject to such conditions as he may prescribe, the head of any agency may suspend any provision of this order (except section 14) with respect to any agency installation or activity which is located outside of the United States.

Approved—January 17th, 1962.

JOHN F. KENNEDY

THE WHITE HOUSE,
January 17, 1962.

5.31 Teachers "To Have the Right Which Other Workers Have Had for Decades," 1973. Dr. Helen D. Wise, President of the National Education Association, testifies before Special Subcommittee on Labor of the House Committee on Education and Labor, 1973. Reprinted in Coalition of American Public Employees, *Federal Bargaining Act for State and Local Public Employees Testimony in Support of H.R. 8677* (Washington, D.C.: CAPE, 1974), pp. 21–22.

In 1973, it should be unnecessary to debate at length the question of whether or not teachers should have the right to engage in collective bargaining with school boards. For almost 40 years employees in the private sector have had the right to bargain with their employers. More than 30 states have enacted legislation providing for some type of bargaining between public employees and their employers. . . . And yet, there are still those who maintain that teachers are somehow "different"—that there is something intrinsic in public education that rules out collective bargaining as an acceptable *modus operandi*. . . . Teacher militancy and unrest are attributed to the efforts of teacher organizations to "take over the schools."

The press of teachers for collective bargaining is not organizationally inspired: organizations do not create need; they respond to need. What, then, has really prompted the movement toward collective bargaining in education? The public focus on teacher demands for improved salaries and fringe benefits tends to present a distorted picture. Money is rarely the sole or even the primary motivating factor. We believe that the root cause is the desire on the part of teachers to have the base right which other workers have had for decades—the right to a meaningful voice in the formulation of the terms and conditions under which they must serve.

We do not maintain that teachers should have this right simply because they want it. On the contrary, it is socially desirable that they have it. The problems facing education are many and complex. If they are to be successfully resolved, it will be necessary to involve the teacher who, because of their background and training, have a special knowledge and competence which enables them to make a valuable contribution. Collective bargaining offers the most effective vehicle for such involvement.

5.32 "On Our Way With AFSCME," words by Joe Ames, sung to the tune of "Panama." In Joe Glazer, ed., *AFSCME Songbook,* American Federation of State, County, and Municipal Employees, 1977.

"You can't fight city hall,"
that's what the politicians said.
"You'll hit a big stone wall,
and get a bloody head."
We did it anyhow,
in our battle to be free.
We're on our way with
A. F. S. C. M. E.

"You can't negotiate,"
that's what all the judges said.
"Not with a sovereign state,"
that's how the law books read.
We did it anyhow,
in our battle to be free.

We're on our way with
A. F. S. C. M. E.
We're on our way,
everybody come along.
We're on our way
everybody sing this song.
We're on our way
to the top and we won't stop
Who says you can't fight city hall,

We'll build the biggest union of all,
I hear those crazy letters calling me,
A. F. S. C. M. E.

5.33   Sen. Strom Thurmond denounces public sector collective bargaining before the U.S. Senate, March, 6, 1975. Reprinted in Ralph de Toledano, *Let Our Cities Burn* (New Rochelle: Arlington House Press, 1975), 152.

A collective-bargaining relationship—any and every collective bargaining relationship—depends on establishing an adversary relationship between employer and employee. Unions, in order to win and hold the loyalty of their members, must demand more than the employer is willing to offer. If a union were to accept only what the employer offered, it would serve no useful purpose for its members. So unions by virtue of their very nature and to preserve their existence must make demands. The only instrument that unions have at their disposal to support their demands is the withdrawal of the services of their members—the strike. The strike is, even when it is peaceful, the use of force. It cannot be defined or construed any other way. No government can call itself sovereign if it permit the use of force to enforce demands against it. We can see from this that there can be no true collective bargaining without strikes and there can be no true government with strikes.

This is the essential question we must face. Are we to have sovereign government, or are we to have public sector collective bargaining? We cannot have both.

6

Era of Economic Change and
Union Decline, Since 1973

The years since 1973 have witnessed vast changes in working-class life in the United States. The globalization of trade accelerated the deindustrialization of the nation. New technologies, especially the proliferation of computers, transformed work processes and moved the economy's center of gravity increasingly away from industrial production toward the provisioning of services. The liberalization of U.S. immigration law in 1965, and the acceleration of immigration, both legal and illegal, from south of the U.S.-Mexico border began to decisively reshape the demographics of the U.S. working class. Together, such changes swept away the two decades of economic stability that most workers had experienced after World War II.

Paradoxically, the new developments that took shape in the late twentieth century contributed to the revival of a number of trends that characterized working-class life in the United States in the late nineteenth century. As a result of plant closures across the industrial heartland insecurity returned to the lives of working people whose families had enjoyed upward mobility and improved standards of living for nearly two generations. The deindustrialization of the nation in turn opened the door to a renewed assault upon unions, the effectiveness of which recalled the open shop drives of a century earlier. Unions recoiled under that assault and saw their relative numbers in the private sector dip lower than at any point since the turn of the last century. Meanwhile, millions of new immigrants, many of whom were illegal, remained beyond the reach of union organizers. Consequently, as in the late nineteenth century, a gap began to widen between the wages and working conditions of native-born workers on the one hand and recent immigrants on the other. These developments further weakened the New Deal political coalition, which was reeling from the upheavals of the 1960s and the ravaging inflation and economic stagnation of the 1970s. A revived conservative movement was perfectly poised to take advantage of this window of opportunity. Politically ascendant conservatives helped to roll back and weaken federal regulatory programs, including those that protected workers' rights and linked their program to an uncritical celebration of the virtues of the free market the likes of which had not been seen since before the dawn of the Progressive era. Meanwhile, most workers saw their real wages stagnate or decline between the 1970s and the end of the century, even as the wealthiest Americans saw their incomes grow at unprecedented rates, creating a gap between the richest Americans and working people that recalled the excesses of the Gilded Age.

The roots of many of these changes can be found in the economic crisis that beset Americans in the 1970s. Fuel crises, triggered in part by embargoes of oil sales to the United States by Arab nations during the 1970s, launched a period of price inflation that only exacerbated the lingering inflationary impact of Vietnam war spending. Not until 1981 did the inflationary wave—which at times reached double-digits—subside. What made the "Great Inflation" of the 1970s different from previous eras of rising prices was that it accompanied not an economic boom but a recession: Between 1973 and the early 1980s economic growth stagnated. Economists termed the resulting economic malady "stagflation," and working—class America bore the brunt of the pain inflicted by it. Prices began to outstrip wages for many workers, especially those who didn't enjoy the benefits of union contracts. Such trends were not significantly reduced during the economic recovery of the 1980s. As a result, the buying power of a typical hourly worker's paycheck in 1990 was 11 percent less than it had been in 1973. Indeed, a 1992 study by the Joint Economic Committee of Congress concluded that between 1979 and 1989, 80 percent of American families saw their wages stagnate or decline.

Economic stagnation for the many was accompanied by unparalleled prosperity for the few. The upper 1 percent of income earners in the United States saw their average income rise by 45.4 percent between 1977 and 1990. Accentuating the growing income divide was the skyrocketing pay of corporate chief executive officers. In 1980 the average American CEO earned 29 times what the average worker in his/her employ earned. By 1990, the ratio had jumped to 113:1. This growing income disparity was uniquely American. The ratio of average CEO income to average worker income in Japan in 1990 was 20:1, whereas in Germany the ratio was 35:1. The growing American disparity in income distribution was in turn reinforced by a resurgence of popular belief in the virtues of the unfettered marketplace. In the writings of authors such as Milton Friedman, George Gilder, and Charles Murray it was argued that any efforts to regulate the free market would ultimately hurt, not help, working people and the poor.

Accentuating the diverging income patterns in the post-1973 United States was the shift from an industrial to a service economy. Industrial plants closed at an alarming rate during the decade of the 1970s. Auto companies were among those most affected by this trend. U.S. automakers were deeply hurt by the high price of gasoline and saw fuel-efficient Japanese imports take a larger slice of the U.S. market. Steel companies that failed to modernize by investing in "basic oxygen process" technology during the 1960s and 1970s also saw foreign-made steel gobble up larger slices of their markets. Taking advantage of improving global communications as well as the cost-saving containerization of transoceanic freight shipping, an increasing number of U.S.-based manufacturers decided to close plants in the United States and relocate production to low-waged countries around the world. The impact of the shift of an increasing share of American manufacturing overseas was most damaging to the economic well-being of America's minority workers. In 1974 there were 38,000 relatively well-paid black steel workers in the United States. By 1988 the number had dropped to 10,000.

Two trends characterized the manufacturing jobs that remained in the United States in the post-1973 era. One trend saw the flight of such jobs from the high-waged North to the low-waged South. By 1980, North Carolina had the highest proportion of blue-collar laborers in its workforce; it also boasted the lowest average hourly wage. A second trend saw the number of non-union manufacturing jobs increase as union manufacturing jobs declined. In 1970 the average union worker earned 19 percent more than her non-union counterpart. By 1980 the differential had grown to 30 percent, offering a significant incentive to employers who sought to go non-union. This trend boded ill for strongly unionized sectors of the economy. The auto industry was one. Between 1978 and 1990, U.S. auto makers saw their share of the domestic market in cars shrink from 83 percent to 67 percent. Meanwhile, Japanese automakers set up non-union production facilities in the United States. Honda opened its first plant in 1982, northwest of Columbus, Ohio. Nissan followed suit in 1983 in Smyrna, Tennessee. Toyota opened a facility in Georgetown, Kentucky, in 1988. And Subaru-Izuzu did so in Lafayette, Indiana, in 1989. These trends combined to isolate union membership in the Northeast, Midwest, and West. By 2002 one-half of the nation's union membership was confined to just six states that together accounted for 35 percent of national employment. In states with large union densities such as California, New York, and Illinois, the union movement continued to exert powerful political influence. But in other regions of the nation it encountered rough sledding. Fast-growing states such as Texas and Florida (the second and fourth most populous in 2000) proved to be difficult terrain for union organizers and organized labor was an overmatched political force throughout much of the New South.

As economic trends shifted in ways that placed increasing downward pressure on workers' wages, political circumstances also worsened for organized labor. President Richard Nixon's Watergate-induced resignation in 1974 and Democrat Jimmy Carter's election in 1976 fueled optimism among some that labor's political clout might help revive a strong liberal movement. Within only a few years it was clear that such hopes would come to naught. The Carter administration soon found itself immersed in the fight against rampant inflation and it increasingly came to see union demands for higher wages as a significant part of the wage-price spiral. The administration consequently adopted a strong anti-inflationary line that led to growing tension between it and the labor movement, the key organizational constituency of the Democratic party. Labor was disappointed in the political initiatives it tried to advance during the Carter presidency. In 1977 a Republican-led Senate filibuster killed the most significant of these: a labor law reform bill that would have corrected the pro-management tilt in labor law enforcement that had become evident since the late 1950s.

As labor's political initiatives stalled, business groups organized as never before to influence the political process. The formation of the Business Roundtable in 1972 marked an aggressive new campaign by corporations to challenge union influence in the political realm. This new offensive saw business funnel huge sums of money into the political process. In the 1972 election cycle, labor and business political action committees contributed to candidates on a roughly equal level, with labor donating $8.5 million and business $8 million. Within a decade the political mobilization of the business community had left organized labor in the dust. In 1982 labor donated some $35 million to political candidates; business gave $84.9 million. The business community's successful mobilization helped it shape the national debate more successfully than at any time since the 1920s. In California, for example, business interests played a leading role in crafting Proposition 13, a successful statewide initiative that offered a politically potent answer to the concerns of inflation-beset Californians: it promised property tax reductions and drastic cuts in public services to inflation-weary voters. Soon a "tax revolt" was gathering force around the country. Among the groups hardest hit by that revolt were public sector unions, which had been the fastest growing part of the labor movement since the early 1960s.

The election of Ronald Reagan in 1980 best symbolized the political transformation of the country. Reagan was the first former union official ever elected to the presidency of the United States (Reagan had led the Screen Actors Guild in the years after World War II), but he was to become the most bitter foe of organized labor since Calvin Coolidge (who was incidentally a hero of Reagan's). Reagan initiated broad tax cuts that lightened the tax burden of the rich more than that of the middle class or working people. He also cut discretionary spending on a host of domestic programs that benefited workers and their families, including food stamps and job training. Perhaps most significantly, he broke a union of federal employees. When 11,500 air traffic controllers who were members of the Professional Air Traffic Controllers Organization (PATCO) struck the Federal Aviation Administration on August 3, 1981, Reagan fired and permanently replaced them. His action was widely interpreted as providing a green light to aggressively anti-union tactics by private employers. In the decade after the PATCO strike a number of large employers in the meatpacking, mining, manufacturing, and transportation sectors chose to permanently replace their striking workers as well. Management's aggressive tactics helped force down the number of significant strikes from 235 in 1979 to a mere 17 in 1999. This trend as much as any other illustrated the marked shift that occurred in the balance of power between management and labor in the last decades of the twentieth century.

The election of Democrat Bill Clinton in 1992 did not represent a significant departure from these unfavorable political trends for labor. One of Clinton's highest priorities was the passage of the North American Free Trade Agreement (NAFTA) over the strenuous objections of unions and most members of Clinton's own party. NAFTA simply accelerated the well-established pattern of manufacturing jobs leaving the United States, much to labor's chagrin. Even so, organized labor's political situation took a dramatic turn for the worse halfway through Clinton's first term when Republicans capitalized on poor Democratic turnout at the polls to take control of both houses of Congress for the first time in a half-century. Behind the leadership of Speaker of the House Newt Gingrich, Republicans attempted to pass several anti-labor measures including the Teamwork for Employees and Managers (TEAM) Act, which would have weakened the Wagner Act's prohibition on the use of company unions for collective bargaining. Although Clinton prevented such legislation from being enacted, labor found itself increasingly on the defensive politically. The disputed election of George W. Bush in 2000 (after a major get-out-the-vote drive by unions helped Democrat Al Gore surge from behind to capture a narrow popular-vote majority) represented a devastating set-back for labor's political influence.

The economic and political changes of the late twentieth century were accompanied by significant shifts in the demographics of the nation's workforce. Three developments combined to foster a dramatic increase in immigration to the United States: the liberalization of the nation's immigration laws in 1965; unfolding economic and political crises in Latin American, Asian, and African nations that sent people from those regions in search of safety and economic opportunity in the United States; and the rise of a U.S. service economy which demanded cheap labor. Declining over decades, the percentage of U.S. workers who were foreign-born suddenly began to zoom upward in the years after 1970. This shift was most visible in the nation's cities, where the overall percentage of the population that was foreign-born grew from 5.8 percent in 1970 to 9.9 percent by 1990. The rise in immigration was even more pronounced in the nation's largest urban areas. The percentage of foreign-born residents in New York's population jumped from 18.2 to 28.4 between 1970 and 1990. Over the same period the portion of Los Angeles's population that was foreign-born jumped from 14.6 to 38.4 percent.

As immigration was changing the face of the American workforce, so, too, was the increasing entry of women into the paid labor force. In 1950, 18.4 million women worked for wages. By 2001 the number had jumped to 66 million. Over this period women's share of the overall labor force rose from 29.6 to 46.6 percent. Still women lagged behind men in earnings. In 2000, women who worked full time, year-round earned 74.3 cents for every dollar earned by men. The rising participation of women in the paid labor force was fraught with contradictory consequences for working-class families. On one hand, barriers to women's entry into a variety of occupations continued to fall as the women's rights revolution of the 1960s permeated American culture. On the other hand, working mothers and fathers often had no choice but to enter the workforce simultaneously since it was increasingly difficult for one parent to earn enough to allow the other to stay home with pre-school-aged children.

Taken together, shifts in the nation's economy, politics, and demographics brought an end to many of the conditions that had fostered the rise of a strong union movement in the years between 1932 and 1973. In the latter years of the twentieth century, organized labor saw its share of the overall labor force decline from 20.1 percent of the overall non-agricultural labor force in 1983 to 13.2 percent in 2002. The resiliency of public employee unions actually camouflaged the degree to which private sector unionism was eroded during these years. By 2000, barely 9.5 percent of private sector workers were unionized (down from a high of 35.7 percent in 1953, a lower proportion than at any time since 1903).

In the latter decades of the century, the union movement attempted to come to terms with new conditions and create solutions to its growing problems. The retirement of the ailing George Meany and the elevation of his lieutenant, Lane Kirkland, to the presidency of the AFL-CIO in 1979 provided an opportunity for labor to reassess its direction. Kirkland worked hard to bring unions like the Teamsters back into the AFL-CIO fold, to reach out to build alliances with other progressive organizations, and to mobilize labor in demonstrations like the 1981 Solidarity Day march on Washington D.C. Yet his efforts produced meager results, as the number of union members continued to decline. The Republican takeover of Congress in 1994 finally discredited Kirkland and triggered a rebellion that ultimately brought John Sweeney, president of the Service Employees International Union (SEIU), into leadership of the AFL-CIO in 1995. Although Sweeney worked hard to revive labor's political muscle and to focus more union resources on the organizing of new workers, he was no more successful than Kirkland in reversing labor's decline.

Nonetheless, as the twentieth century ended, a number of new initiatives promised hope to those who wished to see organized labor reconstitute itself as a potent social force. In many cities around the country labor and church groups combined to pass "living wage" ordinances that mandated that all workers paid by taxpayer-funded municipal contracts must earn wages sufficient to keep them above the poverty line. College students organized successful boycotts of goods produced in exploitative sweatshops and hundred of them flocked into "Union Summer" programs sponsored by the AFL-CIO. The SEIU's "Justice for Janitors" campaign succeeded in making organizing breakthroughs among immigrant custodial workers from Los Angeles to Boston. And at the large rally against the policies of the World Trade Organization that was held in Seattle, Washington, in 1999, union members, environmentalists, and global justice activists stood shoulder to shoulder.

To be sure, significant obstacles continued to impede the revival of organized labor as the twenty-first century began. But the same impulses that historically induced workers to join together to advance their agendas collectively in unions—desires for economic security, a rising standard of living, a semblance of workplace justice, and a voice in determining the conditions under which they labor—operated as strongly as ever in the new century. Although economic, legal, and political forces continued to undermine workers' ability to unionize, there were indications that a broader sense of support for organized labor's revival was taking shape.

FEELING THE ECONOMIC CRUNCH

Beginning around 1973, real wage growth began to stagnate for most American workers. As income inequality grew in the 1970s, resentment boiled among working-class Americans. Document 6.1 helps pinpoint the stagnation of wages in the 1970s and shows how inflation made employees' benefits (especially medical coverage) an increasingly large share of employers' costs. Document 6.2 indicates the degree to which the years since 1979 have led to unequal income growth. And Document 6.3 provides an early example of the ways in which white working people turned frustrations generated from their declining incomes toward perceived enemies ranging from welfare recipients to so-called "tax and spend" liberals. In what ways do the first two documents help contextualize the sentiments voiced in the third document?

6.1. Growth of average hourly wages, benefits and compensation, 1967–1979. From Lawrence Mishel, Jared Bernstein, and John Schmitt, *The State of Working America 2000/2001* (Cornell University Press, 2001), p. 116. Reprinted from Lawrence Mishel, Jared Bernstein, John Schmitt, and the Economic Policy Institute, The State of Working America, 2000–2001. Copyright 2001 by Cornell University. Used by permission of the publisher, Cornell University Press.

Measured in 1999 dollars.

	Wages and Salaries	Benefits	Total Compensation	Benefit Share of Compensation
1967	$13.42	1.66	15.08	11%
1973	$15.51	2.54	18.05	14.1%
1979	$15.69	3.43	19.12	17.9%
1989	$16.89	3.81	20.70	18.4%
1999	$19.50	3.59	23.09	15.6%

6.2 Rate of Growth in Family Income by Quintile,1947–1999. From Mishel et. al, *The State of Working America 2000/2001*, p. 55. Reprinted from Lawrence Mishel, Jared Bernstein, John Schmitt, and thee economic Policy Institute, The State of Working America, 2000–2001. Copyright 2001 by Cornell University. Used by permission of the publisher, Cornell University Press.

	Lowest Fifth	Second Fifth	Third Fifth	Fourth Fifth	Top Fifth
1947–1979	120%	101%	107%	114%	94%
1977–1999	−1%	6%	11%	19%	42%

6.3 Economic Roots of Working-Class Anti-Liberalism, 1969. Excerpts from "The Troubled American: A Special Report on the White Majority," *Newsweek*, October 6, 1969, pp. 46–51. Copyright 1969 Newsweek, Inc. All rights reserved. Reprinted by permission.

The disgruntlement of Middle America finds its cutting edge in the nation's traditional working-class—families whose breadwinners have at most a high-school education, old blue-collar jobs and bring home incomes of $5,000 to $10,000 a year. In this supposed age of affluence and upward mobility such families feel trapped in a marginal life. . . .

The root of the problem is that the blue-collar worker, much more than the rest of Middle America is convinced that prosperity is passing him by. Fewer than one in three of the working-class group say they are better off now than five years ago; by contrast 44 percent of the white-collar workers polled feel more prosperous. And the blue-collar group is even less confident about the future. Only 28 percent expect to be better off five years from now. "With the high cost of living and the taxes, we can't survive," said a Brooklyn machinist. . . .

Only 24 percent of the sample [of middle-class Americans] said the government was doing a "good" or "excellent" job of dealing with the nation's problems; two-thirds said "fair" or "poor."

The grumbling is loudest, of course, over the pocketbook issues of taxes and inflation. Despite the vaunted prosperity of the 1960s, one out of every four middle-class Americans said the rising cost of living had forced a cutback on purchases; another 44 percent said they were just managing to stay even. Nearly eight out of ten said Federal taxes were too steep, and 59 percent thought local taxes excessive. . . . The chief complain is not so much the level of taxation as that the government has its priorities wrong. "Nobody has the right to take a hard-working man's money and waste it, but they all do," said Mrs. Margaret Donovan, a housewife in Albany, N.Y., "Our money just isn't used right." . . .

Behind the long counter of the Nuttie Good Tea Room on Main Street in quiet Springfield, Mass., an aproned, open-faced George Yaos, stands frying eggs.

"I've never collected a day of welfare in my life," he says. "In my family, if you stay home and don't work, you're a bum and a criminal. These black guys think they've got it tough. When my father came to this country from Greece in 1910, he could speak five or six languages. People laughed at him and called him stupid."

"There's plenty of work around. These people just don't have backbone. They give them welfare just to keep them quiet."

GLOBALIZATION AND DE-INDUSTRIALIZATION

The globalization of manufacturing and trade introduced new uncertainties into working-class life, as U.S.-based corporations grew increasingly foot-loose in search of cheaper labor markets outside of the United States. Beginning in the mid-1970s plant closings became commonplace in industrial America. As Document 6.4 makes clear, they often came with no warning to the workers whose jobs were sent offshore, bringing great suffering to industrial communities. By the 1980s, workers were increasingly wary of plant closings, but as Document 6.5 shows, they found it nearly impossible to prevent them. In the end they were able to secure legislation that merely called for management to give advance warning of a closing. The passage of NAFTA only worsened the problem for many workers. As Document 6.6 shows, when the workers of a California company named Friction Brake attempted to build solidarity with workers across the border in Mexico, their employer shut down their plant in retaliation. What do these documents suggest about the impact of plant closings on manufacturing workers' outlooks for the future?

6.4   Effects of Plant Closings, 1979. "Statement of Michael Botkin, Portland Plant Closure Committee," *Hearings Before the Subcommittee on Labor-Management Relations of the Committee on Education and Labor of the House of Representatives,* 96th Cong., 2d Session (Washington, D.C.: Government Printing Office, 1980), pp. 435–37.

My name is Michael Botkin. I'm going to try to summarize my statement, brief as it is. . . . Basically, I want to try and deal with the personal impact of a plant closure, having gone through one. On June 13, which was a Friday the 13th, the plant I worked at closed its doors forever. I worked there for 9 years.

When I first applied for that job, the personnel manager went to great lengths to tell me that at my age I should be looking toward the future, and I should work for this company because I had responsibilities, to myself, to my wife, my future family, and to the community. So I went to work for what was to become Gilmore Steel.

The company set forth rules of employee conduct, and I lived and worked under those rules. During the first few months of employment, I occasionally thought of finding other work, but the words of that personnel manager kept running through my mind. Each time I thought, "No, he's right. You have a family. You should stay here." So I stayed. I felt that I had a responsibility not only to myself and my family, but to the company.

But what about the company's responsibility to the workers and to the community? What are the workers from Gilmore Steel to do about finding other work? They have a choice. They can go to work at jobs that pay them half as much as they earned before, or they can retrain for a more profitable line of work.

But who's going to help these people retrain? Not the company. When the employees were terminated, they also terminated the tuition benefits we had. . . .

How are these workers going to afford health care? In the past, the workers at this plant were covered for periods of up to 2 years after layoff. Now, since they were terminated, their coverage ended 1 month after they were terminated. . . .

I'm not talking about people at my plant who think that the world owes them a living. I'm talking about people who want to work. They want a job, a secure job, one that they know is going to be there tomorrow when they go to work; a job that won't disappear because a board of directors decides that there is not enough profit being made.

I think it's time for big business in this Nation to meet some responsibilities to their employees and to the communities. It is time for them to face up to the fact that when they shut the doors of a marginally profitable operation, they hurt not only the workers, but the entire surrounding community as well.

6.5 "We Packed Up Our Shop," 1992. Statement of Bernadette Ford, Former Employee, Electro-wire Products, *Field Hearings on H.R. 3878, The American Jobs Protection Act,* U.S. House Committee on Education and Labor, 102d Congress, 2d Session, 1992, Serial No. 101–109, pp. 78–79.

Ms. FORD: My name is Bernadette Ford, and I was employed at Electro-Wire Products of Owosso for 10 years. I was a quality supervisor and assistant to the quality manager for most of that time. We manufactured wire harnesses for Ford Motor Company and General Motors and air bag harnesses for Packard of California.

Our position in the Electro-Wire Corporation seemed very secure. We had a Q-1 rating from Ford and were well on our way to obtaining the Total Quality Excellence Award, which is the highest award you can receive from Ford. Electro-Wire of Owosso had for the last 5 years been rated either first or second for quality among all the harness builders in the United States. . . .

As I look back, we should have seen the writing on the wall. In about 1984, Electro-Wire opened their first plant in Juarez, Mexico. Our plant manager hung a letter from the mayor of Juarez on the bulletin board stating, he was extremely pleased by this plant and that he could supply an unlimited work force at the pay rate of 53 cents an hour.

After that this letter was a tool used against us to explain the lack of raises and to intimate there were others who would work for less.

Shortly after that we began receiving regular shipments of Mexico's defective material which we had to rework and repair and then return to the Ford assembly plants.

Between 1987 and 1988, the second larger and more modern plant was built in Mexico. Our assembly lines began going there. We still had work, but it became short term or experimental lines. We were more or less the prototype manufacturer for the corporation, meaning we built the sample parts that went to Ford for approval. We set up the lines, worked the bugs out of the production and then sent the work on down.

In December of 1988 or January of 1989, the corporate name changed from Electro-Wire of Michigan to Electro-Wire of Texas. It was also at this time that we began to hear more about financial problems and lack of work from our corporate officials. At the same time the Mexican plants were getting the yearly lines and jobs that had formerly gone to us.

On January 31, 1990, a meeting was called for all the supervisors. Mr. Jerry Tryon, vice-president of Electro-Wire, announced that as of April 2 the doors would be closing on the Owosso plant. We were stunned. We just sat in silence for a long time. No one wanted to go out in the plant and face our workers.

Then, to add insult to injury, over the next 2 months we packed our shop up and sent it to Texas, which then transferred it to Mexico.

Our workers were mainly women, many who were the sole support of their children. We are not a big General Motors or Ford factory. There was no sub-pay or guaranteed 90 percent of our wages for 3 years. We had 60 days to cope with the uncertainty of no longer having a job. At best we could expect 26 weeks of unemployment.

We did receive TRA benefits amounting to 2 years of retraining which helped, but along with that you only receive 1 year of financial aid to help you get through that, and it has limited completion for many sole support students.

When people see on the news that 1000 General Motors workers will be laid off do they realize that thousands of workers at the support factories will be affected? The auto industry is not just the Big Three. General Motors and Ford are supported by hundreds of small, outside suppliers. If the problems of Flint and Detroit are harsh, the outlying counties and small towns such as Owosso are devastated.

During the whole ordeal the only excuse our company had to offer us was that they were forced into this move by competition.

My question is if American companies can take our jobs to Mexico or Korea or any of the other countries now producing American car parts and if American companies can produce the products for less through cheaper wages and fewer benefits to workers, less restriction on pollution or safety requirements, why have the prices of an auto not reflected that savings? Competition? To me it sounds like greed.

As the American auto industry screams foul at the Japanese for taking our jobs away, they themselves are sending thousands of jobs out of this country, and I am upset. How many of those Mexicans or Koreans can afford to buy the cars that they help build? I am sure not very many can. The lack of car sales proves that we no longer can buy them either.

In closing, I would like to ask that our government do something to protect us, the small companies of America. Stop the loss of our jobs due to the greed and irresponsibility of shortsighted companies looking for the fast buck. We must stop blaming the rest of the world for the shape our economy is in and start taking responsibility for our own.

We are the backbone of this country. The statistics on unemployment and welfare show we are being broken. We are a proud, hard working force, and we want to work and contribute. Please give us that chance. Thank you.

6.6 A "Revenge Closing," 1998. From David Bacon, "Revenge-Closing— Cross-Border Organizing Brings Trouble on All Sides," Pacific News Service, September 29, 1998. Available online at http://www.pacificnews.org/jinn/ stories/4.20/980929-closing.html. Reprinted with permission from Pacific News Service.

IRVINE, CA—Late last month, the gate into the Friction auto brake plant here swung shut for the last time, leaving 110 production workers to move on.

It's not unknown for factories in the U.S. to close as production moves south, but this Orange County plant closed in part because its workers reached across the border to help coworkers at a plant in Mexico belonging to the same company.

The story of the two factories shows a new level of union resolve to cross borders in the era of free trade. It is also a stark reminder of the obstacles to these efforts.

Friction belongs to a Connecticut-based transnational auto parts manufacturer, Echlin, Inc. Throughout 1996 and 1997, workers at Echlin's ITAPSA brake plant in Mexico City tried to form an independent union. Last summer, three ITAPSA workers visited their Irvine counterparts to find out about conditions in U.S. plants. They met informally, at lunch time in the street outside the boxy facility.

The workers at Friction, largely immigrants from Mexico, identified with the effort. "We wanted to help the workers there win their rights," says Maria Villela, president of Local 1090 of the United Electrical Workers, the union at the Irvine plant.

The Mexican workers needed all the help they could get. When they tried to join the independent union called STIMAHCS, dozens were fired. An election at the plant last September was won by the government-affiliated union Echlin supported.

After that election, a new tri-national alliance of unions filed a complaint over the violation of workers' rights before the administrative body set up to enforce NAFTA's labor agreement, the National Administrative Office of the U.S. Department of Labor. In March more than two dozen ITAPSA workers and other union officials submitted testimony. Echlin never showed up.

On July 31, that office issued a report, declaring that workers "were subjected to retaliation by their employer and the established union in the workplace, including threats of physical harm and dismissal."

Friction workers in Irvine signed a petition, demanding that Echlin rehire the fired workers and recognize the independent union. Their plant manager, Mark Levy, responded angrily. "He told us we had drawn a line between the union and the company," Vilella recalls.

In February, Echlin formally notified the union it was closing the Irvine plant. The move came as a shock to Friction workers, who have an average of 11 years on the job. "We think it's revenge," says Villela. "We work like crazy here, and make the best product in the industry."

Echlin spokesperson Paul Ryder says the work is being moved to other U.S. factories. "We have over capacity for that product line," he says. "The closure is just the normal course of business."

The company may have other reasons to feel hostility toward the Irvine workers. When they organized there in 1994, Echlin's senior vice-president Milton Makoski commented in a letter to another union, "We are opposed to union organization of our current non-union locations. . . . We will fight every effort to unionize Echlin employees . . . "

He noted that despite "60 years of determined and relentless efforts" by unions, a majority of the firm's employees were unorganized—except for one operation "where the employees, while they were part of the Echlin organization, have elected to be represented by a union." That operation was the Friction plant.

Once organized, the Irvine workers became the spark plug of a NAFTA-zone alliance of unions with contracts in Echlin's factories, including the Teamsters, the United Electrical Workers (UE), the Paperworkers and UNITE in the U.S., and the Canadian Steelworkers and Auto Workers. "Our primary purpose," says Bob Kingsley, UE Director of Organizing, "is to achieve a situation where we're all sitting down at the table with the same company, and bargaining together."

As the U.S. auto industry relies increasingly on parts made in Mexico's maquiladoras, an increased union focus on struggles such as those at ITAPSA may just be beginning. Unfortunately, NAFTA contains no penalties for companies or governments that violate workers' rights. Nor does it provide any protection for workers who take cross-border action to support their coworkers in other countries.

Mexico's labor law is "very advanced and progressive," according to STIMAHCS attorney Eduardo Diaz. But the government, he says, is afraid to enforce it, as its economic policy depends on foreign investment.

U.S. trade policy also seeks favorable conditions for U.S. investment. Corporations like Echlin reap the benefits. According to University of California Professor Harley Shaiken, "in Mexican plants U.S. investors get first-world rates of productivity, and a work force with a third-world standard of living."

To meet this challenge, "a growing number of unions are trying to deal with each other across borders," observes Robin Alexander, the UE's director of international solidarity. "Maybe there is no single answer to their problems, but we won't find any answers at all without looking for them."

Perhaps that was the error of the Friction workers. They looked.

DECLINING SUPPORT FOR THE WELFARE STATE

By the 1980s, working-class support for the defense of the welfare state was evidently declining under the pressures of high taxes, inflation, and stagnating incomes. As Document 6.7 shows, southern blue-collar workers interviewed by Robert Emil Botsch in the late 1970s exhibited little enthusiasm for the idea that the government should provide jobs to those who wanted them. By 1996 opposition to government welfare programs crystallized in the passage of the Republican-sponsored Temporary Aid to Needy Families (TANF) Act, which ended the New Deal era welfare entitlement and placed strict limits on the aid poor families could receive from the government. Document 6.8 provides a snapshot of TANF's implementation in Georgia in 2000. What do these documents suggest about the ways in which the role of the state has changed in the lives of U.S. workers?

6.7 Waning Enthusiasm for the Welfare State, ca. 1979. Excerpts from Robert Emil Botsch, *We Shall Not Overcome: Populism and Southern Blue-collar Workers* (Chapel Hill: University of North Carolina Press, 1980), pp. 57–67. From *We Shall Not Overcome: Populism and Southern Blue-Collar Workers*, by Robert Emil Botsch. Copyright 1981 by the University of North Carolina Press. Used by permission of the publisher.

The Government and Jobs—Are Jobs a Basic Right?

Each of the men in the small group was asked: "Do you think that the government should provide jobs for those who can't find work and who want to work?" This question was followed by: "Do you mind having some of your tax money spent on this kind of thing?" Their answers to these questions as well as some of their comments on other questions reveal how they feel about whether or not a job is a right that should be guaranteed by the government. The opinions of the ten white men cover a fairly wide range. . . .

EDDIE: I would rather see 'em provide jobs for the ones that want to work and can't find it than I would to pay the ones that don't have a job and don't care to find one.

DAVE: Yes, if they really want to work. But I would have to go back and say that I have never seen the time that a person could not find a job somewhere.

QUESTION: So you don't really think it is necessary the way things are now?

DAVE: Well, not the way it is now because—well, back last year when they had all these plants was laid off—Multicorp and everywhere, and everybody claimed they were out of work. We worked down at Master Molding Company sixteen hours a day—first and second shifts and needed help all the time and we very seldom had people come in and ask for a job. A person is not really going to want a job as long as he can sign up and make a living doing it. [Unemployment.] As long as he can do it and have enough money to live off of. I wouldn't if I could do it. I'll be honest with you! I'll be honest with you! I wouldn't go to work if I could do it, if I could live off of it.

QUESTION: Do you think you could get enough off of it?

DAVE: Nope. But I wouldn't be working today if I could. Today is the last day of duck hunting season. I would have been duck hunting!

PAUL: So far as providing jobs. I would have to think on that cause I don't know what that would involve. Now, certainly, if a man wants to work they should help him find one. Now, that's something I must say helped me to decide to vote for Mr. Carter. He says that people that don't have jobs—we're gonna find 'em a job and train 'em for it. Then if they don't want 'em. we're gonna kick 'em off welfare and we're gonna kick 'em off all the money they got comin'. And I agree with that 100 percent. If a man wants to work, let him work. If a man don't want to work, cut off the money you're giving him cause I don't believe in anybody taking a free ride. . . .

MARK: It would be good if we could go back to the old times and teach people how to work for a living.

QUESTION: Do you think some people are sorry and just don't want to work for a living?

MARK: Right.

QUESTION: Is that a cause of poverty?

MARK: No. That contributes to the unemployment rate which makes the economy worse. And you know as far as paying out taxes and welfare, I don't believe in welfare—if a person can't get out and work and the only people that should get welfare is the disabled. That's the only people I think should have welfare.

QUESTION: You don't like giving welfare to those who don't want to work?

MARK: Right. There's blacks and whites out there, and they collect welfare, and, uh, they could work, they could work. They collect that welfare because they just too dang sorry. If I wanted to I could go out here and find some shack and just, you know. I don't know anybody. I'm off to myself. I need welfare. And they'll pay it!

JUNIOR: I think they tryin' to do that now. I think they tryin' about as good as they can do. They's just so many things that take in consideration for that, it's hard to say. The government, they—I don't guess anybody, unless they in it, knows what they talking about cause I'd say I couldn't. They probably trying to get 'em jobs. They could probably, uh, well, the people that want jobs and can't sign or something like this, they got to do somethin'. That's the ones out here robbin' and stealin' right now is the ones that can't get anything. Part of it is just sorryness and a lot of it is just because they can't really find anything.

QUESTION: Would you mind having some of your tax money spent for that kind of thing?

JUNIOR: It'd be better than worrying about them breaking into your house and they shoot you for $20 and steal your car so they can get $200 out of it or something like this. . . .

ALBERT: If people have no place to turn they should have help from somebody.

QUESTION: Would you mind having some of your tax money spent on this kind of thing?

ALBERT: Well, it's going on now. I mean the people on welfare. That's coming out of my tax money. So I think it would be a good thing to do. Well–I kinda think it do and I kinda think it don't. It's kind of hard to answer. But to a certain extent I guess there is no other way. If a person had no other way to turn I guess he would need help from somebody. . . . I guess you could say that people don't care whether you're making it if they are making it. If you got more than enough and if you could share with people and try to make them have just a little more, then the world would be a better place. I mean you can't just go around giving people this just because you got it, I mean. But I don't think people have enough love for one another.

QUESTION: Do you think there is anything government can do to get people to share better with one another?

ALBERT: I don't really think the government can do much. I think they can do things, but, uh, I guess every time you turn around that's who they's blaming, saying that the government ought to do this and the government ought to do that for you. I think maybe they [the government] could do a little more than what they do. I think people can do more for themselves than what they do. I don't think things is always as bad as people make it seem. But I do think that maybe the government can do a little more.

JOHN: According to what I heard, right now there is 1.5 million people unemployed in the U.S. Suppose fifty-two jobs might open up in Furntex tomorrow. You'd be lucky if you could get fifteen willing to work on the job very long. . . . They drafted me from a job when other guys I know, too sorry to work, was on the streets. I went in and came out, and they was still on the streets. They was too sorry to even work in a pie factory—just eatin' pies!

LEWIS: I don't think so. I think some means should be made available for people who can't find jobs to find work, but I don't think government should have a hand in it. . . .

The simple fact that fourteen out of the fifteen men in this group stated that to some extent they favor the government providing jobs for those who want to work and cannot find work could easily lead to an incorrect conclusion unless we listen to their explanations and qualifications. A summary of their opinions on this issue would be close to the following proposition: The government should provide jobs if (1) merit is proved by the potential employee's willingness to take jobs like those that these men have been willing to accept in their lives; (2) jobs such as these are not available (most of the men believe they are available) and there is nowhere else to turn. A majority of these men, both black and white, also believe that government-provided jobs should not be of higher quality than those they endure. Enthusiasm is notably lacking for increasing taxes to finance the creation of such jobs. Junior, who is more enthusiastic than most about the necessity for government-provided jobs, feels that money for such projects could come out of tax money that is "wasted" on such things as "bringing back pieces of rock from the moon."

6.8 The New Welfare, 2000. TANF Fact Sheet, Georgia Department of Human Resources, Office of Communications, May 2000. http://www2.state.ga.us/Departments/DHR/tanf.html.

Temporary Assistance for Needy Families (TANF), commonly known as welfare, is the monthly cash assistance program for poor families with children under age 18. A family of three (mother and two children) may qualify for TANF if their gross income is below $784 a month and assets are worth less than $1,000.

There is a four-year lifetime limit on cash assistance. Work is a major component of TANF; adult recipients with a child over age 1 will be required to participate in a work activity. These work activities help recipients gain the experience needed to find a job and become self-sufficient.

* Total TANF recipients (February 2000): 129,822 (99,817 children; 30,005 adults) Number of cases (families): 53,171. . . .
* From January 1997 to June 2000, the number of families receiving cash assistance has decreased by 53.8 percent, or 61,994 families. . . .

* Average number of families and individuals receiving cash assistance each month:

	1995	1996	1997	1998	1999
Families	139,253	132,627	114,154	84,513	65,198
People	383,177	360,035	302,473	220,417	153,060

* Racial/ethnic breakdown: White: 17 percent; Hispanic: 1.3 percent; Black: 80.9 percent; Asian: 0.3 percent
* The average length of time families with an adult included in the grant have been receiving TANF is 18.3 months. As of September 1999, about 17 percent of all families with an adult had been receiving TANF continuously since January 1997.
* Average monthly cash benefit through February 2000: $223
* Average family size: 3 (mother, 2 children)
* Maximum monthly benefit for family of three: $280
* Poverty level for a family of three: $1,157/month

DISCONTENTS OF FACTORY LIFE

As managers threatened union workers with plant closings in the 1980s, factory life became increasingly pressurized. Managers employed new efficiency techniques, just-in-time inventory methods, and teamwork strategies to try to elicit greater efficiency from their workers. But as Document 6.9 makes clear, these strategies did little to address workers' disillusionment with factory life. In Document 6.10, autoworker and humorist Ben Hamper indicates how cynical many workers became toward the efficiency drives of their employers. The song reproduced in Document 6.11 gives a labor activist's rejoinder to management's plea for "teamwork." Why do you suppose workers would often react with such cynicism and suspicion toward management efforts to foster cooperation, teamwork, and greater efficiency in production?

6.9 An Autoworker's Lament, ca. 1988. Interview with Ramon Reyes, in Richard Feldman and Michael Bethold, *End of the Line: Autoworkers and the American Dream* (Urbana: University of Illinois Press, 1990), pp. 237–44. Reprinted with permission by Grove Atlantic.

In the plant, people constantly call me names. They like to pick on somebody, and I happen to be one of about five Mexicans in the plant. Because of the way I look, they don't consider me 100 percent American. They call me taco bender and wetback and really give me hell.

To me I'm more of an American than anybody in that plant. I was born in this country, and my family goes back three generations in Texas. . . . My oldest brother fought in Korea, and I and two other brothers fought in Vietnam. I went there because I wanted to serve my country. When we got home, they still called us wetbacks. . . .

I was born and raised in Elsa, Texas, seventeen miles from the Mexican border. I was one of ten kids. . . . From the time I was 12 until I was 18, my mother and I and all my brothers were migrant workers every summer. In April and May we hoed beets in Idaho. In June we came to Michigan to pick cherries. In July we picked cucumbers around Alma, Michigan. Then we went to Defiance, Ohio, and picked tomatoes until October, and then we went back to Texas and started school late. . . .

I was a biology freak when I was a kid, and I went to college to be a marine biologist. But I didn't finish. . . . I never dreamed there was anything like assembly-line work. But I wound up with the job, and now here I am on the line, getting called names by some redneck foremen and my fellow workers. . . . But at the truck plant I made over $250 a week. Back home you were doing great if you made $100 a week. . . .

My biggest mistake was ending up at the Ford Motor Company.

The assembly line is very damaging to your self-esteem. You work hard and build a lot of trucks, and that accomplished something; but you don't ever learn how to do anything else. You stay and stay forever, and ever.

I stayed on the Engine Line about six years. My job was to put pressure on the fan belt, tighten it up, pull on the alternator, and tighten that up. Doing that enormous amount of pulling for six years eventually got to my elbow, and I pulled a muscle in it. I filed for workmen's comp and they put me through hell. They tried to fire me. . . .

But after a while they put me on a job nobody wanted: the bracket job. You climbed on top of the Bronco, got inside the truck, and bent down to put insulation brackets on the side; then you'd climb out. In and out, in and out, all day long.

Eventually my back couldn't handle it. . . . I wound up with about two years off from work on medical, unpaid. I only made it because I was single and then didn't need much to live on. . . .

I think there's going to be a revolution in this country. That's the only thing that is going to stop all this bullshit, stop them from putting so much pressure on people to do slave-type work. . . .

The auto companies aren't going to take care of the workers here. That's a joke. . . . We're the last people they'll let retire from the plants. We're the end of the road. . . .

The union has its hands tied in a way during this modernization process. But they also believe this bullshit that Ford is going to take care of the workers, or at least the union.

The company came out with the EI [employee involvement] bullshit. That's where they give the worker a lot of rope and he eventually hangs himself. . . .

They always tell us we have to become more efficient because we're competing with the Japanese. But I don't know anything about

Japanese autoworkers. Maybe they're slaves. Maybe they don't get paid enough. . . .

There are only a few middle-class people left in my neighborhood. The rest are on welfare. The middle class is dying. Pretty soon it's just going to be the rich and the poor, and it'll be like Mexico and South America, where it's a constant war between the rich and the poor. . . .

I consider myself middle-class. . . .

People like me who can afford to pay other people to keep the economy going are going to be chopped off pretty soon. And when we fade away, the whole system will fall. The middle class people are the ones who keep the economy going, who buy the cars and the consumer goods. If everybody goes on welfare, how fast and how far do you think this country will go down? . . . Pretty soon everybody will be out of a job and walking around like a bum. All the stores will be closed, and my neighborhood will look like a ghost town. . . .

6.10 "Up with us, down with them," ca. 1977. An auto worker's report on a labor management quality and production seminar, from Ben Hamper, *Rivethead: Tales from the Assembly Line* (New York: Warner Books, 1991), pp. 44–48. Copyright 1991 by Ben Hamper. By permission of Warner Books, Inc.

During the Summer and Fall of 1977, the truck plant was hummin' six days a week, nine hours per shift. All of this overtime added up to one gorgeous stream of income. . . .

It was during this boom period that I attended my first of the annual "State of the Factory" addresses. The presentation was to keep us informed on just where our plant stood in relation to efficiency, quality rating, cost procedures worker attendance and overall sales. We were also to be apprised on the condition of our dreaded dogfight with the Japanese and, pickups and sub-snuff Ford Broncos.

We were herded next door to this mammoth hangar called the Research Building. I have no idea what kind of research went on there, but it's a fair bet that the place was at least a partial foil for all the legions of smock-clad highbrows who weaved around the assembly line each evening trying their damnedest to look brilliant and concerned about who knows what. I stuck by Bob-A-Lou, who was an old pro at these corporate hoedowns. He told me to settle in for an hour's worth of propaganda, cheerleading and high-tech gibberish that would gladly float right over my head. We made a quick beeline for the free doughnuts and Pepsi. Whatever was on the agenda, it sure beat working.

"There's the Plant Manager now" Bob-A-Lou mumbled through his forth or fifth jelly doughnut. He was pointing toward the stage which, by this time, was completely overrun with about two dozen clones in drab neckties.

"Which one is the chief?" I asked Bob-A-Lou, hopelessly confused.

"The John Wayne look-alike," he said.

"Oh, yeah." I laughed. 'All that's missin' is the pistol and spurs.

"I can positively assure you of one thing," Bob-A-Lou said while assaulting a new doughnut. "Sometime during his spiel, he's gonna tell us that he will be regularly touring the plant, pausing to listen to any of our gripes or suggestions. He will pledge to be visible and accessible. Just remember I told you so."

"Bullshit, I presume."

"You better know it. In all my years here, I've yet to see his face in the factory. He's probably afraid that he'll scuff one of his cuff links or something."

The pep rally began. The Plant Manager started by back-patting everybody in the galaxy. Up with us, down with them! He introduced a steady parade of weasels who dutifully took their bows. The Plant Manager was a very happy man. Outside the back of the building, I could envision a Brinks truck carting away his company bonus. We received jelly doughnuts and warm pop. Up with us, down with them!

He started talking about the enormous popularity of our best-seller, the Chevy Suburban. "We can't even meet the demand for this product," he bellowed. "Do you realize that there are people in New England who have never even SEEN a Suburban!" I took a gulp of Pepsi and wondered to myself. Is there no limit to the human suffering some people must endure? The Plant Manager's Knute-Rockne-reborn-as-poorboy's Leo-Buscaglia-on-the-threshold-of-industrial-Guyana rah-rah speech continued for another half hour or so. As Bob-A-Lou had predicted, the boss started playin' footsie with the workers:

"I plan to make every effort to visit with as many of you as I can. Your input is invaluable to the future of our operations. It is essential that each and every one of us join together in unifying our . . .

"Shut the fuck up," a guy behind me groaned.

The Plant Manager introduced the man in charge of overseeing worker attendance. In contrast, he didn't seem happy at all. The attendance man unveiled a large chart illustrating the trends in absenteeism. With a long pointer, he traced the roller-coaster tendencies of the unexcused absence. He pointed to Monday, which slung low to the bottom of the chart. Monday was an unpopular day attendance-wise. He moved the pointer over to Tuesday and Wednesday which showed a significant gain in attendance. The chart peaked way up high on Thursday. Thursday was pay night. Everybody showed up on Thursday.

"Then we arrive at Friday," the attendance man announced. A guilty wave of laughter spread though the workers. None of the bossmen appeared at all amused. Friday was an unspoken Sabbath for many of the workers. Paychecks in their pockets, the leash was temporarily loosened. To get a jump on the weekend was often a temptation too difficult to resist. The Corporation saw it quite differently.

The attendance man took his pointer, which was resting triumphantly on the snow-capped peak of Thursday evening, and, following the graph, plunged the pointer straight down through Friday, a motion that resembled falling off a cliff. Again, there was much snickering.

"Unfortunately, this is not a subject that lends itself to any amount of humor," the attendance man bristled. "Absenteeism is the single largest factor in poor quality. No replacement, no utility worker can perform your job as well as you. Each time you take an unexcused absence, you damage the company along with the security of your own job!" With that said, he packed up his graphs and charts and stalked off stage to make way for the techno-cretins. The veins in his neck were visible all the way back to the doughnut table.

Hardly anyone tuned in for the technical presentation. It was one long lullaby of foreign terminology, slides, numerology and assorted high-tech masturbation. Why would any of us give a shit about the specifics of the great master plan? We knew what holes our screws went in. That was truth enough. Point us toward our air guns and welders and drill presses and save all the particulars for the antheads in the smocks and bifocals.

"Be sure to help yourselves to the doughnuts and softdrinks on your way out," the Plant Manager shouted as the pow-wow broke up. It was time to pour ourselves back into the mold and attend to our well-paying jobs. Up with us, down with them.

6.11 Criticizing Labor-Management Cooperation Schemes, 1988. "If You Have a Team," from Mike Parker and Jane Slaughter, *Choosing Sides: Unions and the Team Concept* (Boston: South End Press/Labor Notes Book, 1988), p. 55.

If You Have a Team
(to the tune of "Young at Heart")

Fairy tales can come true
it can happen to you
if you have a team
An adversarial mind
changes quickly you'll find
when you're on a team

Though the line speed's extreme
you never do scream
Jobs designed by your team
aren't as hard as they seem

And though you're working faster
every passing day
the company is in your heart—
work feels like play

Don't you know it is worth
all the unions on earth
just to have a team?

The boss is your friend
as long as you bend
on a flexible team

And if you can survive
till you're 55
think of all they'll derive
cause you've eaten this jive

But here is the main bite
they'll shut your plant tight
unless you go along and
vote to have a team.

WORKING WOMEN'S STRUGGLES

Working women played an increasingly important role in the U.S. work-force in the years after 1973. Document 6.12 outlines their growing importance in the overall economy and in the economies of individual families. As women entered the ranks of organized labor in larger numbers, they helped introduce new thinking into trade unionism's ranks. Document 6.13, from a 1975 pamphlet by the Union Women's Alliance to Gain Equality (WAGE), shows how workplace issues can be seen as women's issues; and Document 6.14 briefly lays out a union woman's argument for "comparable worth"—the notion of improving the wages of traditional "women's jobs" to justly compensate women for labor that has been historically devalued simply because it was done by women. As women have entered the wage labor force in increasing numbers they have generally borne a "double burden" by bearing primary responsibility for child raising as well as working for income. The humor expressed in the song reproduced in Document 6.15 barely conceals the dissatisfaction many women came to feel as they shouldered this double burden. What do these documents suggest about the unique challenges facing wage-earning women in the late twentieth century?

6.12 Facts About Working Women, 2003. AFL-CIO, "Facts About Working Women." http://www.aflcio.org/yourjobeconomy/women/factsaboutworking women.cfm. Copyright AFL-CIO. www.aflcio.org.

More women are working than ever before. And they're looking for solutions to the problems of juggling work and family, making ends meet and finding respect and opportunity on the job.

More and More Women Are Working
* Over the past century, women workers have grown steadily in number and as a proportion of the workforce.
* The number of working women has grown from 5.3 million in 1900 to 18.4 million in 1950 and to 66 million in 2001.
* Women made up 18.3 percent of the labor force in 1900, 29.6 percent in 1950 and 46.6 percent in 2001.
* In the United States, 99 out of every 100 women will work for pay at some point in their lives. Regardless of their marital status, the majority of women (except widows)—even those with young children—work for pay.
* 62.1 percent of married women with spouses present, 65.3 percent of married women with absent spouses, 66.8 percent of never-married women and 74.5 percent of divorced women are in the labor force.
* Women are projected to increase their share of the labor force to 48% over the 1998–2015 period.
* 72.3 percent of women with children younger than 18, 78.7 percent of women with 6- to 17-year-olds and 64.6 percent of women with children younger than six were in the labor force in 2000.
* 54.3 percent of women without children younger than 18 were in the labor force in 2000.

More Families Are Maintained by Women
The number and proportion of families in which a woman is the householder and no spouse is present are growing, too.
* In 2000, 12.8 million families were maintained by women, representing 17.8 percent of all families, compared with 5.6 million—10.8 percent of all families—in 1970.
* 78.5 percent of women who maintained families were employed in 2000.

Nonstandard Work
Most "nonstandard" workers (workers who do not hold regular, full-time jobs) are women.
* 55 percent of workers paid by temporary help agencies are female.
* 70 percent of part-time workers are female.

Holding Multiple Jobs
* In 2001, there were 3.6 million female multiple job holders.
* 47 percent of all multiple jobholders in 2001 were women, up from 20 percent in 1973.

Wages and Income
* In 2000, women who worked full time, year-round earned 74.3 cents for every dollar earned by men.
* Over a lifetime of work, the average 25-year-old woman who works full-time, year-round until she retires at age 65 will earn $523,000 less than the average working man.

* Women who worked full time, year-round saw their inflation-adjusted median annual earnings increase by 1.9 percent from 1999 to 2000.
* Median family income (adjusted for inflation) increased only by 0.2 percent between 1999 and 2000.
* 58 percent of the workers who benefited from the last increase in the minimum wage were women.

Benefits
* In 2000, 38.7 million people were not covered by health insurance, or 14 percent of the population.
* 72.4 percent of those with coverage were covered by private plans. Two out of three who have coverage have insurance through an employer.
* In 2000, half of all older women receiving a pension got less than $4,164 per year, compared with $7,768 per year for older men.
* In the Ask a Working Woman survey, 42 percent of working women said they did not have paid family leave, 3 percent said they lacked flexible hours and 21 percent did not have paid vacation time.

Unions Benefit Working Women
* Pay for women in unions is higher than for their nonunion counterparts. In 2001, women union members earned 30 percent more than nonunion women, according to union wage data based upon the median weekly earnings of full-time wage and salary workers.
* Union workers are more likely than nonunion workers to have health and pension benefits. 85 percent of full-time union workers in medium-sized and large private establishments had health benefits in 1995, compared with 74 percent of full-time nonunion workers.
* 87 percent of full-time union workers in medium-sized and large private establishments had retirement benefits, compared with 78 percent of full-time nonunion workers.

Gender and Organizing
Women make up a growing percentage of union membership.
* In 1962, women accounted for 19 percent of union membership. By 1997, 42 percent of all union members were women.
* When they have the opportunity, women consistently are more likely than men to vote for unions.

6.13 Joyce Maupin, "Women's Issues: What Are They?" from Union Women's Alliance to Gain Equality (WAGE), *Organize! A Working Women's Handbook* (Berkeley, CA.: Union W.A.G.E. Educational Committee, 1975), pp. 18–22.

Whether or not an employee must stop work in the fifth or sixth month of pregnancy, even if she wants to work and her doctor says she is able to work, is exclusively a women's issue. Child care, maternity leave, affirmative action, dress codes, benefits for temporary and part-time workers, are issues affecting a great many women and only a few men. They have generally been ignored by a male-dominated union leadership.

After you elect your rank and file negotiating committee . . . one of the first problems will be to convince union members themselves that "women's" issues are important to all workers in the bargaining union, not just women of child-bearing or men of child begetting age. Your shop must believe that child care and paid maternity leave can be as vital as wages. In fact, with taxes taking such a large bite out of each raise, they may be advantageous even from a dollar and cents point of view. The employer will make every effort to divide you by saying that if you demand luxuries like quality child care, you won't get much of a raise. But working people will be more receptive than the boss to the idea that child care is not a luxury.

Once your shop is convinced, how will the negotiating committee go about it? What kind of language do you write to cover these demands? Language itself is the first step. Go through your union contract and change every one-sided sex reference. Not chairman but "chair" or "chairperson." Not he and his—it is always possible to substitute person, employer, or his/her. Some people feel this is trivial, but language is a key to underlying feelings and attitudes. The executive who refers to women workers, some of them in their fifties or older, as "his girls" is revealing his contempt. If you're in doubt, ask yourself why "his or her vacation" sounds alright, while "her or his vacation" sounds odd. . . .

Dress is another issue which is more likely to affect women than men. A woman's appearance has always been a big factor in getting and keeping a job, and the employer's ideas about suitable dress can range all the way from conservative disapproval of miniskirts and pantsuits to a complaint that the skirt is not short enough. Skirts may be required even in very cold and drafty workplaces and around equipment which makes them dangerous. This requirement is particularly aggravating when employees work in a basement office or some other area where they are never in contact with the public. But no matter where a woman works or what kind of work she does, it's a form of discrimination. One young woman, when she was told that the shortest miniskirt would be more acceptable than the attractive pantsuit she was wearing, retired to the ladies room, took off the pants and came out in her jacket. A simple clause like one in an SEIU Local 535 contract can prevent conflict over clothing: "The Welfare Department shall not promulgate a dress code for the term of this Agreement." This clause would also protect a man with a long hair style. . . .

None of these demands are unrealistic. All of them have been won by some workers and you can get them, too. With child care, maternity leave, affirmative action and personal time off, a woman will find her job easier and have some more energy to spare. She can become more active in her union and assume responsibility for union work. She will know how to talk about these issues and draw other women into the union movement. Organizers can stop complaining that women are difficult to organize because many organizers will *be* women.

6.14 For Comparable Worth, 1982. Statement by Elinor Glenn, of the Coalition of Labor Union Women, from Patricia Cayo Sexton, *The New Nightingales: Hospital Workers, Unions, and Women's Issues* (New York: Enquiry Press, 1982), pp. 129–30.

The unions are just coming to understand a slogan that's been emerging in the last five or six years, "equal pay for work of equal value." It's a new slogan for the women's movement. A clerk in a liquor store, for example, gets much more money in many cases than a clerk on a hospital ward. Yet the ward clerk has a much more responsible job. A laborer can get $500 a week and the laundry worker $125 a week, using the same education and skills. One is male, the other female and third world.

There's no reason to encourage our women to think only in terms of non-traditional jobs—climbing up telephone poles or driving a caterpillar. Many women want to be nursery school teachers and nurses. They may prefer that work. Why should they be penalized monetarily for doing "women's work"? Maybe there's a social or cultural reason why women like to do these jobs: mothering, nurturing, working with children, sick people, old people. In the hospitals, one could say, "Well, if we get more men to be nurses then the wages will go up." That proves the discriminatory pattern of the job. Why should wages go up only when men come in? And why should women leave a profession they like because it is paid a discriminatory wage?

We're policing the apprenticeships to see that women are encouraged to enter them. But that will not seriously impact the millions of women workers who are underpaid for their work. Those millions of women workers are not going to be operating engineers or lumberjacks. They are going to be in the mainstream of women's work. When we seriously commit ourselves to fight for comparable worth, the whole pattern of sexism and wages will change.

6.15 "Day Care," 1990. Capitol Steps, Revised by Merlye Korn. From Rebel Voices compact disk, "Warning: Women at Work," Reveille Music, 1996–97.

Sung to the tune of "The Banana Boat Song (Day-o)"

Oh Day, oh Day Care!
Day Care call, wan' de mom go home.

Day, give me Day Care!
Day Care call, wan' de mom go home.

I work all day to pay de tax an' rent.
Day Care call, wan' de mom go home.
Day Care's half of where me money's spent
Day Care call, wan' de mom go home.

When I get to the office an' I jus' show up, (Refrain)
De Day Care call, dey say me kid t'row up, (Refrain)

Chorus

She's 6 month, 7 month, 8 month old. (Refrain)
She jus' cut another tooth, so I been told. (Refrain)
Oh, I wish I had a nanny-man to nanny me Amanda. (Refrain)
Take 'er to the zoo. Amanda want to see the panda. (Refrain)

Chorus

I had to go back to work not'ing changes dat. (Refrain)
Now me kid is acting like de Simpson brat. (Refrain)
When me kid get sick dey t'ink me work should stop. (Refrain)
Dey never t'ink dat way about de kiddie's pop. (Refrain)

Chorus

It's six o'clock and I'm not home. (Refrain)
I read her a story on de telephone. (Refrain)
O if I win de lottery me job I'll surely quit her. (Refrain)
Never worry how to pay anoder babysitter. (Refrain)

Chorus.

NEW IMMIGRANTS

Since 1970, waves of new immigration have changed the demographics of the U.S. working class. Document 6.16 provides an indication of how important the new immigrants became to the U.S. economy by the turn of the century. Concentrated in the low-waged service sector of the economy, these new immigrants were usually exploited by employers. Document 6.17 indicates the kinds of conditions immigrant domestic workers have faced as well as some of the tactics they've used in trying to confront unfair employers. The little legal leverage that immigrants possessed in contesting maltreatment was significantly eroded by the U.S. Supreme Court's 2002 decision in *Hoffman Plastic Compounds v. NLRB,* which held that illegal immigrants could not claim the protection of the National Labor Relations Act. Document 6.18 reports on that decision as it was seen by the United Electric Workers (UE) union. Based on these documents, what would you say the implications are for working-class America of the growth of a large segment of workers with significantly fewer rights than their U.S.-born counterparts?

6.16 The New Immigrant Workforce, 2003. National Immigration Law Center Fact Sheet, January 2003. NILC, Los Angeles, California.

FACTS ABOUT IMMIGRANTS

Immigrant Families Make up an Important Share of the U.S. Population

- According to the 2000 Census, there are over 30 million immigrants in the U.S., representing 11 percent of the total population.
- One in five children in the U.S. is the native- or foreign-born child of an immigrant.
- Immigrants are settling in communities throughout the U.S. During the 1990s, the immigrant population in "new immigrant" states grew twice as fast (61 percent vs. 31 percent) as the immigrant population in the 6 states that receive the greatest numbers of immigrants.
- Immigrants and citizens live together in families: 85 percent of immigrant families with children are mixed status families (families in which at least one parent is a noncitizen and one child is a citizen).
- Between 1970 and 2000, the naturalized citizen population increased by 71 percent.

Immigrants Contribute Significantly to the U.S. Economy

- The National Academy of Sciences reports that, in 1997, the U.S. reaped a $50 billion surplus from taxes paid by immigrants to all levels of government. In New York, also in 1997, $13.3 billion (69 percent) of the $19.3 billion in taxes paid by immigrants went to the federal government in the form of income taxes, Social Security taxes, and unemployment insurance.
- In 2000 the foreign-born population accounted for 12.4 percent of the total civilian labor force.
- In 2000 foreign-born men 16 years old and older had a higher labor force participation rate (80 percent) than native-born men (74 percent).

Immigrants Rely Disproportionately on Low-Wage, Low-Benefit Jobs

- Even though 7.1 percent of all workers are noncitizens, almost 20 percent of all low-wage workers who live in low-income families with children are noncitizens.
- Almost 43 percent of immigrants work at jobs paying less than $7.50 an hour, compared to 28 percent of all workers.

- Only 26 percent of immigrants have job-based health insurance.
- Children in immigrant families make up one-fifth of the low-income children in 20 states.

Immigrant Families Use Benefits at Lower Rates Than Citizen Families, and Benefits Are Not a Factor in Decisions to Migrate to the U.S.

- Use of public benefits by legal immigrant families with children who earn less than 200 percent of the federal poverty level fell sharply between 1994 and 1999.
- In 1999 the rates at which these immigrant families used Temporary Assistance for Needy Families (TANF), Supplemental Security Income (SSI), and food stamps were lower than for low-income citizen households with children.
- Welfare does not drive migration patterns: between 1995 and 2000, the number of immigrant families with children grew four times faster in states with the least generous safety nets like Arkansas and Texas than it did in states with more generous safety nets for immigrants, like California and Massachusetts.

Immigrants Who Are Able to Improve Their English Skills Have Higher Earnings

- Almost 18 percent of persons in the United States over the age of 5 speak a language other than English at home, and almost 8 percent are limited English-proficient (LEP).
- A study by MassINC found that employed immigrants in Massachusetts who are fluent in English earn 33 percent more than immigrants with limited English speaking skills.
- A study in Los Angeles by the Economic Roundtable found that former welfare recipients who were English proficient earned a higher wage than former welfare recipients who did not speak English or who were LEP.
- In a New York City survey of 500 non-English proficient immigrants, 89 percent of respondents were either on a waiting list or wanted to attend English as a Second Language classes at some time in the future.

Immigrant Restrictions on Support Services Hurt Children

- One-third of all children in the country who are eligible for Medicaid, but are not enrolled, are children in immigrant families.
- Even though U.S. citizen children living with noncitizens remained eligible for food stamps, between 1994 and 1999 their participation in the Food Stamp Program declined 42 percent.
- The children of immigrants are more likely to be disadvantaged than the children of natives. They are more likely to be poor (24 percent versus 16 percent); more likely to be uninsured (22 percent versus 10 percent); more likely to have no usual source of medical care (14 percent versus 4 percent); and more likely not to have a steady source of food (37 percent versus 27 percent).

6.17 Travails of Immigrant Domestic Workers, 1996. Excerpts from Doreen Carvajal, "For Immigrant Maids, Not a Job But Servitude," *New York Times,* February 25, 1996, pp. 1, 37. Copyright 1996 by The New York Times Co. Reprinted with permission.

The dirty little secrets behind the closed doors of some upper middle class houses in the suburbs from New York to Los Angeles are the immigrant women who work up to 15-hour shifts, six days a week, for wages amounting to $2 an hour. Some domestic workers are trying to bare those secrets with rebellious strategies ranging from court challenges and professional mediation to self-esteem training and a new, untested weapon of last resort—demonstrations outside the employers' houses. They are receiving encouragement and legal advice from organizations that work with immigrants. . . .

On a Sunday morning at St. Peter Alcantara Church in Port Washington, after Mass and the coffee hour had ended, dozens of Salvadoran women and men lingered to listen to Dina Aguirre deliver a testimonial about her own bittersweet experiences as a domestic in Garden City.

She was dressed for church instead of work, a woman of 20 in a long green dress and black high heels who had moved here seven months ago from Guatemala where she had been studying to be a school teacher. She speaks little English and lacks immigration documents, a résumé that gave her few choices.

"I worked for three weeks without getting paid," she said. "I worked from 7 in the morning to 7 at night and sometimes till 11. I asked the woman to pay me and she said I don't owe you anything because you ruined my blouse." She said "Give me your address, and I will send you a bill for all that you owe me." . . . Ms. Aguirre finally did get a paycheck, but only after suing in small claims court and receiving an award of $600.

Her tactic is increasingly being used by other domestic workers in the suburbs of Long Island who have discovered how difficult it is to make a claim for back wages. In some cases, the women had already turned unsuccessfully to their local police department for help or to the State Department of Labor, where claims can take as long as 18 months to investigate.

But those who win court claims don't necessarily feel victorious; they still have to collect the money.

The calendar belonging to Yanira Juarez, 25, is filled with entries marking the paydays that passed without payment from her employer in Bellport, L.I., where she worked as a housekeeper. Ultimately, she won her claim in court for back wages of more than $2,000, but the award remains unpaid.

"I returned and I returned again with a friend who spoke English to tell her that I needed the money," Ms. Juarez said. "She took my address and said, 'I will send it.' I'm still waiting."

Such complaints are so common that various social agencies have created special units to offer advice and counseling to domestic workers. . . . The Workplace Project on Long Island is . . . circulating an advice comic book about scornful employers and overworked maids, but their proposed solutions are . . . aggressive. They are organizing workers to form "justice committees" of domestic workers who will appear at an employer's doorstep to show their court orders and demand back wages.

6.18 Beyond the Protection of the Wagner Act, 2002. UE Reports on the Supreme Court Decision in *Hoffman Plastic Compounds v. NLRB*, *UE News*, April 2002.

Jose Castro wanted to have a union because he worked in a low-wage shop. Little did he know that his decision to organize would lead to his firing and, 13 years later, a Supreme Court decision that injures the rights of workers to gain union representation.

The Supreme Court, in its *Hoffman Plastic Compounds v. NLRB* decision on March 27, ruled that Castro and other immigrant workers who are fired for organizing a union are not entitled to back pay. The ruling will make union organizing even more difficult.

Castro worked for Hoffman Plastic Compounds in Los Angeles. To gain better wages and conditions, Castro and his co-workers organized with the United Rubber Workers (since merged with the United Steelworkers). Hoffman struck back in January 1989, with what a Supreme Court Justice termed "crude" and "obviously illegal" tactics, including the firing of Castro and three other workers.

The National Labor Relations Board ruled the company's unionbusting was illegal. But companies face no penalties for breaking the law to crush union organizing. The NLRB can only order employers to cease and desist from violations of the law, post a notice of the order, and offer reinstatement and back pay to the victimized workers. That's what the Labor Board did in the Hoffman case.

Hoffman appealed the NLRB's ruling. During the trial that followed, Castro admitted that he lied about his immigration status to get his minimum-wage job. On the basis of that disclosure, the NLRB decided that Castro's back pay would be limited to the period between the date he was illegally fired and the date the employer "discovered" he was undocumented.

That decision had little impact on the injustice inflicted on Castro, but it was too much for Hoffman—and ultimately, for a 5-4 Supreme Court majority.

The Supreme Court concluded that the Immigration Reform and Control Act of 1986 (IRCA) trumps the National Labor Relations Act. IRCA makes it a crime for an immigrant employee to use fraudulent documents in the employment verification process required by the law. (It is not a crime to fire a worker for organizing a union.) The Supreme Court said that technically, a fired worker without papers has not been "harmed" and therefore cannot receive a remedy.

Judge Stephen Breyer, who wrote the minority opinion, rejected this argument. He pointed out that the NLRB had reconciled the two laws by limiting Castro's back pay in line with IRCA. And Breyer argued that denying back pay to undocumented workers illegally fired for union organizing would only encourage bosses to hire such immigrants, since there would be less financial incentive to respect the law.

Prior to passage of IRCA, the Supreme Court in its 1984 *Sure-Tan, Inc. v. NLRB* affirmed the Labor Board's award of back pay for undocumented workers but waffled on reinstatement. Those deported by running afoul of unionbusting bosses would not get their jobs back.

In effect, the Supreme Court has decided enforcement of immigration law is more important than making sure that federal law protects the right of workers to organize. But the Court was only following Congress— according to federal law, it's a crime for worker to use false documents to get a job but not a crime for a boss to fire a worker exercising a fundamental human right, organizing a union.

"This Supreme Court decision is a major victory for every unionbusting boss that breaks the law in order to deprive workers of their right to have a union," says UE Genl. Sec.-Treas. Bruce J. Klipple. "It's a big setback to every unorganized worker who seeks a voice on the job.

"What's more, it's a bonus to every unscrupulous employer who hires undocumented workers on the assumption they'll be less likely to complain about low pay, dangerous conditions and lack of respect," Klipple says.

"Look at the numbers. There's about 8 million undocumented workers in the United States now, and that number is not going to drop," the UE officer says. "If it's riskier for workers to organize, the wages of those workers will remain low, and all of us will suffer."

"UE remains committed to immigrant workers' rights, because we're committed to an aggressive struggle to improve the conditions of all workers," Klipple concludes.

THE PERSISTENCE OF DANGEROUS WORK

When the Occupational Safety and Health Administration was created in 1971, many were optimistic that its police powers would help end unsafe working conditions in the United States once and for all. After decades of budgetary starvation, that hope remains unfulfilled. Dangerous workplaces persist in the United States. Document 6.19 shows that even workers under the age of 18 continue to risk their lives in some forms of work.

6.19   Fatalities among young workers (aged 17 and under) and all workers, 1992–97. Data from Census of Occupational Injuries, reproduced in Janice Windau and Eric Sygnatur, "Profile of Work Injuries Incurred by Young Workers," *Monthly Labor Review* (June 1999), p. 5.

Event or Exposure	Workers Under 18		All Workers	
	Number	Percent	Number	Percent
Transportation incidents	163	40	2,589	41
Highway incidents	70	17	1,304	21
Nonhighway incidents	47	12	396	6
Workers struck by vehicle	25	6	368	6
Water vehicle	9	2	106	2
Railway	8	2	80	1
Assaults and violent acts	82	20	1,247	20
Homicide	72	18	1,003	16
Suicide	3	1	213	3
Animal attack	7	2	29	1
Contact with objects and equipment	82	20	1,004	16
Struck by	36	9	570	9
Caught in	25	6	295	5
Running machinery	17	4	154	2
Collapsing materials	17	4	121	2
Falls	23	6	657	10
Exposure to harmful substances/environments	44	11	588	9
Electric current	25	6	312	5
Caustic / noxious / allergenic substances	9	2	122	2
Oxygen deficiency	10	2	102	2
Fires and explosions	8	2	194	3
TOTAL	403	100	6,313	100

BRAVE NEW WORKPLACES

The advent of the Internet and the spread of computer technology in the 1990s held contradictory consequences for workers. Some privileged technology workers experienced an updated version of welfare capitalism in the informal workplaces of the nation's dot-com industry. As Document 6.20 indicates, workers were often given attractive benefits in return for bone-crushingly long workdays at their computer terminals. At the same time, the new technologies provided managers with more opportunity than ever to spy on their workers and monitor their productivity. On balance, do you think new computer technologies will tend to emancipate workers from drudgery or deprive them of privacy and control over their work lives?

6.20 High-Tech Welfare Capitalism at Razorfish, 2000. Excerpts from "High-Tech Jobs Offer Perks Galore!" *New England Technology Career Finder*, 2003.

At Razorfish, a company with 1,300 employees and offices in seven countries that is involved with inventing and reinventing client companies with web and internet technology, fitness is also important. The company reimburses each employee up to $500/year for anything fitness or wellness related—golf clubs, snowboards, skis, sneakers, health club memberships or anything else that gets people off the couch. Says Mary Jean Langlais, North American HR manager "This speaks to the importance of having a balanced life and to be healthy."

Besides attracting and keeping employees, there is another reason why so many companies are offering these types of perks and bennies–employee productivity. The philosophy is that the more time employees spend on the company premises, the more work they'll do, and the more productive employees will be. And since it rarely matters whether the work gets done at 3 P.M. or 3 A.M., companies may see huge productivity rewards in the long run—especially among unmarried groups.

Razorfish has a "Resources on Call" program so that it's staff can "enjoy life beyond work" says Langlais. Employees in need of anything—someone to run errands, find a daycare provider, a pet sitter, or someone who delivers groceries—can use the "Resources on Call" to obtain a list of resources available in the area that offers whatever service they are looking for. "It saves all the research time so in their spare time, employees don't have to worry about all the legwork and can have some fun," says Langlais.

Equally important, from the corporate viewpoint, is the creativity that such "time outs" can spark. Says one HR professional, "We really want to encourage creativity. We want an environment where our employees pull themselves out of the daily routine. This sparks more creativity, new energy, and better teamwork. These sessions have become very important as several great product development ideas have been generated from this type of atmosphere."

Langlais of Razorfish says "It's a very competitive environment out there. We need to be more creative to find and retain people. But it's absolutely more than money. It's a unique culture and an environment open to creativity. Our clients are looking for the best, most creative business solutions, so we need to provide an environment that brings out that creativity."

At Razorfish, each incoming employee has a career coach. In this program known as the "Fish Hatcher" program "the coaches help new hires to get where they want to go in the company. It's designed to help people be the best they can be and avoid being pigeon holed into one position or to stagnate," says Langlais. "We want our people to continue to grow and develop professionally."

Razorfish also uses general merchandise, weekend getaways and the like as incentives. Through the company's "A Time to Share Award," individuals are recognized for going above and beyond with a company watch and $300 to $500 in gift certificates with a wide menu of options to select from—including cash.

"This is an opportunity for our managers to give on the spot bonuses for employees that go beyond the call of duty and who have exemplified company values," says Langlais. "It gives the managers a tool to recognize their staff without having to wait for the formal review process."

And when it comes to keeping employees fed while on the job, several companies in the area offer free snacks, juice or soda. Among the more interesting elements is a soda machine in Razorfish's NY office. Soda costs 25 cents but if you don't have the change in your pocket, there's no worry. Just call the machine from your phone or cell phone and a quarter will be added to your phone bill and the soda dispensed. . . .

THE NEW ANTI-UNIONISM

By the late 1970s, managers were battling unions with increased aggressiveness. Ronald Reagan's firing of 11,500 unionized air traffic controllers in 1981 energized the business assault on labor unions. Document 6.21 gives one fired controller's response to the president's action. Document 6.22 indicates the steep decline in worker strike activity in response to deteriorating economic conditions and employers' willingness to permanently replace strikers. Because penalties for unfair labor practices were so light, many employers chose to engage in blatantly illegal practices such as the firing and blacklisting of union workers, as Documents 6.23 and 6.24 show. Right-to-work laws continued to hamper labor organizing in the South and West, and as Document 6.25 indicates employers found new allies among conservative Christian organizations in winning passage of such laws. By the mid-1990s, Republicans were attempting to gut the Wagner Act's prohibition on collective bargaining by company unions through the so-called TEAM act. Excerpts of a debate over the TEAM Act conducted in one Congressional hearing are included in Document 6.26. What do these documents indicate about the state of relations between unions and management at the end of the twentieth century?

6.21 "What the founders of our great country did," 1981. Fired PATCO Controller Ronald A. Oberhauser to Ronald Reagan, November 30, 1981, Federal Aviation Administration Records, RG 237, Entry 14, Box 63, file 81-36, National Archives, Washington, D.C.

November 30th, 1981

Dear Mr. President,

My name is Ronald Oberhauser. I am, or I guess I should say, I was an Air Traffic Controller prior to [August] 5th, 1981. That, Mr. President, if you have forgotten was the day myself and my fellow controllers were fired by you.

I am writing to you Mr. President to let you know, contrary to what I feel you believe, myself and a vast majority of the fellow controllers you fired are not now or ever were liars thiefs or subversives trying to destroy the United States Government. I'll challenge our records of government service against you or any of your staff. We've encouraged safety and have been more honest to the American people than you or any of your White House staff. I can only speak for myself when I say, after spending six (6) years in the Marine Corps, during which I spent a year in Viet Nam, and eleven (11) years as an air traffic controller, I never once endangered the lives of my fellow workers or the public which I was serving. My work always came first. That, I know now, was a mistake. It has cost me my family, my home and many years of dedicated public service.

I am about to turn 37 years old and because I took a stand on something I believed in, I must go out and try to find a job where I might build a new career. Sir may I remind you what I did was nothing more than what the founders of our great country did. The only difference is that they won the battle and I and my fellow controllers lost. There has been one other time in my short life that I have seen a group of people criticized, shamed and forgotten, as the striking controllers have been, and that sir is when I returned from Viet Nam.

I am not looking for sympathy, Mr. President. What I am looking for is justice and equality. I was tired of being a second class citizen. Not having the same rights and privileges as other citizens of this country just because I worked for the government. I hope and pray that someday government employees will have those rights. I don't feel Mr. President it will happen in your administration. You sir are cold and unconcerning about the "Common Man."

I am returning to you my 15 year government pin for dedicated service. As long as injustice is being practiced by this or any other administration, I want no reminders of ever being associated with such a group.

I hope Mr. President that you get a chance to read this. I feel it is one of many voices trying to tell you that todays government is not for the working people. It is caught up in its own political rhetoric.

Ronald A. Oberhauser

6.22   The Disappearing Strike, 1947–2000. Statistics on work stoppages involving 1,000 workers or more and lasting for at least 24 hours. Source: U.S. Bureau of Labor Statistics.

	# Stoppages	# Workers (thousands)	# Man/Days Idle (thousands)	Percent of Estimated Working Time Lost
1947	270	1,629	25,720	NA
1948	245	1,435	26,127	0.22
1949	262	2,537	43,420	0.38
1950	424	1,698	30,390	0.26
1951	415	1,462	15,070	0.12
1952	470	2,746	48,820	0.38
1953	437	1,623	18,130	0.14
1954	265	1,075	16,630	0.13
1955	363	2,055	21,180	0.16
1956	287	1,370	26,840	0.20
1957	279	887	10,340	0.07
1958	332	1,587	17,900	0.13
1959	245	1,381	60,850	0.43
1960	222	896	13,260	0.09
1961	195	1,031	10,140	0.07
1962	211	793	11,760	0.08
1963	181	512	10,020	0.07
1964	246	1,183	16,220	0.11
1965	268	999	15,140	0.10
1966	321	1,300	16,000	0.10
1967	381	2,192	31,320	0.18
1968	392	1,855	35,367	0.20
1969	412	1,576	29,397	0.16
1970	381	2,468	52,761	0.29
1971	298	2,516	35,538	0.19
1972	250	975	16,764	0.09
1973	317	1,400	16,260	0.08
1974	424	1,796	31,809	0.16
1975	235	965	17,563	0.09
1976	231	1,519	23,962	0.12
1977	298	1,212	21,258	0.10
1978	219	1,006	23,774	0.11
1979	235	1,021	20,409	0.09
1980	187	795	20,844	0.09
1981	145	729	16,908	0.07
1982	96	656	9,061	0.04
1983	81	909	17,461	0.08
1984	62	376	8,499	0.04
1985	54	324	7,079	0.03
1986	69	533	11,861	0.05
1987	46	174	4,481	0.02
1988	40	118	4,381	0.02

continued

	# Stoppages	# Workers (thousands)	# Man/Days Idle (thousands)	Percent of Estimated Working Time Lost
1989	51	452	16,996	0.07
1990	44	185	5,926	0.02
1991	40	392	4,584	0.02
1992	35	364	3,989	0.01
1993	35	182	3,981	0.01
1994	45	322	5,020	0.02
1995	31	192	5,771	0.02
1996	37	273	4,889	0.02
1997	29	339	4,497	0.01
1998	34	387	5,116	0.02
1999	17	73	1,996	0.01
2000	39	394	20,419	0.06

1. The number of stoppages and workers relate to stoppages that began in the year. Days of idleness include all stoppages in effect. Workers are counted more than once if they are involved in more than one stoppage during the year.
2. Working time is for all employees, except those in private households, forestry, and fisheries.

6.23 Blacklisting, 1989. Testimony of Carol Holman and Steve Lazaer to Hearing of the Commission on the Future of Worker-Management Relations, Louisville, Kentucky, September 22, 1993. Quoted in *Fact Finding Report: Commission on the Future of Worker-Management Relations* (Washington, D.C.: Government Printing Office, 1994), p. 89.

Excerpt of Ms. Holmon's Testimony:
In June of 1998 I was employed by Humana Audubon on Four East. Because of my concern for understaffing and other conditions affecting patient care, I became active in the NPO (Nurses Professional Organization). I openly spoke for the union. . . . On August 1st, 1989, I and my friend, who was also active in NPO were so frustrated and upset with the conditions of understaffing on our nursing unit that we resigned our positions at Humana Audubon. . . .

It was a time of the nursing shortage when all hospitals were desperate to recruit nurses. Jewish Hospital at that time was anxious to recruit nurses and offered a hundred dollars each to all nurses who agreed to come in for an interview. . . . Jewish Hospital hired us for the Transitional Care Unit. . . . We were told to report to work on September 25th.

On September 20th we each received by UPS Next Day Air at our homes the following letter from Jewish Hospital: Quote: "We regret to inform you that we have no position of employment for you." The letter was signed by the vice president of Human Resources at Jewish. My friend and I went to Jewish Hospital and asked to speak with him. He was there, but would not see us. . . .

I had a very good evaluation at Humana-Audubon. . . . Despite this very good evaluation, Audobon marked me as ineligible for rehire on the personnel form. . . .

We know we had been blacklisted. . . . We knew deep in our hearts that there was no reason for this. Someone had to be out to get us. It was very devastating. . . .

Excerpt of the testimony of Mr. Lazar, a former manager in the employee relations department at Humana, Incorporated:

I was present in the office of the human resource director of Audubon Hospital when he received a call from the human resource director of Jewish Hospital about Carol and her friend. The conversation I overheard was directed at the fact that both nurses were considered to be union red hots, very active in the Audubon campaign, extremely pro-union individuals. The Audubon human resources director went so far to say, "You probably don't want them working for you."

6.24 Harassment, 1994. Testimony of Judy Ray, to Regional Hearing of the Commission on the Future of Worker-Management Relations, Boston, Massachusetts, January 1994. Quoted in Fact *Finding Report: Commission on the Future of Worker-Management Relations,* p. 89.

I was a ten year employee of Jordan Marsh, in Peabody [Massachusetts], up until this day after Thanksgiving on which I was fired. I was fired, I truly believe, solely because I was a union organizer within the store. I was a dedicated employee, for ten years, for that company . . .

I cannot impress upon you what an organizer, what an employee who is just fighting for their rights in a campaign goes through this day and age. I wouldn't have believed it, myself. I have been followed, on my day off, to restaurants, by security guards with walkie-talkies. I had an employee, a management person, assigned to work with me eight hours a day, five days a week, who was told he was solely to work on me, to change my ideas about unions.

I was timed going to the bathroom. I could go nowhere in my workplace without being followed. It's a disgrace. It's harassment beyond what I could ever tell you. Unless you have lived through it, you couldn't know what it feels like. . . .

6.25 Christian Coalition Anti-Unionism, 2001. Flyer distributed by Oklahoma Christian Coalition, 2001, in support of Ballot Question 695, to make Oklahoma a right-to-work state. From Gregory S. Guthrie, "Labor Unions: Champions of Social Justice," (M.A. Thesis, Georgetown University, 2002),

p. 74. [On September 25, 2001, 54 percent of Oklahoma voters approved the question, making Oklahoma the 22nd right-to-work State, and the first state to adopt a right-to-work law since 1986.]

Right to Work is Right for Oklahoma
Vote Yes
Tuesday Sept. 25, 2001

Reasons people of faith should vote for Right to Work:

1. Union dues are used consistently to support pro-abortion candidates.	YES
2. Union dues are used consistently to support pro-homosexual candidates.	YES
3. Union dues are used to consistently support candidates who restrict religious freedom.	YES
4. Union dues are used consistently to support candidates who promote increased federal control of education.	YES
5. People of faith who are forced to join unions have no real say in altering how union dues are spent.	YES
6. It is wrong to force people of faith to join a union when their dues are used for offensive and immoral purposes.	YES

6.26 Debating the TEAM Act, 1995. Excerpts of Testimony before the U.S. House Committee on Economic and Educational Opportunities. *Hearings on H.R. 743, The Teamwork for Employees and Managers [TEAM] Act,* May 11, 1995, 104th Congress, 1st Session, Serial 104-18 (Washington, D.C.: Government Printing Office, 1995), pp. 4–6, 34–41.

[Testimony of Michael Morley, Senior Vice President and Director of Human Relations at the Eastman Kodak Company]:

Good morning, Mr. Chairman and Members of the Committee. . . . I am appearing today on behalf of the TEAM Act coalition, . . . a group over 100 trade associations and businesses, both union and non-union, that have a strong interest in expanding employee involvement in the workplace. . . . I would like to make just three points this morning.

First, the time has come for U.S. employment policy to endorse a new approach to employer-employee relations, one that reflects the positive changes underway in the American workplace. Today public policy recognizes only two approaches. One is dictatorial. It is the command-and-control approach which suggests that employees check their brains at the door and do as they are told. The other is adversarial. It is based on a belief that labor and management have fundamentally different interests that can be resolved only through the conflictual process of collective bargaining. We at the Coalition believe the time has come for . . . a third approach, the cooperative approach. . . . Under this approach, teams of employees become much more involved in the workplace in decisionmaking, and developing recommendations to improve the workplace and taking charge of their work lives.

Second, if the Federal employment policy is to accept the cooperative approach to employee relations, an amendment is needed to section 8(a)(2) of the National Labor Relations Act. . . . Why should non-union employee teams be prohibited by law from addressing terms and conditions of employment?

Third, I believe that all of the Members on this committee are supportive of employer-employee cooperation and employee involvement in the workplace. . . . We ask you to act expeditiously to make possible this simple rule of common sense. Make it a reality by passing the TEAM Act.

[Testimony of David M. Silberman, Director, AFL-CIO Task Force on Labor Law]:

Mr. Chairman, on behalf of the AFL-CIO, I want to thank the Committee for the opportunity to testify before you this morning. . . . As I will explain this morning, in fact this bill takes a discredited reactionary approach. If enacted, this legislation would give nothing to employees in the way of "power"; rather, the bill would take from workers their right to independent representation and give *employers* yet another means of maintaining their unilateral power over workers' terms and conditions of employment. . . .

Despite many pious claims to the contrary, H.R. 743 would allow for the return of . . . company unions. . . . In other words, the bill would recognize an at-will management right to create employee organizations and representation plans to deal with the employer on wages and working conditions. Each organization or plan would exist solely at management's sufferance. Management would have carte blanche to establish the organization's mission and jurisdiction; determine the organization's governing structure and operating procedures; write the organization's bylaws; and, most importantly, select the employees representatives. . . .

Indeed, what the proponents of the TEAM Act want is precisely the freedom to recreate the company unions that did in fact exist in the 1920s and 1930s. Today's managers may want to give their employees more responsibility and discretion over their work than did managers raised in the command-and-control tradition—and they are free to do so under current law. But the very last thing that management desires is a genuinely empowered workforce—that is, a workforce which is able to deal with the employer on an equal footing in determining the terms of their employment.

Rather, in championing this bill management seeks what it always has sought: the freedom to create the form—but not the substance—of joint decision-making while at the same time reserving for itself complete and total authority to decide unilaterally how much employees will be paid and to determine unilaterally all other terms of employment. Put differently, management wants the freedom that it enjoyed prior to 1935 to create and control employee organizations . . . as an alternative to independent employee organizations. . . . Such employer control is, in truth, and should remain in law an unfair labor practice.

Efforts at Union Reform and Revival

As unions fell on the defensive in the 1970s, at least two tendencies were evident in labor's response to its decline. Labor activists looked increasingly to strengthen alliances with broad progressive forces; and they also looked inward at ways to address corruption and harmful bureaucratization in some existing unions. In Document 6.27 below, AFL-CIO president Lane Kirkland addresses Solidarity Day marchers in 1981 with a message intended to unite labor, civil rights advocates, feminists, and others against the policies of President Ronald Reagan. Document 6.28 provides a platform of Teamsters for a Democratic Union, the reform initiative that battled against corruption within the union once dominated by Jimmy Hoffa and elements of organized crime. AFL-CIO President John J. Sweeney reflects on a growing alliance between union activists and gay activists in Document 6.29. What opportunities might emerge from labor's coalition-building, and what points of tensions might arise that might complicate relations between the labor movement and a broader progressive coalition? What might be gained by the campaign of groups like the TDU to democratize unions, and what complications might arise from that effort?

6.27 Solidarity Day, 1981. Solidarity Day Address of AFL-CIO President Lane Kirkland, 1981. *American Federationist* (October 1981), pp. 1–2.

We are here today to reaffirm the great goals that have drawn us together, in solidarity, for 100 years.

We are here to answer a challenge to those goals and to all that we have gained together, in solidarity.

President Reagan has told us that he alone speaks for the working people of this country—and that we do not.

He has told us that he has a mandate from the people for what he wills—and that when we pursue our contrary instructions, we are simply "out of step."

The object of governance in America, we are told, is but to raise armies, to foster and nourish commercial enterprise, and to suppress those forces that might check or temper its rapacity.

If you reject the notion that only the State, through its Chief Executive, faithfully expresses your will—look about you. You are not alone.

If you do not embrace the proposition that this President has a mandate to destroy the programs that feed the roots of a decent society, look about you. You are not alone.

If you believe that governments are raised by the people, not as their enemies but as their instruments, to promote the general welfare, look about you. You are not alone.

Behold your numbers, as far as the eye can see. Attend their spirit, vital, strong and free.

Look at your brothers and sisters, by the thousands, still marching—in solidarity down the historic ways of their Capital City.

You are working men and women who have come here with your friends and allies because you care deeply about the course of your country.

You have given up your family days of rest and spent long and tiring hours in buses, trains and cars, from every part of this land, as an act of devotion and testimony.

Your testimony must be heard. The future course of this nation hangs upon it.

You are the people that do the work of America. You run its factories and offices, work its farms, transport its produce, maintain its buildings, teach its children, nurse its sick, clean its streets and fight in its defense.

When something goes wrong in America, you feel it first—before the politicians or the more securely placed. You know it before the pollsters take your pulse.

Something has gone wrong and you know it all too well.

Those who have risen to power in this city have set out to strip our government of any capacity to serve your needs and aspirations.

They have set out to cancel and dismantle the safeguards of a humane society and to commit us to the economic jungle.

They are sacrificing the homes, health and hopes of millions on the altar of crank economic abstractions that defy the laws of simple arithmetic and dismay even their friends on Wall Street, who never allow sentiment to blind them to the bottom line.

Their tax cuts–transferring resources from the common good to the private purses of the rich–are proving the most irresponsible fiscal act in our times–as we said they would.

Their monetary policies are causing record high interest rates—as we said they would.

They have attacked Social Security and other covenants between the people and their government—as we said they would.

Their indifference or hostility to social justice threatens voting rights, women's rights, worker's rights and human rights—and this too we warned, many months ago, would come to pass.

We were right then and we are right today. Attention should, at last, be paid. Labor is here in its one hundredth year, to deliver a simple message to the Administration and to the Congress.

We have come too far, struggled too long, sacrificed too much, and have too much left to do, to allow all that we have achieved for the good of all to be swept away without a fight. And we have not forgotten how to fight.

We are out of step with no one but the cold-hearted, the callous, the avaricious and the indifferent.

We are out front and we shall not fall back to hide and wait for better political weather.

But the winds are changing as they always do. The winter's chill is approaching and the bloom is fading from false mandates.

Today is just a start, but Solidarity is more than just a day. As our brothers and sisters in Poland have shown the world, it is a quality of the human spirit that can never be defeated.

On this historic day of that new start let us all pledge to each other to return to our communities and to build a new mandate for a humane and just America.

Our mandate responds to the call of Gompers, for:

"More school houses and less jails; more books and less arsenals; more learning and less vice; more constant work and less crime; more leisure and less greed; more justice and less revenge."

Let us bind that mandate in the spirit of Solidarity forever.

6.28 The TDU Program for A Democratic Union, ca. 2002. Teamsters for a Democratic Union, http://solidarity.igc.org/teamster/tdu.htm.

The TDU Program for A Democratic Teamsters Union (TDU) is a united rank-and-file movement of truck drivers, dock workers, airline workers, production workers–every kind of Teamster, and spouses, too. The Rank and File Bill of Rights represents TDU's democratic program for reforming the Teamsters:

1. DEMOCRATIC BY-LAWS. All business agents and stewards should be elected. Vacancies in office should be filled by special election within three months. Local union committees should be elected. Contract and strike votes should be by majority (not two-thirds). All contracts should provide for elected officers retaining company seniority.

2. DIRECT ELECTION OF OFFICERS. General President and all International officers should be elected by the membership, with International VPs elected by region. An end to trusteeships and split-off locals.

3. A FAIR GRIEVANCE PROCEDURE. Innocent until proven guilty, right to remain on the job until final procedure completed. Grievance procedure should include right to a speedy trial, arbitration by peers, and the right to strike if necessary.

4. PRESERVATION OF WORKING CONDITIONS. The union's purpose is to expand and preserve what we have, not trade it away for anything less. People come first, not productivity.

5. SAFETY AND HEALTH. We have the right to enter the workplace without fear for our health and leave in the same condition we arrive. Teamsters should have the right, backed up by our union, to refuse unsafe or hazardous conditions. We are not machinery.

6. EIGHT-HOUR DAY AND FIVE-DAY WEEK. Forced overtime and unfair dispatch rules destroy our family life and cost us jobs. No mandatory overtime, "flexible" work weeks, or 70-hour slavery. We are for the advent of the four-day work week. We work to live, not live to work!

7. A DECENT PENSION. Every dollar in the pension fund belongs to us. We are entitled to 25-and-out, cost of living pensions, and union pension trustees elected by the rank and file and retirees to safeguard our money.

8. JUST SALARIES FOR OFFICERS. A union officer can't understand the problems of members who make less than half what he makes. No officer should make more than the highest paid working members in his jurisdiction. No multiple salaries from union, company, or government sources, or special fringes and pensions. Salary increases limited to the average increase for membership, and subject to membership approval.

9. EQUALITY AMONG TEAMSTERS. Bring all wage levels up to the highest standards, not a lot for the few and little for the many. Fight the hardest for the lowest paid.

10. END TO DISCRIMINATION. Employers have used the differences in age, race and sex to divide us for decades. We oppose these injustices and divisions. Support affirmative action to correct past injustices. Employers should bear the cost of their past discrimination, not the members.

6.29   A "Budding Alliance," 2001. John J. Sweeney, "The Growing Alliance between Gay and Union Activists," in Kitty Krupat and Patrick McCreery, eds., *Out at Work: Building a Gay-Labor Alliance* (Minneapolis: University of Minnesota Press, 2001), pp. 24–25.

I still recall the day in October of 1983 when a resolution condemning discrimination on the basis of sexual orientation came up on the floor of the AFL-CIO's Fifteenth Constitutional Convention. Seventeen years ago, the resolution was something of a landmark, a declaration of the labor movement's support for a group of workers whose identity and particular concerns had never been acknowledged or addressed before. At the time, I was president of the Service Employees International Union (SEIU), which had sponsored the resolution. I rose to speak in favor of it. Since that day, I have spoken out many times for the rights of workers, regardless of sexual orientation. And I am proud to say that the labor movement has since made many advances in the fight for gay and lesbian rights.

Seventeen years ago, six of the most respected union leaders in the country joined me in supporting the AFL-CIO resolution on sexual orientation. As I looked around the room, I could sense the hesitation. Union members, after all, aren't much different than the public at large. . . . I knew there were unspoken questions—questions I had heard before and have heard many times since: Is it a good idea to put rights for gay and lesbian workers on the labor movement's agenda? Is it possible to organize workers who can't easily be identified, much less mobilized? Is there enough public and membership support to organize around these issues? And yet, not one convention delegate spoke against the resolution. It passed overwhelmingly.

What happened that day is something I've seen happen in the labor movement many times over the years. When faced with a choice, no matter how difficult, more often than not our commitment to equality floats to the top. Equality is a value Americans hold dear—not only in the labor movement but across the country.

The passage of that AFL-CIO resolution in 1983 was a small but significant first step toward the formalization and nurturing a budding alliance between gay activists and union activists. In 1997, we reached another milestone when the AFL-CIO Executive Council voted unanimously to recognize Pride at Work—an organization of lesbian/gay/bisexual/transgender (LGBT) union members—as an official constituency group of the AFL-CIO, thereby guaranteeing gay and lesbian workers a voice in determining the labor movement's agenda. I don't mean to romanticize the American labor movement or overstate the progress we've made. . . . No one would deny that it's been a slow and painstaking process to get where we are. And we still have a long way to go. Historically, unions have had to be challenged and prodded before opening the door to people their members view as "different." For gay and lesbian workers, that remains a hard reality to this day. But time and again, the labor movement has shown itself capable of broadening to include and represent every class of workers. . . .

FACING THE FUTURE

At the turn of the century, as organized labor struggled to survive, a spate of new initiatives for labor's resuscitation were launched. In Document 6.30 a successful union leader from California's Silicon Valley outlines a program for the revival of unions as training centers for the new economy's skilled workers. Document 6.31 suggests something of the alliance that was emerging toward the century's end between labor and church organizations concerned about the plight of the working poor. Document 6.32 contains the statement of Harvard University students who struck to gain a living wage for their university's employees, a movement that gathered strength on many campuses and in many cities in the new century. Document 6.33 provides the 2002 platform for the Labor Party, a grass roots effort to mobilize workers for political change. Document 6.34, a Bureau of Labor Statistics report on union membership at the end of the year 2003, suggests that none of the new approaches to organization has yet succeeded. Which strategies hold the most promise for the future?

6.30 Controlling the Skilled Labor Market of the Future, 2001. Remarks by Amy B. Dean, President, South Bay AFL-CIO, at the ILO Conference on The Future of Work, Employment and Social Protection, Annecy, France, January 18–19, 2001. Reprinted with permission from AFL-CIO.

I think it is important that, when we talk about the changing borders of the economy, that we talk not only about national borders that have given way to an international economy, but also about borders that are both international and local as well. In other words, while we see that capital roams the globe freely and can move from country to country, at the same time, the economy is rooting itself in regions worldwide. . . .

The second element that I think is the hallmark of the new economy and that is often missed when people talk about the new economy is the way in which the firm is restructuring itself in the production process. I think too often people talk about the new economy as though it were only involving new products and new technologies, but that is not the point. The point is that the firm has begun to restructure itself in dramatic ways that have a huge impact on working people. As we know, and as has been discussed today, no longer do we have vertically integrated sites of production where all the functions of a firm are performed under one roof. Instead we see networks of firms that create an enterprise, usually net-worked at the regional level. This is a very important point. . . .

Lastly, both here and in our country, as well as in others, are notions of justice that have changed dramatically since World War II when we built a social contract that was based, not only on a different industrial model, but also on a different model around social justice.

I think it is those three points, the shifting borders, the restructuring of the firm and changing notions of justice that really do create a good frame-work for analysis.

What does that mean for working families? . . .

If you look at the employment projections between now and the year 2015, according to California's Economic Development Department, 39 per cent of the jobs that will be created over that period of time will require only a few hours of on-the-job training, 25 per cent or more will require a Bachelor's degree or higher, and very little in between. These numbers are nice because they really do demonstrate well the hour-glass nature of the economy: as firms externalise any function that is not core to innovation, we really are left with two kinds of jobs—high skilled and high paid jobs and low-wage service sector jobs with very little in between.

Having said that, then, what does that mean for the role of the next generation of labour market organizations? . . . Just as in the past, as labour organizations have had to restructure in the context of how the economy has restructured, so too must we do that today. I think this is a serious point because we are really only about 40 percent of the way through this industrial revolution. We have not even hit the half-way mark. Technologies like IT and biotechnology are just beginning to emerge, as other kinds of emerging technologies are coming on line, and I think that there are enormous social and political implications for these technologies and the role of unions is key. But I will be the first, as a trade unionist, to say that our organizations are not prepared to be relevant actors in the context of the restructured economy.

I would argue that there are two major ways we have to focus our work . . . Labour unions need to think about themselves in two particular ways: one, as labour market institutions, and two, as social and political actors. In the context of labour market institutions, they must see themselves as playing a coordinating role in the sector, a coordinating role in particular occupations, and seeing themselves as incredible value-added players in those particular sectors. For example, when I say a coordinating role, I mean coordination among the small and medium sized firms within an occupation or within an industry. Playing this role means coordinating all the training players, the community-based organizations, community colleges, and all the different organizations that have an impact on that particular sector. Labour must become the coordinating entity as it moves people from job to job.

Secondly, labour must own the supply side of training in the regional economy. That is the way we will control the supply of labour in these economies—by virtually controlling the supply chain of training. It is important because, as you look at these small to medium sized companies, none of these companies on their own can afford nor have the incentive to train people given that median job tenure in California is only three years. Therefore being able to coordinate and shift costs across the firm becomes an extremely strategic role for labour long term.

Labour must become proficient at being able to broker the supply and demand of labour within a labour market. Yet, I am suggesting nothing different from the ways in which a temporary agency functions. Temporary agencies were created to fill an important niche that client firms needed but are not filling, the niche that the employee side needs. Thus, we have determined that marrying training with job development and placement is an absolute critical core capacity unions of the future must have. . . .

Unions will play a very important role if we can just get it together. I do not say to set forth an immediate task, but rather to recognize it as a challenge for the long haul. Unions will play a very important role in being able to negotiate tensions, as industry will need a significant partner. On the question of what is labour's role as social and political actors—certainly much more than what we are doing now. Labour builds lots of political capital and we do not leverage it for anything useful. I think we have to think about the ways in which the labour movement, not just here but across the world, leverages its political influence. I like to think of it as a continuum of political outcomes. Obviously, the first one is simply meeting our immediate institutional interest but it should not stop there. In fact, if we stop there we are not building our movement.

The second political outcome is that we have got to figure out ways to build our union movement through political influence. I have just described the way unions should operate in the new economy. There are enormous legal impediments in the United States to even being able to function in that capacity. Without getting into a legal conversation, I will provide one example: communities of interest for purposes of bargaining collectively were defined six years ago. This definition presupposes that a group of workers are all housed under one roof working for the same employer. However, we know that is simply not how people go to work. We know that I may go to work under one roof, sitting next to somebody who is employed through some kind of intermediary institution. Although we are all under the same roof, we have multiple employers. Or for that matter, people may be working for the same employer and be spread out across the world. Therefore, redefining what constitutes legitimate communities of interest for the purpose of bargaining collectively, whether we work individually or we work under one roof, is an important reform. There are many others but this is not the point of the topic. The point simply is to say that from the United States perspective, we need a massive overhaul of our labour law if we are going to be able to reform ourselves in the way that I have talked about.

6.31 Churches and Labor Unite, 2003. New Mexico Conference of Churches Statement against "Right to Work" Law, 2003. http://www.nmchurches.org/pprite.htm.

In view of the ethical, as well as the economic and political implications of current proposals for the enactment of a so-called "right to work" law by the New Mexico Legislature, the New Mexico Conference of Churches feels constrained to express its opposition to such legislation for our State.

We begin by pointing out the basic hypocrisy enshrined in the commonly assigned title of this proposed legislation—"right to work." The law, as enacted by some twenty states and as proposed for New Mexico, guarantees no worker or group of workers any rights whatsoever, certainly not any right to a job. What it does do, and all that it does, is to undermine the stability and strength of labor unions and the foundations of the collective bargaining process which are the principal protection of individual workers against potentially capricious hiring and firing practices of management in industrial and service employment situations. An analysis of the nature and history of right to work legislation makes this very clear. . . .

While such laws may not constitutionally deny labor's right to organize freely into unions, they do outlaw a traditional form of union-management relationship sanctioned by long usage in our country, namely, and principally, the union shop where the employee is required to join the union within a certain period of time after being hired. . . .

Claims have been made in support of "right to work" laws that they contribute to the economic development of states and communities on the ground that such laws improve the climate for economic investment and, growth and employment opportunity. It has also been argued that "right to work" would eliminate strikes and other forms of labor unrest and that it would reduce employment. No authentic studies have been adduced to validate these claims over the forty year history of "right to work."

Probably the most effective argument in favor of "right to work" has been that workers should not be deprived of their freedom to choose whether or not to join a union. This plea certainly has a strong appeal to liberty-loving Americans. The counterpoint to this argument, as many a worker has learned to his/her dismay, is that a worker without the protection of a union contract is very much exposed to the whims of management which may and often do deprive him of freedoms far more fundamental than the freedom to elect or reject union membership. The counter argument of the unions on this issue of right to choose or reject union membership is that under labor law, when a union is certified to represent the employees of a given plant or office, the union is required to represent the interests of all workers in the situation equally and without regard to union or non-union membership. In this situation, the unions argue, it is unfair for any employees to accept the protection of the union without sharing in the costs of union operation. . . .

In view of all the factors involved, as we understand them, the General Assembly of the New Mexico Conference of Churches affirms the following positions:

1. We re-affirm and uphold the position which has been widely proclaimed over many years by Catholic, Protestant and Jewish religious forces in the U.S.A. that union organization, union membership and collective bargaining are inherent and inalienable rights of workers.

2. We affirm the moral responsibility of workers who are protected by union contracts to share in the financial cost of the unions which negotiate on their behalf and monitor the implementation of collectively bargained agreements.

3. We affirm that the union shop and other issues of union security should be matters for collective bargaining between management and labor rather than for state or federal legislation.

4. We affirm that the State of New Mexico should not enact any form of "right to work" law. Our conviction is that any conceivable benefits to the state from such legislation would be more than out-weighed by the damage it would do to the integrity of orderly and free collective bargaining between labor and management.

6.32 Students Take Up Labor's Cause, 2001. "United Students Against Sweatshops Statement in Support of Living Wage at Harvard," http://usasnet.org/campaigns/harvardsitinstatement.shtml

May 7, 2001

USAS Statement in Support of Living Wage at Harvard

For the past three years, United Students Against Sweatshops has been organizing on campuses from coast to coast to ensure that the workers making our collegiate apparel are treated with dignity. We define dignity as . . . freedom of association, proper health and safety standards, no forced labor, freedom from abuse, harassment and underage employment. Further, we advocate that a living wage is the only kind of wage that any worker should ever be paid.

It is in solidarity and with full support, that we, the members of United Students Against Sweatshops proudly and strongly offer our solidarity and support to Progressive Student Labor Movement as they enter their fourth week of a sit-in demanding a LIVING WAGE for all employees at Harvard University. As students, we more than understand the pressures of deadlines for papers, theses, and final exams. We respect the utmost dedication it takes for students to transcend their own needs in order to stand with the workers who make their school run.

In our support for students sitting-in at Harvard, we call on President Rudenstine to immediately grant the student's request to pay all Harvard Workers—in-sourced or out-sourced—$10.25/hour plus medical and educational benefits. As an educational institution, Harvard would show the future leaders that the respect of human rights is the bottom line. As a research institution, Harvard will show that as a beneficiary of federal grants, that it respects all the tax paying citizens who work at Harvard.

The right to protest is one of the tenets of the liberal tradition, taught in the very lecture halls at Harvard. We must remember that Boston is the very city where protests that began the revolution that formed this country commenced. We request that Harvard University respects the integrity of the protestors by not sanctioning them for their peaceful and thoughtful actions. If Harvard acted justly, the workers would be able to thrive, and the students would be studying for finals.

As students concerned for justice, we must emphasize that justice is important for all workers whether they make our clothing or clean our classrooms.

6.33 A New Political Vision, 2002. Preamble to "A Call for Economic Justice: The Labor Party's Program," 2002, http://www.thelaborparty.org/ a_progra.html.

We are the people who build and maintain the nation but rarely enjoy the fruits of our labor.

We are the employed and the unemployed.

We are the people who make the country run but have little say in running the country.

We come together to create this Labor Party to defend our interests and aspirations from the greed of multinational corporate interests. Decades of concessions to corporations by both political parties have not produced the full employment economy we have been promised. Instead income and wealth disparities have widened to shameful extents.

We offer an alternative vision of a just society that values working people, their families and communities.

We, the members of this Labor Party, see ourselves as keepers of the American Dream of opportunity, fairness, and justice. In our American Dream, we all have the right:

* To a decent paying job and a decent place to live
* To join a union freely without fear of being fired or other retribution
* To strike without fear of losing our job
* Not to be discriminated against because of our race, gender, ethnicity, disability, national origin, or sexual orientation, at work or in our communities
* To free, quality public education for ourselves and our children
* To universal access to publicly-funded, comprehensive, quality health care for all residents
* To retire at a decent standard of living after a lifetime of work
* To quality of life in our communities enhanced by a fully funded public sector.

The Democratic and Republican parties serve the corporate interests that finance them. We oppose corporate power that undermines democratic institutions and governments. We oppose corporate politicians and parties that provide billions in corporate tax breaks and subsidies to the rich, selling themselves to the highest bidder. We reject the false choice of jobs versus environmental responsibility. We will not be held hostage by corporate polluters who poison our workplaces and our communities. We reject the redistribution of billions of dollars of wealth from poor and working people to the rich. And we reject every opportunist who plays the race, gender, or immigrant card to keep us from addressing our real needs, and the needs of our families and communities.

Our Labor Party understands that our struggle for democracy pits us against a corporate elite that will fight hard to retain its powers and privileges. This is the struggle of our generation. The future of our children and their children hangs in the balance. It is a struggle we cannot afford to lose.

6.34   *Union Members in 2003*, Bureau of Labor Statistics (Washington, D.C.), January 21, 2004, http://www.bls.gov.newsrelease/pdf/union2pdf.

In 2003, 12.9 percent of wage and salary workers were union members, down from 13.3 percent in 2002, the U.S. Department of Labor's Bureau of Labor Statistics reported today. The number of persons belonging to a union fell by 369,000 over the year to 15.8 million in 2003. The union membership rate has steadily declined from a high of 20.1 percent in 1983, the first year for which comparable union data are available. Some highlights from the 2003 data are:

- Men were more likely to be union members than women.
- Blacks were more likely to be union members than were whites, Asians, and Hispanics or Latinos.
- Nearly 4 in every 10 government workers were union members in 2003, compared with less than 1 in 10 workers in private-sector industries.
- Nearly two-fifths of workers in education, training, and library occupations and in protective service occupations were union members in 2003. Protective service occupations include fire fighters and police officers.

Membership by Industry and Occupation

In 2003, workers in the public sector had a union membership rate more than four times that of private-sector employees, 37.2 percent compared with 8.2 percent. The unionization rate for government workers has held steady since 1983. The rate for private industry workers has fallen by about half over the same time period. Within government, local government workers had the highest union membership rate, 42.6 percent. This group includes the heavily unionized occupations of teachers, police officers, and fire fighters. Among major private industries, transportation and utilities had the highest union membership rate, at 26.2 percent. Construction (16.0 percent), information industries (13.6 percent), and manufacturing (13.5 percent) also had higher-than-average rates. Agriculture and related industries had the lowest unionization rate in 2003—1.6 percent.

Among occupational groups, education, training, and library occupations (37.7 percent), and protective service workers (36.1 percent) had the highest unionization rates in 2003. Natural resources, construction, and maintenance workers and production, transportation, and material moving occupations also had higher-than-average union membership rates at 19.2 percent and 18.7 percent, respectively. Among the major occupational groups, sales and office occupations had the lowest unionization rate—8.2 percent.

Demographic Characteristics of Union Members

In 2003, union membership rates were higher for men (14.3 percent) than for women (11.4 percent). The gap between men's and women's rates has narrowed considerably since 1983, when the rate for men was 10 percentage points higher than the rate for women.

Blacks were more likely to be union members (16.5 percent) than were whites (12.5 percent), Asians (11.4 percent), or Hispanics (10.7 percent). Union membership rates were highest among workers 45 to 54 years old.

Full-time workers were more than twice as likely as part-time workers to be union members.

Union Representation of Nonmembers

About 1.7 million wage and salary workers were represented by a union on their main job in 2003, while not being union members themselves. About half of these workers were employed in government.

Earnings

In 2003, full-time wage and salary workers who were union members had median usual weekly earnings of $760, compared with a median of $559 for wage and salary workers who were not represented by unions. The difference reflects a variety of influences in addition to coverage by a collective bargaining agreement, including variations in the distributions of union members and nonunion employees by occupation, industry, firm size, or geographic region. (For a discussion of the problem of differentiating between the influence of unionization status and the influence of other worker characteristics on employee earnings, see "Measuring union-nonunion earnings differences," *Monthly Labor Review*, June 1990.)

Union Membership by State

In 2003, 33 states reported lower union membership rates, while 15 states and the district of Columbia registered increased rates. Two states reported no change in their union membership rates from 2002 to 2003. Twenty-nine states had union membership rates below that of the U.S., while 21 states and the District of Columbia had higher rates. All states in the Middle Atlantic and Pacific divisions again had union membership rates above the national average of 12.9 percent, while all states in the East South Central and West South Central divisions continued to have rates below it.

Four states had union membership rates over 20 percent in 2003—New York (24.6 percent), Hawaii (23.8 percent), and Michigan (21.9 percent). This is the same rank order as in both 2001 and 2002. All four states have had rates above 20 percent every year since data became regularly available in 1995. North Carolina and South Carolina continued to report the lowest union membership rates, 3.1 and 4.2, respectively. These two states have had the lowest union membership rates each year since the state series became available.

The largest numbers of union members lived in California (2.4 million), New York (1.9 million), and Illinois (1.0 million). About half (7.9 million) of the 15.8 million union members in the U.S. lived in six states (California, New York, Illinois, Michigan, Ohio, and Pennsylvania), although these states accounted for just over one-third of wage and salary employment nationally.

The number of union members in a state depends on both its union membership rate and the size of its employed workforce. Texas had only about one-fourth as many union members as New York, despite having 1.2 million more wage and salary employees.

312

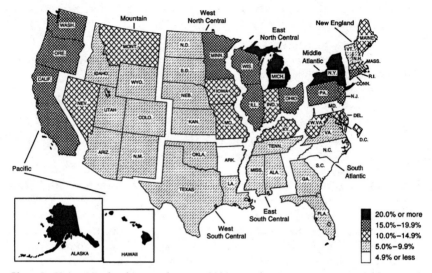

Chart 1. Union Membership rates by state, 2003 annual averages (U.S. rate = 12.9 percent)

INDEX